Nihilism Now!

Also by Keith Ansell Pearson

GERMINAL LIFE: The Difference and Repetition of Deleuze

Also by Diane Morgan

KANT TROUBLE: The Obscurities of the Enlightened

Nihilism Now!

Monsters of Energy

Edited by

Keith Ansell Pearson

and

Diane Morgan

First published in Great Britain 2000 by
MACMILLAN PRESS LTD
Houndmills, Basingstoke, Hampshire RG21 6XS and London
Companies and representatives throughout the world

A catalogue record for this book is available from the British Library.

ISBN 0–333–73292–8

 First published in the United States of America 2000 by
ST. MARTIN'S PRESS, INC.,
Scholarly and Reference Division,
175 Fifth Avenue, New York, N.Y. 10010

ISBN 0–312 23209–8

Library of Congress Cataloging-in-Publication Data
Nihilism Now! : monsters of energy / edited by Keith Ansell Pearson and Diane
Morgan.
p. cm.
Includes bibliographical references and index.
ISBN 0–312–23209–8 (hardcover : alk. paper)
1. Nihilism. I. Ansell-Pearson, Keith, 1960– II. Morgan, Diane, 1963–

B828.3 .N447 2000
149'.8—dc21
99–088249

This book is printed on paper suitable for recycling and made from fully managed and sustained
forest sources.

10   9   8   7   6   5   4   3   2   1
09   08   07   06   05   04   03   02   01   00

Printed and bound in Great Britain by
Antony Rowe Ltd, Chippenham, Wiltshire

Contents

Notes on the Contributors

Eliot Albert recently completed his PhD, 'A Schizogenealogy of Heretical Materialism: Between Bruno and Spinoza, Nietzsche, Deleuze and other Philosophical Recluses', at the University of Warwick. He organised the 'Deleuze/Guattari and Matter' Conference at Warwick in October 1997 and is editor of the forthcoming collection *Materialist Cartographies*. He currently teaches at Goldsmith's College, University of London.

Keith Ansell Pearson is Professor of Philosophy at the University of Warwick and is the author and editor of books on Nietzsche and Deleuze. He is currently working on a series of essays on Bergson and Bergsonism in relation to questions of matter, time and evolution. He serves on the editorial board of *Nietzsche-Studien*.

Richard Beardsworth is Associate Professor of Modern European Philosophy at the American University of Paris. He is author of *Derrida and the Political* (1996) and *Nietzsche* (1997), and is general editor of the journal *Tekhnema: a Journal of Philosophy and Technology*.

David Boothroyd is Senior Lecturer in Cultural Studies at the University of Teesside and co-founding editor of the electronic journal *Culture Machine* (http://Culturemachine.tees.ac.uk). His work has been published in several journals and collections and he is currently working on a monograph, *Culture on Drugs: Narco-cultural Studies of High Modernity*.

Howard Caygill is Professor in Historical and Cultural Studies at Goldsmith's College, University of London. He is the author of *Art of Judgement* (1989), *A Kant Dictionary* (Blackwell 1995), *Benjamin and Colour* (1998) and co-editor (with Keith Ansell Pearson) of *The Fate of the New Nietzsche* (1993). He is currently writing a book, *Lévinas and the Political*.

Justin Clemens and Chris Feik have worked together and apart on literature, nationalism, and Romantic aesthetics. They dwell in Melbourne and have both taught at the University of Melbourne.

Daniel Conway is Professor of Philosophy and Director of Graduate Studies at Penn State University. He is the author of *Nietzsche and the Political* (1997) and *Nietzsche's Dangerous Game: Philosophy of the Twilight of the Idols* (1997).

Catherine Dale recently completed her PhD thesis 'Antonin Artaud and Philosophy: The Problem with Thought' at the University of Western Sydney.

Joanna Hodge is Reader in Philosophy and Director of Research at Manchester Metropolitan University. She is on the editorial boards of *Women's Philosophy Review* and *Angelaki*. She wrote her doctoral thesis in Oxford on the concept of truth in *Being and Time* and is the author of *Heidegger and Ethics* (1995). She is currently working on the question of time in contemporary thought and on a book entitled *Derridean Temporalities*.

Daniel Katz is currently 'Maître de Conférences' in the English Department of the University of Picardie in Amiens, France. He is the author of several articles on Beckett and other major modernists, along with the recent book, *Saying I No More: Subjectivity and Consciousness in the Prose of Samuel Beckett* (1999).

Suhail Malik teaches in the Department of Visual Arts at Goldsmith's College of the University of London.

Diane Morgan is Senior Lecturer in Cultural Studies at University College Northampton. She has written several articles on subjects ranging from Hamann, Büchner, architecture and transgender and is the author of *Kant Trouble: the Obscurities of the Enlightened* (2000).

John Protevi teaches in the Department of French and Italian at Louisiana State University, Baton Rouge. During 1995–6 he was a Leverhulme Research Fellow at the University of Warwick. He is the author of *Time and Exteriority: Aristotle, Heidegger, Derrida* (1994), and of a number of articles on ancient Greek philosophy, classical German philosophy, and contemporary French philosophy. His next book will be on Deleuze and Derrida.

Introduction: the Return of Monstrous Nihilism

Keith Ansell Pearson and Diane Morgan

> We lack creation. We lack resistance to the present.
> Deleuze and Guattari, *What is Philosophy?* (1991)

Have we had enough? But enough of what exactly? Of our mourning and melancholia? Of postmodern narcissism? Of our depressive illness and anxieties of not 'being there' any longer? Enough of enough! We now ask: what of the future of the human and of the future of the future? Is it now possible to produce revitalised ways of thinking and modes of existing that have digested the demand for transhuman overcomings and so are able to navigate new horizons of virtual becoming? Is it possible to save thought from its current degenerative and vegetative state at the hands of a smug and cosy postmodern academicism? Can we still invent new concepts?

If one follows certain influential contemporary accounts, it would appear as if the experience and question of nihilism have become *passé*. Is not the urgency informing the question of the 'now' of nihilism redundant and otiose? For Jean Baudrillard, for example, there is now only the simulation of a realised nihilism and little remains of a possible nihilism (a nihilism of the possible) in theory. In relation to previous forms of nihilism – romanticism, surrealism and dadaism – we find ourselves in an 'insoluble position'. Our nihilism today is neither aesthetic nor political. The apocalypse is over, its time has gone and lies behind us:

> The apocalypse is finished, today it is the precession of the neutral, of the forms of the neutral and of indifference. (Baudrillard 1994, 160)

Baudrillard goes on to make the claim, terrifying in its full import, that all that remains is a 'fascination' for these indifferent forms and for the operation of the system that annihilates us.

Surely, Baudrillard is being ironic when he claims that this mode of nihilism is our current 'passion'? How can one be passionate about indifference and one's own annihilation? As Baudrillard acknowledges, this is the nihilism of the observer and accepter. It is the nihilism of the passive nihilist who no longer aspires towards a transcendence or overcoming of the human (condition), but who simply announces and enjoys its disappearance, the spectator watching the spectacle of his own demise.[1] History, politics, metaphysics, have all reached their terminal point, and willing nothingness appears to be the only desire of the will available to the postmodern mind:

> The dialectic stage, the critical stage is empty. There is no more stage... The masses themselves are caught up in a gigantic process of inertia through acceleration. They are this excrescent, devouring, process that annihilates all growth and all surplus meaning. They are this circuit short-circuited by a monstrous finality.　　(Baudrillard 1994, 161)[2]

Perversely perhaps, our desire in this volume is to inspire a return to the energetics of Nietzsche's prose and the critical intensity of his approach to nihilism, to restore a sense of his hopeful monsters and to give back to the future its rightful futurity. How can there be a sense of 'monstrous finality' without an ambiguity of meaning? It is precisely the double-nature of nihilism that is destroyed by the postmodern single-minded immersion in the melancholia of the system. Of course, there is no final catastrophe. But there are great expectations, an experience of the great noontide, the premonition that 'he must come one day', this victor over God and the cult of nothingness (Nietzsche 1989, II §24). In marking so carefully and demandingly a distinction between *active* nihilism and *passive nihilism*, Nietzsche was presenting and staging an important dialectic of nihilism *and* cultivating a *critical* nihilism too:

> Nihilism. It is *ambiguous* (*zweideutig*):
>
> A.　Nihilism as a sign of increased power of the spirit: as *active nihilism*.
> B.　Nihilism as decline and recession of the power of the spirit: as *passive nihilism*.
>
> It can be a sign of strength: the spirit may have grown so strong that previous goals ('convictions', articles of faith) have become incommensurate (for a faith generally expresses the constraint of conditions of existence, submission to the authority of circumstances under which one flourishes, grows, gains power). Or a sign of the lack of strength to posit for oneself, productively, a goal, why, a faith.
> 　　　　　　　　　　　　　　　(Nietzsche 1968, §22 and 23)

Of course, for Nietzsche there is something peculiarly specific about the modern experience of nihilism in its affective aspects. Nihilism emerges as a psychologically necessary affect of the decline of belief in God. The displeasure with existence has not become any greater than previous times, it is simply that we moderns have come to mistrust any 'meaning' in suffering and in existence itself. One extreme position is now succeeded by another, equally extreme position, one that construes everything as if it were *in vain*. It is this 'in vain', and in particular its tie with *duration*, which constitutes the character of 'present-day nihilism' – or this, says Nietzsche, is what requires a demonstration. The problem is twofold, therefore: it involves a mistrust of all previous valuations that borders on the pathological (all values are now seen as lures that 'draw out of the comedy but without bringing it closer to a solution'), and, secondly, 'duration "in vain"', without goal (*Ziel*) or purpose (*Zweck*), is the most paralyzing idea' (Nietzsche 1968, §55). In short, we understand we are being fooled and yet lack the power *not* to be fooled. We have become the victims of an excess of knowledge that does not enable us to orient and comport ourselves in newfound conditions and we currently lack the resources to create new modes of knowing and acting. Hence we find ourselves trapped in paralysing forms of nihilism. Importantly, Nietzsche draws our attention to the fact that 'active nihilism' presupposes a degree of 'spiritual culture', while our feeling of spiritual weariness that has culminated in 'the most hopeless skepticism regarding all philosophy' is also a sign of our by no means low position as nihilists: to be a nihilist is to be in a 'relatively well off' position, spiritually and culturally speaking (Nietzsche 1968, §55).

It is the attempt to cultivate an active nihilism – the active 'force of destruction' as Nietzsche calls it (Nietzsche 1968, §23) – which, we are told by the likes of our Oedipal master thinkers, is no longer an option for us:

> There is no longer a stage, not even the minimal illusion that makes events capable of adopting the force of reality – no more stage either of mental or political solidarity: what do Chile, Biafra, the boat people, Bologna, or Poland matter? All of that comes to be annihilated on the television screen.   (Baudrillard 1994, 164)

But this self-serving and self-satisfied melancholic nihilism, on full display in all its terror and ugliness in a passage such as this, can be shown to rest on a disavowal of the *energy* of its own investment in inertia.[3] This is not a 'perfect' nihilism, the kind that Nietzsche invited us to cultivate and work through, but an easy and lazy one. It is nihilism reduced to a coping strategy. It is a modish nihilism that reflects little more than the cynicism of the isolated and disenchanted intellectual. It is a nihilism without germinal *life*. It is a nihilism that deserves to die.

By contrast, the essays gathered in this volume are an attempt to respond to Nietzsche's laments in *The Will to Power* about an ethico-political and philosophical 'loss of stimulus', a certain lack of vigour and rigour, a creeping apathy and laziness in 'our' thinking and approach to life. In some sense, 'nihilism' is always 'now', always pressing and urgently calling for our attention. Nietzsche contended that nihilism is a 'normal condition' always lurking on the horizon, not simply an exceptional state of emergency. However, he also described it as a pathological transitional stage one necessarily experiences once traditional values disintegrate under the pressure of disillusionment and distress (Nietzsche 1968, §13). Nihilism is marked by a traumatic split from conventional assurances which forces the question *Wozu?* what is all this about and where are we heading (Nietzsche 1968, §20)? It is the contemporary specificity of such questioning that this present volume addresses while appreciating the always ongoing nature of such speculations.

The concept of nihilism has the status of an 'event' owing to the fact that it cannot be made reducible to or equivalent with any actualised state of affairs. Whereas, culturally and socio-politically, a disjunction between the tired vocabulary 'we' have at our disposal to interpret reality and 'our' actual experience of reality is felt, the event of nihilism announces 'in a hundred signs' a pregnant future which opens novel and exciting lines of thought and life. The conceptual tools at 'our' disposal are found to be inadequate, in need of a re-energising 'revaluation' and 'transvaluation'. It is a thinking of the event as both virtual and spectral that enables us to bestow a germinal life upon nihilism. Of course, nihilism is linked with a state of affairs, but it is only when treated as an event that the history of nihilism can be rendered intelligible and passable; indeed, that nihilism can be given a history. Nietzsche's analysis of the ambiguous signs of nihilism is informed by a complex temporal dynamic. As an experience it appears as a force that comes, like a shockwave, from the future, destabilising established values and petrifying ossified forms of life. In fact, however, nihilism for Nietzsche has been with us for some considerable time, existing spectrally as if it was a ghost of life that haunts the living dead and concealed in the strata of time, part of a virtual becoming in which the precise points of actualisation cannot be predicted or foreseen in advance simply because they are contingent in relation to a whole series of disparate forces.[4]

Nihilism is implicated in a complex virtual history that a naively empiricist historiography finds itself unable to recount. Strangely perhaps, and paradoxically enough, it is the event which is able to give embodiment to the state of affairs (to give 'meaning' to an experience, in this case, that of nihilism as the devaluation of values). The event is double, at least: extracted from the state of affairs it is linked with it discloses the possible of the possible and as *monstrous* – 'the future exists in a hundred signs' (Nietzsche 1968, Preface §2) – and by giving a virtual and dynamic body to the state of affairs, it harnesses the forces that transversally communicate across the strata of geological time. To construe history in this way is, for Nietzsche, the task of universal self-determination:

Direct self-observation is not nearly sufficient for us to know ourselves: we require history, for the past continues to flow within us in a hundred waves; we ourselves are, indeed, nothing but that which at every moment we experience of this continued flowing. It may even be said that here too, when we desire to descend into the river of what seems to be our own most intimate and personal being, there applies the dictum of Heraclitus: we cannot step into the same river twice... there exists a subtler art and object of travel which does not always require us to move from place to place or to traverse thousands of miles. The last three centuries very probably still continue to live on, in all their cultural colours and cultural refractions, close beside us: they want only to be discovered. In many families, indeed in individuals, the strata still lie neatly and clearly one on top of the other: elsewhere there are dislocations and faultlines....

(Nietzsche 1986, section II, §223)

With the conceptual invention of nihilism Nietzsche gathers together, then, a set of disparate and dissonant forces that are at once historical, geological, ethical and philosophical. Regarding the necessity of nihilism's coming and arrival, he will not rest content with quick fixes or easy solutions, or with cavalier and hasty attempts to bypass it. The latter only serve to exacerbate the problem. Of course, on one level – that of the human itself, of human comprehension and incomprehension – the experience of nihilism is caught up in a pathology. In this regard it can be likened to a conceptual storm in an existentialist's tea-cup. When confronted with a world that has been unanchored and that can now exist only as acentred, any control system, from the state imperium to the human mind, will inevitably undergo a crisis state. Nietzsche rightly draws attention to the fact that nihilism is an account of our *idealism*, and one aspect of his philosophical task as he sees it is to draw out the necessary conclusions from Kant's Copernican revolution in thought. These conclusions, however, only take us so far and the distance travelled may not be very far at all. Idealism (including postmodern relativism and so-called 'perspectivism'), considered as a philosophical stance, may simply be part of our transhuman adolescence and, as such, come to be seen as belonging to the immature part of our enlightened, but overhuman, becoming.

The essays collated here testify to the virtuality and germinality of the event of nihilism, especially in the dimension of its monstrous ambiguity. In the opening essay of the volume Eliot Albert contests the accuracy of our reading of a Nietzschean modernity in terms of Copernican and Kantian revolutions. If there is an exacerbation and intensification of these modern elements and tendencies in Nietzsche's thought it is not in the direction of some self-serving anthropologism. Albert contends that Copernicus' revolution was not a radical one since its essential ambit was to place the Sun in relation to the cosmos in exactly the same terms that had been assigned to the privileged Earth. The effect is still to think of a centred and hierarchical cosmos well-regulated by negative feedback and harmonious equilibriums. The conservative nature of Copernicus' theory especially comes to light when the contrast is made with the heretical ideas of Giordano Bruno (1548–1600). Kant's separation of faith and knowledge, of metaphysics and science, was a half-hearted attempt to preserve a transcendent realm from a genuine attack and innovation. Inevitably in the hands of Nietzsche its conceits are relentlessly and remorselessly exposed, and this forms an essential part of Nietzsche's cheerful atheism. Here atheism denotes not so much a tragic affliction as the philosopher's serenity and achievement. 'Nothing is true, everything is permitted' (Nietzsche 1989, §24) is the slogan with which the world, immanent, acentred and anomalous, can come into being and give birth to itself.

In his article 'On Nihilism', Baudrillard suggests that nihilism, known primarily in its nineteenth-century guise 'of dark, Wagnerian, Spenglerian, fulginous colours' is no longer an appropriate category of thought for today's millennial society (Baudrillard 1994, 159). Reflecting on the brooding, apocalyptic gloom of the epoch which announced God's death, he recognises that 'it would be beautiful to be a nihilist if there were still a radicality' (Ibid., 163). Similarly, in their work on Nechaev and the other young Russians radicals associated with the 1860s organisation 'The People's Vengeance', Justin Clemens and Chris Feik provide us with an account of a compellingly colourful subcultural movement and at the same time with a way of testing nihilism. They examine not only whether nihilism can be a durable and effective political instrument but also whether the term now has any currency left for us. Central to their analysis is the practice of 'anaesthetics' which they see as challenging the opposition between bureaucracy and aesthetics. By charting how the aesthetic inscription of bureaucratic effects bound the Russian nihilists together, Clemens and Feik are also examining how the community was destined to achieve 'literally nothing', no lasting effects. This form of nihilism, it is suggested, is the demonic creature of modern bureaucracy itself, parasiting its structures but also imitating its organisation. Whereas Hannah Arendt discussed the bureaucrat in relation to the radical 'banality of evil', in this contribution he is seen as starting out as the young nihilist, an idealistic sower of pandaemonium, who ends up unproductively shuffling papers within an unreal bureaucratic structure. Here nihilism indeed appears to have been reduced to a mere administrative 'activity of second rank' which reactively adapts itself to the prevailing conditions of life (see Nietzsche 1989, II §12).

Richard Beardsworth offers a careful and highly inventive reading of Nietzsche's text *On the Genealogy of Morality*. He aims to demonstrate the implication of the question of 'spirit' in Nietzsche's attempt to think beyond or outside metaphysics. His overriding concern is to guard and warn against any easy appropriation of Nietzsche, such as championing the death of God in the name of a monstrous future that it would gaily, but blindly affirm. Of course, the future will be monstrous, it cannot be anything other, but what cannot be naively or blindly affirmed for Beardsworth is some completely ahistorical and unmediated 'Dionysian' sense and sensibility (the world as a monster of eternal self-creation and self-destruction beyond good and evil, for example). What could be more metaphysical than this? In opposition to an affirmation of supposedly timeless condition or truth – the truth which proclaims the world to be will to power and nothing besides – Beardsworth insists upon a reading of spirit in Nietzsche. In this way he is able to demonstrate the need for a more nuanced reading of a principal text like the *Genealogy* than, with the occasional exception, has hitherto been the case. Part of the consequence of such an attentive and vital reading is that the question of the human and its future cannot be discounted or side-stepped in some cavalier and casual manner. If we are to take the question of futurity seriously in both its human and post-human dimensions, then the question of energy cannot be severed from the matter and question of spirit. Thus speaks Beardsworth's challenge.

Pursuing further this excessive, but not unthinkable, logic of the 'monstrous', Joanna Hodge's contribution intertwines Nietzschean pretensions and ambitions with the concerns of Heideggerean thought on the one hand and Freudian thought on the other. Writing from out of a certain prudence and precision, Hodge counsels us to pay attention to the often overlooked fact that Nietzsche's diagnosis of a condition of nihilism to describe the modern malaise was couched in a specific language and idiom, namely, that of a customised German composed of a Lutheran intonation and a distinctly nineteenth-century political lyric. What happens when this peculiar and specific language and style are translated into the flatness of a cosmopolitan English? Hodge, having raised the question in her essay, then devotes the rest of her analysis to combating a certain viral infection prevalent amongst uncultivated artist-types of late modernity, in which not only is Nietzsche's thought trampled over, treated without regard for its time and place, but so is thought itself. Any and all signs of actual and active thinking are in danger of being erased from the memory-banks of the machines of the future. For Hodge the real menace lies in a 'completed' or perfected nihilism that would no longer able to reflect upon itself since it would be *nothing more or other than* nihilism. This is what she calls a 'demonic nihilism', a nihilism that usurps the monstrous (ambiguous, double, two-headed, active and passive, etc.), and destroys all positioning and place. Do we still have ears for Nietzsche and his music? Do we still have the resources to think? Have we become too self-satisfied with and in our nihilism? These are the kind of urgent questions Hodge's essay entices us to confront now.

Suhail Malik focuses his attention on Heidegger's questioning of nihilism, in particular on the configuration of *bios* and the relationship between nihilism and *life* in his thought and its legacy. How are we to think biogenesis? How are we to relate ontogenesis and ontopoiesis? The aim of this exacting contribution is to arrive at the beginnings of a clearer and more precise understanding of nihilism in Heidegger and, in this way, to move beyond what is increasingly becoming a merely conventional reading of our modernity and historicity. Initially this requires a reckoning with Heidegger's most important contentions about Nietzsche: that he is the philosopher of nihilism and of life because he determines both in accordance with a logic of values (devaluation, transvaluation, etc.); and that he approaches the question of 'life' not biologically but metaphysically. Life has no stable order or value for Nietzsche, hence its logic is always one of complication and excess (of course, as Malik concedes in a note, a different biology to the one Heidegger is working with might mean that this conception has to be dramatically revised). Through a careful and attentive unfolding of Heidegger's confrontation with modernity, Malik is able to produce a highly novel and unsettling encounter with some of the essential tropes of our time, such as animalism, anthropocentrism and fictionalism.

Daniel Conway's contribution situates the problematic of nihilism in relation to its transhuman potentialities. How might we construc the advent of this event of all events, nihilism, in other than wholly or simply negative terms, that is, in terms which will take us away from and well beyond our anthropocentric prejudices? This is an important question to ask, simply because there is an ever-present danger in readings of Nietzsche and nihilism that the experience and the event will be interpreted in terms that merely confirm our self-centred prejudices and conceits, and even serve to enhance them: we can no longer conceive of ourselves as the centre of the universe, no longer be sure that evolution has a purpose, let alone a final purpose which might be us. Sly attempts to recuperate some comfort from the darkest hour of devaluation, by steeping ourselves in melancholic reflection on our own existential meaningless, our poignant cosmic insignificance and the cruel tragedy of life, merely serve to reconfirm our narcissism. So the compulsion to think beyond the old morals and values also entails the task of thinking beyond the human condition as we have come to know it and live it. Conway argues that Nietzsche only began in his lifetime to experiment as a self-proclaimed 'first perfect nihilist' and far from accomplished or realised a transhuman mode of thinking. It is important for Conway that as readers of Nietzsche we acknowledge the extent to which his thinking remains contaminated by the decadent forces it endeavoured to overcome. This is to work against the idea of there being any purely transhuman philosophy, that is, one not tainted by human prejudices, delusions and errors. Ultimately, the ones who see themselves as self-overcomers of millennia of morality and Christianity still face the difficult task of overcoming Nietzsche himself – and by extension, nihilism. We self-vivisectionists must still attend to matters of body and soul.

The transhuman is further pursued in Diane Morgan's work on the much neglected Expressionist poet and doctor, Gottfried Benn. While Conway drew our attention to Nietzsche's challenge to view the world 'from inside' as 'will to power and nothing else', Morgan explores the implications of this for a thinking of 'expressivity', conventionally coupled with a prized 'interiority' but now unleashed from its confinement within the strictly human organism.

Indeed, having abandoned our anthropomorphic illusions of being some sort of 'cosmic paraphrase', the affirmative nihilist can instead become, to use Benn's terms, a 'formal naked gestation', journeying through life bearing various 'animal signatures', such as 'flickering cilia'. This piece adopts a conspicuously quasi-apocalyptic tone, one intended to be thought alongside a proposed return to eschatology (defined in the essay as 'the final present') away from the mapped-outness of teleological thought. If, to adapt somewhat Heidegger's melodramatic and hysterical claim, 'only a cilium can save us',[5] then this is only so far as the world of becoming is regarded, not as facing one catastrophic end, but instead as 'a perpetual present made up of one continually changing apocalypse' (Huxley 1994, 10). This distinction between two types of apocalyptic thought is important as it marks the difference between one which could lead, and did lead with Nazism, to a murderously-inclined biopolitics intent on a generalised conflagration, entailing the suicide of the state, and another, yet to be explored, line of monstrous becoming. The second opens itself to the potential of the 'bio-negative' to 'provoke' life into highly bred (*gezüchtete*) forms which ecstatically crash against the barrier of immateriality. This work provides food for a re-thinking of eugenics as the eulogy of *de-formation*, not the search for a teleologically motivated search for 'purity'. It is not enough to dismiss eugenics out-of-hand as the dispensable by-product of repugnant thirties' politics. Indeed, in an age of genetic engineering, ultrasound scans and amniocentesis/fetorcopies, eugenics no longer merely stands at the door, waiting to be let in or denied entry. Hence Benn's work is most timely in its attempts to bring the disciplines of poetry and medicine to bear on present technologised matter(s).

John Protevi's chapter follows up the provocative and perhaps perplexing link between nihilism and fascism made by Deleuze and Guattari in their work *A Thousand Plateaus*. Protevi aims to determine whether describing fascism as a 'realized nihilism' adds anything substantive to our understanding of both or is merely a rhetorical flourish. This requires putting into operation a close reading and careful negotiation with key sections of *A Thousand Plateaus* and its conceptual innovations. However, more than conceptual innovation is at stake here simply because Deleuze and Guattari make the daring – and easily misunderstood – move of construing fascism as a problem of 'pure matter' (as opposed, say, to a problem of cultural and political history or folk psychology). The 'major' contention made is that the analysis has to be on the level of a physics of the materiality and affectivity of bodies. In order to demonstrate this, or at least to begin the task, Protevi has recourse to complexity thinking, utilising the notion of self-organising processes, in order to supplement the new concepts of Deleuze and Guattari (the 'body without organs' and its typologies, stratification and destratification, the 'rhizome', the 'virtual' and so on). The challenge then is to think fascism not reductively or epiphenomenally as ideology but as a phenomenon rooted in the microtextures of everyday life and implicated in actual tendencies of matter and certain assemblages of desire. Conceived in these terms, the task of articulating an ethics of matter that might facilitate the cultivation of a nonfascist way of life becomes perhaps the most demanding ethics imaginable. Protevi concludes the essay with some thoughts on resistance and its various forms and formations. The issue of 'zero' is also at the heart of this configuration of fascism, nihilism and matter. One of the most novel aspects of Protevi's reading is the distinction he forges between a 'lunar' nihilism (the kind diagnosed by Nietzsche, he claims), which is a nihilism of reflection and depression, and a 'solar' nihilism, which is the 'suicidal' and frantic nihilism identified with a fascism that makes 'war' and extermination the sole object of the 'war machine'.

In his chapter Howard Caygill sets out to explore the ambiguity that lies at the heart of any attempt to speak of a survival 'of' nihilism. He draws our attention to the significance of the double genitive here. This may refer to our will and desire to live on and create new values after nihilism has been brought to perfection and fully activated/actualised, or it may refer to its uncanny and perpetual return, that is, that it survives our attempts to overcome it. Caygill thus stresses its performative contradiction – any attempt to revalue values will merely result in nihilism's return is his contention – and speaks of its 'ineluctable modality'. It is not clear whether this is also not to posit it at the same time as an ontological invariant and as part of some insuperable condition. The essay concentrates attention on the binding character of Nietzschean nihilism, which is to refer to it being spellbound to the very thing it wishes to overcome. One set of highest values are devalued only to be replaced by another equally nihilistic positing of highest values, in which those of the spirit and teleology are replaced by those of the body and of immanence. The argument amounts to the contentious claim that any attempt to overcome transcendent philosophies and religions (Platonism and Christianity) necessarily results in a mere inversion. An attempt to affirm life from the point of view of its immanent production is just as nihilistic as the hegemonic attempt to save it for transcendence (as in the sanctity of life doctrine promulgated in the recent Vatican statements discussed in the essay). Caygill wishes, therefore, to show the errors committed in any attempt to overcome nihilism that does so in ignorance of its powers of return and repetition. He locates a 'solution' in Nietzsche's pursuit of 'cheerfulness', a cheerfulness free of the spirit of revenge and its ressentiment towards life (whether its negation or affirmation). A theology –

whether metaphysical or post-metaphysical – of life gives way to a praxis of life as in the example of Christ (treated by Nietzsche himself in the misleadingly titled *The Anti-Christ*). However, Nietzsche also speaks, and as is cited by Caygill in the context of his newfound cheerfulness in the wake of the death of God (and what could be more dead?), of his 'longing' and great 'expectations' that can now be projected and constituted, and one wonders how Caygill's essentially Stoic resolution of the problem and predicament of nihilism can at all access the nature and character of this desire and expectation, of the 'meaning' of Nietzsche's cheerfulness and the nature of the 'new infinite' he looks forward to. Thinking the event of nihilism entails not only an emancipation from fear and anxiety but also an emancipation of desire.

Working through an unusual combination of Bataille, Artaud and Lévinas, David Boothroyd further contributes to the question of ethics and post-humanism by examining the ethical significance of the skin. In so doing he is refusing the reductive conception of the sentient body prevalent in much 'postmodern' thinking. For instance, the performance artist, Stelarc insists that the body and its boundaries are now rendered obselete by new technologies:

> As surface, skin was once the beginning of the world and simultaneously the boundary of the self. As interface, it was once the site of the collapse of the personal and the political. But now *stretched* and *penetrated* by machines SKIN IS NO LONGER THE SMOOTH SENSUOUS SURFACE OF A SITE OR A SCREEN. Skin no longer signifies closure.The rupture of surface and of skin means the *erasure* of inner and outer. As interface, the skin is inadequate   (Stelarc 1995, 91)[6]

Prefacing his piece with a graphic display of torture and reminding us of contemporary acts of dememberment, from Rwanda to Algeria, Boothroyd flies in the face of such reductive analyses and obliges us to consider violence as 'directed against the skin'. The skin remains vulnerable, marking a liminal difference between the same and the other, but it also continues to be undecidable. It once figures as that which binds the 'me' together *qua* existent and that upon which exteriority constantly impinges. Equally it is that which separates me from the Other and that which allows me to feel for the Other and the immediacy of his/her wounding. Even a concentrated examination of scenes of skin systematically being hacked away and punctured over and over again do not lay its significance to rest as death itself, outside of a particular theatre of individuation, is not arrived at. This underlining of the incompletability of negativity, understood as the 'nihilistic will to nothing', permits Boothroyd to propose 'an ethics of carnality', an ethics of 'being-in-a-skin', one that convolutes witness and victim of violence, involuting the perpetrator with the onlooker, doubling the scene of suffering, implicating us within it. The ethical moment is posited as that which interrupts annihilation.

Catherine Dale also focuses on an interruption of sorts, one that is 'rude' and which shouts down pat and formulaic discourses for controlling what is perceived as madness. Artaud is presented as a figure whose controlled (self)-woundings provide us with an aesthetic corollary to Boothroyd's ethically-focused intervention on 'skinihilation'. In a consideration of the feasibility of an re-energetised and re-energising nihilism, one capable of overcoming the inertia of pessimism, she formulates the phrase 'a conceptual turnstile' to denote the processs of conversion at play within Artaud's work. In a confrontation with an aporetic abyss, that is with something – such as that of the 'flickering form of a man burning at the stake' – which cannot be grasped and put into a fully conceptualised form, the absoluteness of life is seen as re-emerging. This absolute life is not one that gets back in return for having traded in one's sentient body to the policemen of morality; this is no religiously-doused life after death. Instead, out of the whirlpool of 'conceptual conversion', with its unexpected inversion of respectable behaviour, its rude outrage and wilful aggression, bursts a scarcely containable life, one that is constantly in motion, involuting joy with suffering, pain with power. Dale concludes with a reflection on critics' difficulty in reading Artaud and wonders whether this might have something to do with his awareness that reading is itself irreducibly 'rude'.

The concluding chapter by Daniel Katz also concentrates on a modernist writer who is seen as resisting critical appropriation. He rejects a reading of Samuel Beckett which would attempt to recuperate his difficult and elusive *oeuvre* by putting to work the negativity found therein. Katz refuses, and locates a refusal within Beckett himself, a recuperative logic which reduces complex thinking by presenting it as a significant – and thereby positively infused with meaningfulness – staging of the impossibility of meaning. Katz suggests that all too often the specificity of key modernist thinkers has been vitiated by a catch-all formulaic form of criticism which itself could be deemed destructive, if not weakly nihilistic, of crucial aesthetic and philosophical endeavours to maintain a relation to nothing. An archetypal example of such criticism is Adorno's, whose reaction to Beckett's work is summed up in his statement in *Negative Dialectics* that: 'Beckett has given the only appropriate reaction to the situation of the Concentration Camps, that he never names, as if it lay under an image ban *(Bilderverbot)*' (Adorno 1980, 373; 1973, 380). Such a statement tells us nothing about the specific concerns of Beckett (and indeed Adorno's essay on Beckett's 'Endgame' has precious little to do with the play itself and is more pertinent as a reading of French existentialism) and its dogmatic generality might even strike us as dangerous nowadays: a far too great an assumption that the Shoah has become a 'total apriori' for contemporary thinking, that it stands as the 'incommensurable over and above all experience' (Adorno 1997, 313) is, half a century after the events, misplaced and even counterproductive. It can itself become an oft repeated orthodoxy reductively used for politically ends, that falls on deafened and habituated ears. Even worse, the formulaic representation of the Holocaust as the ultimate unnameable can itself produce a form of reactive nihilism, one vividly and provocatively described, for instance, by the Austrian novelist, Elfriede Jelinek in *Wonderful, Wonderful Times* where a gang of young people violently lash out against what they perceive as parental 'swaddling in the human tea-cosy of the murdered, the hanged and the gassed' (Jelinek 1980, 30; 1990, 29). Teaching the younger generations about the Holocaust is meant to inoculate them against a repetition of genocidal history; instead, it perversely becomes a hate-base for neo-Nazi resistance, clearly evident in Jelinek's novel and in our contemporary world. A reiterated putting-to-work of the Holocaust perversely translates it into an ineffectual 'tea cosy' alongside which one lives in the horrors of the everyday, in desperation of some comic reassurance that life is nevertheless still beautiful.[7] While not addressed in these terms in Katz' piece, there is a lot at stake in his insistence on resisting a reading of Beckett which critically appropriates him as either a thinker of absolute nothingless or recuperated meaningfulness and presenting him instead as a demanding thinker of 'enough'.

We return to our beginning: the question of having had enough of melancholia and its dogmatic and uncritical slumbers. If this volume inspires renewed attempts to think and go beyond the human condition, then it will have served its germinal purpose.

English or French spelling of Levinas has been left to individual authors.
The editors would like to thank our copy-editor, Sally Crawford, at Macmillan, for her efficient help with this volume.

Notes

1 Baudrillard's position at this point might well remind one of Benjamin's definition of fascism (1982, 244): 'Mankind, which in Homer's time was an object of contemplation for the Olympian gods, now is one for itself. Its self-alienation has reached such a degree that it can experience its own destruction as an aesthetic pleasure of the first order'.
2 This melancholic nihilism finds echoes in Jean-Francois Lyotard's postmodern fable about evolution, which he reads in terms of the 'inhuman' thesis of negentropic complexification. See Lyotard 1997, 83–103; and for a critical reading of Lyotard's thesis, see Ansell Pearson 2000.
3 For another contemporary thinker's stand against 'postmodern impasses' – understood as 'the paradigm of all submission and every sort of compromise with the existing status quo' – see Guattari in Genosko 1996, 109–14.
4 See also Dawkins (1991, 73): 'the actual animals that have ever lived on Earth are a tiny subset of the theoretical animals that could exist. These real animals are the

products of a very small number of evolutionary trajectories through genetic space. The vast majority of theoretical trajectories through animal space give rise to impossible monsters. Real animals are dotted around here and there among the hypothetical monsters, each perched in its own unique place in genetic hyperspace. Each real animals is surrounded by a little cluster of neighbours, most of whom have never existed but a few of whom are are its ancestors, its descendants and its cousins'.

5   This is a play on Heidegger's 'Only a God Can Save Us' in Wolin (ed.) 1993, 91–116.

6   See also Gibson (1986) on the matrix cowboy's contempt for the 'flesh cage' and 'meat cage' which holds him back from the 'disembodied consciousness' of cyberspace. See Ansell Pearson 1997 for critical revaluation of such approaches to the 'post-human'.

7   This is a reference to Benigni's film 'La vita è bella' (1998), a 'comedy' about life in the Nazi Concentration Camps, which at the moment of writing this introduction has just received an Oscar.

References

Adorno, Th. (1980) *Negative Dialektik* Frankfurt am Main: Suhrkamp (1973) *Negative Dialectics*, trans. E.B. Ashton, NY: Continuum.

(1997) 'Versuch, das Endspiel zu verstehen' in '*Ob nach Auschwitz noch sich leben lasse*': *Ein philosophisches Lesebuch* ed. R. Tiedemann, Frankfurt am Main: Suhrkamp.

Ansell Pearson, K. (1997) 'Life Becoming Body: On the 'Meaning' of Post Human Evolution' in *Cultural Values* vol. 1, no. 2, ed. Scott Wilson, Oxford: Blackwell Publishers Ltd.

——(2000 forthcoming) 'Postdarwinian Evolutions and Postmodern Fables', in L. Hartley and C. Kaplan, *Darwin's Millenium: New Essays on Science and Culture*.

Baudrillard, J. 'On Nihilism' in *Simulcra and Simulation* trans. S.F. Glaser, Michigan: Michigan University Press.

Benjamin, W. (1982) 'The Work of Art in the Age of Mechanical Reproduction' in *Illuminations* trans. H. Zohn, Bungay, Suffolk: Fontana/ Collins.

Dawkins, R. (1991) *The Blind Watchmaker* Harmondsworth: Penguin.

Genosko, G. ed. (1996) *The Guattari Reader* Oxford: Basil Blackwell.

Huxley, A. (1994) *The Doors of Perception and Heaven and Hell*, foreword by J.G. Ballard, London: Flamingo, Harper/Collins.

Jelinek, E. (1980) *Die Ausgesperrten* Hamburg: Rowohlt (1990) *Wonderful, Wonderful Times*, trans. M. Hulse, London: Serpent's Tail.

Lyotard, J.-F. (1997) 'A Postmodern Fable' in *Postmodern Fables*, trans. G. van den Abbeele, Minneapolis: University of Minnesota Press.

Nietzsche, F. (1968) *The Will to Power* trans. W. Kaufmann, NY: Vintage.

——(1986) *Human, All Too Human*, trans. R.J. Hollingdale, Cambridge University Press.

——(1989) *On the Genealogy of Morals and Ecce Homo* trans. W. Kaufmann, NY: Vintage.

Stelarc (1995) 'Towards the Post-human' in *Architectural Design: Architects in Cyberspace* no. 118, Cambridge: Academy Group Ltd.

Wolin, R. ed. (1993) *The Heidegger Controversy* Cambridge Massachusetts: MIT Press.

1

The Shattering of the Crystal Spheres: 'rolling from the centre toward X'

Eliot Albert

> Since Copernicus man has been rolling from the centre toward X.
>
> Nietzsche 1968, §1.5

> Since Copernicus, man seems to have got himself on an inclined plane – now he is slipping faster and faster away from the centre into what? into nothingness? into a *'penetrating* sense of his nothingness'?
>
> Nietzsche 1969 III §25

> Therein we have the reason why every man, whether he be on earth, in the sun,or on another planet, always has the impression that all other things are in movement whilst he himself is in a sort of immovable centre; he will certainly always choose poles which will vary according as his place of existence is the sun, the earth, the moon, Mars etc. In consequence, there will always be a *machina mundi* whose centre so to speak, is everywhere, whose circumference is nowhere, for God is its circumference and centre and he is everywhere and nowhere.
>
> Cusa, *De Docta Ignorantia* Bk. II, Ch. 12

I

Kant claims that his achievement in philosophy is the analogue of that of Copernicus' in cosmology. Colloquially this carries the sense of a major paradigmatic shift in perception: since Kant is claiming for his achievement the status of a rupture with the past, a clean break. The problem with this claim, however, is revealed as soon as one begins to examine the cosmological, metaphysical and concomitant political charge of Copernicus' work. It then becomes apparent that Kant's claim is not really as apocalyptic, as cataclysmic, or as revolutionary, for the terms, conventions, limits and possibilities of thought as he would wish us to think. It is ultimately in

Bataille's sense, comical. 'No one can say without being comical that he is getting ready to overturn things: He must overturn, and that's all' (Bataille 1991 20/10). Put otherwise, in the line of thought being followed here, Kant's thought is characterised as being a 'renovated theology' (Deleuze 1983, 93). In consequence, far from constituting the invention of a thought that would escape State-form and 'blast open the continuum of history' (Benjamin 1973, 264),[1] Kantianism is taken to be a clandestine means of reinstating transcendence.[2] The link between the State-form and transcendence is the compliment to the intimacy that can be explored in an abstract diagram of immanent critique and philosophico-political heresy; this intimacy is not accidental but constitutive; the State-form in its different manifestations through history is sustained by transcendence.[3] Deleuze and Guattari capture the issue thus:

> Whenever there is transcendence, vertical Being, imperial state in the sky or on earth, there is religion; and there is philosophy wherever there is immanence.   (Deleuze and Guattari 1991, 46; 1994, 43)

An understanding of this abstract diagram of power and transcendence is the necessary precondition of accepting Kant's claim to be Copernican; it does of course give that claim an entirely different, negative or strictly delimited value. We can accept Kant's claim to be Copernican insofar as Copernicus' revolution is understood as merely having carried out a cosmic swapping of places: that is to say, he places the Sun in the centre of the cosmos, where the Earth had been. Copernicus, in other words, replaces geo- with the still more ancient heliocentrism,[4] and trades one variant of hierarchical thinking for another; he leaves in place the clockwork mechanisms of the Ptolemaic cosmos, preserves the crystal spheres, allows them to continue floating in the ether, and allows them to continue playing the resonating music that had entertained despots and popes, and stupefied the subjected for a millennum and a half. This celestial symphony is not disrupted until the rude intervention of the apostate Dominican of Nola, Giordano Bruno, and his decision to stop listening to the 'asses dressed up with diadems and hacks decked with rings under the title of doctors' (Bruno 1998, 25). It is only with Bruno that the closed cosmos of the medieval mind is definitively exploded, and it is left to Bruno to venture the possibility of a way of thinking other than the hierarchical, the stratified, for Bruno announces the necessity of thinking the world topologically, rhizomically, and of creating concepts that will reflect the fluid complexity of such a reality, an open conceptual structure, acentric and connected each point to every other by transversal lines, a cosmos and a thought form without a transcendent centre to anchor it. Bruno proclaims an unstable cosmos lacking hierarchy, value and direction, in which meaning does not limit itself, for wherever it goes, always and everywhere it is visible at the centre of the horizon, whether it shifts its observation point on the surface of the earth or on the edges of the universe as it crosses other worlds' (Bruno 1879–91, vol. I pt. 1 204). This clearly is a transformation of Cusa's *dicta* quoted above that God is an entity whose 'centre so to speak, is everywhere, whose circumference is nowhere', into a statement with both cosmological and epistemological ramifications, now, as Nuccio Ordine comments, in Bruno's hands 'the old cosmological concept that relegated the "edges" to a perpetually marginal position falls to pieces, for everything can become the centre, every element can occupy a different place' (Ordine 1996, 166). Deleuze and Guattari's smooth space, or plane of immanence is here perfectly prefigured in Bruno's monistic ontological and epistemological vision, but so too is Nietzsche's perspectivism.[5] When approached in this way it becomes clear quite how these diverse doctrines are all derived from the destruction of transcendental values executed by Bruno's extension of the implications of Copernicanism to their limit, the trajectory performed by the *perfect nihilist* who comes out on the other side of the inevitable event of nihilism.

Crucial to this trajectory is Bruno's adoption and transformation of the system of the Catalan mystic and polymath, Raymond Lull, and in particular of his *ars combinatoria*, so often cited as a precursor of cybernetic machines via its influence on Leibniz' *De Arte Combinatoria*.[6] Lull's breakthrough was to endow concepts with a new fluidity and dynamism utterly alien to the medieval world of hierarchies and categories, for as Spinoza writes 'the order and connection of ideas is the same as the order and connection of things' (Spinoza 1989, E II 7). Lull too postulates a new world, free from 'the restraints of the hierarchical structures of medieval concepts'. The concepts were now understood relative to one another, 'in relationships that were open because they could be reversed' (Roob 1997, 287). Bruno's critique and development of Copernicanism is explicitly carried out on the metaphysical, cosmological, and political planes simultaneously; indeed, as Negri insists in reading Spinoza, the critique of metaphysics *is* political. In Bruno this identity is performatively demonstrated. To trace out these apparently obscure arguments is to dissect the origins, formation and philosophico-political conceptual foundations of modernity itself (a by-product of this analysis is that the terms 'postmodernity' and its cognates must be limited to their origins as terms to describe a particular architectural style; all other uses of them are theoretically naïve and historically ill informed – unless of course one is enamoured of the idea that we *are* going somewhere – by virtue of their being ineluctably tied up with one form or other of teleology, one doctrine or other of universal progress). When we start to look at this birth of modernity, we find coiled in its heart the snake of nihilism; and so to take up, and somewhat distort, a point made by Habermas, we find that this birth has happened again, and again, and again, and every time that the refrain of modernity is played it comes accompanied by nihilism: their relationship, would appear to be symbiogenetic.[7] Nihilism is a constitutively productive element of modernity. It is the recognition of the inevitable coming of this unwanted accomplice that composes one of the elements of Deleuze's understanding of Nietzsche, and it is why he says that 'Nietzsche can think that nihilism is not an event in history but the motor of the history of man as universal history' (Deleuze 1983, 152).

It is not, then, with Copernicus that any sort of threat is posed to the terrestrial order via an onslaught upon its celestial cognate, but with Bruno. The full import of this shift of attribution is considerable and has nothing to do with correcting Kant's use of metaphors, i.e. suggesting that he and other self-aggrandisers no longer think of themselves and their achievements as having the status of the Copernican revolution but rather as being Brunian in their shattering effects. This revolution, both scientific and philosophical, is described by Alexandre Koyré as follows:

> the destruction of the Cosmos, that is, the disappearance, from philosophically and scientifically valid concepts, of the conception of the world as a finite, closed, and hierarchically ordered whole [...] and its replacement by an indefinite universe which is bound together by the identity of its fundamental components and laws, and in which all these concepts are placed on the same level of being. This, in turn, implies the discarding by scientific thought of all considerations based upon value-concepts, such as perfection, harmony, meaning and aim, and finally the utter devalorisation of being, the divorce of the world of value from the world of facts.   (Koyré 1957; 2)

Bruno is acutely aware of Copernicus' limits, and notes them curtly, as follows: he, Copernicus 'did not go much further [away from the common and vulgar philosophy] because he could not plumb and probe into matters to the extent that he could completely uproot unsuitable and empty principles [...] he did not have sufficient means to be able to defeat completely, conquer and suppress falsehood beyond all resistance' (Bruno 1995, 86). The first mention in print of Copernicus' heliocentric thesis was with the publication of his *Commentariolus* in 1514; this publication was followed by a long hiatus in which it was largely ignored, and when Bruno starts lecturing upon its contents and implications, it is not as Copernicus' first acolyte and proselytiser, but as his first and most severe critic (Mendoza 1995, 77), and as such, before the world was able to absorb the implications of Copernicus' system, Bruno was already bringing them news from a much more unfamiliar, disquieting planet: for barely had man been removed from the centre of the cosmos, than Bruno was abolishing the concept of centre altogether: 'Bruno not only anticipated Galileo and Kepler, but he passed beyond them into an entirely new world which had shed all the dross of tradition' (Singer 1950, 49).

Bruno offers a bold precursor of Deleuze and Guattari's demand that philosophy be in accord with the formula 'PLURALISM = MONISM' (Deleuze and Guattari 1980, 31; 1987, 20), as when he notes, explicitly against both Aristotelian and Platonic forms of dualism and transcendentalism, that 'nature descends to the production of things, and intellect ascends to the knowledge of them, by one and the same ladder. Both ways proceed from unity to unity' (Bruno 1998, 93). In this Bruno goes far beyond a naïve empiricism and ventures close to a speculative materialism in his promotion of a monism of modal differentiation. Bruno writes of what is, in effect, the plane of immanence that it is 'complicative [...] one, immense, infinite and comprehensive of all being, and in an explicative manner, it is present in sensible bodies and in the potency and the act that we see distinguished in them' (Bruno 1998, 93). He goes on to note that it is the mark of the feeble mind that it cannot 'understand multiplicity except through many species, analogies and forms [...]. The premier intelligence embraces everything in a single, absolutely perfect idea' (Bruno 1998, 95). This places Bruno directly in the line of univocal ontology, beyond the Scholastic categories, and in touch with a certain nominalistic critique of the Aristotelian architecture of natural species and of the *eidos*. The latter being a critique adopted by Nietzsche following Lange's position that there is 'no such instance of so empty and at the same time crass a superstition as that of Species, and there are probably few points in which men have gone on rocking themselves with such baseless argumentations into dogmatic slumber' (Lange 1879, iii 27).

It is entirely predictable that any discussion of nihilism will have to begin with Nietzsche, and specifically with the writings collected as *The Will to Power*. Nietzsche's characterisation of nihilism is complex, multifaceted, and ranged over several levels, referring to several ontologically distinct objects. Without wanting to attribute to Nietzsche a totalising system, it seems that the constellation of nihilism does indeed knit together several of the most important axes of Nietzschean thought. To put it in his own words, Nietzsche sees himself as 'a spirit of daring and experiment [who] has already lost [its] way once in every labyrinth of the future' (Nietzsche 1968, preface §2) and what he finds there is nihilism. The sustained understanding or diagnosis of nihilism is in a sense the most successful actualisation of one of Nietzsche's definitions of the role of the philosopher: that is as a physician engaged in the diagnosis of the sicknesses afflicting the world in which he finds himself, 'the philosopher as cultural physician'.[8] 'But it is sick, this unchained life, and needs to be cured' (Nietzsche 1983, 120). The philosopher as well as being a physician must be a 'soothsayer-bird spirit' who '*looks back* when relating what will come' (Nietzsche 1968, preface §3), and what this soothsayer sees in this case is a culture which 'has been moving as toward a catastrophe', and that catastrophe is the *advent of nihilism*. The describer of this catastrophe is by virtue of this vision a *perfect nihilist*, that is to say one who has gone through the experience of nihilism, the conflagration of transcendent values, and has left it behind, outside himself. Nihilism then is the diagnosis of our immediate past, and of our immediate present. As for Walter Benjamin, so for Nietzsche, both the past and the future are littered with signs, and speak 'even now in a hundred signs' (Nietzsche 1968 preface §2). The past is a transmitter of oracular wisdom, and it is only the soothsayer who may read this oracle; but a Nietzschean soothsayer, like Benjamin's and Paul Klee's angel of history, is Janus faced, he is orientated simultaneously both towards the future and the past. It is only the soothsayer, the 'architect of the future' (Nietzsche 1983, 94), who knows the present and who may read the oracle; it is imperative that the soothsayer '*looks back* when relating what will come' (Nietzsche 1968, preface §3), the philosopher must be a 'telephone from the beyond' (Nietzsche 1969, III 5), and the news he brings is that of nihilism. For Nietzsche the coming of nihilism, and our experiencing of it is inevitable, unavoidable and necessary; it is so in order that Nietzsche's much vaunted transvaluation of all values may occur: we 'must experience nihilism before we can find out what value these "values" really had – we require, sometime, *new values*' (Nietzsche 1968, preface §4). Diagnosis consists of the elements of etiology and prescription: revelation of the cause of the sickness, anatomisation of the symptoms and prescription of a curative solution. It is for precisely these reasons that Deleuze notes that the 'whole of philosophy is a symptomatology, and a semeiology', and that consequently its object of study, the 'phenomenon [...] is not an appearance or even an apparition but a sign, a symptom which finds its meaning in an existing force' (Deleuze 1983, 3). Nietzsche is immensely precise with each element of his diagnosis of nihilism, and unusually perhaps, no less so in his account of its etiology than in the other two elements. The precise source of nihilism for Nietzsche lies in Nicholas Copernicus' overturning of the Ptolemaic geocentric cosmology, and its replacement with the, in certain senses still more ancient, heliocentric model. As is all too familiar, the immediate consequence of this is that 'the faith in the dignity and uniqueness of man, in his irreplaceability in the great chain of being' became a 'thing of the past'. Copernicus' projection placed man on 'an inclined plane' so that 'now he is slipping faster and faster away from the centre into – what? into nothingness? into a *"penetrating* sense of his nothingness"' (Nietzsche 1969, III 25).

It follows from this that the Copernican revolution needs to be displaced from its principal position in the narrative of nihilism, 'this long plenitude and sequence of breakdown, destruction, ruin and cataclysm' (Nietzsche 1974, §343). As already noted Kant prides himself in carrying out a Copernican revolution in thought, he believes his own achievement to be a seismic event in the possibilities, trajectories and purposes of philosophy, he believes that his *Critiques* represent a shift in philosophy as radical as that represented by Copernicus in cosmology. The Chinaman of Königsberg is of course entitled to his own self-assessment, the problem is that it is not to Copernicus that the revolution that bears his name ought to be attributed, and that hence the event that Kant believes himself to be analogous to is not a revolution but a mere holding manoeuvre on the part of a faltering, crumbling *ancien régime* of thought.

In light of the above, the issue of nihilism, when understood as a diagnosis of Occidental culture since roughly the late-nineteenth-century crisis of faith, must be recast. Classically it has been understood to be precipitated largely by various developments in the natural sciences, critically the Darwinian removal of man from the top of the chain of being, or rather the removal of that 'chain' altogether, and the complete absorption of the ramifications of the much earlier 'Copernican' revolution: the abolition of the geocentrism of the Ptolemaic cosmos, a single gathering wave from the sixteenth to the late nineteenth centuries. However, the advent of nihilism can be refashioned as a constantly recurring refrain in the history of thought. Understood as a persistent scepticism, and as a resolute rejection of all transcendent values, nihilism is absolutely intimate with Deleuze's understanding of philosophy's role as a naturalism, and at the same time a part of Nietzsche's demand that philosophy become both immoral and historical. Although his work hurls countless accusations and critiques against all prior philosophy, it is arguable that there are for Nietzsche two general reasons as to why 'every philosophical architect in Europe has built in vain' (Nietzsche 1982, preface §3). Kant's answer that the reason for this is the absence of a critique of reason is adjudged ludicrous. The first reason, for Nietzsche, is the eternal seduction of metaphysics by morality, and the concomitant preoccupation with truth, against which he 'succeeded in making us understand, thought is creation, not will to truth' (Deleuze and Guattari 1991, 55; 1994, 54). The demand for *historical philosophising* is Nietzsche's response to the second of the generalised forms of the failure of all hitherto existing metaphysical philosophy, that is, that they start out 'from man as he is now and think[ing] their goal through an analysis of him. They involuntarily think of "man" as an *aeterna veritas* [...] they will not learn that man has become, that the faculty of cognition has become' (Nietzsche 1986, §2). This is clearly a charge that can be laid against Kant who acts as if science is and always will be Newtonian science and 'thereby branded as impossible any opposition to classical science that was not an opposition to science itself' (Prigogine and Stengers 1984, 86). Kant is quite explicit about this, and it is clear that his motivation for such a position, and for much else in his system, is derived from the necessity of resisting the implications of a philosophy of nature that has consistently dethroned the sovereignty of man, Spinoza's intention to treat man as if he were dealing with 'lines, planes and bodies' (Spinoza 1989, E III preface) for example.[9] Here is Kant's most forthright statement of the necessity of limiting science:

It is, I mean, quite certain that we can never get a sufficient knowledge of organised beings and their inner possibility [...] by looking merely to mechanical principles of nature [...] it is absurd for men to even entertain any thought of so doing or to hope that maybe another Newton may some day arise, to make intelligible to us even the genesis of a blade of grass from natural laws that no design has ordered. Such insight we must absolutely deny to mankind.   (Kant 1952, §75)

For Nietzsche the event of nihilism leaves the way open for a *chemistry of concepts and sensations*, which in contradistinction to the frozen ontological and epistemological eternal verities of metaphysics will recognise that:

everything has become: there are no *eternal facts*, just as there are no absolute truths. Consequently what is needed from now on is *historical philosophising*.   (Nietzsche 1986, §2)

The dawn of nihilism, then, construed as a thinking of 'existence as it is, without meaning or aim, yet occurring inevitably without any finale of nothingness' (Nietzsche 1968, §55), is a part of that virulent materialism that runs through Occidental civilisation in perpetual, absolute opposition, destroying idols, pronouncing the end of ideals, renouncing states, smashing superstitions, engaging in an indefatigable 'practical critique of all mystifications' (Deleuze 1969, 378; 1980, 279), from Sextus Empiricus to Lucretius, Bruno to Spinoza, Marx to Nietzsche.

In this way, Kant's self-proclaimed revolution can be imagined as an attempt to cancel time; and the critiques can be envisaged as a massive dam built to hold back the horrors of a world without meaning, a world torn from its hinges (the most profound interpretation of Hamlet's time 'out of joint'). Kant himself is adamant that the 'concept of noumenon is thus a merely *limiting concept* [...] and it is therefore only of negative employment' (Kant 1929, A 255/B 311) or even more determinedly 'it is not indeed in any way positive' (Kant 1929, A 252). The Kantianism system, then, is a sea-wall built to ensure that 'the voyage of our reason may be extended no further than the continuous coastline of experience itself [...] a coast we cannot leave without venturing upon a shoreless ocean which [...] compels us in the end to abandon as hopeless all this vexatious and tedious endeavour' (Kant 1929, A 395). In other words to accept the decentring of man and the necessity of a transvaluation of all values implied by a Brunian Cosmology would, for Kant, unleash once again the corrosive speculations of those '*sceptics* [that] species of nomads' who 'despising all settled modes of life, broke up from time to time all civil society' (Kant 1929, A ix). And that, needless to add, was not an option that Kant would countenance. Copernicanism was already conceptually discredited, although as is evidenced by Kant's claim to its mantle, not politically and culturally redundant. Its ontological foundations were shattered, its empirical suppositions super-seded by the scope of Bruno's epoch leaping imagination, even before its general acceptance. The Vatican had in fact developed a far more perceptive assessment of the metaphysical, ontological and political stakes involved in the Copernican 'hypothesis' than Kant ever did.[10] The Vatican's censorship body, the Index Congregation, characterised the Copernican enterprise 'as simply a *doctrina Pythagorica'* (Lange 1879, I 232), and as a consequence didn't find it necessary to place the *Book of the Revolutions of the Heavenly Spheres* on the Index of proscribed books until seventy three years after its 1543 publication, and sixteen years after Bruno's murder. Indeed as Koestler shows there is 'evidence of early benevolent interest in the Copernican theory [...] by the Vatican' (Koestler 1959, 155). The Catholic hierarchy, then, was fully cognisant of the fact that the threat posed by the Coperni-canism of its author was minimal – the old Canon Copernigk stayed in his isolated tower and troubled no-one, unlike the seemingly fearless Nolan driven by an *eroico furore*, which had both Apollinean and Dionysian dimen-sions 'the former because it was a passion for truth and knowledge, the latter because it led to death and resurrection' (Mendoza 1995, xxiv)[11] harboured no reticence about promulgating his disdain for the established order. The canon, on the contrary was never persecuted; he was in fact fêted, even encouraged, by elements reaching as high up the Vatican hierarchy as the pope himself, and to reciprocate for this patronage, it is the pope's name that is found on the dedications page of the *Book of Revolutions*. No such collusion occurs with Bruno, whose purpose is explicitly revolutionary and directed to the destruction of dogmatically imposed ideas and values. So if Kant can ignore Bruno, if he can write as if Bruno had never happened, and if he can pretend that the revolution really does happen with Copernicus he can keep the old order intact. As Nietzsche points out:

> since Kant, transcendentalists of every kind have once more won the day – they have been emancipated from the theologians: what joy! – Kant showed them a secret path by which they may, on their own initiative and with all scientific respectability, from now on follow their 'heart's desire'. (Nietzsche 1969, III §25)

That is, they can sustain the existence of the transcendental without having to resort to the theological: garb themselves with the cloak of revolution and simultaneously reconstitute a different 'regulative fiction', a new form of 'police supervision' (Nietzsche 1974, §344). In Nietzsche's judgement, then, Kant is subject to the rebuke that he had himself directed at those he dubbed 'pretended *indifferentists*', that they 'fell back [...] into those very metaphy-sical assertions which they profess so greatly to despise' (Kant 1929, Ax). As has already been indicated, Nietzsche's diagnosis of nihilism is tripartite, the third part being prescriptive: for after the revaluation of all values comes the formation of new ones. The programme of the *perfect nihilist* is inscribed, Nietzsche reminds us, on the title page of his 'gospel of the future' and it is *The Will to Power: Attempt at a Revaluation of All Values* (Nietzsche 1968, preface §4), Nietzsche lives through, indeed escalates ('You ain't seen nothin' yet'), the necessary event of nihilism, and drags something shining and new from the catastrophic wreckage, the psychic detritus of having been Christian for two thousand years. Unlike Kant, Nietzsche understands that the disarmed depth charge dropped by Copernicus had been surreptitiously retrieved, rewired and given a depleted uranium warhead of immense destructive power by Bruno. Kant retains, claws back, the centre that Bruno had abolished. In constructing the standpoint of the transcendental, Kant reformulates the Renaissance Humanist vision of human dignity, to follow Nietzsche, the Kantian supposition of the scientific human subject deciphering natural law, the subject of the critical epistemology 'was immediately employed by man for his own self-glorification' (Nietzsche 1990b, §106). The Kantian critical enterprise keeps man in thrall of the pathological desire for centring that still orders the healthy human psyche, the 'coming of Spirit apprehending itself' (Prigogine and Stengers 1984, 89) in Hegelian language, the psychoanalytic subject on the Freudian couch. This drive for there *to be* a centre is a veritable, persistent, pernicious pathology. Witness, for example, the history of languages of the self predicated as they are upon the equation of health with centredness, balance, symmetry (that is, conventional ideas of beauty and current spurious attempts to calculate the physical average of the perfect face based upon the deviance of the proportions of facial features from a statistical norm). This pathology is cauterised at source by Bruno and his relentless pursuit of the 'universe that has lost all *centre* as well as any figure that could be attributed to it' (Deleuze 1993, 124). In philosophical history there are two types of hermit or recluse: first is the voluntary like Kant, and second those condemned to exile, the heretical, the outcast. Contrary to his own belief that he is 'a solitary by instinct who has found his advantage in standing aside and outside' (Nietzsche 1968, preface §3) it is to the latter type that Nietzsche truly belongs:

> These outcasts of society, long persecuted and sorely hunted – also the enforced recluses, the Spinozas and Giordano Brunos – in the end always become refined vengeance-seekers and brewers of poison.
>
> (Nietzsche 1990a, §25)

II

As has repeatedly been intimated, it will not be enough for Nietzsche to simply recognise the necessity, the repetition, and the event of nihilism, one must go beyond it, and take its implications on board in the task of creating *new values.* '*Radical nihilism*' is the conviction of an absolute untenability of existence when it comes to the highest values one recognises; plus the realisation that we lack the least right to posit a beyond or an in-itself of things that might be 'divine' (Nietzsche 1968, §3). The basis for this revaluation, for this living through, lies in a dizzying perspectivism and a defiant cheerfulness that enables one to approach the 'gloom without any real sense of involvement and above all without any worry and fear *for ourselves*' (Nietzsche 1974, §343). Related to this, and presumably with the just quoted passage from *The Gay Science* in mind, Deleuze and Guattari make a very simple yet astounding comment about what is commonly held to be the archetypal, the pinnacle event of nihilism, they write that 'for philosophers neither atheism nor the death of God are problems [...]. That philosophers still take the death of god to be a tragedy is astonishing. Atheism isn't a drama, but the philosopher's serenity and philosophy's achievement' (Deleuze and Guattari 1991, 89; 1994, 92 *my translation*). Now this idea eliminates whole currents of thought past and present in both analytic and continental philosophy, burdened as they have been by the weight of the past, by what Nietzsche on occasion calls 'the shadow of God'. This truly philosophical attitude, described by Deleuze and Guattari is precisely what Nietzsche means by cheerfulness, and Spinoza by joy. This cheerfulness is the only way to confront the 'monstrous logic of terror' (Nietzsche 1974, §343) entailed by the destruction of transcendent values, and of the consequences of 'the death of god'; Nietzsche says:

> They are not at all sad and gloomy but rather like a new and scarcely describable kind of light [...] We philosophers and 'free spirits' feel, when we hear the news that the 'old god is dead', as if a new dawn shone upon us; our heart overflows with gratitude, amazement, premonitions, expectation. At long last the horizon appears free to us again, even if it should not be bright; at long last the horizon appears free to us again, even if it should not be right, at long last our ships may venture out again.
> (Nietzsche 1974, §343)

As we have seen, the most striking result of Bruno's radicalisation of Copernicus is the restriction of the Canon's work to a mere cosmic swapping of places. The Nolan on the contrary eliminates the entire medieval machinery, with its armillary spheres, its fixed firmament, hierarchies and centres and replaces it with an infinite, acentric, topological smooth space.

> You will no longer say that there is an edge or limit either to the extent or motion of the universe; you will esteem the belief in a *primum mobile*, an uppermost and all containing heaven, to be a vain fantasy.
> (Bruno 1950, 361)

It is with this invective that Bruno admonishes those who still hang onto a medieval or even a Copernican cosmos, and he might have added with Nietzsche and Admiral Turenne, 'You tremble, carcass? You would tremble a lot more if you knew where I was taking you' (Nietzsche 1974, 277).[12] It is this abolition of the cosmological *primum mobile*, that had lead Bruno to the requisite perspectival and historical approach to epistemology that Nietzsche prescribes. Two options for knowledge are posed in the aftermath of the event of nihilism. For Nietzsche both must be avoided with equal vehemence; on the one hand, there is the stifling atmosphere – one that had made Kleist so suicidal – of Kantianism's 'gnawing and disintegrating scepticism and relativism' (Nietzsche 1983, 140), an atmosphere of scepticism in which 'no one can live' (Nietzsche 1990b, §84), and on the other, the pathological *'belief in truth* [which] makes its appearance as a social necessity [and] has a *moral* origin' (Nietzsche 1990b, §91). Nietzsche's response to both of these dire options 'lies not in *knowing*, but in *creating*' (Nietzsche 1990b, §84). One of the clearest statements as to what Nietzsche means by this is as follows:

> For the plant the world is thus and such; for us the world is thus and such. If we compare the two perceptual powers we consider our view of the world to be the more correct one, i.e. the one that corresponds more closely to the truth [...] The natural process is carried on by science. Thus the things mirror themselves ever more clearly, gradually liberating themselves from what is all too anthropomorphic. For the plant, the whole world is a plant; for us, it is human.   (Nietzsche 1990b, §102)

It is a constant of Nietzsche's critique of Kant that the latter remains ahistorical, that his philosophy is 'entirely outside the historical movement; without any eye for the actuality of his time [...] way off when it comes to great historical values' (Nietzsche 1968, §95, 101). Directly tied to this is Kant's reinvention of the sovereign human subject, his reinscription in the centre of the knowable cosmos though the invention of the categories of reason, the Kantian basis of the anthropocentric platitude, *man is the measure of all things* – the 'hyperbolic naïveté of man' (Nietzsche 1968, §12), the quintessence of humanism against which Bruno had so diligently fought, and against which he posed with Nietzsche, man's 'smallness and accidental occurrence in the flux of becoming and passing away' (Nietzsche 1968, §4).

Since the result of nihilism is the recognition of the destruction of man's privileged position within the acentric, valueless, non-hierarchical entanglement that is the world (and that Nietzsche warns against and actively seeks to circumvent) the possibility is that his analysis, his diagnosis of nihilism, will be taken for a merely negative platitude. Indeed, he writes that 'nihilism is not just a collection of speculations around the theme "all is in vain!": it is not just the thought that everything deserves to be destroyed: the nihilist helps to destroy' (Nietzsche 1968, §102; 1995 §24 *my translation*), and having destroyed, rebuilds.[13]

Notes

1 In 'Thesis XVI of the 'Thesis on the Philosophy of History', Walter Benjamin writes that it is the task of the historical materialist critic to be 'in control of his powers, man enough to blast open the continuum of history'. Another thesis elaborates on this theme, emphasising that historical materialism is not a passive empiricism, but a constructivism, 'based on a constructive principle'. It seeks to 'blast a specific era out of the homogeneous course of history [...] a specific life out of the era or a specific work out of the lifework'. Again, 'the awareness that they are about to make the continuum of history explode is characteristic of the revolutionary classes at the moment of their action' (Benjamin 1973, 263).

2 For a detailed exposition of the concept of 'State-form', its differences from the classical Marxist model, and the necessarily transcendent nature of State thought, see Hardt and Negri 1994, especially the section 'Genealogy of the Constituent Subject' (308–13).

3 The construction of this abstract diagram was one of the principal objects of my thesis, 'A Schizogenealogy of Heretical Materialism...' (Warwick 1999), especially in the section entitled, 'Theses on Brunian Materialism in Deleuze'. See also Negri (1991; 1994) on the identification of politics and ontology in Spinoza and Descartes in particular.

4 Frances Yates offers a detailed account of the long history of heliocentrism, paying especial attention to the role of the sun in Neoplatonic and Neopythagorean mysticisms. As an index of quite how artificial the boundaries were between 'science and Hermeticism in the Renaissance' she writes that 'Copernicus' discovery came out with the blessing of Hermes Trismegistus upon its head, with a quote from that famous work in which Hermes describes the sun-worship of the Egyptians in their magical religion [...] And at the crucial moment, just after the diagram showing the new sun-centred system comes a reference to Hermes Trismegistus on the sun' (Yates 1991, 155).

5 For Deleuze and Guattari, philosophy is characterised as a constructivism with two interconnected yet distinct elements: 'the creation of concepts and the laying out of a plane' of immanence, this latter 'constitutes the absolute ground of philosophy, its earth or deterritorialisation, the foundation on which it creates its concepts' (Deleuze and Guattari 1991: 44; 1994: 41). Philosophy in this sense is coterminous with immanence, it is not that immanence is one concept among many that one can choose to think or not, at the same time it is not a master key, for 'whenever immanence is interpreted as immanent *to* Something, we can be sure that this Something reintroduces the transcendent' (ibid., 48; 45); rather philosophy is defined by immanence in contradistinction to the transcendent which characterises religion. 'Whenever there is transcendence [...] there is religion; and there is philosophy whenever there is immanence' (ibid., 46; 43). There is no one plane of immanence; it is the mark of great philosophers, as opposed to the 'functionary' (52; 51), Nietzsche's 'officially recognised guild of pseudo-thinkers' (Nietzsche 1983, 190), that they invent their own plane of immanence. It is this invention of planes that gives the specific mode of philosophical time as *stratigraphic*, for it is not a question of a linear succession, a list of names of the dead

(a Necronomicon), but rather an interlacing of planes, no longer characterised by before or after, but rather above and below. 'Philosophy is becoming, not history; it is the coexistence of planes, not the succession of systems' (Deleuze and Guattari 1994: 59; 1994: 59).

6   Recall that Norbert Wiener acknowledges Leibniz as the 'patron saint for cybernetics' (Wiener 1994, 12) for two reasons: first, for anticipating mathematical notation and second for constructing an early symbolic logic; but one can also construe a third reason, and that is for the implications of Leibniz's thought for the mechanical actualisation of thought 'in the metal'. However, as Ernst Bloch argues, the credit here should go to Lull, whose combinatory circles take pride of place as the first abstract diagrams of a calculating device, and now 'Lull's arithmeticised dream has been turned into a whole intellectual industry, with speed as witchcraft' (Bloch 1986, 652). Both Yates and Bloch show that a considerable part of Bruno's work, principally his earlier texts on mnemonic techniques, constitute an attempt to improve upon or rationalise the Lullian art. It should though be borne in mind that, as with all of the other figures cannibalised for Bruno's syncretism, his interpretation of Lull is 'even more peculiar, and more remote from the medieval Lull, than [that found] in normal Renaissance Lullism' (Yates 1996, 207). Once again then we see Bruno's decisive stamp on one of the key figures of the Deleuzian genealogy. Bruno's influence on Leibniz extends to other areas too as is evidenced by the frequency of his appearances in *The Fold: in brevis*, the Leibnizian monad is taken from Bruno, principally for its role in the transformation of 'Neoplatonic emanations [...] to a large zone of immanence' (Deleuze 1993, 24); the supposition of a universal parasitism is Brunian; as is the Leibnizian *complicatio*.

7   In what is, I suppose, a landmark essay 'Modernity: an Incomplete Project' Jürgen Habermas notes the frequency, dating back to the fifth century, of the use of the term 'modernity' to denote 'the consciousness of an epoch that relates itself to the past of antiquity, in order to view itself as the result of a transition from the old to the new' (Habermas 1985: 3).

8   See the collection of aphorisms under this title in Nietzsche 1990b: 69–76.

9   For an account of the role that the rising tide of Spinozist-inspired *Naturphilosophie* had upon much of Kantianism, see Beiser 1987, chapter on 'The Rise of Spinozism in Germany 1680–1786' which gives a vivid account of the terror that Spinozist materialism and atheism inspired in the forces of authority, and principally in Kant.

10 Between the completion of the manuscript of *The Book of the Revolutions* in 1530 and its eventual publication, Copernicus vacillated, terrified by the possible consequences of the public availability of his book and his neurotic obsession with maintaining a Pythagorean secrecy. Like Copernicus, Darwin too vacillated in publishing his genuinely revolutionary findings, unlike Copernicus, Darwin *was* genuinely terrified about the social, political and religious conflagration that his work might, and did, spark. Darwin's fears are minutely detailed in the magnificent biography by Desmond and Moore (1997). When Copernicus' book was eventually published it came with a preface by the cofounder of Lutheranism, Andreas Osiander, who, unlike his colleagues, Luther himself and Melanchton, was favourable to Copernicanism. There is some historical controversy as to Copernicus' attitude towards this preface; indeed, it is not even certain that he was in any position to read it, as the first printed copy of his book arrived only hours before his death by which time his mind had become as unhinged as the

Earth soon would be. The point of this preface, and my sole reason for mentioning it, is that it describes the contents of the *Revolutions* as 'hypotheses [which] need not be true nor even probable' (the full text of the preface can be found in Koestler 1959, 573 fn9).

11 *Eroico furore* is the title of one of Bruno's books, the most recent English translation of which is that by P. Memmo, see Bruno 1964.

12 This quotation has a page reference, rather than a section number as is usual with Nietzsche because it is the motto of book five 'We Fearless Ones' of *The Gay Science*. According to Walter Kaufmann's commentary, this splendid quotation comes from the Vicomte de Turenne, the great seventeenth-century French general.

13 That 'Nietzsche was aroused from his dogmatic slumber by Darwin' (Kaufmann 1962, 142), is a commonplace. But what is less remarked upon is that while Nietzsche has a long and sustained engagement with Darwin, it is substantially a Darwin mediated through the book that Nietzsche called variously a 'treasure house' and 'the most significant philosophical work to have appeared in the last hundred years', i.e. Lange's *History of Materialism*. There is a small but growing literature on the influence, upon Nietzsche, of Lange's astonishing and compendious three volume work, from which I have consulted Stack 1983 and Ansell Pearson 1988. A detailed examination of the complex set of relationships – Nietzsche and Lange, Nietzsche and Darwin – is beyond the scope of the present chapter. However, in a larger work, currently in progress, I go on to examine some aspects of the latter. I deal in particular the resonances within Nietzsche's diagnosis of nihilism and his coterminous project of perspectivism of Darwin's horrendous realisation that 'it is absurd to talk of one animal being higher than another [. . .] *We* consider those, where the intellectual faculties [are] most developed as highest – a bee doubtless would [use] instincts [as a criterion]' (Darwin quoted in Desmond and Moore 1997, 232). One of the principal objects of Nietzsche's implacable philosophical scorn is the skin of humanism that binds the dominant traditions of philosophical history, an anthropomorphism stretched between Plato and Kant. This humanism which grounds an instrumentalism ('to "humanise" the world, i.e. to feel ourselves more and more masters within it' (Nietzsche 1968, §613) towards the cosmos is skewered by Nietzschean perspectivism and its speculations upon the possibilities of nonorganic perception and nonhuman senses. Indeed, Nietzsche suggests that: 'other interpretations than merely human ones are perhaps somewhere possible' (Nietzsche 1968, §616). The existence of such senses is now supported by solid empirical evidence ranging from deep sea fish that can see light at wavelengths well beyond the range perceptible to the human, to the sonic abilities of bats and dogs, and beyond the senses to von Uexküll's writing on the temporalities of different organisms from the tick to the tree and to bacteria. The line of thought opened here, has, it can be argued, culminated in what Ilya Prigogine has called 'the end of certainty'. In Prigogine's interpretation, quantum mechanics is the apotheosis and actualisation, of the analysis of nihilism and its transvaluation that we have developed out of Nietzsche. Prigogine writes that 'we are on the eve of the "probabilistic revolution", which has been going on for centuries. Probability is no longer a state of mind due to our ignorance, but the result of laws of nature' (Prigogine 1997, 132): we must henceforth confront not a relativity of truth, but a truth of the relative (see, for example, Deleuze 1993, 20; Deleuze 1985, 191; 1989, 147, and Deleuze and Guattari 1991, 55, 123; 1994: 54, 130).

References

Ansell Pearson, K. (1988) 'The Question of F.A. Lange's Influence on Nietzsche. A Critique of Recent Research from the Standpoint of the Dionysian' in *Nietzsche-Studien: Internationales Jahrbuch für die Nietzsche-Forschung*, Band XVII, 539–54.

Bataille, G. (1991) *The Accursed Share, vol. I: Consumption*, trans. by Robert Hurley, New York: Zone Books.

Beiser, F. (1987) *The Fate of Reason: German Philosophy from Kant to Fichte*, Cambridge MA: Harvard University Press.

Benjamin, W. (1973) 'Theses on the Philosophy of History' in *Illuminations*, trans. H. Zohn, New York: Schocken Books, 2nd edn, 253–64.

Bloch, E. (1986) *The Principle of Hope*, trans. N. and S. Plaice and P. Knight, Oxford: Basil Blackwell.

Bruno, G. (1879 91) *Opera latine conscripta*, ed. by F. Fiorentino, F. Tocco, H. Vitelli, V. Imbriani, C. M. Tallarigo, 3 vols. in 8 parts, Florence: Le Monnier.

—— (1964) *Giordano Bruno's The Heroic Frenzies*, trans. P. Memmo, Chapel Hill: University of North Carolina Press.

—— (1995) *The Ash Wednesday Supper*, ed. and trans. by E.A. Gosselin and L.S. Lerner, Toronto: University of Toronto Press.

—— (1998) *Cause, Principle and Unity. And Essays on Magic*, trans. and ed. R.J. Blackwell, intro. by A. Ingegno, Cambridge: Cambridge University Press.

Deleuze, G. (1983) *Nietzsche and Philosophy*, trans. by H. Tomlinson, London: Athlone Press.

—— (1985) *Cinéma 2: L'image-temps* Paris: Les éditions de Minuit (1989) *Cinema 2: The Time Image*, trans. by H. Tomlinson and R. Galeta, London: The Athlone Press.

—— (1993) *The Fold: Leibniz and the Baroque*, trans. T. Conley, Minneapolis: University of Minnesota Press.

Deleuze, G. and Guattari, F. (1980) *Mille Plateaux: Capitalisme et schizophrénie 2* Paris: Les éditions de Minuit.

—— (1987) *A Thousand Plateaus: Capitalism and Schizophrenia*, trans. B. Massumi, Minneapolis: University of Minnesota Press.

—— (1991) *Qu'est-ce que la philosophie?* Paris: Les éditions de Minuit.

—— (1994) *What is philosophy?* trans. G. Burchell and H. Tomlinson, London: Verso.

Desmond, A. and Moore, J. (1997) *Darwin* London: Penguin Books.

Habermas, J. (1985) 'Modernity: an Incomplete Project' trans. by S. Benhabib, in *Postmodern Culture*, ed. H. Foster 3–15 London: Pluto.

Hardt, M. and Negri, A. (1994) *Labor of Dionysus: a Critique of the State-Form* Minneapolis and London: University of Minnesota Press.

Kant, I. (1929) *Critique of Pure Reason*, trans. N. Kemp Smith, London: Macmillan.

—— (1952) *Critique of Judgement* trans. J. Creed Meredith, Oxford: Clarendon Press.

Kaufmann, W. (1962) *Nietzsche: Philosopher, Psychologist, Antichrist* New York: Meridian.

Koestler, A. (1959) *The Sleepwalkers: A History of Man' Changing Vision of the Universe*, London: Penguin.

Koyré, A. (1957) *From the Closed World to the Infinite Universe* Baltimore: Johns Hopkins University Press.

Lange, F.A. (1879) *The History of Materialism and Criticism of its Present Importance*, one volume edition, trans. E. Chester Thomas, London: Trübner & Co.

Mendoza, R.G. (1995) *The Acentric Labyrinth: Giordano Bruno's Prelude to Contemporary Cosmology* Shaftesbury: Element.

Negri, A. (1991) *The Savage Anomaly: the Power of Spinoza's Metaphysics and Politics* trans. M. Hardt, Minneapolis: University of Minnesota Press.

Nietzsche, F. (1968) *The Will To Power*, trans. W. Kaufmann and R.J. Hollingdale, New York: Vintage Books.

—— (1969) *On the Genealogy of Morals and Ecce Homo*, trans. W. Kaufmann, New York: Vintage Books.

—— (1974) *The Gay Science*, trans. W. Kaufmann, New York: Vintage Books.

—— (1982) *Daybreak: Thoughts on the Prejudices of Morality*, trans. by R.J. Hollingdale, Cambridge: Cambridge University Press.

—— (1983) *Untimely Meditations*, trans. R.J. Hollingdale, Cambridge: Cambridge University Press.

—— (1986) *Human, All Too Human: a Book for Free Spirits*, trans. R.J. Hollingdale, Cambridge: Cambridge University Press

—— (1990a) *Beyond Good and Evil*, trans. R.J. Hollingdale, London: Penguin.

—— (1990b) *Philosophy and Truth: Selections from Nietzsche's Notebooks of the Early 1870's*, ed. and trans. by D. Breazale, London: Humanities Press.

—— (1995) *La volonté de puissance*, in two volumes, trans. G. Bianquis, Paris: Gallimard.

Ordine, N. (1996) *Giordano Bruno and the Philosophy of the Ass*, trans. H. Baranski with A. Saiber, New Haven and London: Yale University Press.

Prigogine, I and Stengers, I (1984) *Order Out of Chaos: Man's New Dialogue With Nature* London: Flamingo.

Prigogine, I. in collaboration with Stengers I (1997) *The End of Certainty: Time, Chaos and the New Laws of Nature* New York: The Free Press.

Singer, D.W. (1950) *Giordano Bruno: His Life and Thought*, includes Singer's translation of Bruno's *On the Infinite Universe and Worlds* New York: Henry Schuman.

Spinoza, B. de. (1989) *Ethics*, trans. A. Boyle and revised by G.H.R. Parkinson, London: J.M. Dent & Sons Ltd.

Stack, G.J. (1983) *Lange and Nietzsche* Berlin: de Gruyter.

Wiener, N. (1994) *Cybernetics: or Control and Communication in the Animal and the Machine*, second edition, Cambridge, MA and London: The MIT Press.

Yates, F. (1991) *Giordano Bruno and the Hermetic Tradition* Chicago: University of Chicago Press.

—— (1996) *The Art of Memory* London: Pimlico.

2
Nihilism, Tonight...

Justin Clemens and Chris Feik

> Under mid-winter light in an antique hall
> 'the fall of because' scrawled on a wall
> suggests why Europe's just a highbrow joke –
> they invented causation in place of hope
> John Forbes

Duped insurgents

What's become of nihilism today? Almost every recent text on the subject is very quickly forced to acknowledge its apparent degradation. Karen Carr, for instance, announces that 'Nietzsche's "uncanniest of all guests", the bane of the nineteenth century, is becoming an unremarkable, even banal, feature of modern life... as its crisis value diminishes, as it becomes accepted with an indifferent shrug,... [Nihilism] devolves into its antithesis: a dogmatic absolutism' (Carr 1992, 10). On Carr's account, something unexpected has obviously occurred, a 'devolution'. Yet if – as Keith Ansell Pearson puts it – 'today it remains as necessary as ever to think through the problem of nihilism and perform Nietzsche's demand for a revaluation of all our values' (Ansell Pearson 1994, 8), then how does this devolution vitiate the forcefulness of the term? For, as the very same texts point out, nihilism is not yet a word that can simply be dispensed with, for nothing else seems quite as appropriate for any possible global critique of contemporary capital, modern technology, Western democratic ideology, nuclear proliferation, ecological mismanagement, global administrative politics, mass-media hyperbole, and so on (see Eden 1983; Gare 1993; Agamben 1991; Darby *et al.* 1989; Critchley 1997).

Nihilism's global im-pertinence, it seems, comes at the cost of its rhetorical distraction. For the term has dropped almost completely out of establishment political discourse in favour of such appellations as 'anti-democratic', 'terroristic', 'fundamentalist', etc. If it is deployed in such situations, it is as an indifferently substitutable term whose value resides merely in its capacity to be chained with a number of other derogatory, supposedly synonymous words. A recent *Economist*, for example, employs this associative procedure in order to describe a 'new terrorism' that replaces revolutionary programmes with a 'nihilist brand of fanaticism' (*The Economist* 1998, 16). Even in those rare public moments when its use does seem absolutely consistent and justifiable, 'nihilism's' force and signification are immediately swept away in and by the startling fact of its appearance at all. Greil Marcus, recalling (as he drives down a freeway) Elizabeth Drew's use of the word 'nihilistic' in the 1980 US Elections, writes:

> What was Drew talking about? She's famous for her reasonableness, her blandness, for numbing transcriptions of interviews and cherry-blossom reports, and as a violation of her normal discourse this word made no sense. It was loud and violent, but like the crash of a falling tree nobody hears. (Marcus 1993, 351)

'Like the crash of a falling tree' . . . the current reality of nihilism is that it is nothing in reality: even the word itself has become as nugatory and inexplicable in its aleatory violence as the unhappy figures and events it and its cognates were once held to designate. On one hand, Marcus is confronted by the apparent impotence of the term, and, on the other, with the fact of its recurrent apparition and unpredictable tiny effects. Indeed, Marcus himself, musing on Drew's utterance, suddenly changes radio stations, and is shocked into automotive immobility by the irruption of Laurie Anderson's 'O Superman' through the speakers.

Marcus's anecdote once again illustrates the almost universal uncertainty regarding the critical purchase of 'nihilism' now. In throwing doubt on nihilism's status as a *politically forceful philosophical discourse*, such a challenge raises a set of valuable questions. Is an attention to nihilism still the most compelling or sophisticated way to characterise contemporary social phenomena? Or does the current situation rather require ways of thinking that depart from the critical heritage in which nihilism has played such a crucial role? Indeed, a willingness to think such questions through, to re-examine the devolution and marginality of nihilism against the background of its institutional and political history, may paradoxically be a condition of returning to nihilism its critical force. In this chapter, we seek to stitch together the apparently incommensurable treatments of the question of nihilism by philosophy and sociology, so as to undercut the standard philosophical sense of the term. Without repudiating the philosophical sense absolutely, we will attempt to show the limits of the uses to which the term has been put by the post-Nietzschean tradition, limits which remained necessarily unquestioned within this tradition. Discerning these limits will then enable us to speak about the historical emergence of political nihilism in a different way – without simply rehearsing inherited philosophical and sociological presumptions about its meaning. Our genealogy seeks to show how and why the philosophical account took the forms that it did and, following on from this, to provide a explanatory diagnosis of the scope and status of nihilism now.

Any attempt to do this must still confront Nietzsche. In the wake of Nietzsche's declaration of the 'death of God', and his concomitant recognition that man would rather will nothingness than not will at all, the quest has been on to supplement his account of nihilism and its genealogy. Despite the distance that these critiques often try to take from Nietzsche as well as from each other, the limits that he delineated with regard to the historical and conceptual determination of nihilism continue to govern the application of this term (see, for instance, Ansell Pearson 1994; Darby *et al.* 1989; Eden 1993; Jonas 1963; Martin 1989; Smith 1996; Ward 1995). Consequently, the post-Nietzschean sense of nihilism invariably boomerangs back upon the following conditions:

1   As an analytic description, nihilism designates the status of the *era* in which *we* are now living, and in which the ungroundedness of every ethico-ontological prescription becomes at once manifest and occluded. One cannot even pose the question of nihilism at all without immediately presuming – and in a variety of ways – that it is, above all, a question of nihilism *today*. However, as we shall explain below, nihilism is *also* held to be non- or a-historical, an 'untimely' designation.

2   As a performative declaration, 'nihilism' is originally both condemnation and injunction: nihilism is that which *must* be overcome or contested, or, at the very least, 'delineated' – even though this involves the paradox that 'nihilism' can only ever be invoked to designate the pressing contemporary im-possibility of every 'must'.

3   The question then arises as to the situation of those who can utter and comprehend the significance of the word at all, and – for Nietzsche as for his heirs – only those who have themselves passed through nihilism are in a position to recognise, affirm and surpass it:

> He that speaks here, conversely, has done nothing so far but reflect...the first perfect nihilist of Europe who, however, has even now lived through the whole of nihilism, to the end, leaving it behind, outside himself. (Nietzsche 1968, 3)

Hence the alienating imperative to embrace nihilism, on one hand, and, on the other, the motivated indifference of the era towards acknowledging its ownmost nature. The era is nihilistic not only because it is witness to the ungroundedness of all values, but also because it cannot recognise this becoming-nothing of its ground.

4 Hence the continuing validity of the word derives from its very appearance as *uselessly indispensable*; a terminological status which then comes to regulate the various positions that can be taken on nihilism now. Nietzsche's argumentative power has been to render the word 'nihilism' irrevocably self-reflexive; as Marcus's anecdote makes clear, even if spoken by an idiot, 'nihilism' now cannot mark anything other – for the few with ears delicate enough to hear it – than *the genuine insistence and persistence of thought in the midst of the disaster itself*. The problem of the 'revaluation of all values' then becomes paramount: where can one look for values, given that *there is no other world but this?* (see Heidegger, 1977, esp. 53–112).

5 Since it is the status of this *this* that remains presently undetermined or indeterminable, philosophers tend to succumb to a romantic *optimistic pessimism* that vacillates uncontrollably between a joyful apocalypticism and a disappointed utopianism – for which the contemporary politico-philosophical calls for a 'community to come' can stand as an index (Lacoue-Labarthe and Nancy 1997; Nancy 1991; Agamben 1993). Such communities, which definitively resist any possible positive predication, supposedly impel us to attempt to think them in and through this very in-accessibility. Nihilism's legacy to the notion of political community has thus entailed a return to traditionally aesthetic motifs (of silence, paralysis, irreducible heterogeneity, etc.). Such a situation is a direct consequence of Nietzsche's own solution to the dilemma, which hinges on aestheticising figurations, notably the *Übermensch* (see Nietzsche 1977).

It remains undecidable, however, whether late Romantic thought of this sort can still offer a genuine way to think beyond the aporias generated by its reliance on nihilism, or whether its indefinitely exciting quasi-apocalyptic hesitations are themselves simple reflex moves of more trivial institutional shifts. Are there other ways of describing the relation between nihilism and State institutions, other than the familiar Romantic denigration of bureaucratic culture? (See on this point the recent, Foucauldian-inflected, work of Hunter 1992a; 1992b; 1996.) What we wish to emphasise in the course of the following account of political nihilism is the integral link between the dissemination of Romantic philosophising and the expansion of Imperial educational bureaucracies. To this end, we return to the emergence of political nihilism in the Russia of the mid-nineteenth century – crucially, a moment when the term nihilism was not simply restricted to philosophical discourse. We aim to show how nihilism emerges as a *cultural youth style*, and how an associated 'war of fictions' is central to its irruption and dissemination across Europe.

'Long hair, blue spectacles and a walking stick'

Russian political nihilism began with a crisis in educational institutions, and culminated in the legend of a demon. Our account focuses on St Petersburg University, whence nihilism was transmitted like a contagion, being dislocated and fictionalised in the process, until finally it found its 'home' in the demonic organisation of Sergei Nechaev.

In the mid-1850s, Russia commenced its Great Reforms, an essential aspect of which was the reform of Russian higher education. The opening up of Russia's universities and institutes had an unexpected effect, however: rather than turning out the intended 'new class' of managers, it produced a 'radical community', known generically as the nihilists.

To understand how this occurred, we must register the situation of Imperial Russia in the mid-nineteenth century. Triggered by defeat in the Crimean War (1856), Russia had finally embarked on its Great Reforms in the mid-1850s. Hopes for reform centred on a new Tsar, Alexander II; it seemed possible a new era of liberalism was dawning. A liberal generation of activists seized the chance to adopt modernising and Westernising models, and quite radical changes to the system of local government and to judicial procedure were initiated. The centrepiece of these reforms was the Emancipation of the serfs in 1861, but the shift from a feudal order demanded sweeping changes to all social institutions (see Seton-Watson 1952, 48).

Concurrent with these events was the reform of the Russian higher education system. Russia lacked a middle class, but in its place institutions such as St Petersburg University were to provide a 'new class' upon whose abilities Tsar Alexander II would draw in managing the processes of reform. With tsarist expectation and the promise of advancement as the bait, from 1855 universities were opened to all who could pass the qualifying examinations. Their intake consequently shifted from a tacit restriction to the gentry to a broader influx of *raznochintsy* – the 'people of various ranks' – made up of 'children of priests, doctors and medical functionaries, marginal landowners, and lower bureaucrats' (Gleason 1980, 120). In the words of Daniel Brower:

> The Russian system of education brought together a diverse student body and offered an intellectual training on the basis of which they were to become constructive members of the state apparatus or to enter professional occupations.   (Brower 1975, 108)

In developing its own Westernised bureaucratic class of 'highly educated career officials' (Orlovsky 1981, 107), Russia was fulfilling a necessary condition of modernising reform. The need for such officials had been anticipated for some time:

A bureaucracy capable of generating policy and an administration efficient enough to implement it became the goal of at least four of the senior
statesmen who served Nicholas I in the 1840s...these four...became
instrumental in shaping the institutional base out of which the enlightened bureaucracy would emerge to produce the broad renovations that
became known as the Great Reforms some twenty years later.

(Lincoln 1990, 25)

There was a sense in which the institutional 'motor' of the reforms – that is,
the bureaucracy – was seeking to reproduce itself, to produce more managers
of the reform process. Students entering higher education after 1855 thus
found themselves in a novel and potentially powerful position: on the one
hand, the Tsar intended that they would help modernise Russia; on the
other, older liberals saw them as the inheritors of the liberalising process
they had already begun.

Such potential power was, of course, tied to the continued expanson of the
reform process. It soon emerged, however, that tsarist approval of 'enlightened bureaucracy' and social reform was waning. Throughout the 1860s and
into the 1870s, many reforms were gradually revoked or watered down. To
take one example, the establishment of local representative bodies led to a
campaign for a national representative institution that terminated in a 'formal and public rebuke' from the Tsar (Gooding 1996, 70). The political
legacy of this retreat was the increasing marginalisation of gentry liberalism,
as the product of a Westernised intelligentsia. By the 1860s, 'the derogatory
verb "to play at being a liberal" (*liberalnichat*)...was widely bandied about'
(Gooding 1996, 70). Although a generation of progressive bureaucrats and
activists continued to work for reform, the gradual reassertion of conservative autocracy seemed to consign them and their work to superfluity.

This sketch, which points to both the felt necessity and the troubled
history of the Great Reforms, therefore concludes with the perception of
their failure, particularly among the youthful 'new class' of the 1860s. The
era of Great Reforms gave way to that of nihilism, which first of all
announced itself as a refusal of both autocracy and liberalism. By the
1860s, it was clear that what universities taught was advancement into the
nobility through the bureaucracy. Radical critic Yossarion Belinski, for example, commented on how men from the 'petty bourgeois, merchant, cle-
rical and even [landowning] noble estates' who enter the bureaucracy 'lose
the crude trappings of these estates and, from father to son, are transformed
into the estates of lords [*barin*]' (Belinski 1953–59, 98–9). But neither the
promise of institutional advancement nor that of liberal reform could be
easily reconciled with the failure of the Great Reforms. Liberal reform had
apparently reached its expiry date, and the prospect of institutional advancement in a state reverting to autocracy was an ambivalent and uncertain one.
The consequence was that nihilism emerged as a politics without a future. Or

rather, less a politics than a style: nihilism in fact appeared as a fashionable label, worn by a disparate group, a kind of cultural youth style linked to the new culture of the opened-up and bureaucratised university. Worth emphasising in this connexion is the characteristic apparel of the young nihilist, which involved a deliberate refusal of the class or 'estate' markers of Russian society. Female nihilists cut their hair short, wore men's boots with plain black dresses, and smoked heavily. The males dressed in the style of the workers, and grew their hair. Furthermore, all nihilists were hygienically suspect. According to Svetlana Boym:

> Ashamed of being too common and unable to be *comme il faut* in the traditional aristocratic sense, members of the Russian intelligentsia, and especially their most radical representatives, the nihilists, fought against *poshlost*[1] through a demonstrative disregard for polite behavior, social mores, and hygiene.   (Boym 1994, 58)

As a corollary to acknowledgement of the *style* of nihilism, it is also customary for commentators to note the relative insignificance of ideas *per se* for the development of nihilism *à la Petersburg* (See Brower 1975, 18–19; Gleason 1980, 133–4). Despite the circulation of Western intellectual currents, and the strong tradition of radical cultural journalism we associate with Belinski *et al.*, nihilism is transmitted as less an intellectual position than a fundamentally aesthetic practice or stance.

What underwrote this stance? We have suggested that it was precisely the institutional context of a university in crisis: the failure of universities to teach either autocratic or progressive narratives of state service. But, complicating this picture, it was precisely the bureaucratic reformation of the self through education that seemed to give structure to the defining fantasy of nihilism: the imagined possibility of a complete break with the existing order to the point of a creation of a self (and society) *ex nihilo*. Kirillov, in Dostoevsky's *Demons*, offers a statement of the metaphysical necessities involved in this break:

> Whoever wants the main freedom must dare to kill himself.... There is no further freedom; here is everything; and there is nothing further. He who dares to kill himself, is God. Now anyone can make it so that there will be no God, and there will be no anything.(Dostoevsky 1994, 115–16)

P.G. Zaichnevsky's underground pamphlet of May 1862, entitled 'Young Russia', took up the question of nihilism and society, urging the necessity of:

> a revolution, a bloody and pitiless revolution, a revolution which must change everything down to the very roots, utterly overthrowing all the foundations of present society.   (cited in Venturi 1960, 292)

Let us examine some further instances of this stance, as stated by some former students of St Petersburg University, so as to begin to locate it in an institutional context. It involves an attitude bluntly enunciated by philology student Dimitri Pisarev in 1861:

> [the] ultimatum of our camp: what can be smashed should be; what stands up under blows is acceptable, and what flies into a thousand pieces is trash   (Pisarev 1934, 66).

Lev Modzalevsky gives us an oedipalised version of this impulse:

> We – youth – boldly and triumphantly denied previous principles of morality and citizenship, although new ones had not yet been found. And in fact no one was in a hurry to find them and all energies were expended on rejection.... Employing the freedom which had been granted to us, to which we were not as yet accustomed, we soon stopped attending the lectures of strict and boring professors, who gave us their knowledge in some kind of dead form....   (Modzalevsky 1917, 136–7)

Another young nihilist, Prokhor Debogory-Mokiyevich, writes in his memoir of a visit to his former headmaster, before whom he paraded with 'long hair, blue spectacles and walking stick', while pretending not to recognise him (cited in Hingley 1967, 25). Nihilist youth here is opposed, first of all, to its own teachers.

Such incidents were part of the hubbub of political activity that came to characterise Russian higher education at this time. A further example will help illustrate the way radicalism was intertwined with educational bureaucratisation, and how nihilism coalesced precisely on the *fringes* of the university, as a radical community that refused to *identify* itself, remaining 'underground' and unrecognisable to the twin political currents of reform and reaction.

St Petersburg University was one of the main sites of student unrest, and in 1861 the so-called 'May Rules' were brought down, which constituted an attempt by fiat to end student corporatism at this and other universities. Petersburg resistance to the new Rules centred on the issue of identification booklets, whose introduction had in fact been suggested by liberal professors as part of an attempt to mediate between students and the ministry of education:

> The idea was that the new regulations should be included in a booklet that would also contain the student's residency permit, grades, and library card – something along the lines of the German university *Studiumbuch*, known at the University of Dorpat as a *Matrikel* and in Russian as a *matrikul*. Thus a convenient symbol of the oppressive new order was

dreamed up by the liberal opposition and issued by the reactionary
authorities.   (Gleason 1980, 153–4)

In October, 1861, after demonstrations and deadlocks, students who had not
accepted their *matrikuly* were dismissed from the university. Ensuing riots
meant that the university was eventually closed until August, 1863. It was
thus the refusal to identify oneself formally to the university that helped
form the students into a cohesive class of New People. And while the
majority of students would repeatedly return to the goal of student corporatism through the 1860s, it became a defining feature of the nihilists that
they continued to refuse to identify themselves in the terms of public and
representational politics. Rather, they established themselves in the form of
underground revolutionary organisations operating on the fringes of the
university.

In this connexion, if we skip forward only a few years, to 1868, we catch
the first public glimpses of Sergei Nechaev attending St Petersburg University. He is admitted under the category of 'free auditor' and chiefly spends his
time there undermining student attempts to form representational bodies,
seeking instead to instal himself as leader of a revolutionary organisation
(Gleason 1980, 346–50). As a free-floating radical, Nechaev had naturally
found his way to Petersburg, described by Dostoevsky as that 'most abstract
and intentional city' (Dostoevsky 1972, 17). As well as 'offering the best
opportunities for young officials to advance their careers' (Lincoln 1990,
19), Petersburg had the most developed radical community. The student
populations of three institutions – the university, the Medical-Surgical Academy, and the Technological Institute – had 'merged into one body, closely
connected by common lodgings, friends, and roommates' (Gleason 1980,
345). Students of the Academy had rented the floor of a nearby house as a
meeting venue. Responding to student radicalism, the minister of war
argued that the students be 'transformed into city residents under the jurisdiction of the general police' (*Central State Historical Archives of Leningrad*,
cited in Brower 1975, 137–8). Such policies encouraged students to move
beyond the sphere of student politics, by displacing them both geograph-
ically and politically.

Before developing this account of Russian political nihilism further, let us
mark some of its central features. We have emphasised nihilism's roots in
youth style, in negation, in the structures of state education. Given that
nihilism lacks the consistency of a politico-philosophical position, it appears
rather as a bundle of claims and dis-identifications, as an emergent term.
Acknowledgement of this status necessarily militates against definition of
nihilism *either* as an identifiable 'philosophical' movement *or* as merely an
anomic subculture. Instead, investigating the receptions and conditions that
determine its appearance, we have pointed to nihilism's regulating fantasy –
the creation of a self and society *ex nihilo* – and to the institutional setting for

its emergence. In emphasising these features, our account opposes itself to the liberal idealism of a critic such as Burton Gleason, who would insert Russian nihilism into the narrative of the evolution of populist conscious-ness in Russia. Gleason puts a reformist, populist, moral slant on Russia's 1860s radical youth movements, whereas it has been argued that nihilism proceeds precisely from a *refusal* of moral and reformist critique.

For somewhat different reasons, our analysis also opposes itself to Marxist accounts that reduce nihilism to a political reflex born of the shift from a feudal order to the capitalist phase of Russian history. Not only do we not trust the generality of great economic phases and the language of class-struggle, but the teleological implications of such accounts also insert nihilism in a trajectory that will inevitably conclude with the triumph of communism, as if one led to the other. Whilst Lenin did indeed admire both Nechaev and Chernyshevsky, what he took from them was not so much a positive political project, but rather a covertly aestheticised conception of revolutionary self- and party-formation (see on this point Schapiro 1986, 188–253 and Figes 1996, 130–3).

Given nihilism's uncertain status as a *political* movement, this inheritance was perhaps to be expected. Party-political claims to nihilism had always to contend with its roots in youth style and its refusal of representational politics. Despite occasional adherence to various doctrines, what bound the radical community of the nihilists together was their practice of an *anaesthethics*. What we are designating by the neologism *anaesthethics* are the effects of a bureaucratic event that, if it is registered aesthetically by the bodies which it affects (i.e. in dress, comportment, corporeal disposition, etc.), nonetheless cannot be easily reconciled with the terms of Romantic aesthetics. Bureaucracy, after all, has consistently been characterised as the opposite or negation of aesthetics; one of the presumptions we are contest-ing is precisely the status of this opposition. Furthermore, this concept of *anaesthethics* helps to distinguish nihilism from those apparently more affir-mative political, social or scientific programmes with which, as we shall see, it is often associated – for example, positivism or utilitarian socialism. Nihil-ism is a shocking event, and not simply a doctrine.

Despite our reference to nihilist style, attention has not yet been given to another aspect of its aesthetic definition. From its inception as a youth style, nihilism was subject to a 'war of fictions'. One can trace the beginnings of this war to Turgenev's novel of 1862, *Fathers and Sons*, which took the label of nihilism and 'fastened... [it] firmly on the younger generation' (Moser 1964, 18).

Fathers and Sons was written out of a fascination – bordering on infatuation – with the political radicals of the generation following Turgenev's: the so-called 1860s men. In depicting this generation, Turgenev portrays his central character Bazarov as a kind of Byronic materialist (Gleason 1980, 72), who spends his afternoons dissecting frogs and his evenings demolishing the liberal illusions of the older generation. Although the novel works with generically romantic elements, it gains its impact from the dissonance produced within this framework by the new nihilist hero, who represents negation and a harshly positivistic realism. In effect, the novel is energised by its willingness to be possessed by the force of nihilism which Bazarov embodies.

As a stance and style, nihilism gained a future from Turgenev: the proto-typical anti-reformism of Bazarov excited debate (Berlin 1979, 280–8) and a proliferation of depictions. The most influential radical response to Turgenev came from Nikolai Chernyshevsky with his novel *What Is to Be Done?* (1863). This novel, a populist, utilitarian socialist answer to *Fathers and Sons*, depicted the exemplary lives of the new people. Among them was an avant-garde Superman figure, Rakmétof, known as 'the rigorist' (Cherny-shevsky 1986, 275), in part for his propensity to sleep on a bed of nails:

> Rakmétof opened the door with a melancholy broad smile... the back and shoulders of his underclothes...were soaked with blood...thou-sands of little nails... Rakmétof had been lying on them all night long.
> (Chernyshevsky 1986, 285)

Later, Lenin took up the title, and the notion of a revolutionary élite; Chernyshevsky's novel, he confessed, had 'churned me inside out' (See Valentinov 1951, 193–216 and Schapiro 1986, 186–252). In Rakmétof, he added, one saw what a 'what a revolutionary *must be like*' (Figes 1996, 131).

Lenin's response was not unusual. Underground groups formed to plan the implementation of *What Is to Be Done?* and from one of these, a group named *Hell* (a cell of a slightly larger group named *Organization*), came a failed 1866 attempt on the life of the Tsar, by Dmitry Karakozov. The con-sumption of nihilist fictions by young nihilists fed back into the evolution of the radical community: the figure of the self-annihilating superman offered to Karakozov, recently dismissed from Moscow University for inability to pay his tuition fees, a solution to his suicidal inclinations and disenchantment with the Russian state.

Contributing to the discussion of nihilism, too, throughout the 1860s, were a series of antinihilist novels, numerous police reports (See Brower 1975, 17, 126, 163), and the internecine feuding of radical journalists (See Lampert 1971, 281–4). A final point to be made in this connexion relates to the crucial formative role played by culture in nineteenth-century Russia. Partly as a consequence of the censorship of open political debate, 'literature became the battleground on which the central social and political issues of life were fought out' (Berlin 1979, 265), and Russia was 'a country so open to literary influence that many individuals would decide to remodel their lives after perusing a single poem, novel or work of political philosophy' (Hingley 1967, 40). Nihilism marked a critical point in this cultural history of aesthetic influence. Like the nineteenth-century category of the aesthetic itself, which resists teaching and paraphrase, the nihilists were born of their own unteachability. Positioned on the fringes of the university, they came to live out the contradictions that fracture the emancipatory dreams of liberal-idealist aesthetics. Their temporal and institutional dislocation made them subjects of a 'war of fictions' and proponents of an anti-Romantic *anaes-thethics*.

But it is a further development from this which demands our attention: the repositioning of the nihilist subject in a mirror hierarchy, an organisation of the anti-State, headed by a demon. The demon – identified as such by Dostoevsky– was Sergei Nechaev, and his efforts to organise nihilism mark a kind of terminus for nihilism as a political movement. Rejoining our historical narrative of nihilism, we thus note the withdrawal of liberal approval and support through the 1860s (see Gleason 1980, 160–79), and the development of nihilism into a kind of Jacobinism, involving secretive groups who fomented in isolation their plans of revolutionary terrorism. It is in the context of terrorist cells that we finally encounter the legendary figure of Sergei Nechaev, writer of the most infamous statement of political nihilism, the *Revolutionary Catechism*.

No one understood better than Nechaev the bureaucratic and educational climate that produced political nihilism. Despite years spent in solitary study of the Gymnasium curriculum, a spell as an elementary-school teacher of religion, and attendance at St Petersburg University, Nechaev repeatedly proclaimed his contempt for academic study, proposing instead the necessity of revolutionary *praxis*. In one manifesto, for instance, addressed to 'the students of Russia', we find the typical declaration that: 'The university now only creates Philistines of science and lackeys of the government' (cited in Venturi 1960, 383). When it came to recruitment of the members of his revolutionary organisation, *The People's Vengeance*, Nechaev presented himself as a self-educated worker-superman, head of a shadowy organisation that students (not authentic People [*narodniki*] themselves) were privileged to assist.

In 1869, Nechaev left St Petersburg University and linked up with Mikhail Bakunin in Switzerland. There they wrote and planned together, and secret organisations were projected, such that:

> Nechaev, the self-styled representative of a non-existent Russian Revolutionary Committee, receive[d] from Bakunin authority to act in Russia as the representative of a non-existent Revolutionary Alliance.
>
> (Carr 1933, 340)

They also found time to co-author the *Revolutionary Catechism*. Nechaev had long recognised the central role of organisation in his nihilistic project – indeed, Lenin would later remark of Nechaev's skills in this regard, 'People completely forget that Nechaev possessed unique organisational talent, an ability to establish the special techniques of conspiratorial work everywhere...' (cited in Shub 1948, 371–2). Organisation was so central to Nechaev's being that he would lament that 'the absence of a plan and of a close organization has paralysed everything' (cited in Venturi 1960, 385). Responding to this deficiency, the *Catechism* offered a sequence of dicta merging negation and bureaucratisation. The revolutionary prototype is famously defined as 'a doomed man [...who] has severed every tie with the civil order, with the educated world' (Dmytryshyn 1967, 241). Supplementing this isolation, though, is the revolutionary organisation:

> *Paragraph 9*: [...] Revolutionary comrades [...] should if possible discuss all major problems jointly and resolve them unanimously. In the execution of the jointly agreed upon plan, each member should act independently. In the execution of a number of destructive actions, each member must act alone, seeking advice and comradely help only when it is essential to the total success.

> *Paragraph 10*: Every comrade must have under his control several revolutionaries of second and third ranks [...] He must consider them as a portion of a general revolutionary capital entrusted to his disposal. He must dispose of his part of the capital economically, striving always to get most advantage from it.   (Dmytryshyn 1967, 243)

In such passages, Nechaev outlined the management structure and principles by which nihilism could be promoted.

By August, 1869, it was time for *praxis*, and Nechaev travelled to Moscow and began to enrol real members in his fictional organisation. *The People's Vengeance* never realised more than a few dozen members, most of whom came from the Petrovsky Agricultural Academy. But having joined such a cell, the young nihilist became what he or she had always been intended to be: the anomic member of an enormous unreal bureaucratic structure. That this structure did not in fact exist only made it more authentically nihilist. Nechaev had *People's Vengeance* letterheads and membership cards printed, to impress potential financial contributors (Gleason 1980, 369). Events took a more serious turn when Nechaev determined that one member, Ivan Ivanov, was unreliable:

> He summoned the members closest to him and said that the central committee (a theoretical institution to which he often appealed) had in its possession evidence which proved Ivanov's intention of denouncing the society. He added that in view of the delicacy of the matter such evidence could not be produced. It was unanimously decided to suppress Ivanov.   (Venturi 1960, 380)

The next evening Ivanov was strangled, then shot through the head by Nechaev and four accomplices in the grounds of the Petrovsky Academy. His four colleagues were soon arrested, but Nechaev escaped to Geneva, travelling to London and Paris, before finally being arrested and extradited from Zurich in 1872. He died in prison in 1882, having become a legend among the new generation of radicals, with whom he managed brief contact in 1881 from prison.

E.H. Carr comments of Nechaev that: 'In a meteoric career, which ended at the age of twenty-five, he achieved literally nothing' (Carr 1933, 335) – a fitting testament for this bureaucrat/revolutionary, one might conclude. But Dostoevsky offers a more instructive analysis of Nechaev's significance. In the novel *Demons* he fictionalised the Nechaev case, depicting small-town life, in particular its 'lost boys', as possessed by a foreign and demonic force. Nechaev, or Peter Verkhovensky as he is called in the novel, appears both a self-made demon and an unlocalisable figure of possession and pandemonium. Dostoevsky thus established the legacy of nihilism for the twentieth century, presenting the demonic Nechaev as its ultimate product. Our account echoes Dostoevsky: Nechaev is, finally, *nihilism itself* because he closes the gap between 'bureaucracy' and 'culture', offering the exemplary statement of both nihilist management-structure and nihilist selfhood. Though he achieves 'literally nothing', his legendary life and pamphleteering have the effect of solidifying nihilism's identity as a mode of terroristic negation that takes its form from the abstract protocols of bureaucracy itself.

Ethos anthropo daimon

The question still remains, not only as to why Dostoevsky would consider *demonology* the most apposite resource for figuring nihilism, but why his figurations also proved so influential – even determining – for subsequent accounts. Why was it necessary that the monsters of nihilism be modeled, whether consciously or implicitly, on a subjacent paradigm of the demon?

In *Paradise Lost* Milton coins a new name for Satan's 'high capital': *Pandaemonium*. As always with neologisms, its roots are very old; it literally transliterates from the ancient Greek as 'all the daemons'. Pandaemonium is the place where all the demons can, according to their own laws, make complicated plans, plot effectively, strategise creatively, and regulate one another without interference from God. Yet, despite its rigorous organisation, Pandaemonium is not a State, it is not the harmonious *Polis* or *Civitas Dei*, but a revolutionary Counter- or Anti-State constitutively arrayed against its glorified others. It is, in its dark and seething heart, dedicated to the overthrow of established laws, conservative knowledges, moral strictures, supposedly immutable and correct social practices, and so on. Pandaemonium is the final end, the dream of total knowledge, all the demons unleashed everyelsewhere, all at once.

In characterising nihilism, Dostoevsky thus has recourse to an abiding ontotheological motif within Western metaphysics and aesthetics – that of demonology[2]. (Other writers who return to the demon, in very different ways, include Bulgakov 1988; Gillespie 1995; Krell 1992; Sologub 1990; Witkiewicz 1985.) Dostoevsky goes on to use Russian nihilism as the basis for a judgement on the modern state, which stands revealed for what it is in the reflected dark light of nihilism – a kind of erratic non-place, which spreads the heresy of reason-over-God.

But this is a familiar story, nihilism embracing and announcing the death of God, and so on. We note that nihilism's status as a *politically forceful philosophical discourse* is tied to its ability to foster pandaemonium. Its twinning with bureaucracy is what places it at the heart of the modern state, giving it its essentially modern character. Demons, in this regard, are merely *functionaries*. Our argument has so far shown that the character of nihilism is formed in the interactions of state bureaucracies, especially educational ones, with their subjects. These interactions tend to produce characteristic figures or types, paradigms of professionalism or contestatory force (see Macintyre 1985, 27–31; Deleuze and Guattari 1991 on the question of such characteristic-conceptual figures). They give rise to the paradoxical aesthetic community of Russian 'political' nihilism and, shortly afterwards, to the character of the perfect nihilist embodied by Nietzsche – whose own overcoming of nineteenth-century academia reproduces the very genealogy we have given for Russian nihilism (see Macintyre 1990, 32–5).

To this genealogical account, there is of course an easy rejoinder: that the philosophical discourse of nihilism projects an analysis and embodies an injunction that cannot simply be disarmed by analysing the conditions of its emergence. But to argue in this manner is to misunderstand the point of our genealogy, which registers nihilism's effect *on philosophy* as precisely rendering im-possible analyses that take their own rational force for granted. Nihilism radically questions all procedures of rational justification. Philosophy – including the philosophical discourse of nihilism – is thereby invited to recognise its insufficiency, and to open itself to an ongoing revaluation of its terms of reference, or else to affirm a blindly absolutist allegiance to the philosophical injunction. What, however, gets recurrently elided in such self-negating critiques are the institutional conditions of philosophical discourse itself. On this account, then, the post-Nietzschean sense of 'nihilism' – outlined in the opening section of this chapter – has been one of the central ways that philosophy has blinded itself to its own contexts, and in the guise of its most thoroughgoing (auto) critique. By contrast, we have tried to show – both through an immanent destruction of the term, and through an analysis of its material conditions – that nihilism *is* its history, a history involving both Nechaev *and* Nietzsche, and the institutional imbrication of these figures with the training of bureaucrats and teachers.

Our conclusions can be most efficiently summarised in the form of a neo-Nechaevean revolutionary catechism:

1   The nihilist, aesthete-philosopher, and bureaucrat are characteristic figures of modernity, embodying representative life-practices.
2   They are linked practically, pedagogically and conceptually, and their fortunes are directly aligned with the expansion and new centrality of governmental organisations and pedagogical institutions in the nineteenth century.
3   The bureaucrat is, as the usual complaint has it, paid for *producing nothing* – monitoring, sorting, writing, testing the mutable and impersonal processes of his or her own de-regulated habit itself. In bureaucratic activity, furthermore, a distinctively modern *ethos* – that is, a place and way of life – elaborates itself, and extends its influence.
4   The nihilist is an unemployed bureaucrat or, more precisely, the nihilist is that individual produced in and by an unforeseen interruption between pedagogical training and professional employment. In this sense, modern power is in the business of training nihilists, and does nothing else: bureaucracy, in fact, comes to function as a *daimonios topos*.
5   The nihilist – trained to do nothing other than nothing, but presently unremunerated for it – *finally* attempts to reveal that this nothing-masquerading-as-everything *is* nothing precisely through its destruction. Nihilism, in other words, terminates in pure *politics*: it insists on prosecuting the nothingness of every existing social bond.
6   However, there is no direct nor inevitable route between bureaucracy and nihilism, ethics and politics; rather, as we have argued, this route can be traversed only by way of *anaesthethics*. The anaesthethics of Russian political nihilism names a paradoxical form of pre-political community, in which youth style marks a dislocation and dis-identification from state reform processes.

This chapter's closing point concerns the status of this catechism. Following Nechaev, nihilism in its manifold forms has regularly taken as its generic mode the *terminal diagnosis*: 'The nihilist is a doomed man', for instance, or 'God is dead'. But, as we began this chapter by noting, nihilism's diagnoses have become unavoidably self-reflexive: following its contemporary apparition as irremediably banalised, the term's diagnostic force has itself been placed in doubt. In fact, our chapter has shown why we do not believe in such diagnoses anymore, and why the continuing attempts to prosecute them ironically end up proving mere intra-institutional repetitions of their predecessors.

Yet there may well be nihilists again, and, as always, the state will have a hand in it. A recent article by Geoffrey Hosking in the *Times Literary Supplement* excites suspicion in this regard. Hosking – the well-respected author of a standard university textbook on Russian history – has recourse to a now-familiar progressive narrative of State service when he suggests that:

> The Russian government could do a great deal to promote civil peace and national solidarity by investing substantial sums in culture, education and learning, which it has shamefully neglected in recent years. George Soros has already done much in this direction. If one or two of the leading Russian financial magnates could bring themselves to follow his example and invest in a peaceful Russian civic nationhood, they would also be promoting their own interest in the stability needed for sustained economic growth. Alas, that kind of far-sightedness is in short supply among the 'new Russians'. (Hosking 1998, 13)

Thank God for that shortsightedness among the new Russians. From our point of view, Hosking's recipe would produce nothing other than a fresh batch of nihilists.[3] Perhaps that's no bad thing; at least you could be sure they'd know how to dress. But our fundamental point remains: wherever bureaucrats and teachers are trained, these institutions will inevitably produce their own Nechaevs and Nietzsches.

Notes

1 An untranslatable term related to kitsch in its association with bourgeois sentimentality, and explored at length by Nabokov and, more recently, Svetlana Boym. See Boym 1994, 41–66 and Nabokov 1944, 70.
2 Our remarks must be distinguished here from those of Michael Gillespie, who also focuses in some detail on the image of the demon in Romantic nihilist thought. Whereas Gillespie, in complete accord with a dominant traditional strain of Romantic interpretation, identifies the truly great individual with the forces of night, our work aims to show, on the contrary, that the demons of nihilism are irreducibly plural. Nihilism is a question of pandaemonium; it is not simply a face-off of individuals (whether these are considered persons, forces, laws, etc.).
3 In noting this, we wish merely to point out the inevitable result of Hosking's prescriptions, rather than to make descriptive or predictive claims as to the possible consequences of the actual political ferment in Russia today.

References

Agamben, G. (1993) *The Coming Community*. Trans. M. Hardt. Minneapolis: University of Minnesota Press.
——(1991) *Language and Death: The Place of Negativity*. Trans. K.E. Pinkus with M. Hardt. Minneapolis: University of Minnesota Press.
Ansell Pearson, K. (1988) *An Introduction to Nietzsche as Political Thinker: the Perfect Nihilist*. Cambridge: Cambridge University Press.
Belinski, V. (1953–59) 'Tarantas' in *Polnoe sobranie sochinenii*. Moscow.
Berlin, I. (1978) *Russian Thinkers*. Harmondsworth: Penguin.

Boym, S. (1994) *Common Places*. Massachusetts: Harvard University Press.
Brower, D. (1975) *Training the Nihilists: Education and Radicalism in Tsarist Russia*. Ithaca and London: Cornell University Press.
Bulgakov, M. (1988) *The Master and Margarita*. Trans. M. Glenny. London: Collins Harvill.
Carr, K. (1992) *The Banalization of Nihilism: Twentieth-Century Responses to Meaninglessness*. Albany: SUNY Press.
Chernyshevsky, N. (1986) *What Is to Be Done?* Ann Arbor: Ardis Publishers.
Critchley, S. 1997.*Very Little...Almost Nothing: Death, Philosophy, Literature*. London: Routledge.
Darby, T., B. Egyed, and B. Jones, eds (1989) *Nietzsche and the Rhetoric of Nihilism: Essays on Interpretation, Language and Politics*. Ottawa: Carleton University Press.
Deleuze, G. and F. Guattari. (1991) *Qu'est-ce que la Philosophie?* Paris: Les éditions de Minuit.
Dmytryshyn, D. ed. (1967) *Imperial Russia*. New York: Holt, Rinehart and Winston.
Dostoevsky, F. (1972) *Notes from Underground/The Double*. Harmondsworth: Penguin.
—— (1994) *Demons*. Trans. R. Pevear and L. Volokhonsky. New York: Knopf.
The Economist. 15/8/1998. 'The New Terrorism' 15–17.
Eden, R. (1983) *Political Leadership and Nihilism*: a Study of Weber and Nietzsche. Tampa: University Presses of Florida.
Figes, O. (1996) *A People's Tragedy: The Russian Revolution 1891–1924*. London: Cape.
Forbes, J. (1998) *Damaged Glamour*. Rose Bay: Brandl and Schlesinger.
Gare, A. (1993) *Nihilism Incorporated*. Bungendore: Eco-Logical Press.
Gillespie, M. (1995) *Nihilism Before Nietzsche*. Chicago: University of Chicago Press.
Gleason, B. (1980) *Young Russia*. New York: Viking.
Gooding, J. (1996) *Rulers & Subjects: Government and People in Russia 1801–1991*. London: Arnold.
Goudsblom, J. (1980) *Nihilism and Culture*. Oxford: Basil Blackwell.
Heidegger, M. (1977) *The Question Concerning Technology and Other Essays*. Trans. and Intro. W. Lovitt. New York: Harper and Row.
Hingley, R. (1967) *Nihilists*. London: Weidenfeld and Nicholson.
Hosking, G. (1997) *Russia: People and Empire 1552–1917*. Massachusetts: Harvard University Press.
Hunter, I. (1992a) 'Aesthetics and Cultural Studies' in L. Grossberg *et al.* (eds), *Cultural Studies*. New York: Routledge.
Hunter, I. (1992b) 'The Humanities without Humanism', in *Meanjin*, Vol. 51, No. 3, 479–90.
Hunter, I. 1996. 'Four Anxieties About English', in *Southern Review*, Vol. 29, No. 1, 4–18.
Jonas, H. (1963) *The Gnostic Religion: the Message of the Alian God and the Beginnings of Christianity*. Boston: Beacon Press.
Krell, D.F. (1992) *Daimon Life: Heidegger and Life-Philosophy*. Bloomington: Indiana University Press.
Lampert, E. (1971) *Sons Against Fathers: Studies in Russian Radicalism and Revolution*. London: Oxford University Press.
Lincoln, W.B. (1990) *The Great Reforms: Autocracy, Bureaucracy and the Politics of Change in Imperial Russia*. DeKalb, Illinois: Northern Illinois University Press.
Macintyre, A. (1985) *After Virtue: a Study in Moral Theory*. 2nd edn. London: Duckworth.
Macintyre, A. (1990) *Three Rival Versions of Moral Enquiry*. London: Duckworth.

Marcus, G. (1993) *Ranters and Crowd-Pleasers: Punk in Pop Music 1977–92*. New York: Doubleday.

Martin, G. (1989) *From Nietzsche to Wittgenstein: the Problem of Truth and Nihilism in the Modern World*. New York: Peter Long.

Modzalevsky, B.A. (1917) 'Kistorii Petersburgkago universiteta, 1857–1859g. Iz bumag L.N. Modzalevskago', *Golos Minuvshago*, No. 1.

Moser, C.A. (1964) *Antinihilism in the Russian Novel of the 1860s*. The Hague: Mouton & Co.

Nabokov, V. (1944) *Nikolai Gogol*. Norfolk, Conn.: New Directions.

Nancy, J-L. and P. Lacoue-Labarthe (1997) *Retreating the Political*. ed. S. Sparks. London: Routledge.

Nancy, J.-L. (1991) *The Inoperative Community*. trans. P. Conner *et al*. Minnesota: University of Minnesota Press.

Nietzsche, F. (1956) *The Birth of Tragedy/The Genealogy of Morals*. trans. F. Goffing. New York: Doubleday.

Nietzsche, F. (1968) *The Will to Power*. Trans. W. Kaufmann and R.J. Hollingdale. New York: Vintage Books.

Nietzsche, F. (1972) *Twilight of the Idols/The Anti-Christ*. trans. with commentary R.J. Hollingdale. Harmondsworth: Penguin.

Nietzsche, F. (1977) *Thus Spoke Zarathustra*. trans. R.J. Hollingdale. Harmondsworth: Penguin.

Orlovsky, D. (1981) *The Limits of Reform: the Ministry of Internal Affairs in Imperial Russia, 1802–1881*. Massachusetts: Harvard University Press.

Pisarev, D. (1934) *Izbrannye sochineniia* [Selected Essays], Moscow.

Schapiro, L. (1986) *Russian Studies*. London: Collins Harvill.

Seton-Watson, H. (1952) *The Decline of Imperial Russia 1855–1914*. London: Methuen.

Shub, D. (1948) *Lenin*. New York: Doubleday.

Sinel, A. (1973) *The Classroom and the Chancellery: State Educational Reform in Russia under Count Dmitri Tolstoi*. Harvard University Press: Massachusetts.

Stites, R. (1978) *The Woman's Liberation Movement in Russia*. New Jersey: Princeton.

Smith, G.B. (1996) *Nietzsche, Heidegger and the Transition to Postmodernity*. Chicago: The University of Chicago Press.

Sologub, F. (1990) *The Petty Demon*. trans. with intro. by S.D. Cioran. London: Quartet.

Valentinov, N. (1951) 'Chernshevsky I Lenin', *Novyi Zhurnal*, 26.

Venturi, F. (1966) *Roots of Revolution: A History of the Populist and Socialist Movements in Nineteenth Century Russia*. New York: Grosset and Dunlap.

Ward, J.F. (1995) *Heidegger's Political Thinking*. Amherst: University of Massachusetts Press.

Witkiewicz, S.I. (1985) *Insatiability*. trans. L. Iribarne. intro. C. Milosz. London: Quartet. *Central State Historical Archives of Leningrad*, f. 908, o. 1, d. 125, l. 82. 'Revoliutsionnoe I studecheskoe dvizhenie 1869 goda' [The revolutionary and student movements of 1869], *Katorga I ssylka*, No. 10 (1924).

3
Nietzsche, Nihilism and Spirit

Richard Beardsworth

> We must learn to 'read'.
>
> Heidegger, *Nietzsche*

Introduction

In the posthumous notes gathered under the title *Will to Power* (Nietzsche 1968b) Nietzsche lays out a typology of 'nihilism'. Nihilism constitutes, first, and foremost, the terms of a diagnosis of metaphysics in general: for Nietzsche, the metaphysical division between the transcendental and the empirical enacts a devaluation of life as such and is motivated at a deep level by the 'will to nothing'. Nihilism serves, second, as a descriptive term to designate the process of the self-devaluation of metaphysical values (1968, §2): in this second sense, the term marks the historical coming-to-be of metaphysics *as* the (historical) event of nihilism. Third, bestriding actively this process of self-devaluation, nihilism designates *qua* 'radical' nihilism an active conviction in the untenability of metaphysical values and, therefore, a will to truthfulness. Since this will is still predicated on faith in truth, it is itself vulnerable to further destruction (§3). In the fourth and fifth senses of nihilism, nihilism is situated by Nietzsche as a response to the above three 'cultures' of nihilism. This response is couched within what Nietzsche calls a diagnosis of *spirit* (§7, §12, §14, §22): on the one hand, 'passive' nihilism accompanies the second sense of nihilism, the designation of a decadent, exhausted world that has no meaning and no value, it is the nihilism of the spirit of 'what for?', the nihilism of *taedium vitae*; on the other hand, countering passive nihilism, 'active nihilism' describes the gesture of active destruction of metaphysical valuation and is seen 'as a sign of the increased power of the spirit' (§22), a prelude, that is, to the transvaluation of values.

According to this typology the term 'nihilism' for Nietzsche describes either a state of thinking and/or culture (the health or otherwise of values that situate the place of the human in the world) or the nature of human response to this state. The two cannot of course be separated from each other: human response to the way in which humankind values itself in the world forms part of that very valuation, and vice versa. And yet the distinction remains important since, for Nietzsche, the way in which we ourselves value the devaluation of values orients and sustains the way in which we respond in turn to this devaluation, be it actively or passively. In this context three things stand out in this typology that I wish to expound before moving to the theme and orientation of this chapter.

First, for Nietzsche, the culture of 'valuelessness' and 'meaninglessness' that constitutes nihilism (in the second historical sense) is the consequence of the fact that the metaphysical categories of 'unity', 'being' and 'purpose' that we have projected onto the world to date are no longer able to articulate the world and the universe convincingly. Nihilism as a historical event of thinking and culture within history defines, in other words, the end of a *fiction*. In the brief, but eloquent, 'How the "Real World" at last Became a Myth: History of an Error' in *Twilight of the Idols* (Nietzsche 1968a, 50–1) this fiction comes to an end with Kant: the fiction, that is, that the categorial thoughts of the human have formal 'objective' status (transcendental idealism). The nihilistic senselessness of existence does nothing but translate, in this context, for Nietzsche, the 'all too human' shock that metaphysical categories do *not* articulate the world. In this sense, nihilism as a historical event of thinking and culture is nothing but the *reverse* side of nihilism *qua* metaphysics, that is, the institution of these categories in the first place.

Thus, second, active nihilism *qua* an active, affirmative force of destruction, is necessarily concerned with nihilism in the first general sense: the nihilism of metaphysical schematisation and valuation as such. It is, in other words, necessarily concerned with the fact that metaphysics is *to begin with* 'nihilistic', with the fact that splitting life into two worlds, two instances or two principles (the empirico-transcendental divide from Plato to Kant), metaphysical thinking and practice *deny life*.

Third, the thinking and culture of nihilism in the first general sense consequently marks a period of history in which the human believed that its own categories of thought organised and oriented the world. The thinking and culture of nihilism in the second historical sense does nothing but mark, therefore, a moment in this history (its end) *when the forces of the world have become too complex to be convincingly organised and synthesised by the force of human thought*. Both nihilisms are therefore not only symmetrical forms of each other: more importantly, their symmetry testifies to the fact that the human is now explicitly exceeded by the forces of which it is at the same time the vehicle. In this sense nihilism in the second sense is nothing more than the inverted, and therefore misrecognised realisation *within* metaphysics ('nihilism' in the larger sense) that *the human is not the dominant force among all other forces in the world*.

Nietzsche's typology of nihilism *qua* a diagnosis of the necessary failure of human force to organise all other forces as well as a response in *spirit* to this failure lead, therefore, to three questions:

1 How do we – as philosophers and as people concerned with, and situated in culture – think with, between and beyond the categories of metaphysics in such a way as to articulate the now explicit complexity of the world and the universe that defies these categories?
2 In what sense, for Nietzsche, are this living and thinking a furtherance of 'spirit'?
3 And therefore, what does Nietzsche mean in the first place by the term 'spirit', if spirit is no longer to be understood as a metaphysical concept, designating what is opposed to the body and matter, that has precisely oriented metaphysics' disavowal of the forces of the world? For, in this sense, 'spirit' would appear a difficult candidate to mobilise in order to forge a philosophical response to this emerging complexity.

Before untying the implications of these questions and laying out the concerns of this chapter in their context, let us first remind ourselves – in the context of the title of this volume – that the final posthumous note at the end of the *Will to Power* volume describes the world sprung from the categories of 'unity', 'being' and 'purpose' as, precisely, 'a monster of energy without beginning, without end; a firm, iron magnitude of force that does not expend itself but only transforms itself' (Nietzsche 1968b, §1067, 549–50). The note stresses that this non-entropic world is one of ebb and flow in which the play of forces lies in the movement back and forward between greater complexity and renewed simplicity, a world, of 'eternal recurrence' and 'self-creation', to which Nietzsche brings the new 'values' of 'will to power' and 'eternal recurrence'. These values mark the difference of force and energy that emerge through the active destruction of nihilism in the general sense alluded to.[1] Nietzsche writes:

> [This world is] my Dionysian world of the eternally self-creating, self-destroying, my 'beyond good and evil' without goal, unless the joy of the circle is itself a goal. This world is the will to power – and nothing besides! And you yourselves are this will to power – and nothing besides! (ibid.)

Now, we have just maintained that, for Nietzsche, passive or active, nihilism constitutes the *working-out* of the categories bequeathed by metaphysics: passive, it designates a state of distress before the loss of a world simplified, under the categories of reason, for the sake of life; active, it affirms the world, from underneath these categories, as a world of becoming, finding its increased energy from the very denial of this truthful world. In the above quotation, following upon the movement of active nihilism, the world (or rather, the universe) is now thought from underneath these categories *as* a monstrous, repetitive cycle of energy whose characteristics are designated in terms of 'will to power', 'eternal recurrence of the same' and the affirmation of the self-destroying and self-creating cycles of energy.

In the following I want to suggest that both this response to nihilism and, first and foremost, the initial understanding of nihilism as such – typologized above from the notes of *Will to Power* – constitute a simplification of an important level of Nietzsche's. Focusing on this level, we will see that a certain Nietzsche constantly unmakes and complicates the distinctions and re-evaluated concepts that nevertheless fuel the epistemological and ethical horizons of a major part of his philosophy. As a result of this complication, on the one hand, one can neither stay with Nietzsche's diagnosis of metaphysics nor accept his response to it since his text shows that these terms of diagnosis and response do not work in the first place. On the other hand, I will show that Nietzsche gives us at the same time the terms within his diagnosis of, and response to the 'all too human' that opens up a way of thinking the complexity of 'now' that maintains the relevance of Nietzsche's thinking of the human and overhuman. I will show that these terms emerge out of the way in which, often beyond himself, Nietzsche opens up an immanent relation between 'genealogy', 'energetics' and 'ethics'. It is this relation which the body of this chapter will be concerned to untie from out of Nietzsche in the knowledge that much recent work with and without Nietzsche has wished to problematise these kinds of relation, considering them as Platonic, Hegelian, mimetic or meta-theoretical.[2] It is thus the major, if implicit supposition of this essay that such a problematisation has been misplaced.

I wish to suggest, then, in the following that this opening up of the relation between the genealogical, the energetic and the ethical, in the context of going beyond the human, is to be traced in Nietzsche's understanding of 'spirit'. I wish also to suggest that it is precisely by pursuing this opening through Nietzsche's understanding of spirit that the complexity of force with which we are all concerned today can be interestingly articulated philosophically, and, perhaps, culturally. We saw above that, for Nietzsche, 'spirit' is common to both active and passive nihilism, standing, therefore, outside the terms of his own typology of it. Standing outside these terms, 'spirit' can be seen, on a careful reading of Nietzsche's work, to articulate an understanding of life, of force and energy that lies prior both to metaphysical conceptualisation and to its inversions and destructions. 'Spirit' is in this sense a useful to term to use, from out of the context of Nietzsche's philosophy, in appraisal of the 'now' of culture and philosophy since it precisely *articulates*, and *responds to* (albeit indeterminately) the way in which the human has had, over the last three hundred years, to abandon the fiction that the forces of the world (within which the human is itself inscribed) can be synthesised by human thought and practice.

Before turning to the text that is most interesting in this regard, *On the Genealogy of Morality* (Nietzsche 1994), let me first give a definition of Nietzsche's understanding of 'spirit'.

Spirit and Spiritualisation

In § 230 of *Beyond Good and Evil* Nietzsche writes:

> That commanding something which the people [*das Volk*] calls 'spirit' [*der Geist*] wants to be master within itself and around itself and to feel itself master: out of multiplicity it has the will to simplicity, a will which binds together and tames, which is imperious and domineering. In this its needs and capacities are the same as those which physiologists posit for everything that lives, grows and multiplies. The power of the spirit [*Die Kraft des Geistes*] to appropriate what is strange to it [*das Fremdes sich anzueignen*] is revealed in a strong inclination to assimilate the new to the old, to simplify the complex, to overlook or repel the wholly contradictory; just as it arbitrarily emphasizes, extracts and falsifies to suit itself certain traits and lines in what is strange to it, in every piece of 'external world'. Its intention in all this is the incorporation [*die Einverleibung*] of new 'experiences', the arrangement of new things within old divisions – growth; more precisely, the feeling of growth, the feeling of increased power [*Kraft*]. This same will is served by an apparently opposing drive of the spirit [*ein scheinbar entgegengesetzter Trieb des Geistes*], a sudden decision for ignorance, for arbitrary shutting-out, a closing of the windows, an inner denial of this or that thing, a refusal to let it approach, a contentment with the dark, the closed horizon: all this being necessary according to the degree of its power to appropriate [*seiner aneignenden Kraft*], its 'digestive power' so to speak [*seiner 'Verdauungskraft'*] – and indeed the 'spirit' resembles most a stomach [*und wirklich gleicht 'der Geist' am meisten noch einem Magen*]. This will to appearance, to simplification [and also] to the mask, in short to that which is on the surface, is counteracted by that sublime tendency in the person of knowledge which takes and *wants to* take a profound, and many-sided and thorough view of things: as a kind of cruelty of the intellectual conscience and taste which every brave thinker will recognize in himself. In fact, it would be nicer if, instead of with cruelty, one credited us perhaps with an 'extravagant honesty' [*eine 'ausschweifende Redlichkeit'*] – we free, very free spirits [*uns freien, sehr freien Geistern*]. (Nietzsche 1973, 141–2; 1988: 168–9)

'Spirit' is initially placed here in inverted commas as if it was a common understanding of the notion that Nietzsche is alluding to, one of popular parlance. According to the metaphysical tradition, and more specifically within the tradition and culture of Christianity following John, Paul and

Augustine, spirit is opposed to matter and to the body. Following this opposition the term accrues to itself the highest values of human conduct: 'love', 'wisdom', 'mercy' are often thought of as the highest 'spiritual' values. It is, for Nietzsche, this notion of spirit that has been devalued by the end of the nineteenth century and of which *passive nihilism – a recession in the power of spirit – is itself a consequence.* The notion of 'spirit' that interests Nietzsche here would at first sight seem, then, to be a somewhat straightforward inversion of the metaphysical hierarchy of the supersensuous and the sensuous. Considered as a process of digestion, of assimilation and rejection, upon which the metabolism and, therefore, the unity of the living organism is predicated, spirit, together with the values flowing therefrom, is described by Nietzsche as a 'stomach'. Nietzsche consequently looks to physiology to give us its description and account. If 'spirit' is indeed stomach, then Nietzsche has simply reduced, the argument might go, spirituality to a biological process of digestion, biologising culture and flattening the work of spirit to the most simple affective mechanisms. The result is a return to the notorious 'blond beast' or the 'beast of prey' of Nietzschean legend. Such would be the risk, for example, that Heidegger attempted to twist Nietzsche from in casting this 'biologism' within a metaphysical ontology and epistemology (see Heidegger 1991b, especially 39–111). So, *contra* Heidegger's reading, in what way does this paragraph intimate a conception of spirit prior to and beyond the distinction between the sensuous and supersensuous within which the metaphysical opposition between spirit and matter falls?

An indication is given in the second part of the quotation. We recall that in the earlier 'Trilogy of Free Spirits', *Human, All Too Human* (Nietzsche 1986), *Daybreak* (Nietzsche 1982) and *The Joyful Science* (Nietzsche 1973), 'free spirit' designated at least three things: first, a concern to demystify faith through the critical use of reason; second, an energetic disposition of abounding force; and, third, the concern to resituate reason within a larger economy of the senses. It is precisely this latter aspect that 'spirit' (in quotation marks in the above paragraph) designates. The physiological designation of spirit as a 'stomach' is therefore to be taken *neither* literally *nor* metaphorically. If 'spirit' is considered as a process of digestion, of assimilation and rejection, upon which the metabolism and the unity of the living organism is predicated, then, for Nietzsche, spirit, in the traditional sense of what is distinct from the sensuous, is *one type* of *digestion of the world*, one in which its digestive function is, precisely, foreclosed. 'Spirit' in the traditional sense thus disavows its 'mechanics': its genealogy, its organisations, and the whys, wherefores and 'hows' of its decisions and choices. The point has several implications.

First, and most locally: the second definition of nihilism designated the self-devaluation of metaphysical categories. Since one such category *as a* value is often called 'spirit' within the tradition, then nihilism is itself a response *within* the economy of a particular (metaphysical) understanding of spirit. This is also the reason why spirit (in the wider sense we are reaching) stands outside either passive or active nihilism, since they are in turn *types of spirit*, types, that is, *of either smaller or larger systems of digestion*. Thus, to return to the terms of my introduction, Nietzsche's re-organisation of spirit goes beyond, indeed renders nonpertinent his own typology of nihilism, as well as his response to it *qua* active nihilism, since each type of nihilism is a minor economy of spirit within processes of spiritualisation that exceed it. It is these processes that need to be assumed for a new spirit to emerge. This will become all the more clear as we proceed.

Second: spirit is not being reinterpreted here along the lines of an empiricist reduction of the metaphysical, one that loses the necessity of philosophical transcendence – an interpretation that Heidegger believed in the thirties Nietzsche's thought risked condoning unless it was 're-spiritualised' philosophically (Heidegger 1991b)[3]. Rather, for Nietzsche, spirit as the process of the living as such opens up *in the first place* the distinction between spirit and matter that accompanies the logic of metaphysical thinking. The re-evaluated term 'spirit' is in this sense a metaphor for a process of differentiation between an organism and its 'environment' (its *Umwelt*).

Third: it is not however a metaphor, for Nietzsche, if spirit in the traditional Pauline sense is only a more 'spiritualised' form of digestion, willfully or habitually unaware of its processes of functioning. The above metaphysical distinction *between* spirit and matter is thus an interpretation of 'spirit', one that forecloses it. Spirit in this deeper Nietzschean sense is something like the metabolic order of the human organism in general, one from out of which particular metabolisms emerge (that which demands a distinction between spirit and matter, that which despairs of the distinction, that which wishes to get behind the distinction, and so forth). 'Spirit' in this sense is therefore neither literal (since the 'literal' is only one form of emergence of 'spirit') nor metaphorical (since there is nothing literal about 'spirit' in the first place, and since to rework 'spirit' behind and beyond its metaphysical determinations is to exceed the distinction between the literal and the metaphorical and place this thinking within a historically informed thinking of spiritualisation).

Fourth: in this context a *free spirit* is a person who has an enlarged sense of the self's relation to its *Umwelt* through recognising the intrinsic relation between the sensuous and the rational. In the experience of this recognition a free spirit becomes less appropriating, more abounding in energy. A 'free spirit' comes, in other words, from knowing where spirit comes from in the first place, how it evolves and what forces are in play behind our conceptual determinations of the world. Now, in this sense, and at this level of the text, Nietzschean genealogy, Nietzschean energetics and the transvaluation of traditional ethics are seen to be *inseparable* elements of a general philosophy of life *qua* 'spirit'. The following will constantly reiterate this last point: it not only suggests that the systematic register of Nietzsche's thinking remains to be read, it implies, *contra* the gesture of much recent philosophizing on Nietzsche, that it is in this systematic register that the importance of Nietzsche's thinking for us today is to be found.

A 'free spirit' constitutes therefore the transvaluation of both the popular and traditional senses of the terms 'spirit' into an embodiment of 'spirit' that is an enlarged digestion. 'Free spirits' are an advanced form of the primary level of 'spirit' *qua* digestion, one that appropriates less than more. The process that takes us from the primary level of 'spirit' to that of a 'free spirit', Nietzsche calls 'spiritualisation' (*Vergeistigung*) (a term most frequently used in *On the Genealogy of Morality*). Spiritualisation is, for Nietzsche, the process of the evolution of life. In the third essay of *On the Genealogy of Morality* Nietzsche calls it the 'law of life, the law of *necessary* "self-overcoming" in the essence of life' (Nietzsche 1994, 126). As Zarathustra had already put it in the second book of *Thus Spake Zarathustra* 'spirit is the life that itself cuts into life [*Der Geist ist das Leben das selber ins Leben schneidet*]' (Nietzsche 1961, 127). I will return to this comment later. Let me end this section by formulating the above points in more definitional terms.

For Nietzsche, 'spirit' designates the emergence and stabilisation of the nervous system as a whole, one not simply prior to, but engendering and always exceeding, towards greater complexity, the metaphysical divisions between 'spirit' and matter, consciousness and instinct, intelligence and affect, the brain and the stomach. 'Spirit' is a 'biological' concept to the extent that it is particular to all living organisms; it is not biological to the extent that it is defined by its own history which is nothing other than the history of its own spiritualisation. As the emergence and stabilisation of the nervous system as a whole, spirit is the history of its own evolution, of the relation drawn between the organism and its *Umwelt* and of the modifications that this relation undergoes over time – an evolution that precisely *leaves* the domain of the biological over time *through* these very mediations. The human organism is the result of this evolution of 'spirit'. Not that 'spirit' was there in the first place, as Hegel posits in both a similar and very different reading of spirit. 'Spirit' is simply the best term by which to articulate the complexity of its own becoming. Re-evaluated by Nietzsche, twisted out of the determinations of metaphysics and plunged back into history, 'spirit' thereby becomes, for Nietzsche, both *a genealogical concept* and *a vector of re-evaluation*, bringing together – and this is again the important 'systematic' point – the epistemological, ethical and speculative aspects of Nietzsche's rethinking of the categories of unity, substance, causality and purpose. In this sense, not only is nihilism, then, to be articulated within the overall economy of 'spirit', but 'spirit' is another way of understanding will to power as the 'self-sublimating' (Nietzsche 1994, 126) law of life. In this sense, in turn, 'spirit' anticipates a re-evaluation of values that cannot be definitively described in terms of a 'Dionysian world of will to power' (Nietzsche 1968,

§1067) *without losing the mediations of the process of spiritualisation.* As our reading of *On the Genealogy of Morality* will now show, it is these very mediations that point the way beyond the fiction of nihilism towards the over-human in the first place.[4]

On the Genealogy of Morality (I)

It is well known, particularly after Deleuze's *Nietzsche and Philosophy* (Deleuze 1983), that *On the Genealogy of Morality* is the work in which Nietzsche gives the most sustained account of his genealogical re-evaluation of metaphysics. This valuation plunges metaphysical values into an open 'field' of forces from which emerge their re-evaluation and transvaluation as types of force. The work thus articulates more than any other text the said relation between genealogy, energetics and ethics. In this sense this particular work is of immense interest both from the perspective of spirit and spiritualisation and in the context of nihilism and its aftermath. That said, *On the Genealogy of Morality* is also a highly ambiguous text, one in which Nietzsche's genealogical and energetic valuation, re-evaluation and transvaluation of metaphysical thinking and practice end up in the worst impasses of philosophical and moral speculation. In my reading of the *Genealogy* I wish, first, to situate the terms of the genealogical and energetic valuation of the first essay of the work and suggest the limits of these terms. I will then show in what ways the second essay overcomes these limits, all the while suggesting what implications this overcoming has for Nietzsche's philosophy of life, spirit and affirmation as a whole. I will thereby seek to show through the reading of this one text, (a) what complications to Nietzsche's thinking are necessary if Nietzsche is to help us think the future of thinking and culture, and (b) how Nietzsche himself helps us into this future by intimating himself where these complications arise.

In the first essay, ' "Good and Evil", "Good and Bad"' the Christian values of 'good' and 'evil' are historically relocated in a cultural battle between two systems of valuation (§§5–11). The valuation 'good and evil' is interpreted as a priestly, then as a Judaic re-evaluation of the noble valuation 'good and bad': this re-evaluation is a struggle of forces. For Nietzsche, what is good is originally what is noble, that is, what discharges spontaneously, what is oriented towards the outside. The bad in this schema constitutes that which blocks the path of this original affirmation. In the valuation 'good and evil', what is bad in the first valuation becomes good in the second (interiorisation and delay) and what was good in the first (discharge) becomes not simply bad, but 'evil'. Evil is that which willfully refuses the distinction between the emerging inside and outside upon which the new notion of the 'good' is predicated (a subject and its acts, choice between nature and culture): it is thus on this very distinction that the Christian concept of original sin, following Paul and Augustine, is possible.[5] This

re-evaluation is thus not simply a change of *signs*, but a different organisation of *force* from one system of valuation to the other, an organisation of
force predicated on the differences of flow of energy between the human
organism and its environment (what becomes the difference *between* the
inside and the outside). In the first valuation what is good moves from inside
to outside, with little understanding, and need for understanding, of any
limit between the two. In the second valuation, what is good is what has
sanctified the difference that has emerged between the two.

Thus what is good in the first valuation is not simply bad in the second.
For this good to become 'evil', the active type must be confronted with a
choice of whether it uses its force or not. The re-evaluation of the good
depends therefore on the prior division between a subject and its effects.
For Nietzsche, it is through this strategy of separation, and through the
consequent concept of 'choice', that the Judaic re-evaluation imposes
upon activity the invitation to nonactivity and reactivity. The invitation is
disguised under the new value system of an 'agent' free from, and responsible for its acts, that is, of a 'subject'. As a result, seen both genealogically
and energetically from the perspective of force, the active force of immediate
discharge (the strong) yields to the reactivity of the weak, transforming this
force from its direction outwards into a disposition of force that only *reacts*
to other forces, to other events from within its own interior organisation. In
the first noble valuation, bad is nothing but a secondary effect of good
whereas in the second *ressentiment* valuation, good is situated as the opposite
of evil, as something only ever to come, projected into a world beyond life.
The split of the forces of life into two worlds is thereby formed and confirmed. There is a lot to say about this analysis of force: in the context of my
argument I wish, here, to underline four things.

1 This account of value clearly collapses concepts and the discourses in
   which they function into a field of forces. That is, the first essay shows
   exemplarily how the genealogy of nihilism in the first general sense leads
   to an energetics (to an account of the relation between humans and their
   Umwelt in terms of flows and dispositions of force).
2 This field is considered as the *same* field from one valuation to the next:
   what has changed is not the forces as such, but the *organisation* of these
   forces and their relations with each other. This differential typology of
   force allows Nietzsche in *On the Genealogy of Morality* and elsewhere to
   'destroy' metaphysical distinctions in terms of the *sameness* of forces that
   subtend these distinctions. The typology of force constitutes the theoretical result of 'active nihilism' and serves as a necessary prerequisite to
   any thinking of transvaluation.[6]
3 That said, this typology is at the same time highly ambiguous in its
   relation to metaphysical thinking. For, while reorganising metaphysical
   distinctions in terms of the forces that subtend them, it *also* leads to a

metaphysics of force in which force is *not* articulated *within* its differentiations (what I am calling 'spirit'), but is exclusively thought in terms of *physiological* and *psychological* organisation. This intellectual lapse often leads in Nietzsche's work to an a-historical account of the organisation of force and a simultaneous simplification of the complexity of the formation of philosophical and religious concepts and their cultures. Here in the first essay of *On the Genealogy of Morality*, for example, the move from noble to Judaic valuation is predicated, first, on an unaccounted split between the warrior and priestly nobility and, second, on a clash between different types of culture *as if* the difference *between* the noble and the Judaic could be wholly accounted for in terms of the *organisation* of the *same*. This ends up reducing culture to the 'affective' (the most obvious domain of the energetic within the human). To judge in this way risks anthropomorphising the differentiations of energy *between* the human and its *Umwelt* in terms of a purely human force that stands *outside* its constitutive relation to technical, economic and social forces. Nietzsche's theory of rank, his affirmation of the blond beast, his tendency to anthropomorphise 'will to power' and his notion of 'grand politics' are important examples of this risk and are, therefore, to be understood as the effects of a unilateral understanding of force.

4 (Finally) the reduction of an indeterminate field of forces to a fairly determinate field of human affects within the Judaic re-evaluation arises symptomatically at the very moment that Nietzsche wonders *how humankind can emerge from out of the Judaic revaluation*, that is, *how the human can leave nihilism* (in the general metaphysical sense of 'will to nothing'). This means, positively, that the emergence from out of nihilism is nothing but a question of re-organising the forces underlying the metaphysical re-evaluation of the noble valuation. It is not a question of inventing the new as such: the overhuman is *already* with us in this sense. The reduction means negatively, however, that the said exit from nihilism risks being located by Nietzsche in a *move back* to the 'original' valuation, the original noble affirmation of force. At such moments the active destruction of metaphysics ('active nihilism') becomes a pure regression to the fiction of spontaneous discharge. In other words, the overcoming of nihilism does not follow the Nietzschean 'law of life' (self-sublimation of force *qua* spirit) but constitutes a straightforward inversion of the priestly/Judaic re-evaluation. It is these moments of panic on Nietzsche's part, or rather, within this panic, of his *desire for the metaphysical purity of force*, that motivate the representation of the 'blond beast' as the future of the human and of the moral. They have lead both to a rejection of Nietzsche's philosophy of life *qua* pure force and to the partly justified accusation that Nietzsche flattens crucial distinctions between culture and biology.[7]

What constitutes the whole problem here is, first and less importantly, the re-evaluation and transvaluation of Judaic valuation and, second and more importantly, Nietzsche's very understanding of active and reactive force. A response to this re-evaluation is not to be found in the first essay except phantasmatically, in terms of a return to a fictive historical point of pure discharge (the blond beast of §11). Whenever this phantasm invades the text, Nietzsche simplifies his own digestive system, his own 'spirit' and repeats the terms of the metaphysical appropriation of the world and life in terms of the 'pure'. That is to say, 'spirit' in the large sense we are unravelling is reduced to a pure reversal of 'spirit' in the metaphysical sense, an inversion that does nothing but repeat in inverse form the desire for the pure.

The 'Second Essay: "Guilt", "bad conscience" and related matters' provides, however, the terms of an answer. For it precisely undercuts and goes beyond the very analysis of active/reactive force that underpins the schema of the initial two antagonistic valuations (noble/priestly, Roman/Judaic). In the second essay not only is there not an initial opposition between active and reactive forces, the organisations of force are immediately posited beyond biological, physiological and psychological force to include other types of force (notably technical). Moreover, these organisations are seen to form a *mediated* history of the organism in its relation to the environment from which, precisely, distinctions like the physiological, the technical, the psychological, the social *emerge in the first place*. These constitute crucial advances upon the schemas of force of the first essay, intimating, ultimately, a serious reconfiguring of Nietzsche's own schemas of valuation and re-evaluation. Let us see how and why.

On the Genealogy of Morality (II)

In the second essay there are two sites in which the opposition between the active and the reactive breaks down, intimating a rethinking of the field of forces beyond the purely affective and suggesting a line of thinking that sublates the 'spirit of revenge'. The first is the sovereign individual (§§1 and 2), the second is the community that lets its malefactors go unpunished (§§10 and 11). I turn first to the sovereign individual. Its description is preceded by a crucial, dense paragraph on the faculty of promising with which we must begin.

For Nietzsche, the specificity of the human in contrast to other animals lies in its ability to *make promises*. A promise, for Nietzsche, is the ability to hold the discharge of one's force until later. In §1 of ' "Guilt", "bad conscience" and related matters' he writes:

> A promise . . . is by no means merely a passive inability to be rid of an
> impression once it has made its impact, nor is it just indigestion caused by

giving your word on some occasion and finding that you cannot cope, instead it is an active *desire* not to let go . . . really it is the *will's memory*: so that a world of strange new things, circumstances and even acts of will may be placed quite safely in between the original 'I will', 'I shall do' and the actual discharge of the will, its *act*, without breaking this long chain of the will. But what a lot of preconditions there are for this! In order to have that degree of control over the future, man must first have learnt to distinguish between what happens by accident, and what by design, to think causally, to view the future as the present and anticipate it, to grasp with certainty what is end and what is means, in all, to be able to calculate, compute – and before he can do this, man himself will really have to become *reliable, regular, automatic* [*notwendig*], even in his own self-image, so that he, as someone making a promise, is answerable for his own *future*! (Nietzsche 1994, 39; 1988, 292)

Whereas in the first essay the affirmation of force was considered in terms of conducting one's force immediately towards the outside, here the very withholding of one's force, the temporal gap 'Between the original 'I will', 'I shall do' and the actual discharge of the will, constitutes the very possibility of the human: promising. Promising is the memory of this delay of force: that is, the will's memory. Thus, firstly, if the human is for Nietzsche predicated on such deferral and retention, from the very beginning of this second essay we have not only moved beyond the affirmation of the intense, spontaneous and instinctive to be found in the first and third essays. We have also moved beyond any notion of a purely active force. That the specificity of the human lies in the very deferral of force means that force in humans can *never* be purely active. This is not to say, however, that animals, indeed any organism, do not defer either. Deferral is the very possibility of life. It means that the process of differentiation particular to the human is particularised through *the way in which* human animals *organise* their force, that is, in Nietzschean terms, 'will', or, in the terms of this essay, have *spirit*. It is on the basis of this organisation of force that willing is possible *in the first place* and that, therefore, a distinction is possible between a will and its acts. Other organisms may indeed come to have spirit in this way. For the moment, however, only the human organises itself accordingly, although this understanding of 'willing' means inversely that the human is precisely constituted from the first through forces that are not human. This is, precisely, the ambivalence of spirit.

The implications of these points for the oppositions of the first essay should be clear. It means that the notion of a pure active force as such is a fiction. As I have already suggested, this fiction always risks returning Nietzsche to metaphysics when he wishes to destroy metaphysics in the horizon of the transvaluation of pure activity (a destruction that returns him all the more roundly to the metaphysical). It means furthermore that the psychological phenomenon of a human 'will' is *the historical result of the organisation of force.* Thus to talk about will, as Nietzsche does, as the organisation of forces means necessarily to talk about the psychological in terms that are at one and the same time psychological *and* historical. (I understand 'historical' here in a sense that includes what Nietzsche still calls the 'pre-historical', a nineteenth-century concept which is predicated on a prior and too unilateral understanding that the historical is dependent upon the written trace.)[8] This paragraph on promising shows, in other words, that an energetics consequent upon genealogy *must* work prior to and beyond the historically late and relative distinction between the 'inside' and the 'outside', 'internal' and 'external' force, 'psyche' and 'environment'. That said, the distinction between a will and its acts that allows for promising, and that promising in turn reinforces, nevertheless means that *all* the *ethically* oriented concepts that Nietzsche is so eager to destroy in the first essay, as he pitches the noble against the morality of the slave, the spirit of Rome against the *ressentiment* spirit of Judea, are concepts that constitute the *specificity* of the human as such *prior to any relative distinction between the active and the reactive.* As a result, these concepts cannot be considered as unilaterally 'nihilistic' or 'reactive' although they remain too simple both to account for their genealogy and to continue to structure the moral interpretation of the world as such.

Categories, then, that Nietzsche so often wishes to get behind as 'epiphenomenal', or worse dismiss as 'useless' and purely 'fictitious' (see particularly 1968b, §§545–70), or account for, as we saw in the first essay, in the exclusive terms of the psychology of *ressentiment*, these categories are located here *within the formation of memory.* Since this formation marks the process of hominisation as such (there is no human organism without the differentiations of memory), categories that emerge within it cannot be either simply 'active' or 'reactive'. Thus, the categories against which Nietzsche sets much of his thinking – causality, finality, purpose, the subjectivity of will – are the result of a long process that designates the human as such and therefore designates them *as also* active, even if, at the same time, they prejudge how to articulate the subphenomenal. This means finally that just as one cannot oppose the active to the reactive one cannot simply oppose, as many passages of Nietzsche do (especially, again, in the posthumous notes, *Will to Power*) the categorial to what lies underneath or beyond it.

Let us recall at this point, for the sake of clarity, the argument at the beginning of §13 of the first essay: ' "Good and Evil", "Good and Bad" '. Nietzsche writes:

> There is nothing strange about the fact that lambs bear a grudge towards large birds of prey: but that is no reason to blame the large birds of prey for carrying off the little lambs. It is just as absurd to ask strength *not* to express itself as strength, *not* to be a desire to overthrow, crush, become

master, to be a thirst for enemies, resistance and triumphs, as it is to ask weakness to express itself as strength. A quantum of force is just such a quantum of drive, will, action, in fact it is nothing but this driving, willing and acting, and only the seduction of language (and the fundamental errors of reason petrified within it) which construes all action upon an agency, a 'subject' can make it appear otherwise.   (Nietzsche 1994, 28)

On the basis of a passage like this, it has often been argued that Nietzsche's questioning of 'cause and effect' in the moral sphere removes the very site of resistance to all forms of particularism, that is, the transcendental subject of modernity, 'condition' of the formal subject of law upon which the constitutions of democracy and the Enlightenment culture of universal rights is predicated.[9] Thus, to 'destroy' the relation of cause/effect removes the possibility, so the argument goes, of accounting for events in terms of a subject prior to those events, an account on the basis of which injustice can be measured in relation to a formal subject of political and ethical law. The above passage from the second essay of *On the Genealogy of Morality* situates both the relation of cause/effect and the economy of force subtending it in a more complicated process of differentiation than is offered by the notions of active and reactive force.

What we see here is that, for Nietzsche, moral responsibility is not simply an economy of affect. It does not simply constitute the effect of an inversion of force that creates the interiority from which the soul and subjectivity emerge, one as a result of which the 'subject' can be separated from its 'acts'. Rather, responsibility ensues from a 'series of preconditions' that must make man determinate and determined for *creative* situations to emerge in the first place. The separation of the becoming of force into a subject and its acts is not, in other words, the result of a psychological force (the ruse of *ressentiment*); it is the effect of a series of forces, both human and nonhuman, 'immaterial' and 'material', that give rise to the notion of subjectivity. This is a crucial argument the implications of which are not to be lost sight of.

It means, first, that subjectivity is a force determined by other forces. It is here that Nietzsche's genealogical and energetic critique of Kantian transcendental/formal subjectivity is itself most forceful. For it does not say that this subjectivity is a 'useless fiction' but circumscribes it within historical parameters, the force of which can themselves, however, no longer resist the increasingly complex forces of the contemporary world. It means, second, that these other forces need to be accounted for within the general field of forces in which Nietzsche's theory of energetics is interested. And it means, third, prior to and beyond the particular context of the formation of subjectivity, that it is only *through* regularisation and through determination that the irregular, singular and creative in the human can come forward in the first place.[10] This argument not only exceeds the terms of Nietzsche's distinction between the active and reactive, it also calls for a recasting of the relation between his understanding of democracy and aristocracy (selection). What, then, are these 'preconditions'?

In paragraph three of the second essay Nietzsche responds that they lie in *mnemotechnics*. He writes: 'Perhaps there is nothing more strange than [the human's] technics of memory.... A thing must be burnt in so that it stays in the memory: only something that continues *to hurt* stays in the memory' (Nietzsche 1994, 41). Most commentators of this passage have focused their attention on the resultant cruelty that underlies, for Nietzsche, ethical concepts like conscience and responsibility. In this perspective it is often argued that Nietzsche's concern is to show how the most spiritual ethical concepts are predicated on the most violent history of affect. Hence the importance of Nietzsche's aside that Kant's categorical imperative 'smells of cruelty' (ibid., 45). What is underestimated in this appreciation is the fact that this passage records a widening of the energetic account of concepts in terms of affects into one that includes *technical forces*. The force behind our metaphysical valuations is not just affective for Nietzsche, it is also technical. Thus, if the 'will' is a result of 'memory', and 'memory' is the result of both cruelty and the technical organisation of our bodies – that is, our corporal forces – then the will, and its accompanying concepts (purpose, intention, finality and promising) derive from an energetic disposition between outside and inside that is *at the same time* affective and technical.

In the terms that Nietzsche most often uses in the 'Trilogy of Free Spirits' and the *Genealogy*, the open field of forces behind metaphysical valuation are simultaneously 'psychological', 'physiological' and 'historical'. Here I wish to orient the term 'historical' towards the technical. Thus, again, what organises the field of forces underlying a discursive field of valuation ('good and bad', 'good and evil', optimism, pessimism, nihilism) cannot be exclusively discussed in the too human terms of a 'priestly caste', or 'an ascetic priest', or noble 'artists and statesman', but must be described, in part, in terms of a relationship between technical object and affect out of which the human organism differentiates itself to begin with. This process is that of 'spiritualisation'.

Several things are absolutely determining in this relationship. First: it is one that is under constant change. Nietzsche's tendency, therefore, to reduce it either to blocks of cultural types (the Noble, the Roman, the Judaic) or to a purely affective economy constitutes a short-circuiting of the historical forces in play within the field of forces subtending metaphysics. It is at such moments of short-circuiting that the biologising Nietzsche returns to the surface. Thus, again, *contra* Heidegger, the way to counter the reduction of culture to nature in Nietzsche is not to re-spiritualise his biology, but to show the way in which in the first place his understanding of life, and of the particularity of human life from within the economy of the organic in general, exceeds and accounts for the metaphysical understanding of spirit. To do this would show that, for Nietzsche, a vast 'spiral' runs from the most primitive organic systems of digestion and metabolism, enlarging out more and more widely through instances of deferral and differentiation like technics, language and social institutions to those organisms whose digestive systems can *promise* (humans).[11] When Nietzsche maintains that 'spirit is a stomach', it is this spiral of spiritualisation that he has in mind. The accusation that Nietzschean physiology is, therefore, reductionist, empiricist and naturalist, while undoubtedly justified by several levels of Nietzsche's text, misses this very spiral in which the most complex level of Nietzsche's texts is interested. These paragraphs on the formation of the faculty of promising are one such example.

Second: the technical organisation of the will presupposes neither the will nor the faculty of promising to be formed. *Such a will and faculty emerge out of this history of mnemonics.* Nietzsche's account of the emergence of responsibility exceeds the opposition between the active and reactive by showing from the beginning that any spirit *prior to being active or reactive* emerges from this technico-affective history of cruelty and interiorisation. We can therefore confirm that when Nietzsche projects this history of interiorisation onto the reactive soul, he betrays a drive to separate out the historical from the psychological and the physiological. As a result of this separation the energetic field in which Nietzsche is interested is impoverished, and the risk returns of separating force from its historical differentiations, that is, *from the multiplicity of forces in which any force necessarily operates.* It should also be clear by now that this drive to separate in Nietzsche's text is one of appropriation that marks a particular period of spiritual evolution, digestion and categorisation, one within which Nietzsche remains caught at the very moment that he gives us the terms by which to exceed it: metaphysics. We can thus characterise this period by both by a particular organisation of force that projects outside of the human forces that constitute it in the first place.

In this sense *Nietzsche's genealogy of memory, will and responsibility call for further genealogising, his notion of force for further differentiation in order for the human to be convincingly situated within forces that exceed and constitute it at one and the same time. Only on this basis can the transvaluation, the 'overhuman', open up as an ethical and cultural possibility for the human.*

To say as much only begins to do justice to these opening paragraphs of the second essay that have been too often poorly read. This conflation of forces, together with the expansion of the terms of energetics by which one reflects upon it, foreground above all the nature of the *immanent* links between the genealogical, the energetic and the ethical. The ambiguity of Nietzsche's transvaluation of metaphysical values is to be situated and untied here: this transvaluation is again not, as Heidegger and others have contended, a question of positing new values *after* the destruction of metaphysics. Rather, these values emerge as a transvaluation of the latter *from within* this *expanded* energetic analysis. In other words what is to be stressed in reading Nietzsche today is at one and the same time, first, the analysis of everything in terms of force and, second, the analysis of this very force in terms of a historically differentiated, changing and expanding complex of forces, in which no particular force or analysis of force predominates.

An indication of this immanent method is to be found in Nietzsche's portrait of the sovereign individual in the second paragraph of this essay, one that emerges from out of the above understanding of constraint, cruelty and determination. Let us now turn to it.

In §2 of the second essay Nietzsche writes:

> The immense amount of labour involved in what I have called the 'morality of custom' [*Sittlichkeit der Sitte*], the actual labour of man on himself during the longest epoch of the human race, his whole labour *before history*, is explained and justified on a grand scale... by this fact: with the help of the morality of custom and the social straitjacket, man was *made* truly predictable. Let us place ourselves, on the other hand, at the end of this immense process where the tree actually bears fruit, where society and its morality of custom reveal what they were simply *the means to*: we then find the *sovereign individual* [*das souveraine Individuum*] as the ripest fruit on its tree, like only to itself, having freed itself from the morality of custom, an autonomous, supra-ethical [*Übersittlich*] individual man with his own independent, durable will, who has *the right to make a promise* [*der wirklich versprechen darf*] and has a proud consciousness quivering in every muscle of *what* he has finally achieved and incorporated [*in ihm leibhaft geworden ist*], an actual awareness of power and freedom, a feeling that man in general has reached completion.... The 'free' man, the possessor of an unbreakable, durable will thus has his own *standard of value*.... [He] gives his word as something which can be relied on, because he is strong enough to remain upright in the face of mishap or even 'in the face of fate'.... The proud realization of the extraordinary privilege of *responsibility*, the awareness of this rare freedom and power over himself and his destiny, has penetrated him to the depths and become an instinct, his dominant instinct. What will he call his dominant instinct, assuming that he needs a word for it? No doubt about the answer: this instinct the sovereign individual calls his *conscience*.   (Nietzsche 1994, 39–40/1988, 293–4)

This extraordinary passage resumes many themes to be found elsewhere in Nietzsche's writings that look forward to the energetic disposition of the overhuman. There is much to analyse: I will again be brief within the context of the argument. The mastery over both one's own internal forces and external forces (*amor fati*) is seen here as a process of spiritualisation, the precondition of which is determination and constraint. Rather than succumbing to this constraint, (the 'reactive'), the sovereign individual *transforms* it in such a way that the forces organising its will are, in the very process of organising it, *re-organised by this will*. The process is in this sense 'dialectical', but not if a dialectical relation presupposes the two terms to be dialecticised. For neither the forces, nor the sovereign individual's will precede each other in their direction; their space of mutual determination is created in the process. The process is dialectical in the sense, therefore, of the pre-eminence of this space over the terms to which it gives rise and, as a result of which, these terms are radically unstable, mutually defining instances.[12] *It is this space that is active and pregnant with the future.*[13] What is, therefore, singular about this passage is that Nietzsche places here the process of re-evaluation of metaphysics, particular to the overhuman, within a historical process of differentiations of energy, which differentiations emerge from out of a 'dialectical' relation between the human organism and the technical. The sovereign will is thus considered as the digestion of a whole history of labour upon human affects that allow for the organisation of time, of memory, of promising, and, therefore, of willing. The sovereign will presupposes and transforms in turn this history. Nietzsche calls this transformation 'incorporation' (*Einverleibung*), the most interesting concept in Nietzsche to mark spiritual digestion.

This transformation is thus the incorporation of constraint to the extent that the individual's very mastery over this constraint becomes a form of responsibility that in turn becomes its dominant instinct. In the first essay the exclusively psychological terms of Nietzsche's re-evaluation of the Judaic schema of valuation precipitated Nietzsche into an affirmation of noble instincts and discharge. Here, a much more complex process of re-evaluation is being written out: the instinct of the sovereign individual is not a regression to the 'natural' beneath the shame and nihilism of the 'civilising' process, it is precisely its transvaluation *qua* overcoming. This transvaluation is, in a logic close to that of Hegelian *Aufhebung*, something like the articulation of a new space of invention through and beyond the distinction between the 'natural' and the 'constraining'. As a result this individual has all the properties of a subject responsible for its acts, depreciated in the first essay, and that of a noble individual overflowing with energy and force. Indeed, the sovereign individual's responsibility can be seen to be nothing but an enlarged understanding of subjective responsibility: it is therefore neither a regression to the premodern nor a simple destruction of Enlightenment law. This is another reason why, precisely, one cannot stigmatise subjectivity as unilaterally 'reactive': *subjectivity is the very precondition of the one who goes beyond the law.*

With this history of sovereignty periods of history that Nietzsche wished to destroy as 'nihilistic', as denying the becoming of life, are consequently retained: first, in the sense that they form a necessary part of the history of life, second in the sense that, as a necessary part of the history of life, they are a precondition to their own overcoming. As a result, from both the perspective of an expanded energetics that conflates the historical and the psychological and from the perspective of an expanded conscience that reevaluates, within its very practice, the traditional opposition between instinct and conscience, the opposition in the first and third essays between the active and the reactive is not made obsolete, but is itself returned to a particular history within this expanded energetics. As is now clear this expanded energetics is both the law and process of life ('the cutting of life into life') and the description of this process and law. And it is in this direction, I am arguing, that the law of 'will to power' and the 'eternal recurrence of the same' (the law of difference and differentiation) need to be articulated if they are to have purchase, as epistemological and ethical transvaluations, on the complexity of force that makes up the 'now' of human history.[14]

This way of situating the law of life becomes all the more clear in our second example from the second essay of *On the Genealogy of Morality*, the community that lets its malefactors go unpunished (§§ 10 and 11).

On the Genealogy of Morality (III)

To approach the description of this community we need first to elaborate the genealogy of guilt. Nietzsche's genealogy of the moral value of 'guilt' is situated within an overall history of 'cruelty' spoken of in terms of the pleasure yielded by festivals of pain. As should now be clear, however, to read this genealogy in predominantly affective terms would be precipitate because of the history of memorisation within which these affects are situated. In this context the fact that Nietzsche takes the feeling of 'guilt' back to a relationship of debt between creditor and debtor is rather important. For this relationship is located within an economic order in which – and here the history of the sovereign individual dovetails with that of guilt – *promises are made*, suspending the immediacy of barter exchange. Little has been made of this point in Nietzschean literature: its implications are important. To promise an exchange of goods over time is to defer the immediate action of transaction: this deferral creates inversely and retrospectively a constraint upon the will and a sense of obligation. The deferral is an act of memory, and the sense of obligation a consequence of it. Thus, if the promise is not kept, a debt is owed.

Now, at first, pressed against the material nature of this contractual relationship, this debt (the goods to be exchanged) is one engaging the very body of the debtor.

> The debtor, in order to inspire confidence that the promise of repayment will be honoured, in order to give a guarantee of the solemnity and sanctity of his promise, and in order to etch the duty and obligation of repayment into his conscience, pawns something to the creditor by means of the contract in case he does not pay, something which he still

possesses and controls, for example, his body, or his wife, or his freedom, or his life. (Nietzsche 1994, §5, 44)

This engagement reflects the level of materiality at which the contractual relationship is set. The equivalent puts a clear limit to the process of deferral between the creditor and debtor and is itself one between a particular object and the debtor's whole life: exchange is predicated on the *finitude* of one of the parties precisely because the relationship remains essentially riveted to matter. As Nietzsche put it earlier, 'The worse man's memory has been, the more dreadful his customs have appeared' (1944, §3, 42). Thus at this stage of history and of memory, punishment is not meted out to punish the miscreant for the act performed since his or her will has not yet become organised enough to attribute to it *responsibility*. Punishment is meted out as an equivalent of the crime. We are at the stage the 'premoral', as Nietzsche calls it in *Beyond Good and Evil*, in which the origin of the action, its 'causal agent', is not yet the category of intentionality by which the action is judged, nor so much the action itself, but its *consequences* for the *community at large* (1973, §32, 45). This means that the return anger against the miscreant or debtor can fall as much upon the family of the latter as upon him or herself. Crime remains within the economy of blood-debt and revenge. In this economy of law neither the creditor or community, nor the debtor or miscreant are powerful: the spirit of material revenge is a very weak spirit, poor in overflowing energy and force.

In §9 of the *Genealogy* Nietzsche situates this analogy between community and creditor in stark terms. Like the premoral creditor, the community cannot afford, either, to defer the relationship between itself and a member. The analogy records at this level of history an equivalence in turn between the economic and the legal. Economic and legal relations are still within the same economy of spirit. This spirit is one of exclusion in order for the metabolism of the community to be maintained. We have already it met at the level of popular parlance (Nietzsche 1973, 141–2). The smaller the economy of this metabolism, the greater the punishment:

> The immediate damage done by the offender is what we are talking about least: quite apart from this, the lawbreaker is a 'breaker', somebody who has broken his word *to the whole*, in connection with all the valued features and amenities of communal life which he has shared up till now. [Assaulting the creditor therefore as much as failing to repay the benefits granted him] he is now reminded of how important these benefits are. The anger of the injured creditor, the community, makes him return to the outlawed and savage state from which he was sheltered hitherto. Punishment at this level of civilization is simply a *mimus*, a copy of normal behaviour towards a hated, disarmed enemy who has

been defeated, who has not only forfeited all rights, but all mercy as well. (Nietzsche 1994, §9, 50)

In the first essay, we recall, Rome is the culture most closely associated with noble affectivity, one defeated by the Judaic spirit of revenge. Here, however, in this genealogy of guilt in terms of debt and credit, it is precisely Rome's code of the Twelve Tables that expands *the economy of equivalence between credit and debt.*

> I regard it as definite progress and proof of a freer, more open-handed calculation, of *a more Roman* pricing of justice, when Rome's code of the Twelve Tables decreed that it did not matter how much or how little a creditor cut off: *si plus minusve secuerent, ne fraude esto* ['If they have cut off more or less, let that not be considered a crime']. (*ibid.*, §5, 44)

Since the immediate equivalence between deed and punishment or action and reaction is *also* thought by Nietzsche in terms of an economy of revenge, the above comment on the legal culture of Rome shows that it is Rome that takes us out of the spirit of revenge at a material level, just as it was the economy of equivalence that took us out of immediate anger and discharge (§4). 'Rome' thus constitutes in the *Genealogy* both a type of nobility *prior to* the revenge structure of Judaic *ressentiment* (§12 of the First Essay) and a step forward in the *Vergeistigung* of cruelty that, beginning with the precedence of equivalence over discharge, 'runs through the history of higher culture' (§6). This radical incompatibility between these two positionings of 'Rome' within the overall spiritualisation of spirit suggests the following.

Just as with the sovereign individual, so with the cultural type of 'Rome' it is *a priori* impossible to separate the interiorising history of *ressentiment* from the interiorising history of sovereignty. As with the sovereign individual, it is not a question here of the fact that the referent of these terms circulates between them, making nonsense of any conceptual stability among the terms 'Noble', 'Judaic', 'Barbarian', 'Roman', 'Blond Beast', 'Sovereign Individual'. Rather, this circulation constitutes the symptom of an economy of spirit and spiritualisation, an economy within which 'internal' and 'external' forces make up the simultaneously diachronic and synchronic 'field' of energetics to which genealogy leads us back. If Nietzsche is not in control of this economy, his text acts it out. But to say this does not mean that we stay with the text – as if it gives the law: rather, Nietzsche's textual contradictions invite us to explore further the economy of spirit.

From this perspective, *contra* large tracts of Nietzsche's diatribe against Kant, Enlightenment formalism and modern democracy, the history of the spiritualisation of cruelty will give full importance to the emergence and spiritual dignity of the concepts of 'intention', 'purpose', 'subjectivity' and 'responsibility'. As we indicated above in reference to §32 of *Beyond Good and*

Evil, they form part of the 'moral' stage of humankind, a stage predicated on a particular organisation of force (economic, technical, social and affective). Within this history these concepts – or rather values *qua* understandings of the human and its relations with itself and its internal and external environment – stem from a history of calculation, inference and judgement in which the malefactor is divided into a subject and his or her deeds. This separation, within this history, cannot be seen as an act of revenge against nobility *without separating*, in turn, the historical from the physiological and psychological. The large tracts of Nietzsche's work that do this are both reducible to the decadent spirit of the *fin-de-siècle* and, more importantly, to a symptom of a more general drive to re-appropriate this very history *in order to* exclude himself from it. In so doing, Nietzsche falls victim to its limited spirit of digestion all the more.

The above separation between subject and deed is, then, from the perspective of the general economy of spirit, confirmed as an act of spiritual progress out of the more immediate relations of credit and debt. This progress is that of the progressive 'mastery' of the community over the energies flowing through it. This progress is by no means necessary: Nietzsche's understanding of spirit is not evolutionist. Historical regression is possible at any moment within the processes of spiritualisation. This mastery is, however, something that takes us to the limit of human possibility: it takes us, ultimately, that is, from out of the 'human' towards the 'overhuman'. This is how Nietzsche begins to describe this process of mastery within one of the most interesting paragraphs of his whole work:

> As a community grows in power, it ceases to take the offense of the individual quite so seriously, because these do not seem to be as dangerous and destabilizing for the survival of the whole as they did earlier: the wrongdoer is no longer... cast out, nor can the public vent their anger on him with the same lack of constraint, – instead the wrongdoer is shielded by the community from this anger, especially from that of the immediate injured part, indeed is given protection.... An attempt to localize the matter...; above all the will [*der Wille*] manifesting itself ever more distinctly, to treat every offence as something that *can be paid off*, so that, at least to a certain degree, the wrongdoer is *isolated* from his deed – these are the characteristics imprinted more and more clearly into the penal law over its development.   (ibid., §10, 50–1)

The separation through judgement and inference of doer from deed is the same separation that will give rise later to the construction of legal systems that institute the deferral of immediate discharge, reaction and revenge and lead to Enlightenment law. These legal systems, Nietzsche argues in §11, are the creation of the *stronger* wills that 'put an end' to the spirit of *ressentiment* (p. 53) by 'lifting the object of *ressentiment* out of the hands of revenge' (ibid.) and providing for it a context in which it can be evaluated *impersonally* (p. 54). Nietzsche is of course right to add at this point that these systems are themselves partial restrictions of the will to life. That said, this is a very different account of the relation between law and life, separation and force than the one that in the same essay, the same movement of thought, opposes the will to power to law and the *ressentiment* constraints of democracy (§7) and which in the first essay maintained that Enlightenment law was a development of the spirit of revenge. Whereas the legal system is in these accounts *reactive*, here it is seen as precisely *active*. We have, as a result, a potentially very much more interesting account of the relation between law and force.

It should be clear, then, (as above) that we should not stay with, or refashion this type of contradiction as something radically ambiguous or undecidable: a temptation in much recent Nietzschean scholarship when re-addressing such moments in Nietzsche's work. *The contradiction ensues from thinking force outside its differentiations, thinking it in abstract.* Whereas, then, Nietzsche's anti-Enlightenment-ism works within a restricted, abstract economy of force that is unable to relate life to law, and force to history, the former relates to the two within a concrete, historically mediated economy of spiritualisation in which the law of life is 'life itself constantly cutting into life'. At one end of this process of spiritualisation stands matter, at the other sovereign responsibility. The separation of force into a subject and its acts is, within this spectrum, not the result of reactive activity as such, but one consequence of the very law of life upon which human force is borne.

In this context, finally, what would be a community, for Nietzsche, that has overcome both the pre-moral (pure discharge) and the moral (the passage from equivalence to legal systems as such): what he calls in §32 of *Beyond Good and Evil* the 'extramoral'? What would be a community articulated through the value of the 'overhuman'? The continuation of §10 indicates what this further *Vergeistigung* of justice might imply:

As the power and self-confidence of a community increase, the penal law always becomes more moderate; every weakening or imperiling of the former brings with it a restoration of the harsher forms of the latter. The creditor always becomes more humane to the extent that he has grown richer, finally, how much injury he can endure without suffering from it becomes the actual measure of his wealth. It is not unthinkable that a society might attain such a consciousness of power that it could allow itself the noblest luxury possible to it – letting those who harm it go unpunished. 'What are my parasites to me', it might say. 'May they live and prosper: I am strong enough for that!' Justice which began by saying 'Everything can be paid off, everything must be paid off', ends by turning a blind eye and letting off those unable to pay – it ends like every good thing on earth by sublimating itself [*sich aufhebend*]. The self-sublimation of justice – we know what a nice name it gives itself – *mercy* [*Gnade*]: it remains of course the prerogative of the most powerful man, better his way of going beyond the lawn [*sein Jenseits des Rechts*].   (ibid. 1988, 308–9)

The *Aufhebung* of justice – the going beyond the law – translates the ability to bear more and more, without suffering therefrom, events which come from outside. It is the ability not to be touched by outside, while at the same time transforming this outside. This ability, the most spiritual form of which constitutes, in collective form, the community Nietzsche describes above, is the same as that which brings to fruition the making of promises. It is the late, historically given fruit of the spiritualisation of processes of memory, that is, of something like the 'dialectic' between organism and environment. The analogy I am making between sovereign individual and community is justified by the fact that both are thought as organic growths assimilating events in such a way that their energetic disposition becomes more dispensing, less appropriating. That growth depends on the history of interiorisation, on what, on other occasions, Nietzsche calls 'nihilism'.

And yet the growth is precisely a constant self-overcoming, what Nietzsche calls here 'self-sublimation'. The re-evaluation of Judaic *ressentiment* is the self-sublimation of the legal system, not a regression to a pure force prior to it. This self-sublimation is in turn the re-evaluation of *mercy* which, allied to pity within the Christian schema of valuation, could only be thought by Nietzsche as Christian (egoistic) altruism at the level of the moral. Mercy here, in contrast to the 'mercilessness' of the primitive community, is the overhuman transvaluation of this mercy into altruistic egoism: the letting go of the other precisely because the community has gained a nonappropriative mastery over its own will. It is this that its legislator embodies through its act of mercy. In *Thus Spake Zarathustra*, this gift is called, precisely, 'love' (see especially 'Of Love of one's Neighbour' and 'Of the Bestowing Virtue' in Nietzsche 1961, 86–8 and 99–104) . Genealogising and sublating – and not destroying and reversing – the Christian love of one's neighbour, Nietzsche's understanding of the loving person is that of someone so sure of themselves, so aware that they are incorporating forces beyond them *as* themselves that *they are able to give to others*. The love of the other is, for Nietzsche, predicated on this rich egoism. It is the same rich egoism that takes one beyond the law.

In one of Nietzsche's earliest works *Human, All too Human* and in his last published work during his lifetime *The Antichrist(ian)* this nonappropriative mastery is constantly described as a new form of 'asceticism', one in which 'constraint' has been incorporated, re-evaluated, as 'instinct'. This form of asceticism is the apex of what Nietzsche understands by spirituality. It is, in a sense, the self-overcoming of the 'ascetic priest' of the third essay of *On the Genealogy of Morality*. I quote:

> The most spiritual [*geistigsten*] human beings, as the *strongest*, find their happiness where others would find their destruction: in the labyrinth, in severity towards themselves and others, in attempting; their joy lies in self-constraint: with them asceticism becomes nature, need, instinct. Knowledge – a form of asceticism. They rule not because they want to [*wollen*], but because they *are*.   (Nietzsche, 1990, §57)

This paragraph needs little comment in the context of my argument as a whole. Suffice it to make three remarks. This asceticism of love was, as mentioned above, what marks the free spirit of the 'Trilogy of Free Spirits'.[15] As the re-incorporation of self-constraint and self-cruelty, it also harks back to the 'free, very free spirits' of *Beyond Good and Evil* with which we began, those who exceed the economy of appropriation through an 'extravagant honesty' (1973, 143). This confirms one of the major theses of this essay: *the ethical perspective of spirit both emerges out of Nietzsche's genealogical method and energetics and orients the future of our understanding and practice of force*. In this sense, it is again a severe under-reading of Nietzsche's work to sever the genealogical and energetic perspective from the ethical. As I said towards the beginning of this essay, spirit is at the same time: (i) the way in which to think an organism's relation to forces both within and without it; (ii) the very growth of that relation; and (iii) the way in which Nietzsche speaks of the renewed incorporation, internalisation of that relation when it has undergone structural change. As such, it is both a descriptive term and the vehicle of re-evaluation: the object of genealogy and the object of the ethics that this genealogy necessarily intimates. As such it collapses, without conflating, and re-organises, without destroying, the conceptual distinction between affirmation and negation.

Conclusion

In the penultimate paragraph of the second essay of *On the Genealogy of Morality*, Nietzsche writes:

> We moderns have inherited millennia of conscience-vivisection and animal-torture inflicted on ourselves. For too long, man has viewed his natural inclinations with an 'evil eye', so that they finally came to be intertwined with 'bad conscience' in him. A reverse experiment should be possible *in principle* – but who has sufficient strength? – by this, I mean an intertwining of bad conscience with *perverse* inclinations, all those otherwordly aspirations, alien to the senses, the instincts, to nature, to animals, in short all the ideals which up to now have been hostile to life and have defamed the world. To whom should we turn with *such* hopes and claims today? But, some time, he will have come to us, the redeeming man of great love, buried in this reality so that he can return from it with

the *redemption* of this reality: redeem it from the curse which its ideal has placed on it up till now.   (1994, §24, 70–1).

I wish to draw this essay to a conclusion from out of this last quotation.

Several things are striking in the paragraph and relevant to our overall argument. First, the 'overman' is seen as a future horizon that will redeem our natural forces from the weight of conscience. Second, this future is one of the re-evaluation or transvaluation of the re-evaluation of Judaic *ressentiment* in the first essay; it promises, in other words, the future beyond the 'will to nothing' or nihilism that frames the *Genealogy* as a whole. Now, from the perspective of the work of the previous pages on the *Genealogy*, it should be clear that both the terms, the concepts and the logic of this paragraph are phantasmatic. It should also be clear that its phantasmatic status is predicated on the desire for pure force, a desire that this essay has rewritten within an historical economy of spirit, predicated itself on an expanding complex of forces within which any one force cannot be isolated in abstraction. Thus the figure in front of whom Nietzsche falls silent in the following paragraph (§25) and whom he passes over to Zarathustra to prepare, 'one with more future' than himself, this figure (the 'overman' in these terms) is a *fiction* that comes out of the logic of opposition according to which Nietzsche opposes 'natural inclinations' to 'conscience'. We have seen, however, that the most interesting levels of this very same work dissolve this logic and its oppositional terms into a field of forces that exceeds and accounts for, in the first place, what we understand by 'inside' and 'outside', 'psyche' and 'environment', 'the natural' and the 'cultural', the 'affective' and the 'technological', etc. I have argued, rather, that these instances grow out of a process of 'spiritualisation' that at the same time is always already beyond these instances. In this sense, and at the very least, *there is no redemption to come* because *there is nothing to be redeemed*. Redemption and its related values (of which nihilism and optimism are two) are themselves instances of the human that grow out of 'spirit', as 'it' in turn outgrows them.

Thus, once one has shown that in Nietzsche pure, spontaneous discharge and the history of subjectivity cannot be separated and that, more importantly, the traits of the overhuman and the history of subjectivity cannot be separated either, but rather are to be rethought within the history that makes them inseparable, much of Nietzsche's text has immense interest for us today. It does not have interest, however, in the context of nihilism, but in the context of dispersing the phantasms of nihilism and placing them in relation to the forces that organise and disrupt these phantasmatic separations to begin with. It is here that Nietzsche still has much to tell us. For what comes out of our reconfiguring of Nietzsche following these complex moments of his work is, at least, four things. I will conclude upon them.

First: force is to be understood as a complex of forces that can only be broken down into unilateral forces at the risk of analytical and ethico-political poverty. Human appropriation of these forces in the name of the human is one such culture of poverty: it is the culture of metaphysics. Nihilism as the inversion of this appropriation is another.

Second: this complex is to be understood *historically* as an increasingly complicated vortex of forces. Hence the need, after Nietzsche, and within the terms of knowledge, to rethink the relations between the humanities and the sciences such that their immanent links can be articulated to the benefit of each separate discipline and field of knowledge. For it is in this constellation of disciplines that a refined, modest understanding of the human will emerge and could have interesting cultural effects.

Third: the end of metaphysical thinking and valuation does not betoken its destruction (as an easy reading of Nietzsche might think), but its re-inscription, rewriting and 'sublation' within this vortex. One result of this re-inscription is not a disempowering sense that the human is only part of this vortex, despite being the major vehicle of it, but *an empowering sense of the indeterminacy of relations to emerge.* This empowering comes, in other words, from human modesty (something that the West and its globalising models have still to learn and, that, therefore, must be fought for). Nietzsche calls this sense 'free spirit'.

And therefore, fourthly: we should affirm the fact that the forces giving rise to the human also exceed the human, that 'spirit' makes the human all the while unmaking it. Affirming this, one can then begin to articulate the relations between our lives and the forces that constitute them in less phantasmatic ways than those discourses and symbolic forms, which either refuse such a genealogical understanding of the human or short-circuit the work to be done, have offered in the past or at present offer. The market is today flooded with both reactions which constitute, at a deep level of the human psyche, panics before the complexity of force. To try and 'incorporate' this complexity (in the Nietzschean sense of *Einverleibung*) constitutes, in turn, an immense cultural adventure. This adventure is an eminent, ethical possibility of 'spirit'. It is where, in Nietzschean terms and to conclude, the systematic relations between 'genealogy', 'energetics' and the practice of 'mercy' and 'love' await a future.

Notes

1   The most important elaboration of these values in terms of this difference remains Deleuze's *Nietzsche and Philosophy* (Deleuze 1983). For Deleuze, 'eternal recurrence' describes and affirms the 'sameness' of the recurrence of difference and of the relations of difference between forces, and 'will to power' marks the genetic element within this differential of force and forces. As the reader will quickly surmise, one of the aims of this chapter is to complicate the way in which a Deleuzian type reading of force locates force within its immanent determinations.

2   See, for example, J.F. Lyotard's *Just Gaming* (1985) for an eloquent refusal, predicated on the philosophy of Emmanuel Lévinas, of immanent relations betweenthe epistemological, ethical and political.

3   On this move, Jacques Derrida's *Of Spirit. Heidegger and the Question* [Derrida 1989] constitutes a fundamental reading of Heidegger. It does not engage, however, in the context of Heidegger's *Auseinandersetzung* with Nietzsche, with the latter's own understanding of spirit. The lack of engagement testifies on several levels to the way in which deconstruction has always read Nietzsche, be it to say something else than Heidegger, in the wake of Heidegger's thought. Jacques Derrida's interview with me in the *Journal of Nietzsche Studies* (Beardsworth 1994) is instructive in this regard.

4   My restricting the Nietzschean concept of 'spirit' to the neuronal complex and its historical avatars seems to exclude what we call 'inorganic' matter from it. This is both true and not true. While 'inorganic' matter is not yet spiritual in the above sense, spirit both depends on 'inorganic' matter in the first place to undergo its own process of spiritualisation (a Marxian point born out by much contemporary thinking of biology and technology) and is itself inorganic matter *prior to* the process of spiritualisation (a point that, of course, destroys the coherence of the term 'inorganic'). Thus, with the Nietzschean definition of spirit, there is no absolute distinction between the inorganic and the organic. *This is not to say*, however – and this is precisely my point in relation to the tendency prevalent in contemporary philosophising to collapse historical mediations, be it from a Derridean or a Deleuzian point of view (and the collapse is very different in each) – that there are not crucial differences within the processes of spiritualisation that are to be assumed genealogically and reflectively in order for the future of spirit to be articulated.

My argument presupposes, therefore, the following: (i) matter becomes spirit, but no matter becomes spirit in the Nietzschean sense unless it becomes endowed with a neuronal complex; and (ii) Nietzsche inevitably philosophises best when he is talking about *life*: inevitably because the move *from* the physical *to* the biological is extremely difficult to think through. Nietzsche never articulates this move, although he is happy, especially in the posthumous notes, to talk about forces in the physical universe and forces in the biological universe in the same breath (see, for example, my first quotation from Nietzsche above on the 'Dionysian world of the eternally self-creating, self-destroying'). To do this in one breath seems to me a serious mistake *if* one is unable to show the move, the mediation, from one realm to the other. It is not surprising that Nietzsche cannot 'genealogise' that move: no experimental or theoretical physicist, no experimental or theoretical biologist to my knowledge has yet done so, precisely because, while *necessary* for us *to think reflectively*, and increasingly so, the move is extremely difficult to think through concretely and, for the moment, an impossibility to put into practice. It may well be that the terms of debate concerning this move are becoming more clear, with the work, among others, of von Uexküll (1934/1965), Maturana and Varela (1980, 1987), Morowitz (1992) and Rosen (1991). However we understand the specificity of the biological, emerging as a greater complexity of forces from out of the physical – in terms, that is, of metabolism and 'self'-organisation, 'self'-repair or reproduction – it is one thing to think this specificity; it is another, however, to articulate it. In this sense, to simulate life on a computer falls very short of the needed mediations to say *what life is and how it operates* (compare, here, the Santa Fe school under Stuart Kauffman). Further, to base one's philosophy *on* such simulations, *on* such modellings and on their predictions is, again, to move too quickly over the very distinctions that need to be maintained on the basis of a broad 'historical' sameness. Despite, therefore, my respect and admiration for work going on around Deleuze at present concerning matter and life, I strongly believe that, without a thinking of such mediations, the philosopher and critic risk falling into a transcendental illusion (in the Kantian sense), if they do not give more hypothetical and *regulative* weight to the concepts that they are forging between the 'natural' sciences and between these sciences and the humanities. This is far from a conservative point. Relations between these disciplines, their fields and their conceptual inventions are absolutely crucial. To nurse these relations in the belief of a general sameness of growing complexity is one thing: to believe, however, that these relations exempt us from fleshing out what allows for them in the first place is another. I believe that it is one task of the philosopher today to underline both the necessity of the sameness between matter and spirit and the necessity of the differences within this sameness. If this task is both epistemological and ethico-political, then the implications of Nietzsche's understanding of spirit allow us to see the continuing importance of the Kantian critical distinctions for speculative orientation in the sciences. And this despite, precisely, Kant's metaphysical understanding of reason, form and matter. This is a point of which philosophers need to be careful, when moving behind, and rightly so (!), the transcendental aesthetic and analytic of the first *Critique* in order to open up, with the contemporary sciences, what lies behind Kant's critical Newtonism.

My thanks to Keith Ansell Pearson for asking me to be clear on how and why I hold to keeping spirit to the nervous system.

5   The concept of original sin presupposes this distinction since without it one cannot think evil as the perversion of the will ; it also however deepens the distinction since, as is well known, without the Christian culture of original sin, the modern notion of subjectivity would have not emerged.

6   Perhaps the most eloquent elaboration of this sameness of force is to be found in J.-F. Lyotard (1993). Compare also my own *Nietzsche* (1997).

7   Compare Henry Staten's work on this desire for the proper in Nietzsche (1990). Staten's concomitant running together of the economies of the active and reactive is not accounted for, however, in term of the historical nature of force. In this sense his deconstruction of Nietzsche remains abstract and over-textual. It is not by chance also that his use of libidinal economy to account for his work effaces, precisely, the historical mediations of force. This effacement will always be the risk of an exclusively 'psychoanalytic' understanding of affect, as is clear, also, from Jean-François Lyotard's overall uses of Nietzsche and Freud in both his earlier and later philosophy.

8   To reduce the historical to the written trace and to demarcate what lies prior to it as 'pre-historical' is to consider trans-individual historical processes of memorisation simply in terms of the objective. This is to short-circuit the relations between affect, psyche and technology in which Nietzsche, for one, is precisely interested. If above, I criticised, therefore, Lyotard and Staten for often reducing force to the affective, those within recent and contemporary philosophy that predicate trans-individual processes of memorisation upon the written sign or the technical object move too quickly in the opposite sense. This seems to me to be the major problem, despite their brilliance and crucial differences with each other, with Derrida's elaboration of transcendental difference in his introduction to Husserl's essay 'The Origin of Geometry' (Derrida 1978) and with current reworkings of Husserlian phenomenology in terms of technology (Stiegler 1996a and 1996b).

9   In France the greatest proponents of this thesis are Luc Ferry and Alain Renaud.
    That they have little time for Nietzsche and recent 'continental' philosophy's
    interest in both Nietzsche and Heidegger is not surprising. The wish here to re-
    evaluate Nietzsche outside the terms of Heidegger's reading is predicated, in turn,
    on my belief that the most forceful understanding of Nietzsche's re-evaluation of
    the subject still awaits.

10 This point is brilliantly elaborated in the context of Heidegger's understanding of
    determination and exactitude by Bernard Stiegler in *Technics and Time, 1. The Fault
    of Epimetheus* [Stiegler 1998].

11 I am grateful to my friend the biologist John Stewart for the term 'spiral'. For an
    attempt to use biology to rework contemporary hermeneutical themes in terms of
    this spiral, see, co-written with Pierre Clement and Ruth Scheps, his very fertile
    'Une interprétation biologique de l'interprétation' and 'La phylogenèse de l'inter-
    prétation' in Jean-Michel Salanskis, François Rastier and Ruth Scheps, *Hérmeneu-
    tique, textes, sciences* (1997).

12 Just as this essay has clearly taken distance to Deleuze's understanding of force, so,
    here, it must question the opposition that Deleuze makes between Nietzschean
    affirmation and Hegelian dialectic (Deleuze 1983, 145–80). That Nietzsche deter-
    mines the 'law of life' as the 'self-sublimation of all things' (Nietzsche 1994, 126),
    that he understands spirit as 'life that itself cuts into life' (Nietzsche 1961, 127) can
    only suggest that the relations between Hegel and Nietzsche are from the first not
    ones of opposition, whatever the necessity of the distinction between the field of
    phenomenology and that of energetics. That said, Deleuze's anti-Hegelianism is
    probably best accounted for in terms of the French mourning of Marxism
    although, importantly, it is Deleuze's anti-Hegelianism that provides the intellec-
    tual context to his underestimation of mediation.

13 Again, Deleuze is therefore too quick to place consciousness, history and memory
    within the field of the reactive, and too quick to argue that the only true 'science' is
    one 'where there is no consciousness' (Deleuze 1983, 42). Neither consciousness
    nor the unconscious, neither the categorial nor the subphenomenal is what is of
    interest: what is of interest is both the relation between the two and the way in
    which this relation is formed, and changes, historically. Although Deleuze's
    polemical point can be again placed in the context of the political and ethical
    consequences of Marxist 'phenomenology', his insistence on the truth of the
    subphenomenal anticipates his philosophies of intensity and affect in, respect-
    ively, *Difference and Repetition* (Deleuze 1994) and *Anti-Oedipus* (Deleuze and
    Guattari 1984). Again it is not a question of saying that this insistence is wrong
    as such, but of articulating, in historical terms, the necessity of the relation, and
    the critical importance of the space between, the phenomenal and nonphenome-
    nal, the categorial and the intense, etc. A critical reading of *A Thousand Plateaus*
    (Deleuze and Guattari 1993), the most ambitious and historical of Deleuze and
    Guattari's works on force, would be of value in this context.

14 'Eternal Recurrence' and 'Will to Power' are, of course, re-evaluated categories
    whereby Nietzsche also wants to think forces prior to life. However, as note 3
    argued at length, to talk about force at a both physical and biological level in
    terms of these categories *risks* losing the very mediations that are crucial to these
    forces' very definition. It seems to me, then, that to use these categories to define
    the sameness of these forces, at the risk of losing the way in which force buckles
    back on itself, through interaction with other forces, to become another force, is
    still too universalising, too philosophical in the classical sense. The danger of such

universalisation is transcendental illusion: the belief that we are talking philosophically about something real – be it here often 'subempirical' – that needs much greater work before we can designate it with concepts that have an *immediate* epistemological and ethical vocation. Hence my preference for the terms 'spirit' and 'spiritualisation': they are more historically rich and flexible, less homogenising in their articulations of difference, less heroic in tone, more inviting of slow, but decisive change. I am well aware, however, that the question of the specificity of the 'inorganic' together with that of its emergence into the 'organic' remain with this choice. These questions are, for me, as I argued in note 3, to be retained in their difficulty. It is retaining this difficulty, not the converse, that will allow for the most powerful inventions.

15 Any attempt, and there have been many from the fifties to today, to divide Nietzsche's writings into an earlier and later philosophy and ethics would seem therefore misguided from the perspective of 'spirit'.

References

Beardsworth, R. (1994) 'Nietzsche and the Machine', interview with Jacques Derrida. *Journal of Nietzsche Studies*. Issue 7. Spring 1994.

——(1997) *Nietzsche*. Paris: Les Belles Lettres.

Deleuze, G. (1983) *Nietzsche and Philosophy*. trans. H. Tomlinson. London: Athlone Press.

——(1994) *Difference and Repetition*. trans. P. Patton. London: Athlone Press.

Deleuze, G, and Guattari, F. (1984) *Anti-Oedipus. Capitalism and Schizophrenia*. trans. R. Hurley, M. Seem and H.R. Lane. London: Athlone Press.

——(1993) *A Thousand Plateaus. Capitalism and Schizophrenia*. trans. B. Massumi. Minneapolis: University of Minnesota Press.

Derrida, J. (1978) *Edmund Husserl's Origin of Geometry: An Introduction*. trans. by John P. Leavey. Lincoln and London: University of Nebraska Press.

——(1989) *Of Spirit. Heidegger and The Question*. trans. G. Bennington and R. Bowlby. Chicago: University of Chicago Press.

Heidegger, M. (1991a) *Nietzsche. Vols I &II*. trans. D.F. Krell. San Francisco: Harper.

——(1991b) *Nietzsche. Vols III & IV*. trans. D.F. Krell. San Francisco: Harper.

Lyotard, J.-F with Jean-Loup Thébaud. (1985) *Just Gaming*. trans. W. Godzich. Manchester: Manchester Unversity Press.

——(1993) *Libidinal Economy*. trans. I. Hamilton Grant. London: Athlone Press.

Maturana, H. and Varela, F. (1980) *Autopoiesis and Cognition: the Realization of the Living*. Boston Studies in the Philosophy of Science, t. XII. Boston: D. Reidel

——(1987) *The Tree of Knowledge. The Biological Roots of Human Understanding*. trans. R. Paolucci. Boston and London: Shambhala.

Morowitz, H.J. (1992) *Beginnings of Cellular Life. Metabolism Recapitulates Biogenesis*. Yale: Yale University Press.

Nietzsche, F. (1961) *Thus Spoke Zarathustra*. trans. R.J. Hollingdale. London: Penguin.

——(1968a) *Twilight of the Idols/The Anti-Christ*. trans. R.J. Hollingdale. London: Penguin.

——(1968b) *The Will To Power*. trans. W. Kaufmann. New York: Vintage.

——(1973) *The Gay Science*. trans. W. Kaufmann. New York: Vintage.

——(1974) *Beyond Good and Evil. Prelude to a Philosophy of the Future*. trans. R.J. Hollingdale. London: Penguin.

——(1982) *Daybreak. Thoughts on the Prejudices of Morality.* trans. R.J. Hollingdale. Cambridge: Cambridge University Press.

——(1986) *Human, All Too Human.* trans. R.J. Hollingdale. Cambridge: Cambridge University Press.

——(1988) *Sämtliche Werke. Kritische Studienausgabe. Band 5.* hrsg. von G. Colli and M. Montinari. München: DTV/de Gruyter.

——(1994) *On The Genealogy Of Morality.* ed. K. Ansell Pearson. trans. C. Diethe. Cambridge: Cambridge University Press.

Rosen, R. (1991) *Life Itself. A Comprehensive Inquiry into the Nature, Origin, and Fabrication of Life.* New York: Columbia University Press.

Salanskis, J.-M., Rastier, F. and Scheps, R. (1997) *Hérmeneutique, textes, sciences.* Paris: Presses Universitaires de France.

Stiegler, B. (1996a) *La technique et le temps: Tome 2. La désorientation.* Paris: Galilée.

——(1996b) 'Persephone, Oedipus, Epimetheus'. trans. R. Beardsworth. *Tekhnema: Journal of Philosophy and Technology.* 3: 69–112.

——(1998) *Technics and Time, 1. The Fault of Epimetheus.* trans. R. Beardsworth and G. Collins. Stanford: Stanford University Press.

4
The Monstrous Rebirth of Nihilism

Joanna Hodge

Paradoxes of Nihilism

There is the difference of a century to be marked between Nietzsche's post-humous reflections on the necessity to expedite the devaluation of all values, and the current widespread reception of those reflections in the various celebrations of nihilism, both active and passive, which are spread out all around and about at this new turn of a century. There is then a paradox here: for the announcement which Nietzsche himself declares to be before its time is now supposed to have arrived, and in circumstances very different from those of Nietzsche's solitary, rigorous self-questioning. The essay which follows explores the implications of this transposition of nihilism from a solitary thought, for the main part developed in posthumously published manuscripts and only obliquely indicated in some of the most highly wrought texts of the tradition, defying one might suppose easy appropriation, to a commonly acknowledged theme.

There are two further dimensions of this transposition: one is the transition from Nietzsche's discretely customised German, a startling combination of Lutheran intonation and nineteenth-century political lyric, into the flatness of a cosmopolitan English; and the other is the transition from a nihilism as a question of the formation and indeed deformation of intellectual values, or indeed of Greek excellences, into the nihilism explored by Heidegger, which, in its emphasis on a spreading wasteland, and its emanation in the spread of technology, reveals a further devaluation of all values, as the reduction of Greek excellence to no more than the values which solve equations. These two transitions, of a thinking from a solitary to a collective domain; and from an intellectual to the technological sphere, are of some significance. These shifts, I suggest, in realising Nietzsche's thought, threaten to accomplish its abolition, thus having the form of a computer virus, which as it declares its presence, wipes all systems of registering presence from the machine.

The danger is that where Nietzsche understood a completed nihilism to make way for a new formation, there is a possible form of completed nihilism which is just that: nihilism. The question to be posed in this essay is whether Nietzsche's or perhaps Zarathustra's teaching concerning nihilism may not still or all the more so have failed to find an adequate hearing, whether the very widespread nature of the reception indicates exactly a loss in transmission so total as to pass for the main part wholly unremarked: that thought can no longer take place. This is Heidegger's hypothesis, explored at some paradoxical length in the 1951–52 lectures, *What calls for thought?* This hypothesis is attributed by Heidegger in those lectures to Nietzsche, quoting: 'woe to he who hides the wasteland within' (Heidegger 1954, 12; 1968, 30). The thought then would be that the posthumous moment of Nietzsche has still not come, and will not come while its signature of futurity is still misunderstood as that which comes later in time, as opposed to that which marks the openness of the horizon, thought as futural.

This chapter explores the paradoxes of the becoming commonplace of nihilism, via these three paradoxes: that Nietzsche supposes his own thought as a non-arrival, as posthumous; that the thought of nihilism is supposed all the same to have arrived, and is relayed as though it had arrived and were well understood; and that Heidegger explores this non-arrival through the thought of nihilism as the spread of technology in a form which then generates a non-arrival of thinking. This has led to the monstrous rebirth of the thought of nihilism in a form no longer, or not yet thought, in a form beyond the active and passive nihilisms of *The Will to Power* (1901), to which I shall give the name demonic nihilism, one which carries the force of its name and destroys all positioning. This then would suggest that the operations of thought as captured in the image of the computer virus presents the form of a specifically modern form of sensibility, basic to the present age, the computer virus, as a transcendental aesthetic which gives thought not as Kant would have it, as infinitely self-replicating, but as self-destructing, wiped from the screen simultaneous with its first appearance on that surface.

It is helpful to identify two possible symptoms of a resistance to a thinking capable of a move beyond demonic nihilism before turning to a discussion of how this strange reversal of Nietzsche's purposes might have taken place. These two symptoms of resistance can be thematised in relation to two sets of Freudian themes: mourning and melancholy, and desire and the drive. There is resistance to any radicalisation of the Freudian theorising of desire, which is continually returned to a presumption of a basic state of lack, echoing the Schellingian theme of the eternal deficiency of being, and to a reading of the death drives as connected up to a destructive negative energy, as discussed by Freud in 'Civilisation and its Discontents' (1931). The task then is to retrieve a positive destructive energy, like that flagged up by Heidegger in the opening sections of *Being and Time* (1927) where he calls for a destruction of the history of philosophy to release thinking into the future; and that announced by Walter Benjamin when he calls for a destruction of the Heideggerian melancholy. The theme of mourning and melancholy is interrupted by Hölderlin's and indeed Nietzsche's affirmations of deaths which defy mourning.

The task of this essay then is to trace out the bivalence of the theoretical initiatives of Heidegger and of Freud, which appear at first glance more radical than the thinking of Nietzsche but which in fact return thinking to Nietzsche rather than going beyond him. This danger of falling behind the gesture of hoping to exceed is one which Heidegger diagnoses in his essay, the letter on nihilism, 'The Question of Being' (1956). These bivalencies if affirmed in one way can open out a modality of affirmation but they more usually get caught back up into the modalities of *ressentiment*. Thus in this essay I shall pursue the line of enquiry which supposes that a Nietzschean nihilism arrives in transposed guise in the thinking of Freud and of Heidegger, and that a Nietzschean critique of Freudianism would separate out the strand of *ressentiment*, presumably to be predicated on an introjection of a socially established view of the secondary status of being a Jew, from the affirmative transcription of this social view into a capacity to reject not just the evaluation but the social norms which produce it. It would be worth considering what the Nietzschean genealogical critique of Heidegger would look like.

The gesture of affirmative self-transformation is evident in Freud's writings most of all in his 'An Autobiographical Study', where he states:

> When in 1873, I first joined the University, I experienced some appreciable disappointments. Above all I found that I was expected to feel myself inferior and an alien because I was a Jew. I refused absolutely to do the first of these things. I have never been able to see why I should feel ashamed of my descent or, as people were beginning to say, of my 'race'.
> (Freud 1993, 193)

Freud thus does not disavow the feeling of being an alien, while clearly affirming his sense that his understanding of the human psyche is infinitely in advance of any of his contemporaries. This is his sense of his own posthumous status, arriving, like Nietzsche, after his own death. Nietzsche, as Freud's friend, would presumably have encouraged him to mobilise the ambivalence between the two reactions to prejudice, acceptance and defiance, to turn the residual reactive element into the critical reappropriation of circumstance, a lesson of course which should not be lost on others, similarly positioned, or indeed on those immobilised by that other lethal mechanism of *ressentiment*: discipleship. The relation between Heidegger and his most faithful critic, Derrida might be read to advantage as replicating such a Nietzschean critique of Freud, perhaps permitting a release of

Heideggerianism from its immobilisation as received wisdom. The question how thinkers such as Nietzsche, Freud and Heidegger are to remain uncontaminated by the complicated resentments generated by the mechanisms of a mass reception is a major issue for intellectual work today. The operations of posthumous critique might be one route to keep access to their work open: to permit their predecessors to put the work of the late comers in question, and above all to disrupt the thought that those who come later are thereby the wiser. The first section of this essay examines the origin of the thought of a monstrous rebirth of nihilism, as demonic, in Nietzsche's *The Birth of Tragedy*; the second explores the ambivalent take up of nihilism in the writings of Heidegger and of Freud, of radical phenomenology and of psychoanalysis; and the third locates the thought of nihilism as the irreversible destruction brought by technological disaster, one symptom of which would be the failure to distinguish between Nietzschean and Heideggerian nihilism.

Nietzschean Prelude

> From the smile of this Dionysus sprang the Olympian gods, from his tears sprang human beings. In this existence as a dismembered god, Dionysus possesses the dual nature of a cruel, barbarized demon and a mild, gentle ruler. (Nietzsche, 1987, Vol. I: 72; 1967: 73)

This demonic nihilism takes the form, while losing the energy, of that aspect of Dionysus named in the tenth section of *The Birth of Tragedy* and cited at the head of this section, in the sentence: 'In this existence as a dismembered god, Dionysus possesses the dual nature of a cruel, barbarized demon and a mild, gentle ruler'. This dualism marks up the difficulty of thinking both Dionysus and nihilism, for that thinking overcomes resentment only if held as a set of counterpoised forces, within a single structure. The moment that these forces become elements detached from each other and are allowed to separate off, they become liable to fetishisation as single moments, no longer held in tension with a counter force. Thus the structure named 'Dionysus', and indeed that named by Nietzsche 'nihilism', can cease to be thought within a dynamic of becoming and instead become immobilised: they can become forces of *ressentiment* and the moment of becoming goes missing, lost in transmission. The mildness of the ruler is thus mild only if it arises out of a self-relation produced from mastering cruelty and wildness. Once that ruling is detached from the moment of self-ruling and self-mastery, it is re-articulated as a relation between self and Other, with an imposition of will no longer reflexively and productively, producing a self, but, instead, negatively and inhibitingly, imposing constraints on others and limiting the provocative self-challenging of Nietzsche's imagination.

Nietzsche indicates this danger of the rule of the Olympian gods, becoming vulnerable through losing connection to the chthonic powers of the Titans:

> The defiant Titan Prometheus has announced to his Olympian tormentor that some day the greatest danger will menace his rule, unless Zeus should enter into an alliance with him in time. In Aeschylus we recognise how the terrified Zeus, fearful of his end, allies himself with the Titan. Thus the former age of the Titans is once more recovered from Tartarus and brought to light.   (Nietzsche 1987, I: 73 ; 1967: 74)

The Olympian gods inaugurate their own demise when they cease to perfect themselves in competition with the other groups in their domain: the chthonic gods, the titans, the giants, even the heroes, and instead attempt to impose a law on these other groups, in the vain hope thereby of reducing chance to order, as though that law might take the place of the throw of chance with which all processes take their inception and maintain their momentum. At this moment the hierarchies of self-esteem begin to be established and the task of self-overcoming goes missing. Once separated from each other, there is then more to be feared from the mild, gentle ruler than from the cruel and barbarised demon. Taken separately these two both become figures of *ressentiment*; while taken together they can generate will to power, self-overcoming, and an affirmation of an eternal return of the same. This duplicity reduplicates itself at every level: Dionysus is a double image; Dionysus is doubled and redoubled by Apollo as god of individuation and just boundaries and thereby as revealing the chaos, within the bounds of which such order is precariously imposed:

> Whoever understands the innermost kernel of the Prometheus story – namely the necessity of sacrilege imposed upon the titanically striving individual – must also immediately feel how un-Apollinian this pessimistic notion is. For Apollo wants to grant repose to individual beings precisely by drawing boundaries between them and by again and again calling these to mind as the most sacred laws of the world, with his demands for self-knowledge and measure.
> (Nietzsche 1987, I: 70; 1967: 72)

But these repeated demands for self-knowledge and measure are required only because such repose is grasped in the teeth of more powerful forces of disruption. Thus those willing to accept this granting of repose are surrendering their relation to the forces which might permit an arrival of Nietzschean nihilism. Granting repose to others disempowers both those others and the figure of Apollo itself, cutting them both loose from the energetics of these powers of disruption and the forces of chance.

Nietzsche's own critical edge is put in jeopardy by the attempt in the immediately preceding paragraph to align a positive, original sacrilege with men and with Aryan strength, and to align a negative original sin with women and with a Semitic tradition of *ressentiment*. Even Nietzsche, and so, all the more so, even Nietzscheans, cannot hope to have definitively freed themselves from the workings of *ressentiment*, for the sense of an unpaid debt in being born oscillates in value back and forth between forming a spur to activity and generating a cause for *ressentiment*. This splitting into Aryan masculine sacrilege, a pre-hellenic paganism, and feminine semitic sin is the splitting of the fetishist, not of the Nietzschean: for it rigidifies rather than displaying the workings of positive forces. These two forces could be productively entwined and mutually provocative, even in one human being, rather than distributed to two distinct groups of human beings, male and female, Aryan and Semitic, thus set in rigid opposition, stalling any thought of development. The account of time implicit in this structure is similarly un-Nietzschean, for there is a hypothesis of an original purity before the advent of Christianity and Judaism. Such original purity is as incompatible with the thought of eternal return as is the thought that the later in time are somehow more illuminated than their precursors. The insight that Nietzsche's most distinctive thought must destroy the values of its bearer is one not foreign to Nietzschean thinking, now distinguished from Nietzsche's actual thoughts, and is remarked by Heidegger in his reading of the inevitability of Nietzsche's collapse. The forces at work imply a metempsychosis, a rebirth, which is no respecter of identity.

In *The Birth of Tragedy* Nietzsche attributes a dual nature to Aeschylus' Prometheus: 'So the dual nature of Aeschylus' Prometheus his nature which is at the same time Dionysian and Apollinian, might be expressed thus in a conceptual formula: 'All that exists is just and unjust and equally justified in both' (Nietzsche 1987, I: 71; 1967, 72). But such a conceptualisation misses the point that the thought is possible only as a consequence of a play of counterpoised forces held in place within a process of self-overcoming. Above the struggle of divinities and morals Nietzsche perhaps surprisingly enthrones divine necessity, as eternal justice:

> The immeasurable suffering of the bold 'individual' on the one hand and the divine predicament and intimation of a twilight of the gods on the other, the way the power of these two worlds of suffering compels a reconciliation, a metaphysical union – all this recalls in the strongest possible manner the centre and main axiom of the Aeschylean view of the world which envisages Moira enthroned above gods and human beings as eternal justice. (Nietzsche 1987, I: 68; 1967: 70)

Here then is an idealised feminine force, by contrast to the despised feminine force of original sin. Moira, fate or destiny, is the law of chance which

all the forms of law attempt and fail to supersede. The notion of a metaphysical union gives the thought away: it is a thought of *ressentiment*. A
more thoroughgoing Nietzscheanism would need to think these two aspects
for a thinking of femaleness together as symptoms of the Nietzschean unresolved resentment against the chance of birth. The rebirth can only be a
rebirth into ressentiment if that chance remains a cause for resentment.

In their attempt to impose a law, the Olympian gods, or indeed Nietzsche
and Nietzscheans, reveal their own advancing twilight, their downfall resulting from an unresolved resentment at an inability to bridge a gap between
their powers and their ambitions. The invented law cannot compete for
exhaustiveness with the law of the fates which proposes eternal justice.
Nietzsche says as much:

> The philosophy of wild and naked nature beholds with the frank undis-
> sembling gaze of truth the myths of the Homeric world as they dance
> past: they turn pale, they tremble under the piercing glance of the god-
> dess-till the powerful fist of the Dionysian artist forces them into the
> service of some new deity.   (Nietzsche 1987, I: 73; 1967: 74)

The fantasy of the goddess of destiny is thus transposed into a fantasy goddess
of truth, and then into a fantasmatic female philosophy: Boethius' pale
consolation. This transition from the goddess of destiny before whom all
tremble to the comforter of scholars in trouble is indeed a monstrous rebirth.
The erotics of the philosophical seminar are revealed as the happily post-
poned union of the male seeker of wisdom and his feminised object of desire.
This reveals the necessity of unthroning the fantasised, fetishised figure of
Moira. Nietzsche is endorsing a law of female exclusion which can no longer
be permitted to pass without question. The gap between invented law and
what there is, between a law of custom and artifice and the law of this wild
naked nature, is one which for Nietzsche is both the spur to thought and so
often its undoing. This gap opens out as a gap between thought and outcome.
In failing to fill it in and to secure a transition from thought to accomplishment to contentment, often, instead of giving thanks for the spur to renewed
effort, new dawns, new activity, there are the two other possible common
responses, even amongst would be Nietzscheans: a despair at failure and a
self-deception that there has been success. Apollo is also the dream-interpreter, and is no less the duplicitous god than is Dionysus. The imposition of
order and harmony in the Apollinian gesture of individuation is a deceit
whose status becomes clearer in the light of the following:

> the one, truly real Dionysus appears in a variety of forms, in the mask of a
> fighting hero, and entangled as it were in the net of the individual will.
> The god who appears talks and acts so as to resemble an erring, striving,
> suffering individual. That he appears at all with such epic precision and

clarity is the work of the dream-interpreter Apollo, who through his symbolic appearance interprets to the chorus its Dionysian state.

(Nietzsche 1987, I: 72; 1967: 73)

This Apollo holds out the hope of a renewed transition from a dispersal of forces to reformulation of a self-empowering order:

And it is this hope alone that casts a gleam of joy upon the features of a world torn asunder and shattered into individuals; this is symbolized in the myth of Demeter, sunk in eternal sorrow, who rejoices again for the first time when told that she may once more give birth to Dionysus. (ibid.)

Or, as the other, sexually unprejudicial version would have it, she may once more give birth to Persephone, mistress of destiny. Nietzsche thus controls and contains any restitution of positivity to female and feminine forces, to a female line, Demeter and Persephone, insisting instead on Demeter's relation to Dionysus, returning again and again, to the twin masculinities of Dionysus, Prometheus, Apollo, as dream tellers and law givers: Persephone reborn as Dionysus. An enthusiasm for Nietzsche at the end of this century which fails to problematise the effort Nietzsche makes to control and contain the traces of female power in Greek mythology is complicit in his inability to accept the arbitrary chance of birth.

This duplicitous Nietzsche is at work in the ambiguous evaluation to be attached to his diagnosis of nihilism: the question is whether his diagnosis of nihilism permits a rebirth of Nietzsche as once again empowered to bring about cultural transformation, pushing tendencies already at work to a point of crisis from which it must reemerge renewed and strengthened; or whether it entails a rebirth as a monumental parasite on the energies of transformation, blocking the promised opening of futurity. I shall pursue this question here by setting up a split inheritance of Nietzsche's themes between the psychoanalysis of Freud an the ontologising of Heidegger, which are further split between the duplicities of Apollo, as a schema of thinking the ambiguous inheritance of Freudian psychoanalysis, part ego bound, part dream interpreter; and the duplicities of Dionysus as a schema for thinking the ambiguous inheritance of Heidegger, part Nazi stooge, part inventor of the future. The problematic can be sketched out in terms of a shift of register from an analysis of transition and inheritance, in affirmative Nietzschean mode, to that of the politics of resentment at work in the analysis of debt and transmission.

Freudian manoeuvres, Heideggerian ambivalence

Enter: for here too the gods are present
(Aristotle *De partibus animalis* 1,5, 645 a 17)

This is a phrase which both Freud and Heidegger cite: Freud in his 'Auto-biographical Study', in Latin, to announce the possibility of making sense of psychic pathology (Freud 1993, 195); Heidegger in the 'Letter on Humanism' (1946). It comes from the story told by Aristotle, in *De partibus animalium*, concerning Heraclitus' response to the puzzlement of his visitors. Heidegger remarks:

> The vision of a shivering thinker offers little interest. At this disappointing spectacle even the curious lose their desire to come any closer. What are they supposed to do here? Such an everyday and unexciting occurrence – somebody who is chilled warming himself at a stove – anyone can find that at home.   (Heidegger 1967, 186; 1998, 270)

More significantly Heidegger and Freud share an ambivalence in their receptions of Nietzsche's thought. Heidegger's ambivalence is stretched out at length in his lectures on Nietzsche from 1936 to 1944, where Nietzsche is set up as both the last metaphysician and as the thinker whose thought defies Heidegger's attempts to impose a history of being on the history of philosophy. That of Freud is expressed more guardedly.

It is however tellingly revealed in Freud's 'On the History of the Psycho-analytical Movement' (1914):

> In latter years I have denied myself the very great pleasure of reading the works of Nietzsche, with the deliberate object of not being hampered in working out the impressions received in psychoanalysis by any sort of anticipatory ideas.   (Freud 1993, 73)

Freud makes this remark in the course of reaffirming a debt to Breuer and of attempting to write Jung out of the history of psychoanalysis. This suggests that the debt to Nietzsche can be expressed because the energy of repression is all directed towards denying the disappointment arising from the break with Jung. It is an odd remark in various respects for clearly such a precaution must always come too late, for the writings, once read, cannot fail, either to suggest or fail to suggest themselves as models; cannot fail to emerge or fail to emerge out of the unconscious resources into which they have presumably sunk. This connection between work, debt and grief, leads into the problematics of mourning and melancholy; whereas a counter-posed, more Nietzschean, series would read playfulness, inheritance, cheerfulness. This Freudian disavowal leads to a domestication of playfulness, away from its full Nietzschean consequences in the dismemberment of Dionysus, a domesticated pleasure which then give rise to an even more fearful death drive. This work of disavowal is conjoined to that of deferred effect: what is in question here in relation to the problematics of nihilism is the temporality of the already too late and the temporality of postponement, the after effect of the Freudian *Nachträglichkeit*, which I shall seek to connect up to the Nietzschean problematics of posthumous (*nachgeboren*) existence in writing. This posthumicity provides a limit case for the Freudian temporality of the after shock, of deferred action.

In lecture thirty-one, 'Dissection of the Personality', of *The New Introductory Lectures* (1933), the relation to Nietzsche appears in less convoluted form. Freud writes:

> We perceive that we have no right to name the mental region that is foreign to the ego 'the system of the *Ucs.*', since the characteristic of being unconscious is not restricted to it. Very well; we will no longer use the term 'unconscious' in the systematic sense and we will give what we hitherto so described a better name and one no longer open to misunderstanding. Following a verbal usage of Nietzsche's and taking up a suggestion by George Groddeck (1923) we will in future call it the 'id'.
>
> (Freud 1975, 104)

By contrast, in the 1923 version of this account, 'The Ego and the Id', only Groddeck is acknowledged as a precursor. In the very next lecture, in *The New Introductory Lectures*, 'Anxiety and Instinctual Life', Freud gives a summary of the results of his paper, 'The Instincts and their Vicissitudes' (1915), in which the pleasure principle and the principle of avoiding displeasure begin to come apart, such that the death drives might emerge as the separate, separable laws of psychic functioning, which Freud both affirms and denies in 'Beyond the Pleasure Principle' (1922). In his reading of this, 'To Speculate – on Freud', Derrida elegantly shows this text performing its own hesitation (Derrida 1978, 257–409). Derrida positions this performance in relation to a question about the status of philosophy today, contrasting the movement of non-completion in Freud's writings as distinct from the foreclosing movement of Hegelian dialectics and of Lacanian affirmations of Hegelian dialectics, which serve to immobilise rather than releasing both Freud and thinking more generally. Derrida insists on Freud's self-avowed avoidance in relation to a certain kind of philosophy and specifically to an avoidance of Nietzsche.

Derrida cites the passage from the 'Autobiographical Sketch', first published, in English, in 1927, in which Freud remarks:

> I read Schopenhauer very late in life. Nietzsche, another philosopher whose guesses and intuitions most often agree in the most astonishing way with the painfully laborious findings of psychoanalysis was for a long time avoided by me precisely on that very account; I was less concerned with the question of priority than with keeping my mind unembarrassed.
>
> (Freud 1993, 244)

This, as Derrida remarks, is set up in the context of the disclaimer: 'Even when I have moved away from observation, I have carefully avoided any contact with philosophy proper' (Derrida 1978, 243). There is a double duplicity here: for Freud re-enacts Nietzsche's duplicity by the denial of any influence from Nietzsche. The duplicity in the workings of the pleasure principle, the reality principle and the death drives replicates the duplicities of Nietzsche's Dionysus, who is both life affirming and self-destructive, and replicates the duplicities of Dionysus' erasure of Persephone, the goddess of destiny. The unravelling of a single principle into an affirmation of multiplicity of counterpoised principles, in both affirming suffering and in a will to avoid suffering, is at work in the transition from a Nietzschean affirmation of nihilism as life enhancing and the reaffirmation of this Nietzschean affirmation in the present context, which has become life denying. The thought would be that what Nietzsche calls ecstatic nihilism takes on a different value. Nietzsche mentions ecstatic nihilism in *Will to Power*:

> A pessimistic teaching and way of teaching, an ecstatic nihilism, can under certain conditions be indispensable precisely to the philosopher – as a mighty pressure and hammer with which he breaks and removes degenerate and decaying races to make way for a new order of life, or to implant into that which is degenerate and desire to die a longing for the end.   (Nietzsche 1968, §1055)

Ecstatic nihilism, then, stands out from the general decline and posits the thought of a regeneration: but what if there is no re-emergence? This hope that an ecstatic nihilism might work as principle of selection between that which is decaying and dying and that which is life affirming assumes that degeneration is only partial. This ecstatic nihilism presupposes rather than wagering the potential of self-affirmation.

In the context of a widespread reception of nihilism this ecstatic nihilism becomes demonic destroying all life and thought in its destruction of supposed degenerate and decaying races: for this is the whole of humankind. This becomes the thesis of Freud's 'Civilisation and its Discontents' (1930), the performative paradoxes of which would repay the same degree of attention as Derrida brings to bear on 'Beyond the Pleasure Principle'. The doctrine of eternal recurrence is then to be counterpoised to Freud's principle determination of time as the law of the posthumous effect, one which will work in a direction unexpected by any would be instigator. Eternal recurrence presupposes its own continuation, while concealing the death of its bearer; deferred effects presupposes that death. Freud both formulates the divine law of necessity, the unsustainability of pleasure, and the eternal recurrence of its disruption by the double take of a love of destiny, *amor fati*, which affirms that unsustainability. This Nietzsche introduces as follows:

Such an experimental philosophy as I live anticipates experimentally even the possibilities of the most fundamental nihilism; but this does not mean that it must halt at negation, a No, a will to negation. It wants rather to cross over to the opposite of this – to a Dionysian affirmation of the world as it is, without subtraction, exception or selection – it wants the eternal circulation – the same things, the same logic and illogic of entanglements. The highest state a philosopher can attain: to stand in a Dionysian relationship to existence – my formula for this is *amor fati*.

(Nietzsche 1968, §1041)

This is perhaps the stance of Freud's 'Psychoanalysis: terminable and interminable' in which the death drive is counterpoised to the life affirmations of analysis as interminable. Nietzschean affirmation is less far from Freud's engagements with everyday grief and suffering than from the various Platonic strategies of avoidance and disengagement. Nietzsche like Freud privileges technique over *theoria*, by contrast to the Greek preference for *theoria* over technique.

In this section I am introducing Freud's ambivalence in relation to Nietzsche to suggest that an internal splitting of the pleasure principle into the pleasure principle and the reality principle, the principle of aggression and a death drive, re-enacts the splitting internal to Nietzsche's Dionysian principle. The greater difficulty of holding the divergent strands of the Freudian principle together leads to a loss of capacity for *amor fati*, and a loss of hopefulness with regard to the outcome of a devaluation of all values. As a result, memory for Freud becomes all the more inextricably connected up with mourning lost emotional investments rather than with celebrating the possibility of disinvestment and reinvestment, and rather than being transformable as it is with Nietzsche into the form of forgetting which permits reinvention and an affirmative relation to the future. This theme of a devaluation of memory, from an affirmative to a life-denying value, can already be traced at work in the poetry of Hölderlin, in the much read Ode to Memory, 'Mnemosyne', which – as I read it – celebrates those who need no mourning. Heidegger takes up this theme, in the opening pages of his *What calls for thought?*, and he describes 'Mnemosyne' thus:

Mnemosyne, daughter of Heaven and earth, bride of Zeus, in nine nights becomes the mother of the nine muses. Drama and music, dance and poetry are of the womb of Mnemosyne, of memory. It is plain that the word means something other than the merely psychologically demonstrable ability to retain the past in representation. Memory thinks what has been thought. But the name of the mother of the muses means 'memory' not as an arbitrary thinking of any thought. Memory is the gathering of thinking to that which everywhere might be thought in advance. Memory is the gathering of directed thinking (*Andenken*).

(Heidegger 1954, 7; 1968, 11)

Mnemosyne, like Prometheus, belongs to the order of the titans: pre-olympian powers allied with the chthonic order of cyclical generation and decay. Heidegger continues:

Under the heading, 'Mnemosyne', Hölderlin says: 'We are an uninterpreted sign': We? Who? We, the human beings of today, the human beings of a today which for a long time, and still longer, preserves a duration, for which no calculation of time can ever bring a measure.

(Heidegger 1954, 7; 1968, 11)

This then is a gathering of thought, an overcoming of forgetting, for which there is no temporal measure, which in effect takes place in some temporal continuum other than a continuum, susceptible to measurement, rather as though alongside chronology, alongside the sequential time of conscious calculation, there were to be another unintended time of simultaneous dispersion and gathering. This sets up a distinction between on one side a time of generation and decay, invoked by Nietzsche in his analysis of the need for devaluing values to be precipitated into their full decline, and a time without such internal sequential structure, where there is no order of one after the other, to be constructed out of an alternation of generation and decay, and where dispersion and gathering might be simultaneous or in a relation of desynchronised syncopation.

The model for such thinking would be the disaggregation of time in the Freudian model of the experience of consciousness into a conscious time and a time of the unconscious, which has no such temporal ordering. Both of these structures, of Heideggerian thinking of incalculability and of the Freudian unconscious appear to destabilise the possibility of the Nietzschean affirmation, which has to presuppose that the time of Dionysian dismemberment can be brought within a single time of cyclical repetition.[1] The key term through which the affirmation of Nietzschean nihilism and the aporetics of Freudian and Heideggerian thinking come apart is then repetition, for the Nietzschean term permits a reunification of temporalities in eternal recurrence of the same; whereas the reunification of temporality is thinkable in the Freudian and Heideggerian models only in terms of the mortality of the individual, whose death does not stand outside time, as unmournable, but which becomes rather a sign of the irretrievable mournfulness of human existence. Only Nietzsche, I suggest, with his account of posthumous existence can affirm the Hölderlinian thought of the death which defies mourning. The challenge of responding to Nietzschean nihilism is thus suspended by Freud in the form of his reflections in 'Civilisation and its Discontents', which cannot be as affirmative as Nietzsche's working with nihilism; and by Heidegger in his diagnoses of a crisis of technology, which displays the similar degree of passivity. The difficulty then may be precisely the splitting of a response to Nietzsche into these two opposed registers: that of psychoanalysis and of psychic pathology, and that of a diagnosis of the current condition of metaphysics. An escape from the completion of nihilism in this demonic form may require a knitting back together of these divergent strands, divergent responses to Nietzsche's invocation of the monstrous forms of Dionysus.

Afterthought

This Europe, in its ruinous blindness forever on the point of cutting its own throat, lies today in a great pincers, squeezed between Russia on one side and America on the other. From a metaphysical point of view, Russia and America are the same; the same dreary technological frenzy, the same unrestricted organization of the average man.   (Heidegger 1959, 37)

The published version of *Will to Power* begins with the remark 'Nihilism stands at the door: whence comes this uncanniest of all guests?' (Nietzsche 1968, §1). In his 1956 letter to Ernst Jünger, Heidegger comments:

You know that an estimation of the situation of human beings in respect of the movement of nihilism and within it demands an adequate determination of essence. Such knowledge is lacking in many places. This lack clouds the view in estimating our situation. It makes the judgment of nihilism superficial and the eye blind to the presence 'of this strangest of all guests' (Nietzsche, *Will to Power* The Plan WW XV p. 141). It is called the strangest because as the unconditional will to will, it wants homelessness as such. Therefore, it does not help to show it the door because it has long since and invisibly gone right through the household.
                                                    (Heidegger 1967, 386–387; 1998, 292)

Heidegger's question might then be thought to be: how is nihilism to be judged? Heidegger's contention is that the essence of nihilism is the affirmation of value, in Nietzsche's writings, in which the history of metaphysics culminates. This affirmation of value makes way for theories of matter, of what there is, as mathematical functions, tracking the movements of elementary particles, with the philosophical slogan: to be is to be the value of a variable. This for Heidegger erases the givenness of interpretation and thinking as an activity pursued or not pursued, consciously or unconsciously, thoughtfully, or unthoughtfully, by human beings, to whom is given the determinacy required for thinking, interpretation, evaluation.

Nihilism, then, for Heidegger, is created by human beings to control and eradicate what is distinctive about human beings: the ambiguous relation to time and the openness of our destinies. It becomes general, and not specific to the task of evaluation, as it is for Nietzsche. In the workings of technical control over the relations in which human beings find themselves, the human is subordinated to the deployment of techniques which at first were developed by human beings in order to explore the potential of the human. The end of technique, the exploration and invention of human capacity, thus becomes detached from that end, and what it is to be human is first taken for granted, then forgotten and, at the limit, destroyed. But this is a forgetting which does not permit the development of specific complexity, as with Nietzsche, but its disambiguation into a theory of complexity, and a single theoretical location for the human, as taken for granted and erased. These relations of technical control increasingly present human beings with no option of taking up an abode, but only of living on a borderline between the human and the technical. The destiny of Nietzschean thinking and that of Heideggerian thinking become indistinguishable one from another: they are all simply emanations of a single humanness.

This impact of technology is that which Heidegger hoped in the 1935–36 lectures *Introduction to Metaphysics* might be held at arms length, sustaining a Germany 'between' Stalinist electrification and American capitalism. This is the diagnosis of the emergence of a single set of electro-technical relations as the fields of force within which human being, its possibilities and its future are held. This shift of register from a diagnosis of the workings of evaluation for the purposes of the reflections of a private all too private scholar to the mass diagnosis of Heideggerian hitlerism renders Nietzschean nihilism all the more dangerous and all the more inaudible. The principle claim here then is that Nietzschean and Heideggerian nihilisms are utterly distinct; that their interdependence is one of conflict and unease rather than of compatibility and cohesion within a single account of a destiny of philosophy and of the human; and that the failure to think this unease is the failure of thinking of the present day, in which Heidegger diagnoses a withdrawal of thinking. Only by distinguishing between the human, all too human of Nietzschean thinking and the monstrous rebirth of nihilism as Hitlerism, by distinguishing between the intellectual struggles of Nietzsche and those of Heidegger can an erasure of all distinctions in a transcendental aesthetic of the computer virus of an instant destruction of thought by thought be held at arm's length.

The ease with which Heideggerian appropriation erases the distinctiveness of Nietzsche's thinking suggests that the source for rescue is not to be found in Heidegger's reading of Nietzsche but perhaps rather in the Freudian refusal to read. Heideggerian forgetting is marked by the will all the same to leave a mark on all previous thinking, while the Freudian thought of technique is not a thought of thinking at all. It is neither a Heideggerian retrieval nor a Platonic recollection restoring a lost continuity but a breaching and broaching of patterns, which make innovation, both of the past and of the future, thinkable. It is then perhaps the Freudian strategy of avoiding Nietzsche which permits a reactivation of the Nietzschean thought, rescuing it from the immobilisations of *ressentiment* and reception, more readily than the Heideggerian attempt to think beyond Nietzsche. The strategy of avoidance permits the thinking of Nietzsche all the same to permeate and work productively against the grain of Freud's own expressed thought. The Heideggerian strategy of confrontation, the attempt to reduce all thinking to the single grid of the history of being, leads to a mutual assured destruction of the thinking of both Nietzsche and Heidegger, and indeed of thinking at all.

Notes

1 For more on this Heideggerian thinking of time, see Joanna Hodge, 'Heideggerian Temporalities: Genesis and Structure of a Thinking of Many Dimensional Time', in *Research in Phenomenology*, volume XXIX, forthcoming, 2000

References

Derrida, J. (1978) 'To Speculate – on Freud' in *The Post Card from Socrates to Freud and Beyond* trans. A. Bass, Chicago: University of Chicago Press.

Freud, S. (1975) *New Introductory Lectures* Penguin Freud Library Vol. II. Harmondsworth: Penguin.

—— (1984) 'Beyond the Pleasure Principle' in *On Metapsychology* Penguin Freud Library Vol. XI. Harmondsworth: Penguin.

—— (1985) 'Civilization and Its Discontents' in *Civilization, Society and Religion* Penguin Freud Library Vol. XII. Harmondworth: Penguin.

—— (1993) *Historical and Expository Works on Psychoanalysis* Penguin Freud Library Vol. 15. Harmondsworth: Penguin.

Heidegger, M. (1959) *Introduction to Metaphysics* trans. R. Manheim. New Haven: Yale University Press.

—— (1954) *Was Heißt Denken?*, Tübingen: Max Niemeye (1968) *What is called Thinking?*, trans. J. Glenn Gray, New York: Harper and Row.

—— (1967) 'Zur Seinsfrage' and 'Brief über den Humanismus' in *Wegmarken* Frankfurt am Main: Klostermann (1998) 'The Question of Being' and 'Letter on Humanism' in *Pathmarks* trans. W. Mcneill, Cambridge: Cambridge University Press.

—— (1967) 'The Birth of Tragedy' and 'The Case of Wagner' ed. W. Kaufmann, New York: Vintage.

—— (1968) *Will to Power* trans. and ed. W. Kaufmann, New York: Vintage.

Nietzsche (1987) 'Die Geburt der Tragödie' in *Nietzsche: Kritische Studienausgabe*, Vol. I, eds Colli and Montinari. Munich/Berlin: dtv/ de Gruyter.

5
Nihilism and Life: Cosmobiology and Ontopoiesis in Heidegger's *Nietzsche*

Suhail Malik

I

For Heidegger, modernity is characterised by the comprehension of life in nihilism. This is, moreover, human Dasein's metaphysical culmination. As such, it is the end of a history inaugurated *with* the Ancients (if not *by* them) and whose 'extreme point', as we will see Heidegger calling it, is reached with Nietzsche. Nihilism is thus an extremity for human Dasein and for the comprehension of life in general. It is the extremity of metaphysics.

However, simply assuming 'the end of metaphysics' on this basis, as is now common enough, obscures what sense such a determination has for Heidegger (as the historical-metaphysical culmination of nihilism). And such an assumption also pre-empts any hesitation as to *whether* it suffices to characterise modernity by nihilism. Without a clearer understanding of nihilism as it is proposed by Heidegger, the sense and history of modernity remain at best *conventional*, as does the philosophical-metaphysical (self-) comprehension of 'the end of metaphysics'. The understanding of such an 'end' is crucial for the contemporary context and reception of Heidegger's work and life too. For what is involved in Heidegger's extended considerations of nihilism is a philosophical-historical relation and thinking of Nazism, a reflection that is articulated through the interpretation of *Nietzsche*. The reason is partly strategic: as is well known, the adoption of Nietzsche as a precursor of Nazi ideologies was occasioned mainly through Alfred Baeumler's espousal of Nietzsche's philosopheme of the will to power as the exaltation and strengthening of life through biological-racial purification, and the concomitant superiority of such a national-racial life.[1] The interpretation of Nietzsche is a way for Heidegger to draw out the sense of both nihilism as *the* history and metaphysics of the West and, concomitantly, the wider historical-philosophical determination of Nazism, specifically with regard to the determination of life. In addition, it allows Heidegger's own moves with respect to Nazism to be elucidated.[2]

The present discussion will be primarily concerned with Heidegger's interpretation of Nietzsche's comprehension of life. This is not at all to denigrate
the importance of the contexts and histories just mentioned. On the contrary, the more extensive implications and congruences are developed here
in order to articulate what is *today* a major philosophical, technoscientific
and, in the limited sense, political issue with those historical-metaphysical
concerns. The issue here is life as such. The following exposition brings the
Nazi programme of racial breeding into focus as a primary concern for
contemporary determinations of life *and* for historical-philosophical reflection on them.

II

The apparently conceptually (if not historically) thin correlation between
nihilism and life can be clarified by turning to the 1940 retrospective on the
four major lecture courses on Nietzsche. These lectures were themselves
contemporaneous with the Nazification of formal institutional power in
the 1930s (they begin two years after Heidegger's aborted rectorship of the
University of Freiburg of 1933–34). The retrospective from 1940 is one of a
series of mostly undelivered treatises in which Heidegger continues to
develop the reflections on Nietzsche and metaphysics until the mid-1940s,
revising them for publication in 1961. In it, Heidegger distinguishes
Nietzsche's conception of nihilism from every 'doctrinal tenet – especially
[from] what a superficial understanding of the term would lead us to imagine, namely, the dissolution (*Auflösung*) of everything into sheer nothingness' (Heidegger 1961b, 275; 1991a, 202–3).[3] Taking instead the statement
by Nietzsche from Spring–Fall 1887 (compiled as §2 of *The Will to Power*) as
the basic premise of the interpretation, Heidegger remarks that for Nietzsche
nihilism is not a total and negating 'dissolution' but rather 'the process
(*Vorgang*) of the devaluation of the previously highest values' (Heidegger
1961b, 275; 1991a, 203). As a 'process', nihilism does not then mean a
collapse of *all* values *at once*. It is instead a history: the history of Western
metaphysics and, concomitantly, Western history is a history of devaluation
of values.

Though Heidegger specifies moments in this historico-philosophical process of devaluation in the successive names of the supersensible 'true being' –
'God as the Christian Creator and Redeemer, the supersensibility of the
moral law, the authority of reason, progress, the happiness of the majority'
(Heidegger 1961b, 273; 1991a, 203), and so on –, the more general and
decisive point from Nietzsche's conception is the following:

> the process of devaluation of the hitherto highest values is thus not
> one historical occurrence (*geschichtliche Begebenheit*) amongst many
> others but rather the [historical] ground occurrence (*Grundgeschehen*) of

metaphysically borne and guided occidental history (*Geschichte*).

(Heidegger 1961b, 275; 1991, 203)

In sum, nihilism is for Heidegger the grounding historical occurrence of occidental metaphysics and its history. Nihilism is occidental histori*city*. Moreover, nihilism is an ontotheology in that it is a historical-metaphysical determination of beings as such (ontology) and as a whole (theology).

Though these world-historical concerns seem to be at some distance from the actuality and conditions of life, nihilism and life are in fact synonymous in Heidegger's interpretation of Nietzsche. Their inherent connection is presented in Heidegger's initial interpretation of excerpts collected under the heading 'Principles of a New Valuation' in *The Will to Power*, in the third lecture course on Nietzsche, titled 'The Will to Power As Cognition (*Erkenntnis*)', which was delivered in the Summer semester of 1939. The common articulation of the world-historical occurrence of nihilism and the actuality of life is *value*. For Heidegger, the condition or essence of the 'interrelation' of nihilism and life in value is Nietzsche's quasi-concept of the will to power. However, in order to partially detach the present argument from those concerned with the validity and status of this latter philosopheme in Nietzsche's work and Heidegger's interpretation of it, these issues will not be elaborated here in terms of the will to power.[4] This detachment is made in view of important strategic and critical considerations: it is to allow the wider and less philosophically determined concern under consideration here to be explictly examined, namely, the actuality and ontogenesis of life. Moreover, since the principal interests are, firstly, the prevalent sense and determination of the 'end of metaphysics' as Heidegger has perhaps above all developed it, and, secondly, whether a non-metaphysical comprehension of life then follows, the point at issue here is not Nietzsche's own articulations of life and nihilism but only Heidegger's interpretation of it. That is, the accuracy or tendentiousness of Heidegger's interpretation of Nietzsche's writings or thinking is of no direct relevance to the present discussion.

III

Heidegger's interpretation that *life* in Nietzsche is determined by value has two initial points. Firstly, that 'value for Nietzsche means a condition of life, a condition of life to be "alive" ' (Heidegger 1961a, 488; 1991a, 15). Secondly, however, that 'Nietzsche does not see the essence of life in "self-preservation" ("struggle for existence") as do the biology and doctrine of life of his time, determined as it is by Darwin, but sees it rather in raising (*Steigerung* ['intensification', 'climbing']) over above itself' (ibid.).[5] Heidegger then immediately notes how preservation and 'raising' are but two *aspects* of a coherent (auto-) comprehension of life:

Value, as condition of life, must therefore come to be thought as that which supports (*trägt* ['bears']), furthers and awakens the raising of life. Only what raises life, [that is,] beings as a whole, has value – or better: *is* a value.   (Heidegger 1961a, 488; 1991a, 15–16)

It is this self-surpassing life which constitutes a 'living' life. Valuation is therefore essential to life if life is, in essence, its raising over above itself. In short, values are given or conditioned by life as essentially as they give or are a condition of it. The connection of nihilism and life is then more apparent: in Heidegger's terms, life has an essential unity with nihilism as a transformation of where and what values are. That is, nihilism *is* the transformation of life as such, of *what* it is and of *how* it is.

However, such a general statement does not capture the complexity of Heidegger's interpretation nor, more importantly, the specific determination of life as such. For, to articulate the historical-metaphysical transformation of nihilism, to propound the historical-metaphysical conditions and 'raising' of life, Heidegger must think historical valuation, which is to say the *actuality* of life. But if it is 'biological' thinking 'that interprets (*deutet*) all appearances as the expression of life' (Heidegger 1961a, 517; 1991a, 39), and if life is the condition and essence of life as such, of values and so of the history of nihilism, it would seem appropriate to look to Nietzsche's biological discussions as the clearest expression of an ontotheology, if not as the core of Nietzsche's thinking since that is where its metaphysics would be rooted (Heidegger 1961a, 519; 1991a, 40–1). This is precisely the Nazi adoption and espousal of Nietzsche: as a *primarily* biologistic thinker of life and history. Heidegger refutes such a comprehension of Nietzsche, however. The refutation is in line with a theme that is constant and familiar across Heidegger's works: namely, that science *assumes* the Western metaphysical decision on being(s) but does not think it. In presuming occidental metaphysics – which is but a valuation of what and how beings as such and as a whole are – science implements this ontotheology without question (Heidegger 1961a, 520; 1991a, 42–3). Life is thus a stable value for biology so interpreted.[6] Accordingly, the life 'of' biology does not correspond to life in its essential 'raising'. Biologism understood as the 'transferring [of] determined prevailing views on the living from the realm of the vegetal and animal to other realms of beings such as history (*Geschichte*)' (ibid., 524; 45) confirms furthermore such a stable value and predecision on life. It thus propogates a metaphysical predecision of which it is, as Heidegger puts it, nonetheless 'totally ignorant' (ibid., 525; 45).[7]

In that it does *not* presume what life is as such (what value it is) nor even that life is, in Heidegger's terms Nietzsche's thinking is not scientific but ontotheological. Heidegger affirms that:

> although Nietzsche gives the impression of speaking and thinking bio-
> logically, giving the living and life a direct precedence (*Vorzug*), this
> precedence of life must first of all be grounded upon a ground which
> has *nothing more* [emph. add.] to do with the appearance of life of the
> plant and the animal.   (ibid., 526; 46)

Hence, life (theology) and the living (ontology) are not to be thought
'positivistically', upon grounds of what is already presumed to be (basically)
alive. In the subsequent lecture course on Nietzsche from the first trimester
of 1940, whose principal theme is nihilism, Heidegger extends this argument against the scientific assumption of life to the comprehension of
ontotheology predicated upon the three further dimensions of: natural or
positive theology, psychology (where beings as such and as a whole may be
said to be comprehended by the (human) mind or soul), and cosmology
(where beings as such and as whole are said to comprehended as the physical
or natural totality of the universe). Combining these metaphysical domains
of representing 'beings as a whole' with that of biology, it can be said with
Heidegger that the ontotheology of life cannot be comprehended from even
an extended scientifically determined realm of the living, be it a psychobio-
logy or, more generally, a cosmobiology.

Nonetheless, Heidegger must think life in its actuality. And it is Nietzsche's
comprehension of life in its actuality as *valuation* that allows it to be considered as a principally historical-*metaphysical* issue beyond and outside of
its cosmobiological (pre)determination: as an issue of nihilism. The
prioritisation of metaphysical over scientific enquiry is stressed by Heidegger
from the start of the Summer 1939 lecture course. As its title suggests,
Heidegger initially emphasises this priority by elucidating the ground and
essence of *cognition* which science simply assumes. The focus on cognition
further emphasises the primacy of metaphysical enquiry since the latter does
not assume the 'thematic' predeterminations of cosmobiology (that is, the
living) and, furthermore, it does not assume even the cognition of life in its
actuality as the 'methodological' *condition* of the enquiry into it. That is, the
metaphysical-valuative determination of cognition allows both the thematic
and methodological assumptions of the scientific examination of life to be
put into question. It is thus a 'destruction' of *every* aspect of biology.
Furthermore, if life is not the 'object' of the enquiry but its essence, then
cognition itself is comprehended in terms of value-positing. Cognition –
which is to say, with Nietzsche, life in its valuation – is itself then 'recognised' outside of its metaphysical security, be it a scientific *or* historical-
philosophical security. Such an *essential*-metaphysical determination thus
allows and requires the destruction of the sedimented *historico*-metaphysical
sense of cognition in the Western tradition.[8] With the destruction of cognition it is also the very condition of *valuation* as such, of which de-and revaluation are specific occurrences, which is firstly put under destruction.

Conversely, with the destruction of cognition life as such is also under destruction.

IV

The 'point of departure' for Heidegger's *destructive* interpretation of cognition to its essence in life is Nietzsche's note from Spring–Fall 1887 (collected as §507 in *The Will to Power*). The first couple of sentences of this passage tie the issue of truth directly back to valuation:

> The *estimation of value* (*Wertschätzung*) 'I believe that such and such is so' as the *essence* of *'truth'*. In estimations of value *conditions of maintenance* (*Erhaltung*) and *growth* are expressed. All our *organs of cognition and our senses* are only developed with regard to conditions of maintenance and growth.   (cited in Heidegger 1961a, 509; 1991a, 33)

That is, the destruction of truth and metaphysics requires the destruction of cognition as it is 'posited' through the senses and cognitive organs. In other words, it requires a destruction of *living cognition*, which is to say, giving living cognition its traditional metaphysical name, a destruction of perception (*Wahrnehmung* [literally: 'truth-taking']) and per-ception (*Vernehmung* [more readily translated by 'examination', though 'per-ception' is chosen here with the 'per-' indicating the intensifier of the transitive sense of getting-hold-of which is carried through in the Latin root *percipere*]). In following the destruction of cognition through to the order of living organic perception, Heidegger conducts the destruction of metaphysical cognition not only into and beyond the order of the metaphysically secure register of knowledge with which epistemology is concerned, but also of its cosmobiological determination. Heidegger gives a fuller meaning to this somewhat abstracted sense of per-ception by remarking that in the sedimented sense of Western metaphysics human per-ception is 'everywhere and always' perception of beings (Heidegger 1961a, 528; 1991a, 48). This banal general sense is pushed further by emphasising that, 'conversely, the being as such opens itself only to such a per-ceiving' (ibid.). While this in some ways only reiterates that the condition of any being as a being is per-ception, which is to say belief, it also emphasises that a being 'is' only such a being if it 'opens itself' to being per-ceived in cognition, if *it* is per-ceiv*able*.

This essential conjunction and co-eval 'opening', which is given *and* obscured by value-positing, is brought into clarity by the destruction of its historical-metaphysical determination.[9] Several other names or quasi-concepts are then relevant. Specifically, Heidegger notes that 'grasping and determining beings have since ancient times come to be attributed to perception – to *nous*. We have for this the German word *Vernunft* [*reason*]' (Heidegger 1961a, 529; 1991a, 49). That is, though the historical-metaphysical sense of reason is that it is 'the capability (*Vermögen* [more usually translated from Kant by 'faculty']) of bringing the human before beings and that represents beings as such for the human' through representation (Heidegger 1961a, 531; 1991a, 51), the destruction of cognition shows that it is another name for the more general co-eval 'opening' of per-ception and beings.

The importance of the destruction of cognition then becomes even clearer: the conditions of beings as such and as a whole are essentially determined not by representation but by life in its valuation. Valuation is thus the essence of reason, its condition. Accordingly, the essential compre-hension of nihilism as the history of valuation requires the destruction of reason, of what Heidegger calls 'the most extreme pre-decision as to what being says' (ibid., 531; 51), namely that there *are* beings for human cogni-tion. Heidegger's destruction here is swift: for Nietzsche it is by belief that the true is 'the grasped (*Erfaßte*) in cognition, the being' (ibid., 543; 59), that 'what is' *is*. Belief is the *condition* for the 'belonging-together' of beings and living cognition (for the human), and so of reason. If the destruction of metaphysics, and so of beings thus comprehended, turns on belief as 'grasping in cognition', then the sense of belief can be elaborated by the destruction of reason as valuation:

we say something *is* of that which we *always and in advance* [emph. add.] encounter (*antreffen*) as always already at hand (*immer schon vorhanden*); what always presents (*anwest*) and in such presence (*Anwesenheit*) has constant constancy (*ständige Bestand* ['standing reserve']).

(ibid., 543; 59)

In accord with the world-historical occurrence and process of nihilism, Heidegger's interpretation suggests that belief and valuation for Nietzsche – that is, 'the beinghood of beings' – 'want to say: *constant presence (beständige Anwesenheit)*' (ibid., 542; 60). With this determination of belief as belonging to the metaphysics of presence, the destruction of metaphysical cognition is accomplished.

In interpreting Nietzsche's thinking of life to be confronting the meta-physics of presence *as such*, Heidegger suggests that Nietzsche explicitly acknowledges the Western metaphysical 'pre-decision' on being(s). That is, for Heidegger, Nietzsche stands at the 'end of metaphysics', at its 'most extreme point' in which 'the proper affirmative essence of nihilism shows itself in the light'. This 'affirmative essence' is belief, the 'constant presence' that 'imposes' constancy and firmness in valuation. Correlatively, belief is itself of the utmost or 'highest' value to the living:

the imposition (*Ansetzung*) of the constant and the firm as beings – is a determined *valuing*. Indeed, the constant-firm comes to be preferred as the higher value to the changing and fleeting. The valuing of the value of the constant and the inconstant comes to be guided from the ground-comprehension (*Grundauffassung*) of the valuable and value.

(ibid., 544; 60)

What is most valuable (constant) to life is valuation (constancy). Value (-positing) is the highest value of value(-positing). Such is the 'unconditional[ity]' and 'originary unity' and 'totality' of beings as such and as a whole. For Heidegger, this ontotheology is what Nietzsche calls 'morality'. It is the 'Platonic doctrine' which '*pre*-decides' occidental historical-metaphysics. It is 'the cause of nihilism – in the sense of the imposition of the supernatural ideals of truth, of goodness, and of beauty that are valid "in themselves"' (Heidegger 1961b, 279; 1991a, 206). 'Morality' imposes 'supernatural ideals' as conditions for life in that these values are the constant-firm and always present condition(s) for there even to be cognition or per-ception (as valuation).

V

Nietzsche's importance to ontotheology is then manifest: firstly, it is this *express* sense of valuation/belief as the complete, sole condition and 'cause' of the various historical-metaphysical-moral determinations of being and truth that lets the affirmative 'proper essence' of nihilism be acknowledged *as such*, as 'constant presence'. Secondly, the *revaluation* of values, which is what the destruction of living per-ception involves, 'must [then] be unconditional and place all beings in an originary unity' (Heidegger 1961b, 278; 1991a, 205). The principal point here, however, is that the unconditional, originary determination of the 'one' *and* its revaluation is, for Heidegger, how and what Nietzsche proposes *life* to be in its duality. For, though morality would be the highest and absolute unconditionality of life if life were only the positing of values, with Nietzsche life is at once the positing of values *and* the raising over itself, to the 'extreme' point that it even revalues itself as valuation (such is the destruction of cognition, and Nietzsche's genealogy of historical-metaphysical morality). In other words; (i) for Heidegger it is Nietzsche's comprehension of life that lets the 'affirmative proper essence of nihilism' be historically 'shown in the light'. And if, as has been seen, for Heidegger Nietzsche proposes the *condition* (and value) of value for valuation to be life as revaluation, then, (ii) in its revaluing, life as the value-positing of belief and morality is itself principally determined not by any value but by life *in its living*: 'truth as value is for Nietzsche a necessary condition for *life*, [but it is] a valuation that life carries out so as to will itself' (Heidegger 1961a, 551; 1991a, 67). Hence, (iii) life as a revaluation of previous values at its 'extreme', at the point of its auto-comprehension, is but the revaluation of valuation as such, and hence of life as such. However, (iv) such a revaluation of values is no less the metaphysical history of nihilism. That is, (v) life as such, in its essence, is a nihilism. And this essence, life in its living, is what nihilism affirms in *its* 'proper essence' under the name of 'becoming *(Werden)*'. Such is the co-essential history and historicity of life *and* nihilism and the sense of the 'end of metaphysics'.

The destruction of life does not presume or consolidate the world-historical occurrence of nihilism – morality – as does all historical-metaphysics up to Nietzsche. Rather, it begins from the ' "extreme" nihilism' that 'cognises that there are no "eternal truths in themselves" ' (Heidegger 1961a, 280; 1991a, 207). Extreme, active nihilism, the end of metaphysics, is, however, not simply congruent with the process of the historical-metaphysical process of nihilism since it:

> clears out *(räumt...aus)* previous values together with their 'space *(Raum)*' (the supersensible) and it moves in *(räumt...ein)* primary possibilities of new valuations. With respect to this character of space-generating *(raumschaffenden)* and stepping into the free of extreme nihilism, Nietzsche speaks also of 'ecstatic nihilism' *(The Will to Power, §1055)*. Such [nihilism] affirms... neither a [thing] at hand nor an ideal [which is why it is not historical-metaphysical nihilism] but rather the *'principle of valuation'* [as such]. As soon as this is expressly seized and is properly taken up as the ground and measure of all value-positing, nihilism has found itself in its affirmative essence, has overcome and included its incompletion, and thus fulfils itself. Ecstatic nihilism comes to be 'classical nihilism'. Nietzsche conceives of his metaphysics as such. [_] The affirmative essence of nihilism overall can not be said more affirmatively. [_] Revaluation [now] does not mean only that new values come to be posited in the old and same place of previous values, but rather firstly and ahead of that means *that the place (Stelle) itself comes to be determined anew*.
> (Heidegger 1961b, 281–2; 1991a, 207–8)

The 'affirmative essence of nihilism' is realised as the unconditional *revaluation* of valuation *as such*. That is, the destruction of life and valuation, of perception, has to be determined beyond the *condition* and value of value. This *unconditional* revaluation is but life (as valuation) in its 'classical nihilism'. It is an 'immorality' requiring the 'place' of valuation to be 'determined anew'.

Though this is not directly the context proposed in the Summer 1939 lecture course, it is in fact what is undertaken when Heidegger interprets Nietzsche's note from March–June 1888 (collected as §515 in *The Will to Power*) as a statement on the essential determination of cognition in becoming. The note reads: 'Not "cognising" but rather schematising, imposing *(auferlegen)* upon chaos as many regularities and forms as satisfies *(genugtut)* our practical need *(Bedürfnis)*' (cited in Heidegger 1961a, 555; 1991a, 71). Heidegger's interpretation highlights two aspects here: firstly, chaos is that upon which 'regularities and forms' come to be imposed by per-ception, it is 'what cognition initially strikes (*stößt*), and what comes to strike it first of all, what cognition steps onto (*auftrifft* ['encounters'])' (Heidegger 1961a, 556; 1991a, 71). Chaos is a name for that which comes to be 'encountered' in schematising but which is not itself the 'imposing [of] regularities and forms'.[10] Though chaos is not then entirely other to cognition, its (partial) 'exteriority' to cognition gives a vantage for the latter's destruction.

The destruction of *living* per-ception relies, however, on the second focus of Heidegger's interpretation: the 'practical need' that drives the schematisation of chaos. The point here is straightforward: from Nietzsche's note, cognition is not carried out by a subject, be it transcendental or otherwise. Rather, as Heidegger insists, 'the cognitive is the *praxis* of life' (Heidegger 1961a, 557; 1991a, 72). In this sense of cognition the schematising *praxis* lies behind not just its modern-metaphysical determination as (representational) reason but also 'behind' beings as value-positing, as what and how beings are, as what is given and 'held'. Belief comprehended as the schematising *praxis* of life gets 'behind' beings to the giving of beings *as such*.

VI

The destruction of cognition therefore requires the chaos encountered in schematising *and* the schematising to be 'itself' per-ceived as something other than *already* (in) being. It thereby poses the *question* of being, which question cannot even occur in reason or in any other determination of valuation since 'morality' presupposes being(s), if not presence, as the condition of valuation. By that presupposition, valuation renounces the 'giving-itself' of the given in the 'pure encounter' of *chaos* (Heidegger 1961a, 564; 1991a, 78) whereby being is put into question. By contrast, the issue for extreme nihilism is an 'access' to the 'pure encounter' which does not renounce the question of being. For Heidegger, this access to the praxis of life is to be had in *how* things are given/open to living per-ception. The 'pure encounter' can be addressed through what is 'indicat[ed]' of it in and *as* perception for the living.[11] The advantage in considering the 'indication' of the 'pure encounter' is that by addressing it indirectly from *this* side of reason, the question of being is not thereby pre-empted or simply renounced. Accordingly, the question of being may be able to be accessed, and 'classical nihilism' affirmed, if it comes to be addressed through the trace (*Spur*) of the 'pure encounter' in the domain of valuations, which is to say, living cognition. Heidegger thus asks if the encounter is:

> named by [its] indication in that whereby it comes to be *brought* (*zugebracht*) to us, through sight, hearing, smell, taste, touch and every sort of feeling (*Gespür*)? One names the given the manifold of 'sensations'. Kant

even speaks of the '*throng* (*Gewühle*) of sensations'.

(Heidegger 1961a, 564; 1991a, 78)

It is feelings which 'indicate' the 'pure encounter' and so *pose* the question of being without addressing it as such *nor then renouncing it* by positing being as a value. The 'throng of sensations' which Kant remarks on, for example, allows access to the 'self-giving' in the encounter which constitutes the living being. It is:

> muddle, that which besets, keeps busy, concerns, floods and burrows through us – apparently more exactly one speaks [here] of 'our body' – not only in [this] instant of perception but continually and overall. For at once and together with the given of the named and cited outer sense, [there] urge and stir, drift and float, detain and push, tear and carry the 'feelings (*Empfindungen*)' of 'inner' sense which one establishes – again apparently more accurately and correctly – as body-states.
>
> (Heidegger 1961a, 564–5; 1991a, 78–9)

The body is the category of the 'throng of sensations'. By its 'inner' and 'outer' feelings the body indicates the chaos of the encounter 'behind' the 'belonging-together' of (what is then determined in the metaphysics of presence as) living per-ception and beings. The body is not then something that encounters a chaos merely *external* to it. It is 'in' the chaos, 'is' the chaos – or, at least, it is *of* chaos. Two points follow:

(i) since it is indicated by the (category of the) living body, the chaos of the opening 'is the nearest, is so near that it does not even stand "near" us in standing over against [us], but rather we ourselves are it – as bodily beings (*leiblichen Wesen*)' (Heidegger 1961a, 565; 1991a, 79);

(ii) since the 'opening' encounter of schematisation and chaos is the condition of per-ception, of valuation, and so of life as such, the body is no less a *condition* of the living, if it is to live; if, that is, life is to live:

> Life lives in that it bodies (*Das Leben lebt, indem es leibt*). We cognise by now perhaps very much about what we name the living body (*Leibkörper*) without our seriously having to consider what *bodying* (*Leiben*) is.... It is that *in which* [emph. add.] what we establish of the courses and appearances of the body of a living [thing] first comes to its own [proper] process-character. Perhaps bodying is initially an obscure term, but it names something which the cognition of the living *initially* and *constantly* experience, and must come to be held in consideration.
>
> (Heidegger 1961a, 565; 1991a, 79)

Bodying is obscure because it is dual: while it is that in which the 'process-character' of the living body comes to be (categorially) established, bodying is, on the other hand, chaotically 'behind' such categorisations and fixings. It is obscure to cognition since it is renounced as such by valuation. It is the obscurity in reason of the question of being, of the revaluation of valuation as such, and of the affirmative essence of nihilism for reason. But, for all its obscurity, it is bodying which indicates in turn the 'place' of valuation, and so life, that is to be determined anew according to the 'affirmative essence of nihilism'.

VII

Bodying is not then simply the self-determined individuation of a particular organic unity (which would be its cosmobiological meaning). The living body is rather the chaos that 'strikes' schematising in their co-constitutive 'pure encounter'. However, since chaos is that which 'cognition steps onto', it is not reducible to nor itself constituted by its encounter with schematising. Hence, as much as it is the condition for (the) living as such, chaos also *exceeds* the schematised chaos that is the living body. Chaos in general is the milieu in and through which life comes to be constituted:

> The bodying of life is nothing separated off by itself, encapsulated in the 'corporeal body' in which the living body can appear to us. Rather the living body is at once letting-and going-through (*Durchlaß und Durch-gang*). Through this living body streams a stream of life of which we only sense (*spüren*) a small and fleeting [part], and this again only in accord with the sort of receptivity of the momentary state of the living body. Our living body is involved (*sich...eingelassen*) in this stream of life. That chaos of the domain of feelings which we cognise as the domain of the living body is only *one section* out of the greater chaos that is the "world" itself.   (Heidegger 1961a, 565–6; 1991a, 79–80)

The living body is of the world as a differentiation of it *and* the world is of the living body as a 'greater chaos'.[12] Each is *of* the other. Two points serve to reconnect the argument back to Heidegger's principal concern:

(i) The world-chaos is beings as a whole. The living body determined through chaos thus involves in Heidegger's sense a *theological* deter-mination of living cognition, if not life.

(ii) With Heidegger, then, the essence of living cognition, through its destruction, is a differential constitution of the world-chaos: 'the cog-nised and cognisable is chaos, but we encounter it bodily; chaos is not first encountered in states of the body, but rather our body lives body-ing as a wave in the stream of chaos' (1939, 569/82). Such 'bodying' chaos is thus the *ontological* condition of life. It is the 'opening' of per-ception *and* beings.

It is in this way, in its specific bodying differentiation of a greater chaos, that the living body is 'in' life. Such is the ontogenesis of life in general and as such, which is to say the ontogenesis of the living *and* the world – which is/are always and only individuated worldly life, life in particular.[13] Bodying thus occasions a 'unity' of the differentiated life-world, of beings as such and as a whole, in which there 'comes historically the mastery of the "totality"'. *This* totality is not a morality, and so not a historical-metaphysical nihilism, but a totality in life-chaos without any supersensible condition. It therefore steps into a new, 'wholly other' condition of life *in* the actuality of bodying life.

It is with the ontotheology of *bodying* that the very 'place' of valuation as such 'comes to be determined anew'. What bodying suggests is that this 'place' is but the *praxis* of life, the practical need of life as bodying life in greater chaos: 'what Nietzsche calls "our practical need" stands in essential connection, even in essential unity, with the vitality of bodying life' (ibid., 570; 84), which is to say with chaos and the revaluation of values, with becoming. This is the primary condition and ontotheology for life in its essential becoming in classical nihilism. For Heidegger, bodying-becoming is is how 'Nietzsche conceives of his metaphysics as such'.

However: constituted as it is by the *praxis* of life, Heidegger remarks that bodying-becoming no less determines classical nihilism as a *restitution* of the unifying totality of the life-world. Moreover, since the totality of the life-world in becoming is comprehended on the basis of belief, which is to say *presence*, for Heidegger the ontotheology of bodying-becoming resituates a metaphysics of presence. The argument is that:

> 'life' is the name for *being*, and being means: presencing, insistence, constancy (*bestheen, Beständigkeit*), withstanding (*standhalten*) vanishing and atrophy. If life *is* then this chaotic bodying, if it ought *to be* properly a being, then it must at the same time and equally originarily (*gleichur-sprünglich*) matter to the living to stand up to the urge and the over-urge (*Drang und Überdrang*), so that, namely, this urge does not urge (*drängt*) it to sheer annihilation.   (ibid., 571; 85)

Heidegger then reverses the predication and says why even in the becoming of chaos ' "life" is the name for being' as constancy:

> This [annihilating urge] cannot occur since otherwise the urge urges itself away (*sich selbst verdrängt*) and so could never *be* an urge. Within its essence of the urge over-urging itself lies [an urge] suitable to it, that is, urging, that urges it to *not* succumb to the urging on (*Andrang*), but rather to *stand* in it, and if only so as *to be* able to be urgeable over itself and *itself* over-urge.   (ibid.)

That is, (i) life-chaos 'urges' the schematising of chaos. But, (ii) even as schematising in turn urges against the urging-on of chaos, without it (iii) chaos could not happen *as such*, as urging-on, nor then could life or the world happen. That is, without schematising becoming could not happen. Schematising is the *condition* of valuation *and* becoming. The place of valuation is thereby newly determined. It is the chaotic 'urge' of bodying life (and so of becoming) *as such*. Without the schematising of chaos *in* chaos there would be no differentiation of the greater chaos and no ontogenesis of life as such. Schematising is in this sense the *praxis* of life: *that* there is bodying life.

If schematising is, in short, the differentiation of chaos as bodying *and* (its) urging-on in their unity, then, with that, it is the differentiation – and differential unity – of life as being *and* becoming. But what is important to note here is that being as constancy and presence 'happens', comes to be 'executed', as the 'urge' of life, if and as life happens. Being *qua* presence arises, happens, from and *since* the schematising urge of life, of bodying differentiation in/of chaos.[14]

'Being' is not then presumed, as per Western metaphysical 'pre-decision', but comes to be and is comprehended *from* life as the differentiation of chaos. And since this differentiation – being – is the condition of life as such, of (the) living in its actuality and vitality/essence, Heidegger further notes: '[t]he vitality of a living [thing] does not stop with this delimiting circumscription but rather constantly begins out of it' (ibid., 573; 86).

Heidegger can then elucidate the essential sense of the 'opening' that lies behind (and is renounced by) the metaphysics of presence, be it in the historical-metaphysical designation of per-ception *and* beings, or, in modernity, as reason. In its essence as the *praxis* of life,

> it is not reason itself, not its essence, that develops itself first out of the need of reigning over chaos (*Chaosbewältigung*), but rather that it is *in itself* [emph. add.] already chaos-per-ception (*Chaos-Vernehmung*), in so far as the wild urging-on only comes to be per-ceptual in view of order and constancy and, therefore, as the thus and thus urgent (*Bedrängendes*) [chaos] implies and demands this or that making-firm, this or that schema-forming (*Schemabildung*). (ibid., 576; 88)

In its essence, then, reason is a differentiation of chaos and the urge to differentiate the urging chaos, to *be*. For the human in its modern metaphysical essence/determination, it is life as such, living. Reason – which is essentially practical reason (ibid., 575; 88f.) – lets chaos be 'felt' and per-ceived as chaos, felt and per-ceived by a (human) body, as being, as a (counter-)urge to chaos. Reason is in short the (modern-metaphysical-anthropic) mode of bodying, which only 'shows itself' as such upon the historical occurrence of Nietzsche's classical nihilism. Reason shows itself there as the differentiation of chaos, which Nietzsche calls 'belief'.

VIII

In 1940, Heidegger identifies this revaluation of reason, and the correlative revaluation of the human as the *animal rationale*, as an ontotheology of bodying-becoming. Such an ontotheology leads to the affirmation of the *Übermensch* which:

negates the previous essence of the human nihilistically. Its negation steps upon the distinction of the human, reason. [...] In the nihilistic interpretation of metaphysics and its history, thinking, that is, reason, appears as the ground and guiding measure for the imposition of values. [...] The nihilistic negation of reason does not however eliminate thinking (*ratio*) but rather takes it to be in the service of animality (*animalitas*).

Only, animality is also likewise and already overturned. It no longer obtains as mere sensuality and as the basest in the human. Animality is the bodying-body. This latter name names the distinctive unity of the shaping mastery of all drives, urges, passions that will life itself. Animality lives, as it bodies, in that it is in the mode of [the urge to constancy].

[...] Reason is only a living [reason] as bodying reason. [...] The previously metaphysical essential distinction of the human, rationality, comes to be transposed to animality in the sense of bodying.

(Heidegger 1961b, 293–5; 1991a, 217–18)

What is revalued in *classical* nihilism beyond its determinations in historical-metaphysical nihilism is the essential characterisation of the human. However, the human is now revalued as a bodying-becoming, as an animality that is itself 'overturned' from its metaphysical sense (for example, as somehow in contrast to the human). Animality thus *fulfils* classical nihilism's essential re-placement of the historical-metaphysical determinations of the human.

Heidegger's own exposition of reason in the 'affirmative essence of nihilism' can not be fully developed here for want of space. The following discussion is directed only towards establishing a very partial clarification of Heidegger's interpretation of reason upon the affirmation of the 'extreme' stage of its destruction/revaluation as animality. For this interpretation, Heidegger initially emphasises not the historical-metaphysical comprehension of reason but rather, assuming the accomplishment of classical nihilism, the 'bodily', per-ceptual urge of schematising. This urge is elaborated by giving the 'case' of a tree. Despite changes and 'diverse characteristics' of "objective" conditions such as atmosphere, light, season, and so on, or of "subjective" conditions such as 'the changing perspective of perception', the tree is nonetheless 'yet always this "same tree"' (Heidegger 1961a, 583; 1991a, 95). That is, the tree 'subsists' or perdures, is nonetheless constant, through the always different external and internal 'direct' sensations and perceptual cogitions of it. As the constancy in the per-ceptual chaos, the tree in *its* 'sameness' is for Heidegger not an act of synthesis subsequent to its cognitions but rather the schematising 'urge' that is called reason:

It *is* the 'same', not subsequently (*nachträglich*), in that we establish [this] on the grounds of afterwards adding comparisons (*Vergleichungen*), such that it was after all the 'same' tree, but rather the other way around: our coming-to (*Zukommen*) the tree always already looks out for the 'same'. Not as though the change of aspects escapes us. On the contrary, only if we posit in advance over (*über... hinweg*) the respective diversity of the self-givens such a 'same', that is, a selfsame (*Selbiges*), which is not in any case the at hand self-giving given, are we able to experience the magic of the change of aspects.   (ibid.)[15]

The crucial point here for Heidegger is the co-eval bodying of the tree (a being) *and* its per-ception, which is the 'open' from which the experience arises. Though this is but the differential bodying of the standing-urge in the urge of chaos, the principal point now is Heidegger's characterisation of the 'place' and modality of the 'same':

This positing of a 'same' is a fiction and a sealing-out (*Erdichten und Ausdichten*). In order to determine and think the tree in its each case directly given appearance its selfsameness must have come to be fictioned (*gedichtet*) beforehand. This free forward-positing (*Vorweg-setzen*) of a self-same, that is, of selfsameness, this fictioning character is the essence of reason and thought.   (Heidegger 1961a, 583; 1991a, 95)

That is, reason's always already or forward positing of constancies and schemata in chaos – the 'sameness' of the being and its per-ception – is, in Heidegger's terms (partially adopted from Nietzsche), a fictioning. For Heidegger, then, this 'coming-to' indicates that the essential 'pure encounter' of schematising and chaos is characterised by fictioning. Though it is the body-ing life of the human as *animal rationale*, its ontogenesis and condition, this fictioning is no less the schematising 'urge' of bodying life as such. Hence, the essence and ontogenesis of life and being is a 'forward positing' fiction-ing. This fictioning lies 'behind' the historical-metaphysical determination of the essence and ontogenesis of life, a determination to which cosmobio-logy adheres. Moreover, since the essence and ontogenesis of life are *them-selves* characterised in this way, they too are *fictional*. That is, in its genesis and essence, life and nihilism (and being) happen as and by an *ontopoiesis*.[16] The ontopoiesis of the same, of chaotic bodying, is not at hand (it is not of 'the throng of sensations') nor, in its extreme nihilism, is it an ideal (it is not valuation). It is, Heidegger writes, 'over' the self-giving of the 'pure encoun-ter'.

IX

Heidegger's own determination of the 'place' that lies 'over' the self-giving chaos, which is to be 'determined anew' upon classical nihilism, cannot be taken up here. Rather, the two express 'manifestations' of the ontopoietic condition of life as such which bracket the metaphysical history of nihilism will be highlighted. The first is the historical-metaphysical occasion in which it is the idea for Plato and, in its modern variant, the ' "formative (*bildende*)" ' transcendental imagination of Kant and also German Idealism. The second is Nietzsche's classical nihilism as it is interpreted in the exposition above.

The former manifestation of fictioning has been remarked several times above as the world-historical occurrence and process of nihilism. But it can now also be added that with respect to the ontopoietic essence of life, the specificity of world-historical nihilism is that ontopoiesis is *itself* fictioned as a constant. In the consequent 'self-sameness' of ontopoiesis as a value, and so as *a* being, historical-metaphysical nihilism 'places' ontopoiesis 'above' beings, as always already ahead of – that is, prior to – the 'pure encounter' in chaos. Value and being are then held as the *anterior*, higher essence of ontopoiesis against which ontopoietic bodying-becoming is comparatively inconstant and derivative (though the latter is in fact and in essence the condition of the former). Historical-metaphysical nihilism is thus inaugurated with, and it inaugurates, the 'holding' of the ontopoiesis of life and being as a *transcendental* condition, essence, truth and value of life and being.

On the other hand, Nietzsche's classical nihilism exposes the ontogenesis of life and being as *bodying-becoming* as such. For Heidegger, however, it remains entirely congruent to historical-metaphysical nihilism since Nietzsche too 'must firmly hold to the fictioning character of reason, – that is, to the pre-forming and fore-stabilising (*voraus-beständigen*) character of the determinations of being' (Heidegger 1961a, 586; 1991a, 97): that is, even Nietzsche's determination of bodying is within the metaphysics of presence. However, since fictioning is the 'affirmation of the essence of nihilism' which lies *behind* its historical-metaphysical manifestations, Heidegger goes on to remark that for 'the determination of the *provenance* (*Herkunft*) of this fictioning, pre-forming character differs for Plato and Nietzsche. For Nietzsche, this character of reason is given *with* [emph. add.] the execution of life – with praxis' (ibid.) rather than being itself fictioned as a transcendental value 'above' life's praxis. With Nietzsche the ontopoietic essence of life and reason is therefore *immanent* to life in its actuality. Having noted this difference between Nietzsche and 'Platonic doctrine', Heidegger nonetheless proposes that in affirming classical nihilism Nietzsche assumes and extenuates the *modern* metaphysical determination of life: 'life, however, Nietzsche takes as that which is in the power (*mächting*) of the human itself, installed (*gestellt*) upon itself' (ibid.).

Heidegger's interpretation of Nietzsche here needs special emphasis since it is crucial to the entire sense of what is *in fact* affirmed (rather than asserted) of nihilism and, at once, of *what* and *how* life is thus comprehended. The interpretation here rests on the determination of the ontogenesis of reason as animality, which is also the *ontotheology* of classical nihilism. For Heidegger, this end of metaphysics depends on and *derives from* the modern metaphysical determination of the essence of the human as reason (Heidegger 1961b, 295–304; 1991a, 218–27). As such, it is the 'extreme point' of metaphysics, as Heidegger elaborates in the 1940 overview:

> [o]nly if reason [and thus, in modern metaphysics, the human] unfolds metaphysically as unconditional subjectivity and therewith as the being of beings does the overturning of the previous pre-eminence of reason [and so the human] to the pre-eminence of animality of itself become unconditional, that is, nihilistic. The nihilistic negation of the metaphysical *pre-eminence* of unconditional reason [of the human], of being thus determined – and not its full removal – is the affirmation of the unconditional role of the body as the place of command (*Befehlstelle*) of all world interpretation. (ibid., 300; 223)

Insofar as animality is the unifying 'totality' of the ontopoiesis and ontotheology of life, and is thus the nihilistic negation of the pre-eminence of reason, animality is still determined in the 'place' of historical-metaphysical nihilism, valuation, presence. The place itself is not itself determined anew but only re-placed by an immanentism that is predicated on the 'pre-eminence' of the human. The animality characterising classical nihilism thereby *affirms* the pre-eminence of the human. Animality is then (and however much it may assert or be directed otherwise) an anthropocentrism.

Correlatively, with classical nihilism the human comes to be the 'place of command' over life, where life, as the differentiation of chaotic bodying, is now no less the world. Heidegger remarks in the 1939 lecture course that 'for Nietzsche human life is *only* [emph. add.] a metaphysical point of life in the sense of the "world" ' (Heidegger 1961a, 586; 1991a, 97). Upon this interpretation, it then (famously) follows that Nietzsche's:

> doctrine of the schemata returns to Plato's doctrine of ideas so closely that it is only a determinate sort of overturning (*Umkehrung* ['reversal']) of the latter, that is, it is identical to it in its *essence*. (ibid., 586; 97)

Despite 'overturning' Platonic doctrine, Nietzsche's classical nihilism is for Heidegger yet identical to it in essence since it only duplicates the primarily anthropic determination of life and being. This overturning of reason is how Heidegger interprets the 'humanisation' of which Nietzsche speaks (Heidegger 1961b, 307; 1991a, 229), one which is nonetheless a 'dehumanisation' of life and beings in terms of historical metaphysics in that it 'frees beings from the value-positing of previous human[ity]' towards the onto-theology and -poiesis of animality (ibid.). So comprehended, and even in its dehumanisation, the immanentist bio-ontopoiesis and ontotheology of animality is a (covert) anthropocentric metaphysics.

X

This (partial) conclusion to Heidegger's interpretation of Nietzsche's 'classical nihilism' as the 'end of metaphysics' allows Heidegger to gauge the significance of its historical realisations, most notably Nazism. In the first instance, the affirmation of life as ontopoiesis means for Heidegger that Nietzsche does not think life and the world cosmobiologically but metaphysically. Nietzsche's classical nihilsm 'bring[s] out the complete character of life as a fictioning-commanding' and, with that, 'something else' is to be heard in the word 'biological' than the metaphysical determination of life – 'namely, what *shows* (*zeigt*) the essential traits of fictioning and commanding' (Heidegger 1961a, 615; 1991a, 122). That is, for Heidegger, Nietzsche does not consider life in its bodily actuality, the biological, as the essential condition or determination of life. It is only a 'formal indication' of the *ontopoietic* essence of life as animality. In short, for Heidegger, Nietzsche:

> does *not* think the biological, which is to say, the essence of (the) living, at all biologically. [O]n the contrary, he inclines towards interpreting the biological in the proper and strict sense – vegetality and animalism – *nonbiogically*, that is, *primarily humanly* [emph. add.].   (ibid.)

It is precisely this affirmation of bio-onto*poiesis* that forces a rejection of the Nazi comprehension of Nietzsche as advocating a biologism. With this delegitimisation Heidegger detaches his own thinking (of the metaphysics of presence) and affirmations from collusion with or support of the dominant philosophical espousals of Nazism. At the same time, Nazism could then be characterised as a misapprehension of classical nihilism as a historical-metaphysical nihilism of reason.

But there is an inherent complexity in Heidegger's moves here with respect to Nazism. For as much as the determination of animality in classical nihilism delegitimises the appropriation of Nietzsche's thinking by Nazism, animality is also precisely how, for Heidegger, Nietzsche consolidates the ontotheological unifying totality of modern metaphysics. That is, with the 'primarily human' interpretation of life as such, Nietzsche *affirms* too the fate of modernity as it is realised, most blatantly and at the time of Heidegger's writing, by the ideologies and efficiencies of Nazism:

[t]he classical in this self-stamping of the human which takes the human itself in hand consists in the simple rigor of simplification of all things and humans upon the unity of unconditional empowering *for mastery over the Earth*. The conditions of this mastery, that is, all values, come to be posited and developed through a full-standing 'machinisation' of things and through the breeding of the human.

(Heidegger 1961b, 308; 1991a, 230)

This constitution of the world *and* the human as a generalised bio-ontopoiesis (of a life that is more generalised and differentiated than it is determined by cosmobiology, as, for example, the organic) is what Heidegger calls 'machinisation'. It is congruent to the animality characterising classical nihilism. Machinisation thereby determines life and being to be constituted by a *praxis* of constancy that is itself inherently anthropic. Which is to say that machinisation too is an anthropocentrism.

Heidegger elaborates the actualisation of the 'simplifying' and unifying-total onto-theology and -poiesis of machinisation in the instance of the human:

[m]achinisation makes possible a force-saving, that is, at once force-storing, always everywhere overseeable ministration of beings. [...] The breeding of humans... is the storing up and purification of force (*Kräfte*) in the univocity of rigorously masterable 'automatism' of all dealings (*Handlung*). Only where the unconditional subjectivity of [classical nihilism's animality] comes to be the truth of beings as a whole is the *principle* of a directive (*Einrichtung*) of racial breeding possible, metaphysically possible, that is, not merely from self growing racial formation but rather from the self-knowing *thought* of race. That is, the principle is metaphysically neccesary. Just as much as [animality] is ontologically rather than biologically thought, even more does Nietzsche's racial thought have a metaphysical rather than biologistic sense.

(Heidegger 1961b, 309; 1991a, 210–11)

This is where the full complexity of Heidegger's appraisal of Nazism and machinisation can be registered. For though Nazism can make no valid avowal to Nietzsche's (or Heidegger's) thinking on the presumption of its biologism, it is nonetheless Nietzsche's anthropic determination of life *and* world as machinisation that in fact lends it to the racial ideologies of Nazism. And it does not just support such ideologies; worse still, it enables them by affirming the essence of classical nihilism to be a bio-ontopoiesis. It affirms the essence of nihilism *and* life to be an (anthropic) metaphysics of presence.[17]

If, then, a metaphysical thinking does not suffice to detach Nietzsche from Nazism but rather, on the contrary *gives* the principle for its racial policies, then neither does it suffice for Heidegger to avow a metaphysical thinking of ontotheology in order to detach himself *simply* from an incipient collusion with Nazism. And neither does it suffice to detach Heidegger's own affirmations from anthropic machinisation. Insofar as Heidegger avows the 'fictioning' – or, as Krell translates it, 'poetising' – 'essence of reason'[18] and thereby avows the essential ontopoiesis of being (by the destruction of historical-metaphysical nihilism, for example), so the anthropic metaphysics of machinisation is also affirmed *in a way* (Heidegger 1961b, 330–1; 1991a, 248–9). This is not a matter of choice for Heidegger. Upon the end of metaphysics, upon the assumption of classical nihilism, machinisation/animality is 'metaphysically necessary'. Nazism is, for Heidegger, but a historical instance of this metaphysical necessity which Heidegger takes Nietzsche to be propounding.

XI

For *Heidegger*, however, assuming classical nihilism need not lead directly or *simply* to affirming machinisation/animality. It need not if, as Heidegger proposes (following Kant and Schelling rather than Nietzsche), the essence of ontopoiesis is not itself immanent to bodying (as with animality) but is rather that which is 'in itself *fictioning*', namely, *freedom* (Heidegger 1961a, 611; 1991a, 119). Though there is not the space here to follow through Heidegger's affirmation of freedom,[19] the following can be noted: if the essence of ontopoiesis is freedom rather than bodying, the principle of racial breeding of humans in anthropic machinisation no longer has the character of a metaphysical *necessity*. Rather, machinisation indicates that the 'affirmative essence of nihilism' is freedom, a freeing *for* the 'new freedom in the sense of the self-legislation of humanity' (Heidegger 1961b, 319–22; 1991a, 239–41). 'Freedom' in this sense is neither a transcendental nor immanent condition of bodying, life and being: it is the fictioning 'above' the actuality of chaotic bodying; it is the 'command' of the differentiating counter-urge of chaos.

For Heidegger, then, the realisation of the 'affirmative essence of nihilism' as machinisation/animality has a dual and complex character. As much as it occludes the *free* commanding essence of (historical-metaphysical or classical) nihilism and leads to the principle of the racial breeding of humans, classical nihilism nonetheless indicates and *itself affirms* the ontopoiesis of life and being, be it as the *bio*-onto-poiesis and -theology of machinisation/animality. In other words, anthropic machinisation/animality indicates for the first time the free fictioning essence of being as such, beyond its historical-metaphysical valuation. And it does so *through* animality/machinisation. Classical nihilism thereby gives access to the free commanding essence of being as such. It is an 'indication' to how the free essence of being 'shows itself in the light' (Heidegger 1961b, 324–5; 1991a, 243–4).

Historically and essentially, then, to affirm the free fictioning essence of ontopoiesis Heidegger must at once affirm and, within that affirmation of its essence, *not* affirm 'life in the power of the human installed (*gestellt*) upon itself'.[20] Life *qua* classical nihilism is not to be affirmed *in fact*, for itself (as animality/machinisation), but rather in its essence, for what it brings to light: the anthropic essence and ontotheology of ontopoiesis in its freedom.[21]

XII

However, since the essence of ontopoiesis only comes to light in its essential freedom with the historical-metaphysical realisation of classical nihilism, the 'place' of (re)valuation which is determined anew by freedom is no less anthropically situated than the animality which it is to counterpoint. It follows that the sense and historical actualisation of life as such upon the end of metaphysics as either animality *or* freedom is not determined by whether the essence of life and being is itself more or less anthropically conditioned. Anthropism is not itself at issue unless it is the *fictioning* essence of life, that is, the onto*poiesis* of being, that is in question. Specifically, the issue of anthropism cannot be raised in classical nihilism since it assumes fictioning as the essential condition of life. More generally, however, anthropism is not at issue when the essence of being is held to be an ontopoiesis.

The *issue* of anthropism is, then, one of a discrepancy in the determination and conditions of life as a generalised onto*poiesis* (the 'fictioning' essence of urging chaos) or as a generalised biocosmo*genesis* (its differential bodying-becoming). With Heidegger, the two are identified through 'extreme nihilism', which affirms and makes possible the *metaphysical* principle of racial breeding *as well as* the realisation of a 'new freedom' of being. This identification is a necessity if the essence (of the historicity) of life and being *is* ontopoietic. However: a discrepancy between biocosmogenesis and ontopoiesis, if there is one, would indicate an occurrence and actualisation of life as such whose condition would *not* be fictioning, free or otherwise, nor *principally anthropic*.

We close the present discussion by putting the anthropic assumption of the essence of being – ontopoiesis – into relief. This is proposed from the vantage of the divergence between biocosmogenesis and ontopoiesis, a divergence which is at present only hypothetical:

1 The discrepancy between biocosmogenesis in general and onto*poiesis* in general would suggest that there is no '*necessity*' for the determination and affirmation of the life-world as anthropic machinisation, *however* that affirmation may then be directed. The irreducibility of biocosmogenesis to ontopoiesis would disestablish the necessity of classical nihilism not

because it directly questions the importance of the human as the new 'place' of (re)valuation, but rather because it deposes the entire notion of a historical-metaphysical nihilism as such (of which the anthropism of classical nihilism, and the concomitant 'end of metaphysics' is the 'accomplishment'). In other words, if there is such a discrepancy, the essence of being and life could be characterised by *neither* animality/ machinisation *nor* freedom – and only because differential bodying as the condition of life could not then be at all characterised as a fictioning. The argument here passes through several points discussed above: Heidegger's proposal that the anthropocentric actualisation of life (that is, ontopoiesis as such) is the essence of life in general for Nietzsche is part of the interpretation postulating Nietzsche to presume the (attenuated) trancendental onto-theology and -poiesis which 'characterises' Western metaphysics. In other words, Nietzsche adheres to Platonic doctrine. Accordingly, in the order of *historical* determination, Heidegger interprets Nietzsche to 'overturn' Plato's doctrine. But, precisely, as Heidegger suggests by the destruction of metaphysics, Nietzsche does not. Rather, Nietzsche's destruction of the essence of life, cognition and reason *in Heidegger's interpretation* suggests that Plato's *historically* 'precedent' determination of the essence of life and being is not its *essential* determination. In fact and essentially, *with* Heidegger it is *Nietzsche's* ontotheology of life which is the condition for the world-historical occurrence of nihilism, and hence for Plato's determination of the 'place' of valuation. The situation is then complicated: it is only by subjugating the *essential* constitution of life in its occurrence and actuality (namely, the differential bodying of chaos) to its *historical*-metaphysical determinations (reason in modern metaphysics) that the occurrence and process of nihilism can be itself constituted. That is, nihilism is itself a thought and a 'process' that *follows upon* the specific historical-metaphysical subsumption of biocosmogenesis in ontopoiesis. Or, in terms of world-history, nihilism follows only upon the *assumption* of a quasi-rational ontotheological determination of biocosmogenesis.[22]

2   In other words, the history of nihilism, the (so-said) history of the West together with its metaphysical 'ground occurrence', is itself then a metaphysical ratiocinative fantasm (and no less actual for that). It is an active nihilism in that reason is taken (surreptitiously by Heidegger) to be the primary (and 'highest') onto-poietic actualisation of life as such, even though Heidegger's interpretation need not so determine it (at least, not without giving up the thought of nihilism[23]). It can then be seen that if biocosmogenesis is irreducibe to ontopoiesis but is nonetheless determined from the latter, nihilism *as such* is an attenuation of 'Platonic doctrine'. This is so even *for* Heidegger and the 'new freedom' which is 'indicated' by animality. What is important in this deduction is that nihilism is not an essential attenuation and determination of metaphy-

sics, but a *historical* one. Even in the 'affirmative essence' of the free 'opening' of its futurity, then, nihilism is a historicism.[24] It follows that the anthropism which determines biocosmogenesis to be an ontopoiesis and which, in turn, makes 'possible' the principle of the racial breeding of humans (amongst other manifestations of animality and machinisation in their unicity), is also constituted by a historicism.

3 What then becomes crucial is an investigation as to *whether* biocosmogenesis is irreducible to ontopoiesis or not. For, without the fantasmatic-historical subsumption of the former by the latter, the concomitant fantasm of an onto-theology (in Heidegger's sense) of life, together with its correlative history and process, nihilism, collapses as a thought and as an actuality. As then do the 'unifying totalities' of immanentist animality (the unifying total 'overturning' of *reason*) and machinisation (the consequent anthropic metaphysics).

But this is again only to beg the question as to *whether* there is a discrepancy between ontopoiesis and a generalised cosmobiogenesis. Such a determination cannot be gauged either by metaphysical thought alone (be it transcendentalist or immanentist) or by biology alone. It is rather a discrepancy in and between both the biological and quasi-metaphysical (which is also to say cosmobiological) determinations of life and chaos. The clarification needed here therefore requires further philosophical and scientific research as to what and how biogenesis occurs.

Notes

1 For an extended historically contextual discussion of philosophy in Nazi Germany, see Sluga (1993, esp. Ch. 2) which is partly devoted to Nietzsche's fate in this period as a proponent of a biologico-metaphysical determination of nationalism *and* inter-nationalism. These apparently incongruous comprehensions reflect what is salutary in Sluga's book: that Nazism was not at all a coherent or homogeneous politics, power or thinking but rather riven with conflictual ambitions which were manifest in the academic and institutional struggles over the teaching, doctrine and place of philosophy.

2 These do not necessarily co-incide with Heidegger's own version of what was involved in the affiliation *and* disaffiliation with the Nazi party, namely, with respect to the latter, that 'in 1933–34 [Heidegger] affirmed the social and the national (not the National Socialistic) and negated the spiritual and metaphysical foundations [determined] through the biologism of Party doctrine, since the social and the national, as [Heidegger] saw it, were not *essentially* [emph. add.] tied to the biological-racial world-view' (Heidegger 1991b, 552–3).

3 Standard translations have been used, though sometimes in a modifed form, in this text.

4 On this, see Haar (1993, 1994) and, more convincingly, Müller-Lauter (1974a, 1974b and, especially in this context, 1981/82).

5 There are two specific inter-related contexts for Heidegger's critique of 'preservation' here. Firstly, as stated, Darwinian theory understood as the preservation of

inherited traits in the general 'struggle' of the living. Although this is only a one-sided portrayal of Darwin's niche-adaptation theory, it is a dominant line of Darwinism, proposed *against* preformationism, which can be tracked back via Adam Smith to Hobbesian and Newtonian mechanist views of natural processes. It can be tracked forward into the early part of the twentieth century through the statistically organised response of Galton amongst others to the 'threat' of continuous variation of inherited traits, namely: eugenics (Depew and Weber 1995). That Darwin(ism) may not in fact propose 'preservation' as a condition for the maintenance of the living but rather the contrary to preservation is not the issue here. The second and historically more immediate context for the notion of 'preservation' is Hitler's declaration that '[t]he new State knows no other task than the fulfillment of the conditions necessary for the preservation of the people' (cited in Agamben 1998, Ch. 4 §4.2). This statement is presented by Agamben in a citation from Verschuer's tract *Rassenhygiene als Wissenschaft und Staatsaufgabe* (1936) in which it is appended by the comment: 'These words of the Führer mean that every political act of the national Socialist state serves the life of the people. We know today that the life of the people is only secured if the racial traits and hereditary health of the body of the people are preserved' (ibid.). If Heidegger's remarks can readily be taken to be directed *against* the co-determination of *statism* and life as such (which is what is missed by Agamben's Levinasian critique of Heidegger a few pages later), then these remarks are also counter to the 'totalitarianism' which Agamben finds in Verschuer's comments, that '[t]he totalitarianism of our century has its ground in this dynamic identity of life and politics, without which it remains incomprehensible' (ibid.). Agamben proposes this 'dynamic identity' to be at least characteristic of political organisation in the post-Classical West.

6   A convincing refutation of Heidegger's argument that sciences themselves do not think their metaphysical conditions can not be undertaken here. Suffice it to say that with respect to biology the metaphysical 'stability' of life *as such* is not *simply* taken for granted by recent work in theoretical biology and research in artificial life. The issue of what and how life, if not the living, is constituted is central to these disciplines. In this regard, for four quite distinct if not divergent examples, cf. Kauffman (1993), Rosen (1985), Maturana and Varela (1980), and Langton (1991).

7   Biologism of course persists today, most generally in the name of social or neo-Darwinism. A glaring contemporary example of the 'total ignorance' of which Heidegger speaks is provided by Dawkins (1989), specifically in the notion of the *meme* as a re-iteration of something like genetic transmission between phenotypes or 'replicators' irrespective of the order of biological or cultural complexity.

8   'Destruction' here is to be taken in the technical sense which Heidegger attributes to it: it is an interpretative repetition of historical-metaphysics by which, as Heidegger remarks in §6 of *Being and Time*, the received content or 'the hardened tradition' of historical-metaphysics is thus undone so that 'those originary experiences of the first and therewith guiding determinations of being come to be won' (Heidegger 1927; 1962, H22).

9   The 'open' discussed here is a constant thematic interest from one end of Heidegger's thinking to the other. In *Being and Time*, it is the (ante-predicative) 'existential-hermeneutical "as"' of Dasein's 'concernful understanding' (Heidegger 1927; 1962, §31–3, esp. H 158). The open is Dasein's 'movement of caring'. Kisiel notes, in terms whose importance will become clearer as the main text progresses, that even in the destruction of Aristotle from 1922, Heidegger thinks of the hermeneutic 'as' as the 'way the world has already been interpreted [which] is factically the

interpretation in which life stands' such that 'the world is in and for life' (Kisiel 1993, 256). In 1936 the open is called the *Ereignis*, and in 1946 it is explictly thematised by Heidegger as the 'essence of the human', 'insofar as the human is the ek-sisting one' (Heidegger 1976, 180; 1998, 266). Therafter the open is addressed by Heidegger as the sending or gift of being. The present discussion is directed to examining the limits of the determination of the 'open' precisely when it moves from being an issue of the *Daseinsanalytik* to the essence of (human) life as such for Heidegger.

10 Traditionally, this 'encountered' which is schematised would be designated matter. But, as will be seen, and despite Heidegger's rather hasty formulation just cited in the main text here, the schematising 'imposition' in and of chaos is anterior to the form-matter couplet in that the schematisation of chaos is the condition for the hylomorphic model to be able to be internally demarcated in the first instance.

11 Kisiel (1993) shows the methodological importance of 'formal indication' to Heidegger's early and subsequent destructions of not only historical-metaphysics but also, as in the main discussion here, of facticity. (*Being and Time* is, summarily, the destruction of facticity in that it takes the latter as a 'formal indication' of the question of being for Dasein).

12 As Heidegger points out in the vicinity of this argument, the living being is then something like Leibniz's 'metaphysical points' or monads, 'in which the whole world gather and shows itself in the bounded luminosity of a particular perspective' (Heidegger 1961a, 569; 1991a, 82). Through Leibniz, and for all the evident divergence, Heidegger's determination of the living as a differentiation of chaos (in both senses of the genitive) can be compared with Deleuze–Guattari's (generalisation of Simondon's) critique of the hylomorphic model and dynamic individuation. The latter critique is carried out principally in the notions of 'machinic flow' (Deleuze and Guattari 1972, 43–50; 1983, 36–41), haecceity (Deleuze and Guattari 1980, esp. Chs. 10 and 12), and the functive of chaos (Deleuze and Guattari 1991). Other divergences notwithstanding, the correspondence between what Heidegger is proposing in these lectures and Deleuze's reading of Nietzsche is also suggestive, especially if what Heidegger here calls chaos is instead comprehended as a multiplicity of forces (Deleuze 1962, Ch. 2) and if, as for both Deleuze–Guattari (1981, 209/171) and Heidegger (as will be seen later in the main text in this volume), differentiation is to be assumed and directed along an orientation *counter* to biotic animality. There is space here only to mention that Whitehead's 'philosophy of the organism' and Bergson's philosophy of life are also suggestively comparable to Heidegger's thinking of 'bodying'.

13 The 'artificiality' of Artificial Life research is determined by the generalised and abstract because dis-embodied organisation of dynamic systems. Such systems satisfy other formal criteria for life as the *maintenance* of an individuated system at a variety of levels of complexity and processual determinants. These are principally neo-Darwinian criteria of self-reproduction and adaptation. For example, Langton's influential essay proposes that 'a properly organised set of artificial [meaning electrocomputational] primitives carrying out the same functional roles as the biomolecules in natural living systems will support a process that will be "alive" in the same way that natural organisms are alive. Artificial Life will therefore be *genuine* life – it will simply be made of different stuff than the life that has evolved here on Earth' (Langton 1996, 69). However, the argument of the main text here suggests that it is precisely in assuming life to be only a system of

formal relations and productions corresponding to neo-Darwinian criteria for biotic life, and in thus stipulating abstract determinations as the primary conditions for life (that is, values which 'emerge' and are computationally maintained), that Langton recovers a historical-metaphysical determination of life as such. This unilateral stress on the *principally* formal ontogeny of life is precisely what is put into destruction by Heidegger's interpretation of life in its actuality for Nietzsche as bodying-becoming.

14   Under the name of maintained organisation, constancy is a crucial determination for ontogeny in contemporary theoretical biology too, whether it is that of a complex self-organisation of metabolic processes on the 'edge' of a chaotic distribution of molecular interaction (Kauffman 1993), or that of unified relational dynamic structures at whatever register of actuality and order of complexity (Maturana and Varela 1980), or (following Prigogine amongst others) that of thermodynamically localised 'far-from-equilibrium dissipative structures' (Schneider and Kay 1995). As suggested in n.15 above, constancy is also a central criteria for the determination of the living in some Artificial Life theory. In this context, where it is the metaphysicality of such theories of ontogeny which is at issue, it is important to distinguish those determinations of ontogeny which are principally formal from those which, as Heidegger proposes, are concerned with life *in its actuality*. Such a critical discrimination of the literature is beyond the scope of the present discussion.

15   We leave aside the issue of time and temporality which is crucial to the mediation of the diversity and 'sameness' of the 'change of aspects' in their synthesis as the tree. It will be only suggested here that the 'forward-positing' sameness Heidegger is discussing here is formally close to Dasein's originary temporal anticipation as elaborated in *Being and Time* (Heidegger 1927; 1962, §65), not least in that temporality is there stated to be 'the originary unity of the structure of care' (1927; 1962, H327) which, as suggested in n.9 above, is but the 'open' of Dasein's hermeneutic 'as'. The full elaboration of this hypothetical unicity of the 'forward-positing' synthesis of the 'same' and anticipation as the primal mode of temporality would have to go through Heidegger's destruction of Kant's first *Critique*, showing how the synthesising power of the transcendental imagination is but the 'original temporality' of finite (human) reason (see Heidegger 1973; 1990).

16   The schematising *praxis* of life can be specifically categorised as an onto*poiesis* since its fictioning is characterised by a *finality* (Heidegger 1961a, 588–9; 1991a, 98–100). Briefly, since the essential condition of bodying, beings and per-ception depends on the schematising 'making-firm in advance' of chaos, the latter is always fictioned in 'prospect of constancy'. This is the *'forward*-positing' of a self-same by the *praxis* of life. In terms of Aristotle's categories of coming to be, bodying is thus a *poiesis*. What the destruction of reason makes clear, moreover, is that finality is not one category amongst amongst others *in* reason but rather 'characterises the essence of reason to the ground'. Accordingly, Heidegger cites Nietzsche's statement that 'finality is an effect not a cause': it is an 'effect' of the fact that there is life and being.

17   But since classical nihilism is a 'total' determination of modernity, machinisation/animality does not just characterise Nazism. In particular, Heidegger castigates both America and the USSR in precisely these terms (1953, 28–9; 1959, 37–9). As well as the global anthropic organisation of 'monsters of energy' such as the Rhine dam and atomic power on which Heidegger remarks elsewhere (see Heidegger

1954, 22–4; 1977, 14–16), the unicity of machinisation/animality can also readily be argued to characterise developments in genetic modification, for example. However, for Heidegger Nazism is crucial to future determinations of the unifying totality of being in that its appeal to national Germanic roots indicates another manifestation of ontopoiesis to the one which simply assumes and promotes the (de)humanisation of modern metaphysics. This national-*political* counter determination of ontopoiesis is principally Germanic since the free essence of ontopoiesis is for Heidegger literally a *geo*-historical Euro*centric* realisation (1942, 126–8; 1992, 85–7).

18 As becomes more prevalent from the 1940s onwards and comes to dominate Heidegger's publication record from the late 1950s, particularly through the interpretations of Hölderlin, Trakl and Hebel and the reflections on language.

19 A fuller exposition of 'freedom' in Heidegger's philosophical career would have to pay particular attention to the lecture courses on freedom in Kant's First *Critique* (Heidegger 1988a) and on Schelling (Heidegger 1971).

20 Four standard *topoi* of the Heidegger literature, which are to be found in their unicity in the 1954 essay devoted to the essence of technics, can be taken up at this point: (i) the unifying totality of machinisation of classical nihilism is what Heidegger later calls the *Ge-stell* of modern techincs (Heidegger 1954, 28; 1977, 20); (ii) if classical nihilism is in essence the free fictioning essence of ontopoiesis but is in actuality technical machinisation and not ontopoiesis *as such*, then the essence of (modern, if not histoiical-metaphysical) technics is not itself technical (ibid.); (iii) if the 'new freedom' of ontopoiesis is the primary essence of life and being then, as much as the animality/machinisation of classical nihilism dominates the determination of being at the 'extremity' of the metaphysical history, so its ontopoietic *essence*, which is occluded by that history, comes to be more pronounced in its originary non-metaphysical essence. Or, in Hölderlin's words, '[w]here danger is, grows/Also deliverance' (ibid., 43; 34). The 'danger' here is that of the totality of classical nihilism's non-essential determination of being, whilst the 'deliverance' is the realisation of that essence *as such*, as ontopoiesis. (iv) In its essence, the human (qua living) 'encounters' beings in the 'open' of ontopoiesis, whence (from Hölderlin again), it is '[onto-] poietically [that] the human dwells on this Earth' (ibid.).

The notes for the *Beiträge* explicitly confirm that the matrix for Heidegger's elaborations of the 1950s was in place by the mid-1930s: 'machination (*Machenschaft*) as the essence of beinghood gives a first hint to the truth of beyng (*Seyn*) itself' (1989, §61; 127). The four clichés just noted above follow directly from this determination of what is essentially important about 'machination'. What is emphasised in the main discussion here is that if the free ontopoiesis of the essence of being is to be affirmed then, following Heidegger's interpretation, the anthropic *Ge-stell* of machinisation must also be so affirmed. It is this *duality* of the affirmation of ontopoiesis which remains in the background of the later texts, and which comes to be effectively simplified by the privileging of poetry as the manifest site of ontopoiesis.

21 It is in this sense that Heidegger's destruction of historical-metaphysics and concern for poetry can be taken *in its coherence* with the notorious statement of 1935 that '[t]he works that are being peddled about nowadays as the philosophy of National Socialism have nothing to do with the inner truth and greatness of this movement (namely, the encounter (*Begegnung*) between global technology and modern man)' (1953, 199; 1959, 152). That is, for Heidegger the 'greatness and

strength' of National Socialism is not so much in its (historical-actual) facticity but more in its '*inner* truth and greatness', which is to say in its ontopoietic essence. The issue of whether the 'encounter' mentioned in parenthesis was spoken or not by Heidegger in delivering the lecture in 1935, or even written at the time, is not the concern here (see Editor's comments in Heidegger 1953, 233–4). The comment would in any case be wholly comprehensible in Heidegger's terms at the time, as the citation from the *Beiträge* above makes clear [see n.19 infra].

What is clear, then, is that in no way is 'Heidegger's thought ceded in political *compromise* [emph.add.]' by the support for Nazism, as Fynsk (1993, 69) puts it, and neither is Heidegger 'blind' to 'political realities' in the early thirties. Heidegger's affirmation of Nazism *and* the critique of it are, rather, wholly consonant with his destruction of historical-metaphysics and the affirmation of the ontopoietic essence of being. What compromise there is with respect to 'political realities' is, *in terms of Heidegger's thinking*, instead to be found in the univocal determination of the essence of being in poetry. This latter determination turns away from the historical-metaphysical actuality and contemporaneity of that very essence as a 'classical nihilism'. It is precisely this actuality to which Heidegger is deeply responsive, as outlined, in the decade or so from the early 1930s.

22   The ontopoietic determination of biocosmogenesis is transparently presented in Plato's psychosomatology at the end of *Timæus*. In particular, Plato describes how the intestines are 'turned in coils' by the 'composers of the race (*genos*)' since without this 'foresight' food and drink would 'pass through so quickly that the body would of necessity require fresh nourishment just as quickly, thereby rendering it insatiable. Such gluttony would make [the] whole race incapable of philosophy and the arts, and incapable of heeding the most divine part within us' (73a1–5). For the human, then, philosophy, arts and the theism depend on the intestine. For Plato, however, it is the former which determine the finality of the intestine and are 'higher' than it.

23   This is the specific importance of Hölderlin for Heidegger: the poet affirms the free essence of being as an (onto-)poiesis of reason which is not 'overturned' into the animality/machinisation of classical nihilism. (The proximity of Hölderlin to Kant is important here to Heidegger.) This in turn allows the 'social and the national' to be comprehended through an essential 'commanding freedom' rather than bodying. Nonetheless, and however implicitly, 'poetic thinking' is then wholly coherent with the historical-essential logic leading to the affirmation of Nazism. It re-iterates that affirmation in principle, if it does not instead just presuppose it.

24   To be clear: Heidegger's determination of occidental historical-metaphysics is a histori*cism* and not a 'destinal histori*calism*', as Janicaud (1990) proposes. The latter is a philosophical-metaphysical determination of history whereby it is organised in fact and in meaning in terms of an inner necessity. The force of this critique (which repeats something of Löwith's disagreement of Heidegger) is that such a primarily philosophical-essential or 'transcendental' understanding of world-history 'neutralises both the political field and rational possibility'. The main text of the present discussion shows, on the contrary, that (i) Heidegger's appeal to the free essence of ontopoiesis is an effort to *maintain* the 'political field and rational possibility' be it on a primarily anthropic basis; (ii) Heidegger's thinking of the fate of Western history and metaphysics is not itself organised by an *essential* determination (for which Plato's ontotheology is in fact *derived*

from the valuation Nietzsche proposes to be the condition for the living), much less one that is 'transcendental', but rather by a primarily *historical* determination (that Plato's determination of ontotheology is prior to Nietzsche's in *every* respect); and (iii) whilst these two points could be said to philosophically motivate Heidegger's collusion with Nazism, in terms of Heidegger's own destruction they are nevertheless philosophically unwarranted since, precisely, the 'essential' determination of bodying is anthropically assumed.

References

Agamben, G. (1998) *Homo Sacer: Sovereign Power and Bare Life*, trans. D. Hellier-Roazen, Stanford: Stanford University Press.

Dawkins, R. (1989) 2nd edn. *The Extended Phenotype*, Oxford: Oxford University Press.

Deleuze, G. (1962) *Nietzsche et la philosophie*, Paris: Presses Universitaire de France (1983) *Nietzsche and Philosophy*, trans. H. Tomlinson, London: Athlone Press.

—— and Guattari, F. (1972) *L'Anti-Oedipe*, Paris: Les éditions du Minuit (1983) *Anti-Oedipus: Capitalism & Schizophrenia*, trans. R. Hurley, M. Seem and H.R. Lane, Minnesota: University of Minnesota Press.

—— and Guattari, F. (1980) *Mille plateaux: Capitalism et schizophrénie*, Paris: Minuit (1987) *A Thousand Plateaus: Capitalism & Schizophrenia*, trans. B. Massumi, Minnesota: University of Minnesota Press.

—— and Guattari, F. (1991) *Qu'est-ce que la philosophie?*, Paris: Les éditions du Minuit (1994) *What is Philosophy?*, trans. G. Burchell and H. Tomlinson, New York: Columbia University Press.

Depew, D. and Weber, B. (1995) *Darwinism Evolving: Systems Dynamics and the Genealogy of Natural Selection*, Cambridge, MA.: MIT Press.

Fynsk, C. (1993) *Heidegger: Thought and Historicity (Expanded Edn.)*, Ithica, NY: Cornell University Press.

Haar, M. (1993) *Nietzsche et la Métaphysique*, Paris: Gallimard; (1996) *Nietzsche and Metaphysics*, trans. M. Gendre, Albany, NY: SUNY Press.

—— (1994) *La fracture de l'histoire*, Grenoble: Jérome Millon.

Heidegger, M. (1927) *Sein und Zeit*, Tübingen: Niemeyer.

—— (1953) *Einführung in die Metaphysik*, Tübingen: Niemeyer (1959) *Introduction to Metaphysics*, trans. R. Mannheim, New Haven CT: Yale University Press.

—— (1954) 'Die Frage nach der Technik' in *Vorträge und Aufsätze*, Pfullingen: Neske.

—— (1961a) 'Der Wille zur Macht Als Erkenntnis' in *Nietzsche I*, Pfullingen: Günther Neske.

—— (1961b) 'Nietzsches Metaphysik' in *Nietzsche II*, Pfullingen: Neske.

—— (1962) *Being and Time*, trans. J. Macquarrie and E. Robinson, Oxford: Blackwell.

—— (1971) *Schellings Abhandlung Über das Wesens der Menschlichen Freiheit*, Tübingen: Niemeyer.

—— (1973) *Kant und das Problem der Metaphysik*, Frankfurt a.M.: Klostermann.

—— (1976) 'Briefe über den "Humanismus"' in *Wegmarken*, Frankfurt a.M.: Klostermann.

—— (1977) 'The Question in Concerning Technology', trans. W. Lovitt, in *The Question in Concerning Technology and Other Essays*, NY: Harpers & Row.

—— (1982) *Parmenides [Gesamtasugabe v.54]*, ed. M.S. Frings, Frankfurt. a. M.: Klostermann

—— (1985) *Schelling's Treatise on the Essence of Human Freedom*, trans. J. Stambaugh, Athens, Ohio: Ohio University Press.

—— (1988a) *Vom Wesen der Menschlichen Freiheit*, ed. H. Mörchen, Frankfurt a.M.: Klostermann.

—— (1988b) 'Letter on "Humanism"', trans. F. Capuzzi, in *Pathmarkings*, ed. W. McNiell, Cambridge: Cambridge University Press.

—— (1989) *Beiträge zur Philosophie(Vom Ereignis)* [*Gesamtausgabe v.65*], ed. F.-W. von Hermann, Frankfurt a.M.: Klostermann.

—— (1990) *Kant and the Problem of Metaphysics* trans. R. Taft, Bloomington, IN: Indiana University Press.

—— (1991a) *Nietzsche v.III: The Will to Power as Knowledge and as Metaphysics*, ed. D.F. Krell, trans. J. Stambaugh, D.F. Krell, F. Capuzzi, San Francisco, CA: HarperCollins.

—— (1991b) 'Documents from the Denazification Proceedings Concerning Martin Heidegger' (bilingual), trans. J.M. Wirth, in *Graduate Faculty Philosophy Journal* 14:2–15:1.

—— (1992) *Parmenides*, trans. A. Schuwer and R. Rojcewicz, Bloomington, IN: Indiana University Press.

Janicaud, D. (1990) *L'ombre de cette pensée*, Grenoble: Jérome Millon; (1996) *The Shadow of That Thought*, trans. M. Gendre, Evanston, IL.: Northwestern University Press.

Kisiel, T. (1993) *The Genesis of Heidegger's 'Being and Time'*, Berkeley, CA.: University of California Press.

Kauffman, S. (1993) *The Origins of Order: Self-Organisation and Selection in Evolution*, Oxford: Oxford University Press.

Langton, C. (1996) 'Artificial Life' in *The Philosophy of Artificial Life*, ed. M. Boden, Oxford: Oxford University Press.

Maturana, H. and Varela, F. (1980) *Autopoiesis and Cognition: The Realisation of the Living*, Dordrecht: Reidel.

Müller-Lauter, W. (1974a) 'Nietzsches Lehre vom Willen zur Machten' in *Nietzsche-Studien* 3.

—— (1974b) 'Welt as Wille zur Macht' in *Tijdschrift voor Filosofie*, 3:1.

—— (1981/82) 'Das Willenwesen und der Übermensch. Ein Beitrag zur Heideggers Nietzsche-Interpretationen' in *Nietzsche-Studien* 10/11.

Plato, n.d. (1978) 'Timæus' in *Platonis Opera t.IV*, ed. J. Burnett, Oxford: Clarendon Press.

—— (1998) 'Timaeus' in *Plato: Collected Works*, ed. J.M. Cooper, trans. D.J. Zeyl, Indianapolis, IN.: Hackett.

Rosen, R. (1985) 'Organisms as Causal Systems Which Are Not Mechanisms: An Essay into the Nature of Complexity' in *Theoretical Biology and Complexity*, ed. R. Rosen, Orlando, FL.: Academic Press.

Schneider, E. and Kay, J. (1995) 'Order from Disorder: the Thermodynamics of Complexity in Biology' in *What is Life? The Next Fifty Years: Speculations on the Future of Biology*, eds M. Murphy and L. O'Neill, Camnridge: Cambridge University Press.

Sluga, H. (1993) *Heidegger's Crisis. Philosophy and Politics in Nazi Germany* Cambridge: Harvard University Press.

6

Revisiting the Will to Power: Active Nihilism and the Project of Trans-human Philosophy

Daniel Conway

And do you know what 'the world' is to me? Shall I show it to you in my mirror? This world, a monster of energy, without beginning, without end; a firm, iron magnitude of force that does not grow bigger or smaller, that does not expend itself but only transforms itself. . . . *This world is the will to power, and nothing besides!* And you yourselves are also this will to power – and nothing besides!

Friedrich Nietzsche, The Will to Power, §1067.

The perfect nihilist – the nihilist's eye idealizes in the direction of ugliness and is unfaithful to his memories: it allows them to drop, lose their leaves; it does not guard them against the corpselike pallor that weakness pours out over what is distant and gone. And what he does not do for himself, he also does not do for the whole past of mankind: he lets it drop.

Friedrich Nietzsche, The Will to Power, §21.

This chapter undertakes an investigation of the productive possibilities engendered by nihilism for the experimental project of 'trans-human' philosophy. While viewed by some critics as an event of strictly negative and stultifying consequence, the advent of European nihilism may actually furnish an interpretive context within which philosophers might finally 'let drop' their nagging anthropocentric prejudices. Against the blighted backdrop of European nihilism, that is, philosophers might progress significantly toward (and eventually complete?) the untimely agenda set for them by Friedrich Nietzsche: 'to translate man back into Nature' (Nietzsche 1989, 230), and thus behold the world in its sheer, amoral immanence.

Toward this end, Nietzsche supplies a number of compelling images of the world as he believes it will be viewed by trans- human philosophers: 'the innocence of Becoming', the world viewed 'from inside', as ' "will to power" and nothing else' (ibid., 36), and, finally, as a 'monster of energy' (Nietzsche 1968, §1067). Here it must be emphasised, however, that these vivid images are largely products of Nietzsche's fertile imagination. He has only barely embarked upon the project of exploring the undiscovered country of trans-human philosophy, and his experimental formulations must not be confused with the final realisation of the project. In short, he is not yet the 'perfect nihilist' he takes himself to be. Indeed, the very historical conditions that sanction his explorations also ensure his eventual failure to complete them. Situated within the besetting decadence of late modernity, he cannot insulate his trans-human experiments from his own participation in this decadence. It is entirely likely, in fact, that his beguiling images for the world beheld by trans-human philosophers remain residually anthropomorphic and moralistic. That is, Nietzsche himself may need to be overcome on the way toward a genuinely trans-human orientation to philosophy.

I take as my point of departure in this essay Nietzsche's famous (and widely-misunderstood) pronouncement that 'nihilism stands at the door' (Nietzsche 1968, §1). In proclaiming the advent of 'European nihilism', he does not mean to imply, as he is popularly understood to claim, that humankind now believes in nothing. While this *may* in fact be the response of those nihilists who had fatuously invested their hopes in 'being', 'permanence', 'causality', 'God', 'truth', and all other superlative values, Nietzsche understands nihilism as delivering a single, grand (though generally unappealing) truth – namely, that the world admits of no antecedent moral order or pre-ordained *telos*. The world simply *is*, in its brute, undifferentiated immanence, and it now presents itself as such for investigation by a few intrepid thinkers. It is Nietzsche's hope that he might open the door to nihilism, in order that he and his fellow free spirits might begin to make the acquaintance of this uncanny visitor.

He consequently describes nihilism as 'ambiguous', for it presents to some individuals the opportunity to move beyond the stubborn anthropomorphisms of folk psychology and humanism. Having gained insight into the nullity of all human projections onto the world, nihilists like Nietzsche may now proceed to fashion a post-anthropocentric, or trans-human, orientation to philosophy. Thus oriented, philosophers would presumably be free to explore the undifferentiated plenum of Nature without the distortions introduced by lingering religious and metaphysical prejudices. As a preliminary step toward the realisation of the trans-human orientation to philosophy, Nietzsche offers his own 'hypothesis' of *the will to power*, which purports to behold the world 'from inside', as a lavishly extravagant 'monster of energy'.

I

Toward the end of *On the Genealogy of Morals*, Nietzsche parenthetically promises his faithful readers that he will soon deliver an essay:

'On the History of European Nihilism'; it will be contained in a work in progress: *The Will to Power: Attempt at a Revaluation of All Values* (Nietzsche 1989b, III 27)[1]

Nietzsche's promise was neither reckless nor unfounded. He mentions 'nihilism' on four occasions in the *Genealogy* itself, and his notebook entries from this period indicate that he had in fact embarked upon a genealogical analysis of 'European nihilism'.[2] Yet the promised essay never appeared.

In 1888, in fact, Nietzsche suddenly abandoned the proposed *Hauptwerk* to which this citation adverts in order to take up yet another quadrapartite project,[3] which he provisionally entitled *The Revaluation of All Values*.[4] However, he subsequently abandoned *this* project as well, apparently deciding to allow the 'first book' of *The Revaluation of All Values* – known to us as *The Antichrist(ian)* – to stand as the whole.[5] Nietzsche thus reneged on his promise not once, but twice. Indeed, the year following the publication of his *On the Genealogy of Morals* was the most productive of his life. Presumably, he thus had every opportunity to produce an essay 'On the History of European Nihilism' if he were so inclined. But he elected to direct his energies elsewhere. Any reconstruction of his account of nihilism thus involves a delicate exegetical project, for one must rely extensively on the unpolished, epigrammatic notes from his *Nachlass*. One must also proceed under the caution that Nietzsche himself never executed this project, despite apparently having sufficient time and opportunity to do so.

Let us begin by determining what Nietzsche meant his diagnosis of 'European nihilism' to convey: Who, or what, is this 'uncanniest of all guests' that now 'stands at the door', silently demanding recognition and entry? (Nietzsche 1967ff, Vol. XII 125). Whereas contemporary scholars tend to use the term 'nihilism' rather loosely, to denote virtually any manifestation of cultural disarray, Nietzsche apparently intends something more precise. He alternately refers to nihilism as a psychological state and a physiological condition, both of which are marked by exhaustion, pervasive pessimism, a pandemic dissipation of will, and an unprecedented erethism. We might say, then, that in these notebook entries he equates nihilism with *the experience of decay*.

Having identified nihilism with the experience of decay, Nietzsche immediately cautions us not to mistake this experience for its cause. In a note from 1888, which echoes several others from that year, he writes: 'Basic insight regarding the nature of decadence: *its supposed causes are its consequences*' (Nietzsche 1968, §41; cf. §42–5). He similarly maintains that:

> [I]t is an error to consider 'social distress' or 'physiological degeneration' or, worse, corruption, as the *cause* of nihilism. (ibid., §1)

He consequently ridicules the notion that we might combat decadence simply by easing the discomfort that attends this experience of nihilism:

> The supposed remedies of degeneration are also mere palliatives against some of its effects: the 'cured are merely one type of the degenerate'. (Nietzsche 1968 §42; cf. 1982, 2:11)

As Nietzsche reveals in an early prospectus for *The Will to Power*, the experience of decay thus marks only the 'point of departure' for his investigation into nihilism (Nietzsche 1968, §1). He consequently probes further, in order to determine the genuine cause(s) of the physiological condition he associates with this experience of decay. Toward this end, he investigates the physiological experience of decay not simply as an isolated historical event, but also as the most recent stage of development in a more sweeping historical process. He thus speaks of a uniquely *European* articulation of nihilism and of various eastern varieties,[6] as well as of the logic that informs them all.[7] As Martin Heidegger astutely observes:

> [F]or Nietzsche nihilism is not in any way simply a phenomenon of decay; rather nihilism is, as the fundamental event of Western history, simultaneously and above all the intrinsic law of that history. . . . Nietzsche thinks nihilism as the 'inner logic' of Western history.   (Heidegger 1977, 67)

As these notebook entries suggest, Nietzsche's understanding of nihilism is inextricably linked to his diagnosis of the pronounced decay that besets the epoch of late modernity. While it is customary for his readers to treat 'nihilism' and 'decadence' as roughly synonymous terms of diagnostic evaluation, several notebook entries in fact militate against this interpretation. Nihilism and decadence are indisputably related as characteristic phenomena of the fading lifeworlds of Western European cultures in late modernity, but they are not identical to one another. As we shall soon see, 'nihilism' names a particular cognitive attunement that is possible only under the conditions of advanced decay.

In perhaps his most famous discussion of nihilism, contained in a note from 1886, Nietzsche attempts to explain the differences between nihilism and decadence:

> What does nihilism mean? *That the highest values devaluate themselves.* The aim is lacking; 'why?' finds no answer.   (Nietzsche 1968, §2)[8]

This response to his own query reveals an important and often overlooked aspect of his understanding of nihilism: He neither asks, nor explains, what nihilism *is;* he is concerned instead to discern what it *means [bedeutet].*[9] What the advent of nihilism *means* is that the decay of Western European cultures has progressed sufficiently far that we can no longer invest resolute belief in the values that we formerly regarded as highest. What the advent of nihilism *means* is that our collective search for purpose, meaning, and justification is now futile. That we find ourselves in an unwanted condition of 'aimlessness' *means* that our highest values, which were hitherto responsible for postponing the onset of this condition, have devaluated themselves.[10] The devaluation of our highest values thus accounts for the *meaning* of nihilism, but not for its essence or cause.[11]

According to Nietzsche, the historical devaluation of these highest values is neither arbitrary nor accidental, for they devaluate *themselves*.[12] In an 1886 prospectus for his proposed *Hauptwerk*, he describes nihilism '*as the necessary consequence* of our valuations thus far' (Nietzsche 1967ff, Vol. III2 107). Two years later, in what he once intended as the Prologue to his *Hauptwerk*, he confirms that 'nihilism represents the ultimate logical conclusion of our great values and ideals' (Nietzssche 1967ff, Vol III2 432). The necessity of the devalution of our highest values is thus ensured by an (as yet) unspecified aspect of their internal logic.

The meaning of nihilism apparently comprises the devaluation only of our highest [*oberst*] values. *Oberst* connotes not only a cardinal sense of authority, but a spatial one as well – as if our 'highest' values were also those most distant from us. To explain why our highest values are also our most insubstantial, Nietzsche scrutinises their blighted birth. He blames philosophers for:

> confusing the last and the first. They place that which comes at the end – unfortunately! for it ought not to come at all! – namely, the 'highest concepts'...in the beginning, *as* the beginning...Moral: whatever is of the first rank must be *causa sui*. Origin out of something else is considered an objection, a questioning of value. All the highest [*obersten*] values are of the first rank...and therefore must be *causa sui*. (Nietzsche 1982, 3:4)

Nietzsche thus traces our current alienation from the highest values to a basic (and perhaps pathological) confusion concerning their origin.[13] Owing to what he calls 'the basic fact of the human will', its '*horror vacui*' (Nietzsche 1989, III 1), humankind formerly believed its highest values to have originated *causa sui*, innocent of history and contingency. As a consequence of the decadence that envelopes late modernity, however, we now see these highest values as expressions of particular, historically-specific interests. In a note from 1888 he explicitly links the experience of nihilism to the origin of our *oberst* values:

> Now that the shabby origin of these values is becoming clear, the universe seems to have lost value, seems 'meaningless'.
>
> (Nietzsche 1967ff, Vol VIII2 291–2)

Although all values are subject to historical devaluation, only the devaluation of our highest values, which supposedly originated *causa sui*, is implicated in the meaning of nihilism. (The devaluation of lesser values, whose 'shabby' human origin was never disputed, apparently need not partake in the logic of nihilism.) Once revealed to be all-too-human in origin, these values forfeit their *oberst* status and take their place beside all other 'merely' human values. Formerly relied on to redeem the human condition, the highest values now stand in need of redemption.[14]

This explanation, of course, only raises additional questions about the cause(s) of nihilism. Why, for example, does the *human* origin of these values constitute an objection to their perdurance? At this point in his analysis of nihilism, Nietzsche apparently understands that he can provide no further explanations. He has effectively raised the question of the defining character of the epoch within which he labours, and he realises that he does not command sufficient insight into the nature of the epoch to venture an adequate response to this question. He consequently shifts the focus of his investigation to the decadence that characterises late modernity. Only if we discern the causes of decadence and uncover the laws and regularities that govern its advance can we hope to appreciate why the 'shabby' human origin of the highest values constitutes a fatal objection to them.

Thus we see why Nietzsche was obliged to renege on his promise to deliver an essay 'On the History of European Nihilism'. Any such historical explanation would first require him to divine the nature of the pandemic decadence that threatens to suffocate the epigonic cultures of late modernity. In fact, his failure to discern the historical 'essence' or 'cause' of decadence is important to bear in mind, for it mitigates the success of his most productive experiments in trans-human philosophy. Indeed, his persistent myopia relegates his efforts to 'view the world from inside' to a preparatory status. His successors may someday take their stand 'beyond good and evil', but Nietzsche himself does not.

It is certainly fair to conclude, with Heidegger, that 'Nietzsche never recognized the *essence* of nihilism, just as no metaphysics before him ever did' (Heidegger 1977, 109). It is equally fair to acknowledge, however, that he managed to situate the meaning of nihilism within his investigation of the historical destiny of late modernity, much as Heidegger himself would later identify the thrall of planetary technics as the enframing *Gestell* of modernity. Nihilism is the cognitive legacy of a decadent age, which is characterised by a nearly total eclipse of the dimension of *praxis*. Unable to muster sufficient vitality to act decisively, the representative exemplars of a decadent age inevitably capitulate to nihilism: *they know* that human volition and agency are myths, that human beings cannot alter the destiny of the historical epoch in which they toil, that even the greatest human accomplishments pale against the backdrop of history, that no moral force or law steers the cosmos in a direction hospitable to human beings, and that no god exists who might redeem a decadent epoch from its ownmost plight. They know, in short, that nothing matters. *Einmal ist keinmal.*

II

As a self-avowed 'child of his time' (Nietzsche 1967, 155), Nietzsche is in no position to redeem anyone, let alone modernity as a whole. He consequently places himself squarely within the ongoing crisis of modernity, presenting himself as a decadent who discerns – but cannot alter – the inexorable cycle of growth and decay.[15] As his own diagnosis would predict of him, he is much more a thinker than a doer; his insight into the peculiar conditions of late modernity far outstrips his ability to amend them.[16]

According to Nietzsche, however, his own decadence does not precisely mirror that of late modernity as a whole. He distinguishes himself from (most of) his contemporaries in several respects. First of all, his signal insight into the trans-historical cycle of growth and decay marks him as a nihilist, and he proudly (if mistakenly) identifies himself as a 'perfect nihilist'.[17] Second, his own decadence is accidental rather than constitutive, for it afflicts him only periodically. It thus signifies an underlying condition – as '*summa summarum*' – of health (Nietzsche 1989b, wise 2).[18] He consequently insists that although he is a decadent, he is 'also the opposite [*Gegenstück*]' of a decadent, an opposition to which he traces his copious 'wisdom' (ibid). Third, his underlying condition of 'health' enables him to resist his decay, apparently to his distinct advantage. He similarly attributes his capacity to 'resist' decadence to the salutary residence of 'the philosopher in [him]' (Nietzsche 1967, 155). He is, in his own words, 'at the same time a *decadent* and a *beginning*' (Nietzsche 1989b, wise 1). Because he participates in the decay of modernity only 'as an angle, as a speciality', his decadence is something he can *use* as 'an energetic *stimulus* for life, for living *more*' (ibid., wise 2). Indeed, if he is 'strong enough to turn even what is most questionable and dangerous to [his] advantage' (ibid.,: clever 6), then he can turn even his own decadence against itself. A nihilist is not free to divest himself of the decadence of his age, but he may exploit his decadence for his own limited ends.

Nietzsche's published writings refer only infrequently to the event of nihilism, but all of the relevant passages support an interpretation of nihilism as delivering a historically specific insight into the economy of decadence.[19] On two occasions in the *Genealogy*, for example, he refers to nihilism as the experience that attends his own insight into the inexorable decay of modernity. He describes his historical situation as verging upon a 'European Buddhism' (Nietzsche 1989b, 19), and he notes that we late moderns have finally grown 'weary of man' (ibid., I §12). On two other occasions, he links nihilism to the advent of a 'will to nothingness' (ibid., II §24; III §14), which shelters the final will of any dying epoch or people.

In his notes from the period, he similarly refers to nihilism as the 'psychological state' that accompanies (but does not cause) the exhaustion, pessimism, and dissipation of will that he presents as symptoms of advanced decay (Nietzsche 1968, §12). These notebook entries thus confirm that he understands nihilism as a cognitive product of decadence, as an achievement of insight and recognition:

> Nihilism, then, is the *recognition* of the long *waste* of strength, the agony of the 'in vain', insecurity, the lack of any opportunity to recover and to regain composure-being ashamed in front of oneself, as if one had *deceived* oneself all too long.   (ibid., §12, *emph. add.*)

As this passage suggests, Nietzsche associates nihilism with the recognition of irreversible decay; we should therefore take quite seriously his frequent associations of nihilism with 'sickness' or 'disease'.[20]

Although it is now customary for Nietzsche's readers to conflate decadence with nihilism, it may be more accurate to conceive of nihilism as a particular cognitive product of decadence. All nihilists are also decadents, but not all decadents are nihilists. A nihilist is therefore a particular type of decadent, one who knows that all expressions of strength and vitality, even those that have been accorded a permanent, supernatural status, must eventually decay. Nihilists understand not only that the ages and peoples they represent lack the vitality needed to sustain themselves, but also that this depleted vitality is the natural, ineluctable result of the ways in which these ages and peoples have expressed themselves in the past.

As a nihilist in his own right, Nietzsche knows that nothing endures permanently, that even the greatest human creations must eventually fall, and that no antecedent moral order ensures the happiness – or even the survival – of humankind. The world beheld by the nihilist is none other than the world viewed 'from inside' (Nietzsche 1989a, 36), the world as will to power, which Nietzsche elsewhere describes as an amoral 'monster of energy' (Nietzsche 1968, §1067). He consequently acknowledges the utter lack of supernatural or metaphysical warrant for the superlative values from which modernity (or any age) has heretofore derived meaning and vitality.[21] Like his peripatetic twin 'sons', the Madman and Zarathustra, Nietzsche witnesses the 'death of God' and conveys this obituary to an obtuse, unbelieving audience.[22]

Nietzsche also distinguishes in his notes between 'active' and 'passive' modes of nihilism. He and his unknown 'friends' apparently partake of the former mode, while virtually everyone else partakes of the latter. Nihilism is 'ambiguous', he explains, because it can signify either 'increased power of the spirit, as *active* nihilism', or 'decline and recession of the power of the spirit, as *passive* nihilism' (Nietzsche 1968, §22; see §23).[23] While both forms of nihilism share a common insight into the economy of decay, they differ with respect to the volitional response that is engendered by this insight. Active nihilists are apparently able to affirm the entire cycle of growth and decay, including the inevitable destruction of themselves as 'individual' agents. Passive nihilists characteristically (and involuntarily) generalise from their own decay, projecting it onto humankind as a whole; their own crippled agency proves to them that agency *per se* is now defunct. Active nihilists consequently see decadence as a necessary ingredient of Life, whose rich economy includes, but is not reducible to, their own careers as 'individual' agents.[24] Passive nihilists, by contrast, cannot help but see decadence as the opposite or negation of Life itself.[25]

Whereas active nihilists can afford to behold the world in its painful, amoral immanence, passive nihilists must interpose saving, metaphysical fictions between themselves and the world. Indeed, the moralisation of decadence is itself a result, or by-product, of the attempt by passive nihilists to invest their otherwise meaningless existence with *some* purpose, no matter how perverse. Nietzsche insists that humankind would rather 'will nothingness than *not* will' (Nietzsche 1989b, III:1), a truth that passive nihilists confirm by embracing self-annihilation as the goal that provides them with meaning and purpose. In his notes, he occasionally employs the term *incomplete nihilism* to describe the plight of those passive nihilists who can neither create lasting illusions nor abjure their reliance on them.[26]

The most enduring illusion to which passive nihilists cling is the fiction of individual agency. Rather than revise their guiding prejudices in light of the growing disparity between the cognitive and volitional resources available to them, passive nihilists (involuntarily) insist to the end that they are causally efficient agents, albeit failed ones. Passive nihilists cling tenaciously to the naive voluntarism of folk psychology, despite their realisation that it has culminated in the *absurdum practicum* that now defines their sclerotic existence. Passive nihilists thus view decadence as the product not of one's unalterable destiny, but of one's voluntary elections gone awry. Indeed, moralisations of decadence typically trace the advent of decay to some tragic, misguided choice on the part of oneself or one's ancestors, such that more promising paths of development were temporarily obnubilated and permanently forfeited. The familiar doctrine of original sin represents a typical instance of the moralisation of decadence, for it locates within individual agency a powerful impulse toward a predetermined self-destruction. Passive nihilists thus believe that decadence, although intrinsically worthless in and of itself, performs an invaluable moral service to successor ages and peoples. Decadent ages and individuals stand to posterity as negative exemplars, whose damning mistakes should – and can – be avoided.

Active nihilism is the exclusive province of those exemplary individuals who boast some minimal capacity for squandering their remaining volitional resources. Passive nihilism is the lot of those individuals whose insight into the economy of decadence regrettably coincides with the sheer exhaustion of their native vitality. While active nihilists are enabled as 'squanderers' by their insight into the trans-historical cycle of growth and decay, passive nihilists respond by surrendering to decadence, by expending all remaining vitality in the pursuit of self-abnegation. According to the gospel of passive nihilism, the death of God spells the end not of our crippling guilt, but of all hope that our indebtedness might someday be redeemed. Nietzsche thus insists that most philosophers and priests are passive nihilists, for they treat decay as the definitive objection to existence itself (Nietzsche 1989b, III:11).

Whereas passive nihilists declare their contribution to the enhancement of humankind to be complete, locating their own 'perfection' in their timely demise and extinction, active nihilists seek to continue their explorations of the human soul, even (or especially) in the twilight of the idols. Active nihilists thus pursue heretofore unknown routes to human enhancement, in the face of a self-fulfilling prophecy that proclaims the future course of humankind to be already determined. The volitional resources available to a crepuscular epoch may pale in comparison to those squandered by predecessor epochs, but this disparity alone does not warrant the moralisation that passive nihilists typically attach to it. In an unusually detailed sketch of the active nihilist, Nietzsche explains:

> With a single glance he sees what, given a favorable accumulation and increase of forces and tasks, might yet *be made of man*; he knows with all the knowledge of his conscience how often the type 'man' has already confronted enigmatic decisions and new paths.... Anyone who has thought through this possibility to the end knows one kind of nausea that other men don't know – but perhaps also a new *task!*
>
> (Nietzsche 1989a, 203)

For active nihilists, the *absurdum practicum* associated with decadence presents an unprecedented opportunity to rethink the notion of agency, to philosophise outside the constraints of traditional categories and frameworks, to investigate decadent forms of Life, and to experiment with untested constellations of human powers. At their realistic best, active nihilists conceive of decadence as delivering them a novel (rather than an empty) slate of potentialities, which they might then explore and enact.

The opportunity to investigate unknown forms of Life arises only when the advance of decadence exposes the fiction of individual agency and the limitations of individual 'subjects'. Freed from the tarnished cage of their own individual agency, active nihilists are positioned to attain a better appreciation of their situation within the overlapping economies of Life, Nature, and will to power. That is, they are uniquely enabled by the decay of their epoch to 'let drop' the anthropomorphic prejudices that have recently been exposed as philosophically inefficacious; they consequently find themselves poised on the threshold of a trans-human orientation to philosophy. By continuing their experiments, even throughout the twilight of the idols, active nihilists will succeed neither in defying the trans-historical cycle of growth and decay, nor in developing a cure or treatment for decay. But they may nevertheless bequeath to the founders of the successor epoch an unprecedented insight into the nature and limitations of agency.

As it withers and dies, a decadent people or age enacts a unique sequence of involuntary paroxysms, all of which potentially contribute to our understanding of Life. Even in the twilight of the idols, human beings remain 'incomplete' animals, 'pregnant with a future' that remains to some extent unknown (Nietzsche 1989b, II 16). While this 'pregnancy' may seem destined for miscarriage, active nihilists vow to continue their maieutic efforts and bring this troubled pregnancy to term. In their ongoing efforts to say 'Yes to Life even in its strangest and hardest problems' (Nietzsche 1982, 10: 5), active nihilists explore the possibilities afforded them even by their imminent demise.

III

Although Nietzsche employs a host of concussive images to convey his sense of his unique historical destiny, the signal accomplishment arising out of his engagement with nihilism lies in a distinctly cognitive triumph. By virtue of his immersion in the decadence of late modernity, he sees more clearly than others the peculiar *ethos* of his age (and its ongoing disintegration). In touching off his 'explosion', he realistically aspires not so much to destruction and devastation as to revelation and illumination. While he certainly prefers the muscular image of the archer flexing his bow (Nietzsche 1989a: preface), his own humble quiver contains only signal flares and warning arrows; the strength to dispatch more lethal ordnance lies beyond his diminished capacities.

It is therefore more appropriate to view Nietzsche's vaunted 'revaluation of all values' as a cognitive achievement. Rather than 'break history in two' (Nietzsche 1989b, destiny 8), as he melodramatically promises, his 'revaluation of all values' formally inaugurates the transitional period announced by the advent of European nihilism. Indeed, his contributions to the articulation of a trans-human orientation to philosophy are largely preparatory in nature. Owing to his historical situation in a crepuscular epoch, he remains far too tightly enmeshed in the prevailing prejudices of Western humanism to complete the emigration he recommends 'beyond good and evil'. Despite his best efforts, that is, he is not yet able to 'leave the illusion of moral judgments *beneath* himself' (Nietzsche 1982, 7:1).

Notwithstanding the humanistic encumbrances of his historical situation, however, he is not without valuable resources to deploy. Turning to his advantage the nihilism that darkens the horizon of late modernity, he conducts various philosophical experiments that have been heretofore impossible to undertake. The devaluation of the highest values uniquely positions him to call into question – and perhaps to suspend – several of the hoariest prejudices of Western philosophy and theology. Let us turn now to examine one such crepuscular experiment, in which he attempts to develop his hypothesis of *the will to power*. He intends the will to power, or so I claim, as a trans-human cosmological hypothesis, purged of all taint of moral evaluation and anthropocentric privilege. This cosmology would not only dislodge the human from its accustomed place at the center of the 'world', but also demonstrate that 'human' agency is in fact derivative of a more pervasive, trans-personal agency. To regard the world 'from inside', as ' "will to power" and nothing else' (Nietzsche 1989, §36), would be to command a genuinely extra-moral and trans-human standpoint. This is an experiment, he furthermore believes, that only he can conduct, and only within the advancing penumbra of nihilism.[27]

Nietzsche's experiment with the will to power emerges as the product of his attempt to take seriously the notion that the will is the sole efficient cause of human agency. While introducing his experiment, he claims that:

> The question is in the end whether we really recognize the will as *efficient*, whether we believe in the causality of the will: if we do . . . then we have to experiment with the hypothesis *that the will alone is causal*. 'Will', of course, can affect only 'will' – and not 'matter' (not 'nerves', for example).
> (Nietzsche 1989a, §36, *emph. add.*)

At first glance, this experiment might seem to confirm the popular (and mistaken) interpretation of Nietzsche as a champion of the metaphysical will, for he attempts here to defend his belief in 'the causality of the will'. If 'the will alone is causal', however, then the 'efficient' will in question can no longer be identified with that puny homunculus whose sole power lies in transforming natural impulses into sins.

In order to accommodate his hypothesis that the will alone is causal, Nietzsche must supplant that alleged mover of matter, the metaphysical will, with a more powerful and pervasive agency, which he calls 'will to power'. This he can do, moreover, because the devaluation of the highest values has cast a shadow of suspicion over the allegedly transformative powers of the human will. Nietzsche makes precisely this point in his text-book debunking of 'The Four Great Errors' in *Twilight of the Idols*. He begins by exposing the alleged causality of the will as an external projection of an 'inward fact' – namely, the experience of oneself as a causally efficient agent in the world. The progress of psychology reveals, however, that the meta-physical will, a spectral agency allegedly responsible for translating beliefs into deeds, is nothing more than a 'phantom', a 'will-o'-the-wisp' (Nietzsche

1982, 6:3) that was 'invented essentially for the purpose of punishment, that is, because one wanted to impute guilt' (ibid., 6:7).

In a parlance reminiscent of his famous critique of subjectivity in the *Genealogy* (Nietzsche 1989b, I:13), Nietzsche exposes the metaphysical will as an atavistic fiction of folk psychology:

> The most ancient and enduring psychology was at work here and did not do anything else: all that happened was considered a doing, all doing the effect of a will.... A doer (a 'subject') was slipped under all that happened. It was out of himself that man projected his three 'inner facts' – that in which he believed most firmly: the will, the spirit, the ego. (ibid., 6:3)

He consequently ridicules those 'philosophers [who] are accustomed to speak of the will as if it were the best-known thing in the world' (Nietzsche 1989a, §19). He singles out his *Erzieher*, Schopenhauer, who 'has given us to understand that the will alone is really known to us, absolutely and completely known, without subtraction or addition' (ibid., §19).

Although the metaphysical will is nothing more than an enduring fiction of folk psychology, its currency can be traced to the attempt to account for a phenomenon that Nietzsche takes quite seriously: the experience of oneself as a causally efficient agent. He consequently undertakes to explain the provenance of this experience, but without relying on the metaphysical contrivances of folk psychology:

> The old word 'will' now serves only to denote a resultant, a kind of individual reaction, which follows necessarily upon a number of partly contradictory, partly harmonious stimuli: the will no longer 'acts' or 'moves'. (Nietzsche 1982, 14)

He consequently advances a strictly phenomenalistic account of the experience associated with 'willing', of which the metaphysical will represents a clumsy hypostatization.[28]

Ostensibly freed from the thrall of folk psychology, Nietzsche proceeds to account for the experience of willing without any recourse to the wondrous powers of the metaphysical will. As an implementation of this strategy, he famously wonders whether 'all mechanical occurrences are not ... effects of will' (Nietzsche 1989a, §36), which leads him to the more radical hypothesis that:

> [O]ur entire instinctual life [is] the development and ramification of *one* basic form of the will – namely, of the will to power. (ibid., §36)

His signal contribution to psychology, he explains, is 'to understand it as morphology and *the doctrine of the development of the will to power*' (ibid., §23).

He thus proposes that '*all* efficient force' is, in its most basic form, '*will to power*' (ibid., §36).[29]

In order to take seriously the causality of the will, now understood as the hypothesised will to power, Nietzsche boldly reverses the relation of cause and effect as it has been traditionally understood. He traces the 'Four Great Errors' of philosophical explanation to a common, uncritical faith in the individual subject as the causally efficient originator of action. This account is conducive to error because it confuses the effect or expression of agency – namely, the will – with its cause:

> The will no longer moves anything, hence does not explain anything either – it merely accompanies events; it can also be absent.
> (Nietzsche 1982, 6:3)

Nietzsche is positioned to attempt this momentous reversal only because he toils in the twilight of the idols, wherein the myth of causality has finally exploded itself beyond repair. That is, only an active nihilist can both expose the metaphysical will as a fabrication *and* celebrate this revelation as a new opportunity for philosophical investigation. Indeed, because he no longer believes that the will causes or moves anything, Nietzsche is free to experiment with a cosmology that does not locate in human beings the origin of the 'agency' that is popularly invested in them.

But if the will does not cause action, then the source of the agency attributed to individual 'subjects' must lie elsewhere. Having exposed the 'individual' as a composite fiction of folk psychology, Nietzsche locates the source of the agency popularly ascribed to 'individual' agents outside (and logically prior to) them. The 'individual' human being is not the origin or cause of agency, but its expression or effect:

> When we speak of values, we speak with the inspiration, with the way of looking at things, which is part of Life: Life itself forces [*zwingt*] us to posit values; Life itself values through us when we posit values.
> (Nietzsche 1982, 5:5)

Nietzsche's hypothesis thus suggests that 'individual' human beings are not so much agents of willful volition as patients of will to power, through whom Life expresses itself in the ostensibly subjective positing of values. What philosophers and laymen alike have designated as intentions, choices, decisions, volitions, and other voluntary 'facts' of our mental life may in fact be involuntary epiphenoma of the will to power propagating itself through its unwitting patients. Indeed, this account of the cosmological patiency of all human 'agents' represents one of his most profound contributions to the articulation of a trans-human orientation to philosophy.

This rich passage not only militates against the robust voluntarism that is popularly attributed to Nietzsche, but also suggests a further identification of the primordial agency that 'values through us'. Indeed, his cryptic allusion to Life calls to mind his earlier proclamation that: 'A living thing seeks above all to *discharge* its strength – Life itself is *will to power*' (Nietzsche 1989a, §13). Further embellishing this apparent identification of Life with will to power, he notoriously maintains that:

> [L]ife itself is *essentially* appropriation, injury, overpowering of what is alien and weaker... 'Exploitation' does not belong to a corrupt or imperfect and primitive society: it belongs to the *essence* of what lives, as a basic organic function; it is a consequence of the will to power, which is after all the will of Life. (ibid., §259)

Taken together, these passages situate Nietzsche's hypothesis of the will to power squarely within the context of his experiment in trans-human philosophy. *Life* is his preferred designation for the will to power at its most basic, undifferentiated level of organic ramification. We might say that Life is that which all animate beings, independent of the complexity of their respective morphologies, share as a common link and provenance.[30] At the uniquely human level of organic differentiation and complexity, Life thus functions as the primordial, trans-individual agency that endows individual souls with the vital forces they involuntarily propagate and expend. As a trans-individual agency, moreover, Life operates amorally and independently to cause individuals to posit values. Nietzsche's hypothesis of the will to power thus leads him to adopt the vitalism that informs his post-Zarathustran writings. In these writings, in fact, Nietzsche occasionally figures Life as a transpersonal force that spontaneously overflows itself in a sumptuary expression of its unquenchable vitality.

Rather than abandon his hypothesis that the cosmos in its most basic reality is will to power, he thus shifts his interpretive focus to the uniquely organic ramification of will to power, which he calls Life.[31] This shift not only facilitates the continued development of his experiment in trans-human philosophy, but also isolates the precise interface between the trans-personal will to power and the individual human being. According to Nietzsche, the human soul is indirectly known to us through its observable patterns of instinctual behaviour as an invisible network of drives and impulses. For this reason, he consistently figures the soul in his post-Zarathustran writings as a vessel or capacitor, which amorally discharges its native endowment of vitality, or 'will'. The pervasive, transpersonal agency that suffuses animate entities with vitality is Life, which itself comprises all organic differentiations of the primordial will to power. The 'individual' is therefore nothing more than an artificially designated- albeit functional- configuration of will to power:

> The single one, the 'individual', as hitherto understood by the people and the philosophers alike, is an error after all: he is nothing by himself, no atom, no 'link in the chain', nothing merely inherited from former times; he is the whole single line of humanity up to himself.
>
> (Nietzsche 1982 9:33)

This trans-moral account of the 'individual' human being, Nietzsche furthermore insists, constitutes the logical conclusion of his hypothesis that the will alone is causal.

As this passage suggests, Nietzsche ascribes originary agency only to Life, or will to power. To the 'individual' he attributes only a derivative agency. Indeed, he sees the 'individual' as nothing more than a transient vortex within the amoral plenum of Life. His experiment with will to power thus exposes the uniquely modernist preoccupation with the 'individual', as a (potentially) autonomous, self-regulating subject, as a fatuous piece of voluntaristic *niaiserie*. The Enlightenment project has not so much failed (as Nietzsche's readers often report him to have claimed), as it has never actually been in a position to commence. He consequently observes that 'Today the individual still has to be made possible by being pruned: possible here means *whole*' (Nietzsche 1982, 9:41).

IV

Nietzsche's hypothesis of the will to power thus sanctions a powerful critique of individual agency, especially insofar as the integrity of the 'individual' has been traditionally linked to the causal efficacy of the will.[32] As we have seen, his hypothesis reduces human 'agents' to the embodied media through which the will to power amorally propagates itself. He consequently debunks the purposiveness that supposedly confirms the individual's 'will' to act in a certain way:

> Is the 'goal', the 'purpose', not often enough a beautifying pretext, a self-deception of vanity after the event that does not want to acknowledge that the ship is *following* the current into which it has entered accidentally? That it 'wills' to go that way *because it – must?* that is has a direction, to be sure, but – no helmsman at all?
>
> (Nietzsche 1974, §360)

As a result of this experiment with the will to power, Nietzsche recommends a fairly severe restriction of the domain of individual freedom. As patients of the will to power, individual 'agents' are (at best) able to determine only the specific expression of the vitality they involuntarily propagate. They are in no event able to determine the quantity and quality of this supervening vitality. Directing our attention to 'one of [his] most essential steps and advances', he rehearses the following distinction between 'two kinds of causes that are often confounded':

> I have learned to distinguish the cause of acting from the cause of acting in a particular way, in a particular direction, with a particular goal. The first type of cause is a quantum of dammed-up energy that is waiting to be used up somehow, for something, while the second kind is, compared to this energy, something quite insignificant, for the most part a little accident in accordance with which this quantum 'discharges' itself in one particular way – a match versus a ton of powder.   (Nietzsche 1974, 360)

Only this second kind of cause falls within the legitimate compass of human agency and volition. Indeed, although some exemplary 'individuals' can influence the specific expressions of the vitality they involuntarily propagate, the condition of their souls (including the capacity of expendable resources at their disposal) is a matter of their unalterable destiny.

Lest we dismiss this account of agency and volition as simply too impoverished, Nietzsche cautions us to beware of popular prejudice. Here he replaces his customary discussion of 'causes' with the more experimental (and potentially trans-human) vocabulary of 'forces':

People are accustomed to consider the goal (purposes, vocations, etc.) as the *driving force*, in keeping with a very ancient error; but it is merely the *directing force* – one has mistaken the helmsman for the steam. And not even always the helmsman, the directing force (Nietzsche 1974, 360).

Taken together, these two passages suggest that Nietzsche likens the directing force of agency to a match, and the driving force of agency to a ton of gunpowder. While the directing force of agency is, relative to the driving force, quantitatively insignificant, it is potentially momentous in the qualitative terms that human beings alone find interesting. The humble helmsman cannot possibly generate sufficient steam to propel the vessel he steers, but his steady hand can nevertheless influence the ship's initial course and ultimate destination.

As this analogy suggests, 'individual' human beings are constituted at the intersection of (at least) two lines of force. They consequently do not control (and *a fortiori* cannot be held responsible for) the quanta of force they involuntarily propagate. Under certain conditions, however, they can determine the qualitative disposition of these quanta. Although restricted to a command of the directing force of the agency they patiently enact, some human beings command sufficient volitional resources to determine the specific expressions of their native vitality. Sensing, perhaps, that his critique of agency betrays a residual humanism, Nietzsche furthermore cautions us not to overestimate even this limited sphere of volition. In many cases, he suggests, even the directing force exerted by the helmsman may itself belong to the figments of folk psychology. Perhaps there is no helmsman at all. Perhaps all 'directing' forces are in fact 'driving' forces after all.

Conclusion

As a response to the onset of European nihilism, Nietzsche endeavours to conduct a philosophical experiment that was formerly unimaginable. He gamely endeavours to view the world 'from inside' (Nietzsche 1989a, §36), hoping thereby to articulate a cosmological thesis that might stand as uniquely extra-moral and trans-human.

As he apparently realises, however, the enormity of his task virtually eclipses his own modest philosophical achievements. Supernatural vestiges of the world viewed 'from outside' continue to haunt his experiment with the will to power, causing him to retreat occasionally behind the metaphysical prejudices he has so expertly debunked. Contrary to his sincere intentions, for example, he never actually manages to confront the will to power as a perfectly amoral 'monster of energy'. In his concern to demonstrate that the undifferentiated plenum of Life shelters transient sub-systems amenable to human design, he unwittingly tames the 'monster', yielding in the process a domesticated cosmology that reflects his residual humanistic allegiances.[33]

Despite his wish to dispense altogether with moral evaluations and anthropocentric prerogatives, he apparently cannot help but attempt to preserve a minimal domain of freedom and responsibility, wherein heroic individuals might strategically manifest their own decay for the benefit of those who will follow. Although he acknowledges that a genuinely trans-human account of agency may require him to banish altogether the homuncular 'helmsman' (Nietzsche 1974, 360), he stops just short of doing so, reserving for himself and his fellow 'free spirits' a limited fiefdom of volition and *praxis*. He is apparently not prepared to embrace a cosmology that would require him to forfeit his residual agency, whereby he might fulfil his 'destiny' and steer modernity to a timely close. Poised on the threshold of a trans-human orientation to cosmology, he invariably relapses into the humanism against which he inveighs. In the end, he is not a 'perfect' nihilist after all, for he retains an allegiance to the metaphysics of morals that he struggles to dismantle. Unable in the end to 'leave the illusion of moral judgments *beneath* himself' (Nietzsche 1982, 7:1), he fails to take the recommended stand 'beyond good and evil'.

The limitations of Nietzsche's experiment in trans-human cosmology are apparently attributable not to cowardice, reluctance, or indecision on his part, but to the unique epistemic conditions that characterise the historical situation of his experiment. As he himself would judge of others, he is probably too close to the advent of European nihilism to disentangle himself from the traditions it supposedly brings to a close. He cannot cleanly extricate himself from the apparatus of Western humanism because he does not see clearly enough its contributions to the enframing character of decadence in late modernity. He is able to discern the need for trans-human experimentation in philosophy, but he lacks access to philosophical typologies and vocabularies that are not thoroughly contaminated by the anthropomorphisms he wishes to avoid. Despite his prodigious linguistic talents, he is not sufficiently poetic to elude the metaphysical snares of the language he deploys. But his failure to abjure completely the prejudices of Western humanism should come as no surprise to us, or to him. Having announced the death of God, Nietzsche cautions that 'given the ways of men, there may still be caves for thousands of years in which his shadow will be shown' (Nietzsche 1974, §108). Since he has not yet abandoned entirely 'the ways of men', we should fully expect to find shadows of the dead God flickering on the walls of his (and Zarathustra's) cave. Indeed, we can be certain that the enticing dance of these shadows will complicate any attempt to behold the world 'from inside'.

Nietzsche's experiment nevertheless succeeds in (at least) two ways. First of all, he points the way toward a genuinely trans-human orientation to philosophy. Successor experimenters may not only build upon his progress thus far, but may also treat his failures as occasions for further scrutiny. If nothing else, Nietzsche's successors might set themselves the task of banishing the shadows that continue to darken his cave. That is, the best way to honor his contributions to trans-human philosophy may be to overcome him in the process, legislating on his behalf the self-overcoming he pursued but never achieved. This legislation may in turn require, of course, that trans-human philosophers sever their umbilical ties with Nietzsche, in order that his agenda and authority not merge with the dancing shadows of the dead god. To tarry in the thralldom of Nietzsche is to risk installing him, much as the 'higher men' come to worship Zarathustra's ass, as a quasi-divine authority in the twilight of the idols. Nowhere is this danger more apparent than in an early essay by Deleuze, which approaches hagiography in its apprecation of Nietzsche's de-territorialising accomplishments. In a passage in which he effectively exempts Nietzsche from the limitations of the all-too-human, Deleuze gushes:

> But if Nietzsche does not belong to philosophy, it is perhaps because he was the first to conceive of another kind of discourse as counter-philosophy. This discourse is above all nomadic; its statements can be conceived as the products of a mobile war machine and not the utterances of a rational, administrative machinery, whose philosophers would be bureacrats of pure reason. (Deleuze 1977, 149)

Second, Nietzsche's own failures might be helpful in guiding our attempts to measure accurately the successes and limitations of his successors. Given our own historical proximity to Nietzsche (and *a fortiori* to the advent of European nihilism), a genuinely trans-human orientation to philosophy may yet be impossible for us to achieve. We may be nearly as susceptible as he to unwitting relapses and recidivisms, and our proximity to the event of nihilism may cloud our judgment in ways we cannot yet discern. At the extreme, this danger is perhaps best exemplified in Heidegger's precipitous decision in 1933 to assume the rectorship at the University of Freiburg as a means of covertly shaping the National Socialist movement. Convinced that a world-historical moment of crisis demanded *his* immediate and decisive response, Heidegger indulged his untutored sympathies with National Socialism.[34] Secretly hoping to 'lead the leader' [*den Führer führen*] from within the National Socialist movement, he apparently wished to steer the German *Volk* toward its ownmost spiritual destiny. Of course, this scheme was poorly planned and disastrously executed, as Heidegger himself readily acknowledges. But its perceived urgency at the time can be traced in part to his mismeasure of the historical moment, to his misunderstanding of nihilism, which contributed to the impairment of his judgement.

The world viewed 'from inside' thus remains a project rather than an accomplishment.[35] Indeed, the genius of Nietzsche's hypothesis of will to power lies not in its success in securing for us a glimpse of the world viewed from inside, as a 'monster of energy', but in its suggestion that our failure to do so need not constitute a dead end. He thus invites his readers to collaborate on an experiment that he knows may take centuries, even millennia, to complete. The Platonic sun may be a cold, dead star, but its light will continue to reach – and blind – our eyes for years to come.[36]

Notes

1   Throughout part I of this essay I occasionally draw on reworked sentences that originally appeared in Conway 1992.

2   His self-appointed executors collected his notebook entries relating to nihilism in 'Book One' of *The Will to Power*, under the heading, 'European Nihilism'.

3   For a persuasive documentation of the finality with which Nietzsche abandoned his plans for *The Will to Power* see Magnus (1993, 37–46).

4   In a letter to Overbeck on 18 October 1888, Nietzsche says of *The Revaluation of All Values*, 'There will be four books; they will appear individually [*einzeln*]' (Nietzsche 1986, 8:453).

5   In his Preface to *Twilight of the Idols*, Nietzsche dates his signature with the following inscription: 'Turin, September 30, 1888, on the day when the first book of the *Revaluation of All Values* was completed' (Nietzsche 1982, Preface). In a letter to Overbeck on 18 October 1888, he describes the first book of the *Revaluation* as 'ready for press [*druckfertig*]' (Nietzsche 1986, 8: 453).

6   See the discussion of Buddhism in Nietzsche 1982, 20–3.

7   Heidegger speaks of 'the *inner logic* of nihilism', which he identifies as its 'essence' (Heidegger 1982, 52–7). Heidegger again takes up the question of Nietzsche's nihilism in 'The Word of Nietzsche: God is Dead', where he claims

that 'Nietzsche thinks nihilism as the "inner logic" of Western history' (Heidegger 1977, 67).

8   Nietzsche asks a similar question of meaning in Essay III of the *Genealogy: Was bedeuten asketische Ideale?* Nietzsche's interest in the meaning of nihilism thus links this note thematically to the third Essay of the *Genealogy*, which is devoted to the meaning of the ascetic ideal. Later in the *Genealogy*, he explains his hermeneutic focus: 'It is my purpose here to bring to light, not what this [ascetic] ideal has *done*, but simply what it *means*; what it indicates; what lies hidden behind it, beneath it, within it; of what it is the provisional, indistinct expression, overlaid with question marks and misunderstandings' (Nietzsche 1989, III: 23).

9   Heidegger's concern with the essence [*Wesen*] of nihilism thus misrepresents Nietzsche's interests, and constitutes a significant deviation from Nietzsche's own strategy. Heidegger rightly concludes that 'Nietzsche cannot think the essence of nihilism' (Heidegger 1977, 93), but then Nietzsche's interest lay elsewhere, in determining the *meaning* of nihilism.

10 While Heidegger rightly concludes that 'Nietzsche cannot think the essence [*Wesen*] of nihilism' (Heidegger 1977, 93), Nietzsche's actual interest lies elsewhere, in determining the *meaning* of nihilism. Heidegger's guiding concern with the essence of nihilism thus marks a significant deviation from Nietzsche's own strategy.

11 Here I depart from the account of nihilism advanced by Michael Alan Gillespie in his excellent study. Apparently conflating the meaning of nihilism with its source or cause, Gillespie observes that 'nihilism, according to Nietzsche, is the consequence of the fact that God and all eternal truths and standards become unbelievable. The highest values devaluate themselves' (Gillespie 1995, xi, *emph. add.*). Reprising this account later in his study, Gillespie explains that 'nihilism for Nietzsche is the result of the fact that the highest values devaluate themselves, that God and reason and all of the supposed eternal truths become unbelievable' (Gillespie 1995, 174, *emph. add.*). Gillespie's tendency to conflate the meaning of nihilism with its cause may partially explain why he ultimately finds Nietzsche's notion of nihilism to be insufficient.

12 In the *Birth of Tragedy*, Nietzsche portrayed the devaluation of the tragic worldview as both a consequence of its 'death struggle' with Socratic optimism and as a 'suicide'. He confusedly blamed Socrates and Euripides for impelling the 'deathleap' of tragedy despite his recognition that they were unable to affect tragedy otherwise. In the account of nihilism under consideration, however, Nietzsche suggests that rival configurations of value (e.g. Socratism) function not as causes of devaluation, but as historical catalysts of devaluation that exploit the internal logic of these doomed values.

13 As Heidegger points out, 'The very positing of these values in the world is already nihilism' (Heidegger 1982, 44).

14 Nietzsche argues in *Der Antichrist* that 'all the highest [obersten] values of mankind lack this will [to power] – that the values which are symptomatic of decline, nihilistic values, are lording it under the holiest names (Nietzsche 1982, §6).

15 For the suggestion that Nietzsche's account of decadence itself contributes to an esoteric strategy designed to accelerate the decay of modernity, see Rosen, 191–8.

16 Only in the writings of late 1888 and in those letters inspired by incipient madness does Nietzsche lay claim to any world-historical political designs. For an account of the emergence of politics – thereby eclipsing aesthetics – as the 'master trope' of Nietzsche's thought, see Strong 1998. Turning in 'desperation to politics'

Nietzsche 'at the end of his life . . . thinks that a political act is necessary to make the aesthetic experience possible', which would in turn make 'the recognition of self and other and thus politics possible' (Strong 1998 168–9).

17 In his notes, Nietzsche announces himself (in the third person) as 'the first perfect nihilist of Europe, who, however, has even now lived outside the whole of nihilism, to the end, leaving it behind, outside himself' (Nietzsche 1968, §3). Returning to this theme, he intimates: 'That I have hitherto been a thorough-going nihilist, I have admitted to myself only recently: the energy and radicalism with which I advanced as a nihilist deceived me about this basic fact' (ibid., §25).

18 While recounting his own convalescence, Nietzsche refers to 'periods of decadence' in which he was obliged to forbid himself all feelings of *ressentiment* (Nietzsche 1989 :wise 6). With the passing of such periods, such feelings were not so much harmful to him as simply beneath him.

19 Gillespie persuasively demonstrates 'nihilism is not the central teaching of Nietzsche's thought' (Gillespie 1995, 178).

20 While explaining why we must concentrate on Nietzsche's notebooks rather than on his published works, Heidegger describes 'the two final years 1887 and 1888' as 'a time of utter lucidity and keen insight' (Heidegger 1982, 13). Even if we grant Heidegger's assessment of the period 1887–88, we might wonder why the published works of this period are not of greater value to him. Although Nietzsche's published books from this period say very little about nihilism itself, the account of decadence they collectively essay suggests that he wisely suspended his plans for the envisioned *Hauptwerk*.

21 Nietzsche knows that nothing endures, but he usually presents the truth of this insight as itself enduring. As we have already seen, the truth of his historicism is not itself historical. Heidegger's famous criticism is therefore accurate, for Nietzsche hypostatises the *nihil* of nihilism, transforming it into a thing or being in its own right: 'Yet for Nietzsche nihilism is not in any way simply a phenomenon of decay; rather nihilism is, as the fundamental event of Western history, simultaneously and above all the intrinsic law of that history . . . Nietzsche thinks nihilism as the "inner logic" of Western history' (Heidegger 1977, 67).

22 In Book V of *The Gay Science*, which he added to the 1886 edition, Nietzsche returns to the theme of the 'death of God' (Nietzsche 1974, §343). Reprising the imagery of the Madman passage (ibid., §125), he now implicates himself in the ignorance of the townspeople who are 'responsible' for the death of God. He too has overestimated his ability to digest the meaning of this unprecedented event.

23 The distinction between active and passive nihilism is related, though by no means identical, to the distinction he draws in his published writings between realism and idealism. See Nietzsche 1982, 10:2; 1989b: clever 10.

24 On the productive, purgative functions of nihilism, see Blanchot 1993, 136–51. The active nihilist, Blanchot insists, is distinguished by an insight into the transience of the experience of negation that accompanies nihilism: 'Nihilism is the impossibility of being done with it and of finding a way out even in that end that is nothingness. It says the impotence of nothingness, the false brilliance of its victories; it tells us that when we think nothingness we are still thinking being. . . . Nihilism thus tells us its final and rather grim truth: it tells of the impossibility of nihilism' (ibid., 149).

25 On the necessity of decadence within the economy of whole, and Nietzsche's wavering allegiance to active nihilism, see Staten 1992, 22.

26 In a note in which he introduces the term 'incomplete nihilism', Nietzsche explains: 'Attempts to escape nihilism without revaluating our values so far: they produce the opposite, make the problem more acute' (Nietzcshe 1968, §28).

27 Although the revolutionary nature of Nietzsche's experiment with will to power is widely appreciated, it is also typically held to signal the shipwreck of his otherwise promising philosophical project. Representative of this dominant opinion is the interpretation proffered by Karl Jaspers. Referring explicitly to the hypothesis of will to power, Jaspers concludes that: 'Nietzsche's thoughts about the world' undergo 'self-destruction' (Jaspers 1965, 329–30). According to Jaspers: 'What, in Nietzsche's meditations on truth, was an expressive circle constantly giving rise to new movements of thought, finally becomes, in his thoughts about the world, an annulment of metaphysics now become dogmatic: that of the will to power, as a militant exegesis temporarily believed. Here the contradictions become incapacitating, for there is a dead finality about them that prevents them from giving rise to anything new' (Jaspers 1965, 330).

28 I am indebted here to Mark Warren's excellent reconstruction of Nietzsche's 'phenomenology of agency' (Warren 1988, 126–30).

29 For an ingenious anti-metaphysical interpretation of the will to power, see Clark 1990. According to Clark (1990, 217), the argument in Nietzsche 1989a, §36: 'depend[s] on the causality of the will, something he nowhere accepts'. Clark thus maintains not only that 'Nietzsche gives us very strong reason to deny that he accepts the argument of *Beyond Good and Evil*, §36', but also that his exercise in self-subversion is 'quite deliberate'. Clark assures us that 'Nietzsche is challenging us to look for an explanation' of will to power (Clark 1990, 218).

30 On the relationship of Life to will to power, see Jaspers 1965, 293–302.

31 In a parallel development, his post-Zarathustran writings identify Nature as an even more basic morphological differentiation of the will to power, one that comprises the whole of Life within its boundless economy. Although less fully developed than his discussions of Life, his occasional appeals to Nature represent his most ambitious (and successful) attempts to rid his philosophy of its anthropocentric prejudices. As described by Nietzsche in his post-Zarathustran writings, Nature is unbounded, independent of and indifferent to the peculiar needs and demands of Life. Nature admits of no other, whether hospitable or hostile to Life, that imposes conditions upon the internal regulation of its economy. To those philologically inept 'physicists' who claim to deduce democratic principles from the canon of natural law, he rejoins: '[S]omebody might come along who, with opposite intentions and modes of interpretation, could read out of the same "Nature", and with regard to the same phenomena, rather the tyrannically inconsiderate and relentless enforcement of claims of power' (Nietzsche1989a, §22). For a sustained discussion of the distinction between Life and Nature, see Conway 1995.

32 For a positive interpretation of Nietzsche's critique of individual agency, see Hamacher 1986, 316–23.

33 On this topic of Nietzsche's residual humanist allegiances, his 'remaining caught up in the net of anthropomorphism', see Ansell Pearson 1997, 161–4.

34 I am indebted for this interpretation to Sluga, who convincingly documents Heidegger's moment of 'crisis'.

35 Nietzsche's failure to gain access to the world viewed 'from inside' would appear to confirm Heidegger's famous critique: 'This makes clear in what respect the mod-

ern metaphysics of subjectness is consummated in Nietzsche's doctrine of will to power as the "essence" of everything real' (Heidegger 1977, 83).

36 I would like to thank Diane Morgan and Keith Ansell Pearson for their excellent editorial comments on an earlier draft of this essay. Section I of this essay makes use of some paragraphs that originally appeared in my essay, 'Heidegger, Nietzsche, and the Origins of Nihilism', *Journal of Nietzsche Studies*, 3:11–43. Throughout Sections II–IV of this essay, I rely on reworked materials drawn from Chapters 2 and 4 of my *Nietzsche's Dangerous Game: Philosophy in the Twilight of the Idols* (Cambridge: Cambridge University Press, 1997). I am grateful to Cambridge University Press for their kind permission to reprint these materials in revised form.

References

Ansell Pearson, K. (1997) *Viroid Life. Perspectives on Nietzsche and the Transhuman Condition*. London: Routledge.

Blanchot, M. (1993) *The Infinite Conversation*, trans. Susan Hanson. Minneapolis: University of Minnesota Press.

Clark, M. (1990) *Nietzsche on Truth and Philosophy*. Cambridge: Cambridge University Press.

Conway, D. (1992) 'Heidegger, Nietzsche and the Origins of Nihilism', *Journal of Nietzsche Studies*, Spring Issue III, 11–43.

Conway, D. (1995) 'Returning to Nature: Nietzsche's *Götterdämmerung*' in *Nietzsche: A Critical Reader*, ed. P. Sedgwick. London: Blackwell.

Deleuze, G. (1977) 'Nomad Thought' trans. David B. Allison. In *The New Nietzsche: Contemporary Styles of Interpretation*, ed. David B. Allison. New York: Delta Books.

Gillespie, M. (1995) *Nihilism Before Nietzsche*. Chicago: University of Chicago Press.

Hamacher, W. (1986) ' "Disgregation des Willens": Nietzsche über Individuum und Individualität' in *Nietzsche-Studien* 15.

Heidegger, M. (1977) 'The Word of Nietzsche: God is Dead' in *The Question Concerning Technology and Other Essays*, trans. and ed. William Lovitt. New York: Harper & Row.

Heidegger, M. (1982) *Nietzsche IV: Nihilism*, trans. and ed. D.F. Krell. San Francisco: Harper & Row.

Jaspers, K. (1965) *Nietzsche: An Introduction to the Understanding of His Philosophical Activity*, trans. C.F. Wallraff and F.J. Schmitz. South Bend, IN: Regnery/Gateway.

Magnus, B., *et al.* (1993) *Nietzsche's Case: Philosophy as/and Literature*. New York: Routledge.

Sluga, H. (1993) *Heidegger's Crisis: Philosophy and Politics in Nazi Germany*. Cambridge, MA: Harvard University Press.

Nietzsche, F. (1967) *The Birth of Tragedy* and *The Case of Wagner* trans. and ed. Walter Kaufmann. New York: Vintage Books.

—— (1967 ff) *Werke: Kritische Gesamtausgabe*, eds. G. Colli and M. Montinari. Berlin: Walter De Gruyter.

—— (1968) *The Will To Power*, trans. Walter Kaufmann and R.J. Hollingdale, ed. Walter Kaufmann. New York: Vintage Books.

—— (1974) *The Gay Science*, trans. Walter Kaufmann. New York: Vintage Books.

—— (1982) *The Antichrist & Twilight of the Idols* in *The Portable Nietzsche*, ed. and trans. Walter Kaufmann. New York: Viking Penguin.

—— (1986) *Sämtliche Briefe, Kritische Studienausgabe in 8 Bänden*, eds. G. Colli and M. Montinari. Berlin: Walter De Gruyter/Deutscher Taschenbuch Verlag.

—— (1989a) *Beyond Good and Evil*, trans. Walter Kaufmann. New York: Vintage Books.

—— (1989b) *Ecce Homo* and *On the Genealogy of Morals* trans. & ed. Walter Kaufmann with R.J. Hollingdale, New York: Vintage Books.

Rosen, S. (1989) 'Nietzsche's Revolution' in *The Ancients and the Moderns*. New Haven: Yale University Press.

Staten, H. (1992) *Nietzsche's Voice*. Ithaca, NY: Cornell University Press.

Strong, T. (1998) 'Nietzsche's Political Aesthetics' in *Nietzsche's New Seas*, eds M. Gillespie and T. Strong. Chicago: University of Chicago Press.

Warren, M. (1988) *Nietzsche and Political Thought*. Cambridge, MA: MIT Press.

7
'Provoked Life': Expressing Nihilism

Diane Morgan

Having always forged its way with acausal steps, the brain is the prime example of the pygmy character of causal laws. Faced with the brain, all biological hypotheses fail. According to the work of Versluys, Poetzl and Lorenz, it seems to have developed itself through a saltatory doubling of the neurones accompanied by new formations of the cortical zones. 'Intermediary forms are missing'. Nothing here to do with adaptation, no summation of the smallest stimuli, no gradual decomposition and maturation leading to any purposive adjustment (*Zweckmäßigkeitsumstellung*), *here there always were creative crises*. It is the mutative, i.e. revolutionary, organ par excellence. Its essence was never content, but always form; its means intensification; its demand stimulation. This lodge of rudiments and catacombs brought everything with it right from the beginning; it never had to rely on impressions, it produced itself when called upon. Its predilections were no way limited to "Life" but included lethal factors, hunger, fasting, walking on nails, snake-charming, magic, the bionegative, death.

Benn 'Provoked Life' (1943)

Floods caused by melting icecaps, whole land-masses submerged; the oceans starved of oxygen by burgeoning algae which thrives off effluent; the once innocuous soyabean genetically modified into an insidious, all-pervasive, cancer-provoking substance; clinically brain dead women used as 'alternative reproductive vehicles'; the countryside resounds with the bleats of absolutely identical 'Dollies': such is the future facing us. Cows and chickens transformed into zombie killing machines, whose sacrificed carcases seep into water reserves, polluting the whole ecosystem. Humans are eating their own madness as they tuck into their carnivorous cow-rumps. Something is seriously wrong. But who do we trust to put it right?[1]

Back in the 1920s right through to the 1950s, Gottfried Benn – doctor for skin afflictions, venereal diseases and expressionist poet – faced the daunting future conjured up by such questions. Drawing together his interest for and expertise in the natural science and his after-surgery-hours dedication to lyric poetry, he wrote extraordinary contributions (essays and poems) to the debates around nihilism raging at the beginning of the century. However, perhaps precisely because of the bizarre concoction of modern scientific theories interspliced with expressionist lyricism, he was never just a product of his time.[2] Indeed, this chapter wants to show how Benn's notion of 'provoked life', regarded as the most appropriate retort to the occident's passive slide into a terminal phase, has much to contribute to a thinking of nihilism, now!

Drawing on Newtonian physics, Helmholtz, Darwin and contemporary thinkers of entropy, Benn suggests that the modern world has been strapped down and stretched out by mechanistic-deterministic laws purporting to chart life's progress, whether this be 'upwards' – towards an inevitably ever-increasing sophistication – or downwards – towards an inevitable eventual heat-death.[3] Benn claims that, in the eighteenth century, it was Goethe who first reacted against the iniquitous effects of this 'progressive cerebralisation' of life's movements (Benn 1989a, 203). Goethe resisted such attempts to predict the future by positing teleological ends. Tucked under the auspices of an englobing 'perspective',[4] such as causality, the future is turned into a bigger, better (or, for the pessimists, a weaker, worse) variation of the present. It is not a future at all. For Goethe this mind-set represents a dire failure to confront life's unpredictable vitality. Goethe's crazy project to find the originary plant (*Urplanze*) from which all subsequent flowerings and foliations stem, is a passionate attempt to trace the morphological transmutations of nature, its bizarre interrelatedness, its wacky offshoots, thereby resisting stultifying classificatory compressions into discrete species. Likewise, his dogged pursuit of the intermaxillary bone (the *Zwischenkieferknochen*) was his way of breaking down the barrier between the animal and the human, of resisting the all-too-prevalent tendency to see the human as arising *out of* and *away from* the animal world.[5]

Continuing in his own way such Goethean preoccupations, Benn resists the prevailing platitudes of his time. In 'Problems of the Poetical' (1930) he gives vent to his detestation of what he sees as the Darwinian 'mountaineer-ideal' which regards the Human as the victor of the struggle for existence, brazenly bedecked with 'the scalps of animals' (Benn 1989a, 85). For such a Human, the past is just a 'descendence-slag heap' (Benn 1989a, 86–7) comprising of worthless waste matter eliminated in the rationalised pursuit of a health-oriented 'race consolidation' (*Rassenertüchtigung*).[6] History for social Darwinians is just a high-performance, anthropomorphic 'steeple chase' towards a nebulous concept of excellence (Benn 1989a, 265). Equally, Benn suggests that the concept of evolution has also been used as a comforting 'nightcap' to ward off everything that might disturb the human's sleepy self-assurance that time is on his side, faithfully furthering the race: 'pssh! quieten down! we've got our evolution' (Benn 1989a, 35). Benn, when he is not in his own fascistically bellicose 'period', is also disgusted by the use to which evolution has been put by social Darwinians: relying on a false parallel between organic life and human culture, the expressions 'struggle for existence' and 'survival of the fittest' have been used to justify colonialising war and the systematic elimination of those deemed to be weak.[7]

In the place of such reductive readings of nature, the organic world and humans' place within it, Benn favours a radically different perspective. In 1920, when addressing prospective medical students, he remarks upon the fact that many of them are traumatised and exhausted, have broken limbs and glass-eyes, having been through the 'mud years' (*die Schlammjahren*) of Ypres and experienced the painful impact of so-called (technological and social) advancement (Benn 1989a, 29). And now, here they are, about to embark upon a initiation into the venerable medical profession which, unperturbed by recent events, prides itself on its quest to bolster the human body in the name of health, both individual and national. Surely the whole body politic is sick and gangrenous? Should it continually be patched up and dutifully redispatched onto the assembly-line which carries it ineluctably to meaningless destruction? Benn proposes a revaluation of the future and enjoins the medical students to reconsider their position: where are they heading and why?

To help them on their way, Benn proposes that the modern ego has metamorphosed into something very different from its prior incarnations. Back in the age of 'Enlightenment', preformationists, such as Haller, pre-empted an encounter of the unknown by outlawing any becoming. Development was reduced to a precooked recipe which just needed to be reheated (whether by the male sperm or female egg) in order to be actualised (Benn 1989a, 35). This was one of a whole series of general laws which purported to account for all future development. As we have already seen, Benn sees Darwinism as extending this ignorance of real change with its confident investment in human progress. As a counterpoint to such stolid theories, Benn espouses the viewpoint of someone like Semi Meyer. Instead of seeing future development as neatly encapsulated in prior forms, Meyer's *Problems of the Development of Spirit* explores a development as a principle which does not merely unwind or unfold itself but which instead creatively builds on the available basis in a incalculable fashion (Benn 1989a, 38). Now the spirit can be free as overriding general laws (those grand old narratives) have fallen into disrepute and creation is at last seen to be laden with unforeseeable potential. Unhitched from the reductive burden of general progress, each one of us becomes a (our own) destiny. Benn exorts those medical freshmen to take another look at the quasi-divine authoritative figures to whom they were so grateful for being gracefully received by: 'listen, what a productive flatulence, from behind the truth-drive is discharged and from the front the free research; he wipes himself with the cleanliness of the intellectual attitude held in his right hand and the refusal of all speculation in his left' (Benn 1989a, 38–9). Benn calls on the young students to reject the pontificating staleness of the old and to seize the potential of new ways of looking at the world. Gone are mechanistic-deterministic laws governing your every movement, defunct is inductive reasoning intent on imposing its presumptuous formulae on objects, thereby blinding itself to any vision of difference (Benn 1989a, 171). Phenomena such as Picasso's violins must be seen as axes dealing deadly blows to the old 'reality'. Amongst the debris of a busted cosmos the new generation are free to invent their own pathways (Benn 1989a, 39).

These youthful nihilists stand on the edge of nothingness, where formlessness lurks (Benn 1989a, 39). Hardly surprising that the question urges itself whether it is really worthwhile to carry on the sanitising work of previous years, patching up ailing bodies with injections, ointments, bandages, when the race might be on the very verge of mutating into another form. Benn is a faithful follower of Turgenev's Bazarov when, as a doctor, he throws doubt on our faith in medicine, questioning its pertinence.[8] What is the point nursing back to health this anachronistic little darling of progress when his background remains 'a rotten ideology of positivistic usefulness, the same old worn-out, helpless, run-down hymnology from the cradle to the grave, (constant mollycoddling(with nose-baths and nutritional enemas'? (Benn 1989a, 171). For Benn, one of the defining characteristics of the artistic movement to which he belonged, Expressionism, was precisely a passionate rejection of this thinned-out, reactive type of existence in favour of an intensely 'provoked life'. No longer playing safe, neurotically discriminating between what is 'good' for one's organism and what is 'bad', the nihilistic Expressionist injects himself with whatever produces a highly charged rush.[9] The bionegative stimulates the artist, channelling his energies towards the climax of an intense, formal ex-pression which is catapulted into the formless nothingness confronting him.

The Expressionist flies in the face of the times by exposing himself to such destruction. With a fervour comparable to the dedication of an ascetic holyman, he holds himself out against the horrifying vacuum left behind by the smashed-up edifices of the old realities, absolutely refusing to compromise. Earlier on in the century in his *The Decline of the West*, Spengler had already outlined the reduced options available for the western Man who is resigned to his modern fate:

> The expansive tendency is a fate, something demonic and monstrous, that grabs the last human of this stage of the world's history, forces him into its service and consumes him, whether he wants it or not. Life is the realisation of the possible and for this cerebral human (*Gehirnmenschen*) there exists only extensive possibilities.   (Spengler 1991, 51)[10]

Stretched out of the rack of grand narratives, which run over him in a myopic search of some far-away teleological end, the later day human lacks substance. In this modern world of speed, distance-covering becomes an unquestioned priority. Vast expanses of the earth surface are traversed without affecting the human organism sensually at all. The only receptor left to the human resigned to extensive possibilities is the highly intellectualised brain.

By contrast, the actively nihilistic Expressionist goes for pounding intensity. He is fully aware of that the all too cerebrally accentuated species described by Spengler is most probably doomed to extinction. Benn, with all his medical expertise, predicts that, due to the steady increase in their skull size, *homo sapiens* will eventually die out as their heads rip open and destroy the very pelvic girdles which await their arrival in pregnant anticipation (Benn 1989a, 117 and 452). Even before this apocalyptic end to the race, the human organism will already have been on a steady wane as progressive cerebralisation leaves the other organs, with their attached sensations, to lapse into etiolation.[11] What is needed, as Benn makes clear in 'Provoked Life' quoted above, is to exploit the brain's 'creative crises', its saltational acausality, its punctuated equilibrium.[12] Far from stultifying the organ, and thereby gradually sapping the transformatory vitality of the whole organism, Benn affirms – as we will see – a different approach to the meaning of the human and its place within the evolving world.

Logical thought represents a mere fraction of the brain's inherited characteristics. The vigilant ego is a late and fleeting product of nature for whom the distinction between the inner self and the outside has not always existed. In the prelogical world the brain moved in different organic circles, in those belonging to strange one-eyed sea creatures and fishes with flickering cilia.[13] *Homo sapiens'* descendence from fish with load-bearing fins, who were fortuitously able to scramble to the land thrown up by the receding seas,[14] is treated by Benn, not as an opportunity to eulogise human 'progress', but as a way of thinking the future as monstrously energetic.

Benn suggests that the human 'personality' is all of its evolutionary past. It bears the 'animal signatures' of its former incarnations: having been sometimes akin to the marsupials, sometimes to the mammals, having worn fish scales in the age of the victorious amphibians, fur in the era of the apes, having had a tail, having found itself in amongst the giants. . . . The human 'personality' 'recorded all of these turns' and that legacy of chimeras – half-animal, half-human – is still mysteriously alive within the species (Benn 1989a, 121). Even in this age of highly developed intellects we are still not in possession of the key to the machinations of evolutionary history. Benn remarks:

> We can only say that, within the framework of gigantic telluric-cosmic events, ice-eons and eras of world-conflagrations, the fall of the tertiary

moon to earth, the darkening of the heavens, the cataclysms of fire and cyclons, in ever new spontaneous, evolutive drives [*immer neuen spontanen Entwicklungstrieben*]: half causality, half creation, half geological necessity, half act of transcendence – that, in these ways, the epileptoid mixture of the genesis of our personality was carried out.

(Benn 1989a, 121–2)

Benn detects very little long-term purposive adaptation in nature. Nature is moody, prone to fickleness and organic life's responses are spasmodic, but highly creative.[15] The organism joyfully – Benn goes so far as to suggest, orgiastically – partakes of these incessant reinventions of itself:

We saw in [the (human) organism] the amphibian, the reptilian, the marsupial, the mammalian, the simian: all these stigma of its subjection to a vast principle of tellurian history; all these stigma of its former declines and of its renewed joy in the surges of one great organic motif that always runs through all animal forms of the same geological period, producing a tension that drives contemporaneously living zoological beings away from their characterising specificities towards new corporeal situations and functions. (Benn 1989a, 123)

At the beginning of the quaternary period mammals began to develop the cerebrum which has now become the leading organ of our holocene epoch, making us so proud of our place in the universe. However, the organic signature of previous ages, of the mesozoic era and tertiary period, was also a miraculous creation. It was, according to Benn, the pineal eye. He tells us that this organ:

conferred the vision of nature, the magical feeling, the telepathy and telekinesis with which they [the people of the past] effortlessly moved the enormous stone blocks, rendered somehow weightless, right over mountains and through the waters to build their colossal temples.

(Benn 1989a, 123)

As regards his reflections on the pineal eye Benn would have had a lot in common with George Bataille. Like Benn, Bataille also emphasised this organ's importance and explored its significance in his outrageous essay of the same name:

The eye at the summit of the skull, opening on the incandescent sun in order to contemplate it in a sinister solitude, is not a product of the understanding but is instead an immediate experience; it opens up and blinds itself like a conflagration, or like a fever that eats the being, or more exactly the head. (Bataille 1994, 82)

Bataille suggests that the pineal eye exposes itself to destruction as it expresses itself, as it opens itself up to the solar experience. The pineal eye is reckless in its pursuit of fiery experience, of the very experience which will burn it out, reducing its voracious lust for a vitalised vision to the blackest of blindnesses. Bataille's depiction of this ecstatic, yet volatile, self-destructive, life-form is akin to Benn's understanding of evolution. Instead of a steady, constant, hierarchising growth towards ever-consolidated perfection, Benn also emphasises the instability and contingency of living forms:

> the life that arises from the gullet, organises itself a while to disappear into the inferno, this life will open its jaws against those civilisation-hordes who regard the sea as a nutritional enema with its oyster beds and value fire as a beer-warmer for under their asbestos sheets.
>
> (Benn 1989a, 94)

While in the process of developing a theory about life-forms in this passage, Benn does not miss an opportunity to give self-satisfied evolutionists, those who insist on understanding biology as a unqualified confirmation of Man's progress, a kick up the backside. With this enemy in mind, he would surely have appreciated the force of Bataille's filthy lesson about pineal eyes and their relation to the riotously coloured anuses of apes. Bataille emphasises 'the expressive value of an excremental orifice emerging from a hairy body like a live coal' (Bataille 1994, 87). Undeniably visible on the ape is the 'huge screaming pink anal protrusion [which] stares at the sky like a flower' (Bataille 1994, 85). This rude animal is not to be tamed, will not be summarised into some smoothly linear history of Man's gradual civilisation. The ape with its 'parti-coloured, red or mauve anal baldness' is a freak who troublingly impinges on the human consciousness, sending traumatised young 'innocents' to sob convulsively in secluded lavatories (Bataille 1994, 87).[16] Similarly, Benn aims to sabotage the certainties of smug evolutionists by apocalyptically heralding the reaffirmation of life's cyclical patterns, its ebbs and flows.[17] Working side-by-side with Bataille and his depiction of the scandalous ape and its freakish anus, Benn further underlines the freakish aspect of all life-forms: they are organisations which momentarily inscribe themselves on the surge of life before plunging into formless nothingness.[18] The task facing affirmative nihilists, like Benn, is to redefine the human in the face of such annihilatory forces. The challenge is to rethink the human as an (ever recurring) instant inscribed upon the seething movement of demonic matter.

Benn calls the 'reality' constructed by twentieth-century Europeans a 'demonic concept' (Benn 1989a, 266). As we have already seen with the help of Spengler, the modern world has placed its emphasis on the 'cerebral' (at the expense of other anatomical assets) and on the 'expansive' (long-drawn teleological goals, the stretching- and qualitative thinning-out of space). The human is viewed as completely detached from nature. Indeed the human's task is presented as being that of conquering nature, exploiting its resources and rationalising its moods (Benn 1989a, 207). Benn blames the physicist, Helmholtz, for luring us into the illusion that the world can be wholly understood thanks to generally applicable mechanical laws (Benn 1989a, 208). Darwinism is seen as further bolstering this world-view with its meritocratic vision. Those who are strong and fit will survive in this capitalist world of cut-throat competition (Benn 1989a, 208). Or, more precisely, the mere fact that one is here means that one has already survived the struggle and thereby merited a place in the sun. Benn concludes that the human type which is produced as a result of these ideologies is a: 'materialist and socialist utilitarian type (*Gebrauchstyp*), a montage-type, optimistic and shallow, cynically rid of any idea of fatality, the least possible suffering for the individual, the most comfort possible for all' (Benn 1989a, 226). The human race, having already 'proved' its worth, now has to consolidate its potential by concentrating on solid averages. The race stock must be preserved, not squandered, and, as a consequence, any variation from the norm is to be discouraged.

However, this rationalised, functional world, perpetuated by state-run institutions – whose task it is to protect citizens from anything that threatens their cushioned existence – is under attack. Having dedicated itself to the elimination of the 'bionegative' and to the exclusion of any vestiges of former mythological and biological life-forms, the 'civilised', 'cerebralised' human falls prey to demonic forces. Uncontrollable neurotic symptoms erupt all over him as the repressed returns to haunt his fragile security (Benn 1989a, 239–40).[19] Agoraphobia declares itself in the vast, hollow expanses of the modern city; murderous sex fantasies are acted out as the body lays claim to its ancient rights. Leaving the beyond of lands and times 'forgotten', these forces exact their revenge. They are experienced as something demonic which impinges from without, threatening a cherished inner self; but this 'interiority' is already extenuated. Hollowed out by the crazy processes of 'rationalisation', with their obsessional concern for mass standardisation, the petrified human cannot resist the vindictive onslaught of the demons. The human has stopped short its development by failing to appreciate that inventive new life-forms often arise from daring departures from the norm, not from a reactive defence of the already known. In short, the only way to conquer the demons is to become a mutative monster.[20]

Indeed, although Benn does not quite use these terms, he obliquely confirms this perspective on the overcoming of the demonic throughout his works. As we will see, the mutative monstrous is that which he associates with genial expression. In his essay 'The Problem of Genius', Benn disputes the fact that societal safekeeping could ever foster really creative products. Genius surges forth only where there is the 'abnormality and degeneration' (Benn 1989a, 141); genius is in the first place anathema to society's values and only retrospectively acknowledged as something great. Genius is the mutant child of an improbable coupling:

> As for the parents, it seems that germ-material which is as different as possible is often the starting point for the formation of genius. Blood and race foreignness, e.g. Slavic with German blood: in the case of Nietzsche, Leibniz, R. Wagner; or, also, a marked difference in the characters and constiutions: e.g. an extreme schizoid type matched with a cyclothymic, in short everything which aims for the unmixable (*die Unvermischbarkeit*), the unbalanced (*die Unausgeglichenheit*) bastardisation, insolvable tension.
>
> (Benn 1989a, 133)

Genius is partly a novel concoction of the most disparate elements improbably brought together in a volatile vessel, that of the musician, scientist, lyric poet, philosopher.... The other part comprises of that intrepid surfer on the back of life's primordial, seething movements evoked earlier. Genius is that which is able to ride the wave, 'organise itself a while', before plunging into the infernal gullet that is the beginning and end of life. The genius recognises, and draws on the recognition, that the human is 'mutatively stratified' (Benn 1989a, 669). As discussed above, the human has always been in closest association with manifold other living beings during its evolutionary past and it thereby bears the 'organic signatures' of each transmutational stage. As a consequence of this rich and inexhaustible inheritance, the human, for Benn, is eternal and primordial (*uralt*) (Benn 1989a, 448). If the human is not wilfully reduced to its latter day form, the *homo sapiens* – which is heading for destruction if cerebralisation continues at its current pace – then talk of the 'posthuman' is inappropriate: 'The human race! Immortality within a creative system that is itself subject to further inconceivable extensions (*Erweiterungen*) and transformations' (Benn 1989a, 448). If evolution is not conceived anthropomorphically as a linear march to 'progress', we can begin to start thinking life as evolving in ways which border on becoming monstrous, opening up the human in ways which do not confirm his place in a knowable world according to our conventional categories of thought. Consequently, Benn explicitly rejects the Kantian reading of nature as consisting of 'starry heavens' and 'beaming' humans who, despite being confronted with the 'almost monstrous' sublime, are still assured of basic general laws governing their world. While trying to explain the tortuous urgency of the expressionist movement to the very (in)different world of 1934, he writes:

> And so these generations grew up, those who drank down all substances offering disintegration (*Zersetzung*) and who precisely did not lift their beaming human faces to the starry heavens, rather in whose insides instead chimera and demons fattened themselves and sucked away, seeds of discord, and who, in their hurlings of form (*Formausstürzen*)

and the subsequent periods of lethargy, succumb to *(erlagen)* all the cerebral intoxications of the age. (Benn 1984, 332)

If the human is eternal, there are no guarantees that we will recognise ourselves at all within any future manifestations of our race. We cannot preconceive its future trajectories and symbiotic alliances. However, instead of passively being overwhelmed by a fate, we should become expressionists.[21] Expressionist are those who can conquer the demons by being able to conceive of the living world as a 'monster of energy'. The expressionist is able to think the human 'as arising from and being extended *(ergänzt)* by the mutatively stratified, that is, in ever new transcendental acts and out of ever new creative impulses' (Benn 1989a, 669). The term 'stratified' refers to geological history, itself made up of catastrophic events wiping out whole species, reinventing others along unpredictable trajectories, that Benn so adores describing, for instance in 'Primal Vision'[22]:

> Mass in instincts. Brain bubbles into the drain, germ layers into the flower bed, yolk sacks in the thrust of distance. Heritage of exaltation and intoxications, astral conflagrations, transoceanic decay. Crises, mixtures, third century.... Primeval urges of ageless masses in the sound of the seas and the plunge of light *(Uralte Dränge altersloser Masse im Klang der Meere und im Sturz des Lichts)*. Life wants to maintain itself but also to perish.... From catastrophes that were latent, catastrophes that preceded the word, come dreadful memories of the race, hybrid, beast-shaped, sphinx-pouched features of the primal face. (Benn 1984, 118–19)[23]

The 'primal face' is not actually something to be seen – we cannot regress through time to get at it.[24] 'It' is also not just one thing but already is a sprouting becoming-something-else, the enigmatic offspring from a cross between two or more improbables. What Benn suggests in 'The Incessant' is that the human 'keeps on remembering *(erinnert)* the indissoluble mythical remains of his race' (Benn 1984, 183). What is being proposed here is no mere recapitulation of the evolutionary history of the race at the level of the individual,[25] which would run the risk of reducing the individual to a mere playback machine. The interiorisation implied within remembering *(erinnern)* is what has the power of converting demons into monstrously creative outbursts:

> With what does the human conquer the demonic, not the absolute man, but today's historical man, who no longer lives in the age of monotheistic incantation *(Beschwörung)*, but rather in the epoch after Nietzsche.... The answer reads: contemporary Western man conquers the demonic through form; his demonic nature is form, his magic is the technical–constructive,

his icy-world-teaching is that creation is the demand for form, the human
is the cry for expression (*Schrei nach Ausdruck*)   (Benn 1989a, 485–6)

The demonic is ex-pressed, pressed out, in a tense, formal outbursts which
splatter against the barrier of life's seething movements. Life's prodigious
movements are all too threatening to the conventional human, he who has
for so long used nature as a car park for his 'oyster beds' or a means to heat up
his beer (see Benn, above). Non-humanoid nature appears to the Darwinian
kingpin to be undifferentiated matter, sheer immateriality. The expressionist, on the other hand, sees a chance to test new, tightly-packed, intensely-
charged forms, not in order to communicate something to an audience, not
to pass on a message (*nicht Mitteilung*) but so as to express (*sondern Ausdruck*).
The expressionist is not seeking some sort of participation (*nicht Teilnahme*),
such as a mystical blending or communally shared moment, but instead is
intent on aggravating differentiation (*sondern Differenzierung*) (Benn 1989a,
162). He is not afraid to activate the plethora of individualisms within the
individual, thereby unravelling any intrinsic kernel the subject claims to
possess for itself.[26]. He valiantly confronts the prospect of cataclysmic events
of nature which suddenly overturn years of gradual growing, wiping out
whole species and packing others off along wholly unexplored, new evolutive pathways. In 'Wolf's Tavern' Benn writes at length about the unpredictable, saltational characteristics of natural life:

And is this Nature of yours, I could not help retorting, really natural?...I
can prove that it is unnatural, a thing of leaps and bounds (*äußerst
sprunghaft*), indeed the very textbook example of what one means by
'contrary to nature'. It begins something and drops it, makes a great stir
and forgets. It is unbridled, it exaggerates, it produces fish in incredible
shoals off the Lofotens, or rolling swarms of locusts and cicadas. Or there
is peace on earth, everything has the temperature of the stones, one can
truly give one's attention to the climate, and then the Aaron's rod shoots
up in flower at forty degrees Centigrade, everything is thrown into confusion and the gods insist on warm-blooded animals – is that Nature's
doing, or whose is it? Or take geological folding, densification, unimaginable concentration – one of its methods – is that a simple an natural thing
to do? Or it takes a fancy to send immense tensions charging across
microscopically tiny spaces – is that now the thing to expect? Come to
think of it, was the phenomenon of life not nicely looked after in plant
form? Why set it in motion and sent it out in search of food – is that not a
model of uprooting? As for its creature, Man, does it not plunge him
headlong into anti-Nature, hurling bacteria to destroy him, diminishing
his smell, reducing his sense of hearing, denaturing his eye by means of
optical lenses, so that the man of the future is the merest abstraction –
where are the workings of natural Nature? No, it is some other face that

peers out everywhere, sleeping in the stones, blossoming in the flowers, making its demands in all late forms – a very different face, and the result I arrive at is a strange one.   (Benn 1984,141–2; 1971, 75–6)

No mere passive pastoral, no mere laudatory echo of Man's good feeling about himself and his place on earth; instead nature is most monstrously energetic. Nature is wilful (but with no particular goal 'in mind'), fickle, perverse, exuberant in its fostering of proliferating life-forms, but also deadly when in a fit of destruction. We vainly try to anthropomorphise 'her' just as we attempt to humanise the genial. Indeed Benn reiterates culture's consistent attempts desperately to cover over the nihilism at work within creative work:

Not for an instant are they unaware of the essential nature of their own inner creative substance. It is the abyss, the void, the unsolvable, the cold, the inhuman element.   (Benn 1984: 145; 1971, 79)

For Benn, even Nietzsche is human, all too human, in his wish to avoid a confrontation with the inhuman. Zarathustra is a 'child of nature' who reeks of 'evolutionary optimism' (*Züchtungsoptimismus*), redolent of 'shallow utopianism about the spirit and its realization'[27] (Benn 1984, 145; 1971, 79). Such optimism about the future of the race is deemed to be misplaced as the human is a vestigial survivor of a law which provokes an 'inconceivable metamorphosis' (Benn 1989a, 124). While not exactly doomed to extinction, the human may be reworked in ways which bear no resemblance to the familiar *homo sapien* of today. Only in Nietzsche's later works does Benn sense more of an awareness of the negativity which informs creativity, of the formless negativity in the face of which creativity forms.[28]

On the cultural plane, the inhumanity of creative genius mirrors the monstrous face of the biological. On the technological plane – in the laboratories of the genetic engineers – scientists also imitate nature in all its unnaturalness. Amongst the expressionists and the latter-day eugenicists the realisation prevails that the current human form, that of the *homo sapien*, is transitory. In 1949, Benn apocalyptically announces that the 'style of the future' will be:

that of robots, an art of montage. The human on evidence up to now is finished. . . . The human must be reassembled all over again out of clichés, proverbs, meaningless references, from over-subtleties, broadly based: *a human in inverted commas*. Its depiction will be kept going by using formal tricks, repetitions of words and motives – ideas will be banged in like nails and outcomes hung on them.   (Benn 1984, 471)

Gone is that blessed, incantatory human, mentioned earlier who was able to conjure up the world around himself; whose thoughts and world view are preciously perpetuated in novels; the *bonhomme* we are supposed to patiently get to know intimately, tracing – chapter upon chapter – his steps through a life which seems mapped-out around him, sometimes treating him well, sometimes badly, but anyhow, a life which relates to him as someone special. This human is finished. He is merely an instance of the process of the becoming-something-else. Such a human possesses no absolute value, is not at the centre of things, is a stand-in, is standing in the mutating flow of matter.

For the lyric poet and the eugenicist the way to meet this challenge to the conventional human is through the 'cultivated absoluteness of form... the intensified pushing-forward of the constructive up to the boundary of immateriality' (Benn 1989a, 213). In the relaying of characteristics from one life cycle to another, form presents itself as the only baton which stands a chance of being passed on.[29] Competing with the 'ever new spontaneous, evolutive drives, half causality, half transcendence' (Benn 1989a, 121–2 *quoted earlier*), the poet and the biologist have to try and breed a form that is once tensely disciplined, yet 'epileptoid', not weakly purist but throbbing with the 'bionegative', with vibrantly 'provoked life'.

Having dumped the evolutionary liability of the conventionally sacrosanct humanist self, the lyrical human is free to express itself mutatively. Expression here, as we have seen, is unrelated to the pious niceties of the novelistic age, no precious message from one sentient human to another is meant. The inner is the turned-around demonic energetically projected outwards in tight form, bulging with associative potentiality, not in any anticipation of a sympathetic ear, not with any content in mind. The expression which is pressed outwards did not originate in the inner depths of a human subject. Far from it: 'the way inwards leads to the stratifications of creation' (Benn 1989a, 421) where the human can be tracked down as something at times half-fish, at others almost-ape, feeling its way across bizarre mesozaic landscapes with the help of its pineal eye.

Once the bourgeois ego is declared defunct, there is certainly no way back to that comfortable (*gemütlich*) inwardness kept buoyant by humanists.[30] Speaking as a true modernist nihilist in 'Nihilism and its Overcoming' (1932), Benn writes about the irreversible shift that has occurred from a spatiality which is gathered up around the lyrical solitude of the individual to a projection of space against metallic and glass design (Benn 1989a, 213). Benn does not regret the arrival of this new form of spatiality, indeed he embraces it. In *Double Life* he writes:

> the formal must come, transitory, light and smooth wings, everything that floats in azure, aluminium surfaces, superficialities .. in short, style, the new world, turned outside.   (Benn 1984, 375)

Earlier on in the same essay, he fleshes out the impact of this rethinking of space for the shrinking body:

> Cortex = brain: the cortical wilting of the worlds, the bourgeois world, the capitalist world, the opportunist, prophylactic, antiseptic worlds, beaten by the cloud bursts of the political and the restructurings of power, this arises from Western man's crisis of substance. Inner man is in tatters, more tattered than his body ever was from worms and grenades: fermented, sour, gasified, with rusted slogans in his baggage rack . . . a new man pushes his way in, no longer an emotional, religious, humanist being, no cosmic paraphrase, but the man as naked, formal gestation. A new world is beginning, the world of expression. It is a world of clear, interspliced (*verzahnter*) relations, the interlocking of ground down forces, metallicized and smoothed (*gestillter*) surfaces . . . .
> (Benn 1984, 373)

As we have already seen, for Benn the task is no longer to be, in Heidegger's words, a 'physician of culture' (Heidegger 1978, 387), patching it up, making it better. One of his reservations regarding psychoanalysis is that it attempts just this, always looking backwards doctoring hereditary ills, thereby neglecting the ascendancy of the future. In his notorious reply to Klaus Mann, in 'Letter to the Literary Emigrants' (1933), Benn writes:

> [The essence of Man] is an eternal Quaternary, a horde magic feuilletonistically decking even the late Ice Age, a fabric of diluvial moods, Tertiary bric-à-brac; in fact, he is the eternally primal vision [*Urgesicht*]: wakefulness, day life, reality – loosely consolidated rhythms of hidden creative intoxications.
> (Benn 1984, 298)

The essence of man is not human; it is 'a clod of slime' (*ein Klümpchen Schleim*) (Benn 1982, 47).[31] Instead of this factor dragging us back to some obscure atavism, it should lead the way forward to a cultivation (*Züchtung*) of 'creative intoxications'.[32] The body becomes a malleable surface to be designed to the most extreme of definitions – it must split its sides, cleave in two, spill outwards – if the human is to be equal to the challenge of 'the law of inconceivable metamorphosis'.

Describing the patients he had to treat as specialist for venereal diseases, Benn explores the 'sweet corporeality' of the oozing and unctuous genitals. In his poem 'The Doctor' (1917) a diseased penis has grown over; instead of fecundating his wife the man has poached a grave problem. The disease boils away and one day: 'the crevice and the thrust / will gape from the forehead to the sky' [*Ich ahne: einst / Werden die Spalte und der Stoß / Zum Himmel klaffen von der Stirn*] (Benn 1982, 87). Far from wanting to purge the nation of venereal diseases – whose gradual elimination puts Benn out of work – the doctor-poet (ironically) rants against their 'shameless persecution' by the authorities (Benn 1989a, 34). He mocks the institutionalised policing of 'a few Prussian testicles' which converts the body into an object of social hygiene (Benn 1989a, 35). Indeed in 'Genius and Health' (1930) he traces the intimacy between genial creativity and illness: Baudelaire died of hashish, Goethe was a psychopath and Kant died of arterio-sclerotic idiocy (Benn 1989a, 106 and 137). He concludes the essay with the following lines:

> the body is the last compulsion and the depth of necessity, the monologue of creation and, if it degenerates in a particular way sometimes the premise for genius.   (Benn 1989a, 109)

Degeneration (*Entartung*) is not necessarily an illness to be eliminated but can be a condition to be bred (*gezüchtet*). This would leave the paradoxical possibility open of a different approach to eugenics, of an eugenics which presents itself as a eulogy of *de-formation* as formal expression. A far cry from the criminal use of eugenics as 'ethnic cleansing', this other sort of eugenics would celebrate the hurling of a particular, bionegatively 'provoked', that is, cultivated, form against the 'barrier of immateriality', up to the point where its extreme concentration cracks, disintegrates and sinks back into the mutating flux.

In the 'Of Redemption' chapter of Nietzsche's *Thus Spake Zarathustra* we hear of 'men who lack everything except one thing, of which they have too much' (Nietzsche 1969, 160). The man who has and is an ear, the one who is no more than a great eye or mouth. The cultivation of such deformity, as described by Benn, would imply the concentration of form, the streamlining of creative, formalising energy towards that ear, towards that unique eye, that gigantic mouth, until the intensity of precision becomes so finely defined that it becomes indefinite. It then collapses back into the inhumanly material. However, in a 1867–68 fragment, Nietzsche seems to be suggesting that form possesses only a very limited capacity to overcome the monster which is life and he appears to recommend caution: 'you can draw lots for all forms, but life!' (*Alle Formen können ausgewürfelt werden, aber das Leben!*) (Nietzsche 1933–42, 388). An overestimation of the potential of cultivated form, whether it comes in the shape of lyric poetry or genetic engineering, might just be the same 'evolutionary optimism' so despised by Benn, but in another guise, just one more deceptively savorous to the nihilist's pallet. The promise held out by genetic engineering of being able, in Zarathustra's words, to 'redeem' oneself from chance, by turning every 'it was' into 'I wanted it thus', is maybe just another deluded attempt to rewrite 'life's grandeur' and all that implies – its prodigious creativity, not always traceable to a cause or an end; its horrific cataclysmic events which force a radical reorientation of some species and enforce destruction on others – as a 'grand narrative' of life.[33] Such a narrative would hold out the comforting prospect of a purposeful direction underlying what otherwise appears to be inhumanly nonsensical.

In 'Problems of the Lyric' Benn further discusses eugenics and genetics. He alludes to the 'important work' of the scientist, Alexis Carrel, who after experimenting on organ transplantation ended up working for the Vichy government implementing 'purification' programmes on the mentally ill. Carrel is nowadays celebrated by the Front National as the 'father of ecology' (Bonnafé and Tort 1992, 8).[34] Jean-Marie Le Pen has described eugenics as being necessitated by the development away from natural law, understood as the law of natural selection. According to Le Pen, society has degenerated and thereby ecological balance has to be artificially put right through conscious, planned eugenics. This cannot be accomplished without pain. As Carrel himself wrote in *Man, this Unknown*:

> In order to grow again, man is obliged to renew himself [*se refaire*]. This cannot be done without pain as he is at once the marble and the sculptor. It is his own substance that he has to chip away at with blows of the hammer and send flying before he can wear his real face again.
>
> (Carrel 1935, 327)

This is highly toxic stuff and Benn certainly finds himself in extremely bad company. Indeed, for a time, he explicitly supports the Nazi ideology of racial cleansing and projects such as *Lebensborn* (Aryan breeding farms). However, the quasi-scientific techniques adopted by the Nazis and their collaborators so as to conquer a degenerate nature, a nature that has to be put back on course by man, is otherwise far too positivist for Benn. Technology is not simply a human tool just as it is not simply an invention of modernity; technology has always been part of nature:

> Man behaves according to the creative laws which stand above the atom bomb and uranium ore.. There has always been technology but most people don't know enough about it to know this.   (Benn 1989a, 531–2)

There is no one particular event or invention which offers man the occasion to seize technology and ride it, just as life itself refuses to be tamed. Benn adds that 'the technology established here on earth is lacking in existential significance' (Benn 1989a, 531). There is no privileged moment, such as the moment of fascism, wherein technology reveals itself and offers itself for harnessing so as to hunt down life.

This analysis of Benn's work flushes out one line of argument that is the poet's. Another line, the more familiar one, is also his. It is also the absolute contradiction of the former: that is, it asserts that there precisely is a privileged moment (1933), race (Aryan), era (modernity), regime (Third Reich) and party (NSDAP) and the line which divides the old from the new is there and must be crossed. 'The intermediary realm of nihilism is at an end' Benn affirms in 1933 (Benn 1989a, 488). His angry exchange of letters with Klaus Mann exactly centres on this question of what side of the divide they decide to position themselves – the right or the left. Mann, a youthful enthusiast for Benn's shocking and iconoclastic expressionist poetry, finds his hero affiliating himself with the criminals of the other side. Nihilism is all very well and good if the moment is not a pressingly political one. But now! in 1933, *für die Stunde*, faith in a humanist, *übernationaler Geist*, that dry storehouse of hope, value and ideals, must be opened up, even if only temporarily (Mann 1968, 174). Mann understands Benn's mistaken familiarity with the Nazis to arise from his lack of ideals, from his concentration on the hopeless irrationality of the human psyche. He fails to appreciate the fact that idealism has nothing intrinsically 'leftish', socialist or anti-fascist about it. Benn's 1933 political involvement unfortunately *does* arise very much from a sudden optimistic, idealistic euphoria. For instance, he believed that finally a regime had arrived that would be able to appreciate expressionism: how wrong can you get four years before the 'Degenerate Art' exhibition, an exhibition which included Benn within it?

Barely believing the tales he hears about a Benn turned rabid Nazi, Mann calls on him not to behave ambiguously: 'he who does so will no longer and will never again belong to us'. He should now know where his place is, (that is, amongst the exiles), just as Mann does: 'I now know, more clearly and exactly than ever, where my place is' *(ich weiß] nun so klar und so genau wie nie, wo mein Platz ist)* (Mann 1968, 177). Benn responds by announcing that he too knows where his place is, in Nazi Germany and not in sunny exile on the Riviera (Benn 1984, 296).

Thematically, this altercation between Benn and Mann resembles the far more polite treatment served out to Ernst Jünger's 'Über die Linie' by Heidegger. In his reply, 'Zur Seinsfrage' or 'Über "Die Line"', Heidegger deals directly with in the question of nihilism's status as an event, its taking place. In *Heidegger and Ethics* Joanna Hodge glosses Heidegger's argument in the following way:

> For transition out of nihilism to take place it is not a question of moving from one locality to another, but of transforming the locality in which we already find ourselves, transforming our stance with respect to that locality. (Hodge 1995, 70)

Be this as it may, for Mann and Benn, and many other German writers, the question of nihilism formulates itself precisely as a question of staying in a locality or moving locality, crossing the line which ideally separates countries and their politics from one another. The question being hotly disputed by them in 1933 is whether one should emigrate, what it means to stay in Germany. Later the debate will rage around Klaus' father, Thomas Mann, and his refusal to return to Germany after the war: whether he is still to be regarded as a German writer; whether his 'exile' in sunny California is a betrayal; whether the so-called 'inner emigration' of German writers who stayed in Germany during the war is really tenable as a position not necessarily complicit with, or even as a type of covert resistance against, the dominant regime. All these questions count one's positioning vis-à-vis a specific locality, where one physically stands, as crucial for assessing one's political standpoint.[35] For both Klaus Mann and Benn a clear-cut territorial choice is urgently presenting itself in exceptional circumstances. Both make a decision, one goes left, the other right. Benn's lamentable decision in favour of the right was not just wrong ethically but a puzzling 'misreading' of his own implicit position as evident in his writings. Critics are left to ponder over the poet's enigmatic choice, one that he soon realised, once even the Nazis had rejected his absurd attempts at collaboration, was a terrible mistake.[36]

Out of the depths of Benn's political foulness, arising, not phoenix-like to be reborn and thereby redeemed, but in the very face of this ugliness, let us return to the 'primal vision' evoked earlier. How is the human reconfigured by, or how should he reconfigure himself when confronted with, those 'primeval drives of ageless masses in the sound of seas and the plunge of light'? (Benn 1984, 118–19) One reaction, the one adopted by the Nazis and temporarily by Benn, is to opt for a brutal politics of 'purified' form in the hope that an artificially cultivated body can, in its very exclusivity and 'disciplined' absoluteness, impinge on the germ-plasma and thereby be passed down into the next generation (Benn 1989a, 272–3). This type of eugenics is certainly no eulogy of deformation as an expression of form, mimicking life's movements. Instead it attempts to be a smart outwitting of life's 'degeneration', a 'degeneration' which it can only perceive as noxious for the consolidated, 'healthy' human.

The other response to life, which is also more consistently Benn's, refuses such an ultimately weak reaction. In 1932, one year before his own rampant celebration of 'breeding programmes', Benn suggests that the 'organic substance' has seized up in exhaustion (*organische Ermattung*). In vain do scientists armed with their incubators and breeding farms attempt to force nature, prodding and poking it to yield new varieties as a mainstay against the slide into the undifferentiated state which is heat-death (Benn 1989a, 452–3). In 'Wolf's Tavern' (1936), after his Nazi 'period', he continues this line of thought:

> We are no longer concerned for breeding for a future we can neither await nor utilize, but with our bearing in an eschatological present that has become an abstract experience only (*sondern um Haltung in einer nur noch abstraktiv erlebbaren, finalen Gegenwart*). Thus reads the coded message. Here the certain few come to a halt: before the remote signs that are

dawning steadily nearer, the invisible protagonists of the impending transformation.... Decomposition is palpable, a return to earlier conditions impossible, the substance spent; this is where the Second Law of Thermodynamics applies. The new power is there, holding the cigarette-lighter to the fuse. Whether by moon-plunge or atom-smashing, by entropy (*Vereisung*) or incendiarism, by whatever method it prefers, it is the transformation, the eternal element, the spirit, the antagonist of dreary rationality and mere consumption – in short: the end of the natural view of the world.   (Benn 1984, 146–7; 1971, 80–1)

Benn's abandonment of a fascistically oriented biopolitics is concomitant with his turning away from the teleological (breeding in the name of some distant future) and a return to eschatology (the final present). Shortly before this cited passage Benn has already cryptically evoked the 'coded message' of the 'monstrous alkaloid', which cannot be possessed cognitively, whose formulations may be known but whose substance is withheld 'in all its purity'. Klaus Theweleit suggests that here Benn might as well be talking, however precociously, about DNA:

the monstrous alkaloid.. that will bring about in the human what the human itself has not been able to manage in all its inadequate attempts. Cocaine, caffeine, nicotine, morphine are all alkalides. This is the state of chemistry in 1936, a few years later Benn would have written: 'acids'; LSD as well as DNA, the monstrous acids, that is to say amino acids... which lead humans out of their *Natural History*, which has never been and never will be anything other than *deadly* for them.

   Therefore a substance which structures genes, DNA, which makes itself known to humans [but not knowable] and a hallucinogenic like LSD, that opens up the pathways to the unconscious, are Benn's wishes, when no longer for Frankensteinian/Nietzschean 'breeding', then as fundamental components for the Writing-System Year 2000 (*des Aufschreibesystems 2000*) [the reference is to Kittler's book of the same name].
      (Theweleit 1996a, 749–50)

The 'organic substance', that which has reacted to the prodding and manipulation of the limited imagination of the *homo sapien*, is spent. The monsters of embryology are ineffectual creatures, signs of this human's vain attempts to become the quasi-divine captain's of life. Benn corrects these misguided aspirations by announcing in 'Provoked Life' that:

God is a substance, a drug. An intoxicating substance related to the human brain. This is perfectly possible and more likely than Him being an electrified machine or a Spemannian Triton's larva engendered through grafting tadpole tissue in the buccal zone.   (Benn 1989a, 372)[37]

Fiddling around in laboratories with grafts and transplants, even managing to tamper with DNA itself are 'inadequate attempts' to provoke a transformation of the human. They pale into insignificance when contrasted with the moody (*launisch*) and enigmatic laws of nature. Instead of lamenting a failure to dominate 'our' nature, we should, advises Benn, reorientate our understanding of what it is to be human through a perspectival re-vision (a primal vision) of life itself. This involves a return to our initial quotation from 'Provoked Life' on the nature of the brain.

Benn wants to 'shut off causal rows, turn around entropy and, in continual propagation and increase of improbabilites and complicated orderings (*Kompliziert-Geordneten*) go on to attain the extreme' (Benn 1989a, 392). This necessitates a sudden interruption of the 'progressive cerebralisation' of the brain before it implodes within the reproductive vehicle. The turn-around proposed is more a change in approach than any negentropic clawing back from the immanence of heat-death through complexification. Instead of trying to take the fate of the world on his shoulders by becoming a 'cosmic paraphrase' the human should aim, as we saw earlier, to become a 'naked, formal gestation' (Benn 1984, 375). The world of expression is therefore streamlined, composed of 'clear interspliced (*verzahnter*) relations, the interlocking of ground-down forces...'. Instead of implying complexification, there is a certain simplicity in the 'organic signature' the mutating human is to bear.[38]

The life that wells up 'from the gullet, organises itself a while to disppear into the inferno' is described by Benn as 'seething', 'heaving' – he talks of the *Schwellungscharakter der Schöpfung* – and this gives rise to his *Wallungstheorie*, the theory of turmoil, of congestion and of nomadic journeying (Benn 1984, 274 and 327).[39] It is the reinvented body, including the reactivated brain, i.e.one that can profit from its acausal saltations, its creative crises and craving for provoked life, that is to take us on this congested journey into the unknown human.[40] 'Congestion' implies a crowded collection of things merely heaped together, not bound together by any adhering content. Like an expressionist poem, the force of the evolutionary experience is to come from the impact of intensely expressed form, not from any substantial content or hotly-pursued, linear logic. 'Congestion' also evokes the accumulation of blood or morbid (i.e. bionegative) matter in any part of the body which provokes a violent reaction. Benn explains that: 'Life lasts for twenty four hours and when it arises, it was a congestion' (Benn 1984, 274). Life is an ever-changing concatenation of organic forms and if the *homo sapien*, with his terminal progressive cerebralisation, is to experience this seething intoxication as something other than a negative burning out of current values, then he must himself become monstrous. This reinvention of himself takes him on a journey into the future, (facing ascendance not descendance), through the bizarre backwaters of evolution:

In the sea there are living organisms of the lower zoological system which are covered with cilia (*Flimmerhaare*). Cilia are the animal sensory organ which precedes any differentiation into separated sensual energies; it is the general organ of touch, the link to the environment (*Umwelt*) of the sea. One imagines a human covered with cilia not only over the brain but over the whole organism. (Benn 1984, 273 and 327)

A human bristling with flickering sensory hairs whose energetic lashing drives it through its *Umwelt* offers the prospect of an intense experience of life. Such an experience, while not restoring our defunct values, might save us from a despairing nihilism.

Notes

1 For Benn's quasi-apocalyptic view of the modern world see, for example, Benn 1989, 373.

2 Most commentators end up trying to classify Benn as a 'man of his time', typical of the 1920s (decadent, irrational) Weimar Republic perceived in turn as a mere prelude to 1930s fascism. See for instance, Strauss 1992; Hohendahl 1989.

3 Benn indiscriminately puts Newton, Darwin, Helmholtz and thermodynamics all in the same camp. It is not my intention here explicitly to assess Benn's reductive reading of Darwin (or indeed of Nietzsche). Indeed, it will be implied that Benn disagrees vehemently with a particular current of Darwinism and is in fact, in spite of himself, an interesting reader of Darwin (and of Nietzsche). His theories on evolution bear an uncanny resemblance to those in vogue today, made popular through the work of Stephen Jay Gould. Gould, for instance, has made a strong case for exactly *not* understanding Darwinian evolution as an unrelenting march to progress (see Gould 1997). For another powerful contemporary reading of Darwin, see Ansell Pearson 1997.

4 In 'Fazit der Perspektiven' (1930) and 'Bezugssystemen' (1943) Benn shows himself to be a faithful reader of Nietzsche, exploring his idea of perspectivism. For instance, he amusingly suggests that from within the system of references (*Bezugssytem*) that is inductive thinking, Kant, the thinker of causal-analytical apodeictic necessity, can be regarded as having laid down principles which are binding for us all. However, from a different perspective, outside of this specific *Bezugssystem*, he may just be viewed as a rather strange 'yogi-figure' who lived in climatically disfavoured city, as distant from us as trance-dancers in Bali! (Benn 1989, 392).

5 See Goethe (1995, 111ff) and Benn's interesting essay 'Goethe und die Naturwissenschaften' (1932) in Benn 1989, 175–206.

6 Benn's adhesion to the National Socialist movement presents us with the dilemma of an author who is a terrible misreader and manipulator of his own work. In 'Nihilismus und seine Überwindung' (1932) he criticises Darwinism for its biopolitics, yet, one year later in 'Geist und Seele künftiger Geschlechter' (1922) he is himself advocating 'race consolidation' (see Benn 1989a, 207–8, 255). The two 'Züchtung' essays (Benn 1989: 237–44: 329–32) are further bewildering examples of a complete rewrite of Benn's earlier position. The only commentator I know who has seriously – and in great detail and at great length – puzzled over Benn's 'case' is Klaus Theweleit. See Theweleit 1991; 1996a and b.

7   In 'Zum Thema: Geschichte' (1942) Benn goes so far as to blame Darwin, and Nietzsche, for being responsible for 'millions of deaths' (Benn 1989: 364).

8   See Turgenev (1991: 140): ' "It'll be a comfort to you to know", said Bazarov, "that nowadays in general we laugh at medicine and worship nobody". "How d'you mean? You want to be a doctor, don't you?" "I do, but the one doesn't prevent the other" '. See also Jünger (1952, 20) on 'nihilistic medicine' which he defines in the following way: 'it does not want to cure, but pursues other ends'. Heidegger (1978, 215) further reworks Jünger's definition: 'The young Nietzsche once called the philosopher the "doctor of culture". But now it is no longer just a question of culture. You rightly say "the whole thing is at stake" '.

9   Anticipating Artaud's enthusiasm for the drug, Benn lauds the capacity of Peyote, used by Mexican Indians to strengthen the mythological concept of the body's relation with vital natural forces (see Benn 1989, 94). In advocating the bionegative intoxication of the body as 'damage done to a race can bring it unexpected compensation' (Benn 1989, 376), Benn is echoing Nietzsche's advocacy of 'ennoblement through degeneration' in Nietzsche 1993, 107–8.

10 Spengler uses the terms 'monstrous' and 'demonic' interchangeably. Later in this article I will be distinguishing between them.

11 Diderot (1966: 180–1) anticipates this line of thought (and much else that Benn will be suggesting) e.g.: ' "We walk so little, work so little, but think so much that I wouldn't rule out that man might end by being nothing but a head" '. See also further what he has to say about humans and their relation to hypothetical monsters: 'But the whole is constantly changing.... Man is merely a frequent effect, a monstrosity is a rare one, but both are equally natural, equally inevitable, equally part of the universal and general order... all nature is in a perpetual flux. Every animal is more or less a human being, every mineral more or less a plant...'. Diderot's theories here about the volatile potentiality of evolutionary becoming are interestingly similar to those suggested by Dawkins (1991: 73):

12 See, for example, Gould and Eldredge (1993) for an explanation of 'punctuated equilibrium'.

13 See von Uexküll (1992: 342) on cilia. We return to cilia at the end of the chapter. For Benn on von Uexküll, see Benn (1990: 217–18; 1990: 229).

14 Here I have the rather beautiful passage from Gould (1996: 216) in mind: 'If one small and odd lineage of fishes had not evolved fins capable of bearing weight on land.... If a large extraterrestrial object – the ultimate bolt from the blue – had not triggered the extinction of dinosaurs 65 milliion years ago, mammals would still be small creatures, confined to the small nooks and crannies of a dinosaur's world, and incapable of evolving the larger size of brain that self-consciousness requires'.

15 Benn refers to Nietzsche's description of natural laws as 'moody', prone to sudden panicky movements, in Benn 1989: 87.

16 See Bataille (1985:87): 'she runs to the foul-smelling place and locks herself in with surprise... obscurely, but in ecstasy, she has learned to recognise the face...'. As we will see later Benn also talks of the 'primal face'.

17 See Benn (1990: 231) on life as cyclical.

18 Of course 'moments' in geological time can last a very long time. See for instance Gould (1997: 220) where he points out that the Cambrian explosion lasted 5 million years!

19 See Hillebrand (Benn 1989:749) on the similarities, yet very different differences, between Benn and Adorno and Horkheimer's 'dialectic of the enlightenment'.

20   For a collection of essays on the demonic side of nihilism, see *Evil Spirits: Nihilism and the Fate of Modernity*, ed. C. Blake and G. Banham (Manchester University Press 2000).

21   For Benn (1989: 264) Goethe is an expressionist. He uses the term to describe thought which is no longer individualised but which is a rigorous 'going-to-the-root-of-things' expressed in acausal form.

22   See Ansell Pearson (1997, 96–7) on the importance of geological stratification, which records 'virtual planes of becoming', for Nietzsche's opposition to historical evolutionism or historicism.

23   The Cambrian explosion is the most famous of the catastrophic 'great dyings' as it killed off dinosaurs and permitted the evolution of large mammals. An engaging account of it is provided by Gould in an attempt to show how the 'history of life is not a continuum of development but a record punctuated by brief, sometimes geologically instantaneous, episodes of mass extinction and subsequent diversification' (see Gould 1991, esp. 54).

24   Klaus Mann clearly thinks Benn is regressive and cites the poem 'Gesänge' on primal slime as proof (see Mann 1968, 184–5; Benn 1994, 47). However, the definition of regression given by Deleuze and Guattari is that it is a movement towards that which is the *least differentiated*. Regression is to be contrasted with with 'creative involution', which is a form of evolution which takes place between things which are heterogeneous and not where there is homogeneity (Deleuze and Guattari 1980, 292). In another poem called 'Regression' Benn writes about 'thalassal regression' (Benn 1994, 203). As we will see at the end of this article when he describes the strange creatures with their flickering cilia, the sea for Benn is far from being an undifferentiated mass but, instead, the prime example of heightened, creative intoxication. Indeed, as Deleuze points out in relation to German Expressionism as a whole, the movement was primarily concerned with the vital as sprouting, as a 'pre-organic germinal force, common to both animated and the inanimated matter' (Deleuze 1996, 76). This Expressionist emphasis on germinal life complicates the dominant standard reading of the movement as a preface to fascistic atavism (see note 2, above). See further Benn (1989: 96) on ecstatic germination.

25   See Benn (1989: 118) on recapitulation and Carus.

26   See also Nietzsche 1933–42, 388: 'Every individual has an infinity of living individ. in itself', (*Jedes Individuum hat eine Unendlichkeit lebendiger Individ. in sich*).

27   Benn criticises Nietzsche for directing his writing to a future 'we', for apostrophising a future community of friends, whereas Benn considers himself to be contributing to the 'absolute poem, the poem without hope, directed to nobody' (see Benn 1989, 343 and 529).

28   As is the case with his reading of Darwin, I am not suggesting that Benn is a particularly strong reader of Nietzsche at this point.

29   See Gould (1997, 221–2) on the differences between cultural Lamarkism and natural evolution.

30   See Benn (1989: 489) on 'eine vielleicht sehr schön gewesene deutsche Innerlichkeit'.

31   See also Ansell Pearson (1997, 124): 'our origins are in slime'.

32   See Benn (1989, 488): 'the intermediary phase of nihilism is at an end ... it moves away from descendance towards ascendance'.

33 See Gould (1997) on how 'life's grandeur' is not to be understood as a teleologically oriented grand narrative which endorses our anthropocentric view of evolution.

34 Carrel's book was translated into 19 languages and has sold hundreds of thousands copies. For a shockingly uncritical account of Carrel's life see Christen 1986. For antifascist account of Carrel, see Bonnafé and Tort 1992. Tort also has devoted much of his time to retrieving Darwin's work from the arms of the social Darwinians, for example, see Tort 1997.

35 See Grosser (ed.) 1963 on the postwar Thomas Mann debate.

36 Once again see Theweleit (1991; 1996a and b) who ponders this question at (great) length

37 Spemann's experiments with transplantation revealed that cells form themselves according to where they are situated, and not where they come from, that is, their fate is determined by place (it is *ortsgemäss*) not predetermined by origin (*nicht herkunftsgemäss*). Benn (1990: 227) concludes that skin cells which find themselves transplanted into the brain can adapt to their new location. See also Carrel's amazing (and chilling) 'The Relation of Cells to One Another' where he also states that: 'the fate of a cell is a function of its position' and '[within] the organism, tissue cells actualize only a small part of their potentialities' (Carrel 1930, 210–11). The article begins by questioning whether the processes which bring out and maintain the organism really are purposeful, i.e. teleologically directed.

38 See Deleuze and Parnet (1996, 37–8) for how a simplifying paring-down can be part of a creative involution.

39 See Benn (1995: 20–1) for a consideration of the various permutations of *Wallung*.

40 Here I am suggesting a play on Carrel's title *Man: this Unknown*. For a eugenicist such as Carrel, one who cannot envisage de-formation as form, 'man' is far from being an unknown. 'Purification' programmes exactly purport to know the human as an intrinsic value and they aim to eliminate, not breed, 'monsters'.

References

Ansell Pearson, K. (1997) *Viroid Life* London/New York: Routledge.

Bataille, G. (1985) 'The Pineal Eye' in *Visions of Excess* Minneapolis: University of Minnesota Press.

Benn, G. (1954) *Double Vie* trans. J.-M. Palmier. Paris: Les éditions de Minuit.

—— (1971) *Primal Vision* ed. B. Ashton. NY: New Directions.

—— (1982) *Gedichte* ed. B. Hillebrand. Frankfurt am Main: Fischer.

—— (1984) *Prosa und Autobiographie* ed. B. Hillebrand. Frankfurt am Main: Fischer.

—— (1989a) *Essays und Reden* ed. B. Hillebrand. Frankfurt am Main: Fischer.

—— (1989b) *Un poète et le monde* trans. R Rovini. Paris: Gallimard.

—— (1990) *Szenen und Schriften* ed. B. Hillebrand. Frankfurt am Main: Fischer.

—— (1995) *Le ptoléméen et d'autres textes* trans. H. Feydy, introd. C. Schmiele. Paris: Gallimard.

Bonnafé, L. and Tort, P. (1992) *L'homme, cet inconnu?: Alexis Carrel, Jean-Marie Le Pen et les chambres de gaz*, Paris: Editions Syllepse.

Carrel, A. (1930) 'The Relation of Cells to One Another' in *Human Biology and Racial Welfare* ed. E Cowdry, New York: Paul B Hoeber.

Carrel, A. (1935) *L'homme, cet inconnu* Alençon: Plon.

Christen, Y. ed. (1986) *Alexis Carrel: L'ouverture de l'homme* Paris: Editions du Félin.

Dawkins, R. (1991) *The Blind Watchmaker* Harmondsworth: Penguin

Deleuze, G. (1996) *Cinéma I: L'image-mouvement* Paris: Les éditions de Minuit.
Deleuze, G. and Guattari, F. (1980) *Milles Plateaux* Paris: Les éditions de Minuit.
Deleuze, G. and Parnot, C. (1996) *Dialogues* Paris: Flammarion.
Diderot, D. (1966) *D'Alembert Dream*, trans. L. Tancock. Harmondsworth: Penguin.
Goethe, J.W. von. (1995) *Scientific Studies*, ed. and trans. D. Miller. New Jersey: Princeton University Press.
Gould, S.J. (1991) *Wonderful Life* Harmondsworth: Penguin.
Gould, S.J. (1996) *Life's Grandeur* London: Vintage.
Gould, S.J. and Eldredge, N. (1993) 'Punctuated Equilibrium comes of Age' in *Nature* Vol 366: 223–7.
Grosser, J.F.G. ed. (1963) *Die große Kontroverse: ein Briefwechsel um Deutschland* Hamburg/ Genf/ Paris: Nagel Verlag.
Heidegger, M. (1978) 'Zur Seinsfrage' in *Wegmarken* Frankfurt am Main: Klostermann.
Hodge, J. (1995) *Heidegger and Ethics* London and NY: Routledge.
Hohendahl, P.U. (1989) 'The Loss of Reality: Gottfried Benn's Early Prose' in *Modernity and the Text*, ed. Huyssen and Bathrick, Columbia: Columbia University Press.
Jünger, E. (1952 *Über die Linie* Frankfurt am Main: Klostermann.
Long, R.-C. W. ed. (1995) *German Expressionism* Berkeley: University of California Press.
Mann, Kl. (1968) *Prüfungen: Schriften zur Literatur*, ed. M. Gregor-Dellin, Munich: Nymphenburger Verlagshandlung.
Nietzsche, F. (1933–42) 'Zur Teleologie' in *Historisch-Kriticshe Gesamtausgabe* Vol 3 Munich.
—— (1969) *Thus spake Zarathustra*, trans. R. Hollingdale, Harmondsworth: Penguin.
—— (1992) *Der Wille zur Macht* Frankfurt am Main: Insel Verlag.
—— (1993) *Human all too Human* trans. R. Hollingdale, Cambridge: Cambridge University Press.
Palmier, J.-M. (1983) *L'expressionisme comme révolte* Paris: Payot.
—— (1988a) *L'expressionisme et les arts* Vol I, Paris: Payot.
—— (1988b) *L'expressionisme et les arts* Vol II, Paris: Payot.
—— (1990) *Retour à Berlin*, Paris: Payot.
Raabe, P. ed. (1987) *Expressionismus: Der Kampf um eine literarische Bewegung* Zürich: Arche.
Spengler, O. (1991) *Der Untergang des Abendlandes* Munich: d.t.v.
Strauss, W.A. (1992) 'Gottfried Benn: a Double Life in Uninhabitable Regions' in *Fascism, Aesthetics and Culture* ed. R. Golsan, Hampshire: University Press of New England.
Theweleit, K. (1991) *Buch der Könige: Orpheus und Eurydike* Vol. I, Basel/ Frankfurt am Main, Stroemfeld/Roter Stern.
—— (1996a) *Buch der Könige: Orpheus am Machtpol* Vol. 2x, Basel/ Frankfurt am Main: Stroemfeld/Roter Feld.
—— (1996b) *Buch der Könige Recording Angel's Mysteries* Vol. 2y, Basel/Frankfurt am Main, Stroemfeld/Roter Feld.
Tort, P. (1997) *Darwin et le darwinisme* Paris: Presses Universitaires de France.
Turgenev, I. (1991) *Fathers and Sons* trans. R. Freeborn, Oxford: Oxford University Press.
Uexküll, J von. (1992) 'The World of Animals and Men', trans. C. Schiller in *Semiotica* Vol. 89–4.

8

A Problem of Pure Matter: Fascist Nihilism in *A Thousand Plateaus*

John Protevi

Introduction: Constructing the Concept of Fascist Nihilism

Were the Nazis nihilists? Did they devalue this world in favour of a higher world? Had they lost their belief in a higher world? Did they prefer to fade away in passivity rather than live?

In one sense, the answer to the first question can only be affirmative: yes, the Nazis were indeed nihilists, for they produced death and destruction as the positive goal of their social machine. However, they do not seem to have been the sort of nihilists Nietzsche diagnosed using the last three questions. In so far as one of the clearest expositions of Nietzsche's analysis of nihilism is to be found in Gilles Deleuze's *Nietzsche and Philosophy* (henceforth abbreviated to *NP*), it is thus somewhat surprising that the only occurrence of the term 'nihilism' in Deleuze and Guattari's *Capitalism and Schizophrenia* is in a discussion of Nazism, at the conclusion of the 1933 plateau ('Micropolitics and Segmentarity') of *A Thousand Plateaus*: 'There is in fascism a realized nihilism' (Deleuze and Guattari 1987, 230 henceforth abbreviated to *ATP*).

What justifies this strange usage of 'nihilism' by Deleuze–Guattari to characterise fascism? Is it just a rhetorical flourish, a moralising deprecation? Does calling it a nihilism add to the understanding of historical fascism, and to the struggle against new fascism(s)? To answer these questions – to evaluate its usefulness in this last, most important area – this chapter follows the rhizome in *ATP* of fascism and nihilism. In keeping with Deleuze–Guattari's characterisation of their work, let us put it in practical terms: how should one construct the concept of fascist nihilism in *ATP*? I propose four steps, the last two of which will be dealt with in the body of the chapter.

First, distinguish it from the treatment of fascism in *Anti-Oedipus* (Deleuze and Guattari 1983, henceforth abbreviated to *AO*).[1] Perhaps we owe the impression that *AO* is about fascism to Foucault's preface to the English translation, in which he calls *AO* 'An Introduction to the Non-Fascist Life' (xiii). But in fact historical fascism – as Foucault acknowledges – is explicitly addressed in *AO* relatively infrequently: a few comments on Hitler getting the masses sexually aroused, a note that the fascist state is the most fantastic re-territorialisation of capitalism. In other words, in *AO*, fascism is largely addressed only architectonically, as a pole of desire, an answer to the puzzling question, how does desire come to desire its own repression? Architectonically, fascism is on the side of paranoia and reterritorialisation, the counter pole to schizophrenia and deterritorialisation. In *AO*, then, fascism is paranoia, freezing, the body without organs as catatonia. In *ATP*, however, fascism is distinguished from totalitarianism, which is 'quintessentially conservative' (230). In *ATP*, fascism is too fast rather than too slow: it is cancer, a runaway war machine. Recognising these dangers brings out the 'caution' of *ATP*. In *AO* the task of schizoanalysis is: 'destroy, destroy' (311). In *ATP* we read: 'Staying stratified – organised, signified, subjected – is not the worst that can happen' (161).[2]

Second, distinguish nihilism in *ATP* and *NP*. Nihilism is discussed extensively in the final section of the Nietzsche book, 'Against the Dialectic', but there the context is will, values, life. The key is man and the question of man, while nihilism is the motor of European history. None of these concerns (with the possible exception of 'life'[3]) carry over to *ATP*, whose slogan is 'geography, not history': drawing a map of lines, not tracing a decline or conversion. This is not to say, however, that the 'same' nihilism diagnosed by Nietzsche – let's call it 'lunar' nihilism, the giving over of life to a resigned, reflective freezing – is not also diagnosed in a different framework by *ATP*, as the 'empty body without organs'.

Third, follow the rhizome nihilism–fascism in *ATP* through its two main nodes: (1) as cancerous BwO of the strata (plateau 6: 'How Do You Make Yourself a Body Without Organs'); (2) as danger of the line of flight (plateau 9: 'Micropolitics and Segmentarity'); and the appropriate sub-nodes: (3) the theory of sedimentation (plateau 3: 'The Geology of Morals: Who Does the Earth Think It Is?'); and (4) the relations of war-machine and State (plateaus 12: 'Treatise on Nomadology – The War Machine' and 13: 'Apparatus of Capture').

Fourth, make sure fascist nihilism is discussed as a problem of 'pure matter' (165) rather than cultural history or psychology. As we have insisted, the term 'nihilism' cannot have its Nietzschean context of man, will, and values, nor can fascism be discussed as an ideology ('a most execrable concept' [68]). The key in giving a positive account of fascist nihilism rather than resting content with such negative distinctions lies in the articulation of the work of Deleuze–Guattari with so-called complexity theory, as in the work of Manuel DeLanda (1991; 1992; 1997) and Brian Massumi (1992). On their readings, *ATP* provides materialist diagrams for the construction and evaluation of bodies via mattern–energy flow (the body without organs) and self-organising processes (abstract machines). Fascism thus cannot be a 'psychological category' (Holland 1987, 26) nor does *ATP* contain a 'metaphysics of difference' (May 1997, 175) or of 'forces' (May 1994, 68) – if anything, it is a physics.

With these prescriptions in mind, the paper will follow the following course: first, a discussion of the fascist body without organs; second, the danger of the fascist line of flight; third, a discussion of the complexity theory background to the materialism of *ATP*; fourth, a concluding section considering *ATP*'s contribution to an understanding of fascist 'nihilism now'.

The Fascist BwO

A difficult question: 'How Do You Make Yourself a Body without Organs?' First, you must recognise the practical nature of the question: the BwO is an object of practice; it is produced, starting from the organism. Second, you must notice that the question is badly phrased, a holdover of *AO* terminology that will be corrected in *ATP*: it should read, 'How Do You Make Yourself a Body That Is Not an Organism?'

Let us begin by distinguishing body, organs, organism, *a* BwO and *the* BwO.

1 A body is any economic system considered as a mechanism of appropriation and regulation, a region of matter–energy flow that has a relative consistency even as it is plugged into a network of other flows, slowing some down, speeding others up. A body is a flow regulator. In *NP*, Deleuze used the Nietzschean language of 'dominant and dominated forces', to explain that '[e]very relationship of forces constitutes a body – whether it is chemical, biological, social, or political' (Deleuze 1983, 40). In *ATP*, Deleuze–Guattari maintain the wide range of application of the term 'body', but add the word 'stratum' to designate an economic exchange between similarly constituted bodies with regard to adjacent levels of dominated or dominating bodies. *ATP* also introduces the language of 'content' (the production of formed matters) and 'expression' (the production of functional structures) to explain body constitution and/or stratification (43).

2 Organs are machines, that is, flow/break couplings in which a matter-energy flow is interrupted and part siphoned off to flow in the economy of the body. Organs are a body's way of negotiating with the outside, appropriating and regulating a bit of matter-energy flow. In psychoanalytic terms, organs are 'partial objects' not (yet) connected to a person, mere points of intensity of matter-energy, a place of activity less intense than the surrounding outside but more intense than the body's other organs (with regard to its particular flow, that is). In *AO*, Deleuze–Guattari call organs 'desiring machines'; in *ATP*, they are called 'machinic assemblages'.

3 An organism is a particular organisation of organs, one that is centralised and hierarchical, appropriating the matter–energy of the organs and

funnelling a surplus portion of them to the benefit of a transcendence, a superior body or stratum that has appropriated the organism as a substratum, as labor, as content for its expression. The organism is a stratum on the BwO, 'a phenomenon of accumulation, coagulation, and sedimentation that, in order to extract useful labor from the BwO, imposes upon it forms, functions, bonds, dominant and hierarchized organizations, organized transcendences' (159). An organism is a capture and siphon machine, a particular way of regulating flows: 'that which life sets against itself in order to limit itself' (503).

4 *A* BwO is a destratified body. It is an object of construction, a practice; it is 'what remains after you take everything away' (151). It is not reached by regression, for a BwO is not the infantile body of our past, but the virtual realm of potentials for different body organisation precluded by current organismic organisation. Thus it is reached by a systematic practice of disturbing the current organismic organisation: 'the BwO is not at all the opposite of the organs. The organs are not its enemies. The enemy is the organism' (158). By disturbing the organism, the level of purely distributed, rather than centralised, organs can be reached, sitting upon the matter–energy flow itself. In other words, a BwO is purely immanently arranged production; matter–energy flowing without regard to externally-imposed *foci* that drain off surpluses to a point outside the body. As an object of practice reached starting from the organism, BwO is two-sided: 'it swings between two poles, the surfaces of stratification into which it is recoiled, on which it submits to the judgment, and the plane of consistency in which it unfurls and opens to experimentation' (159). This two-sidedness is not peaceful; rather we find 'a perpetual and violent combat between the plane of consistency, which frees the BwO, cutting across and dismantling all the strata, and the surfaces of stratification that block it or make it recoil' (159).

5 *The* BwO is the 'plane of consistency', the economy of economies, the matter–energy flow of the terrestial/cosmic system: it is 'the Earth'. Thus the BwO is 'that glacial reality where the alluvions, sedimentations, coagulations, foldings and recoilings that compose an organism – and also a signification and a subject – occur' (159).

The relation of *a* BwO and *the* BwO is explored in *ATP* in a Spinozist manner: 'After all, is not Spinoza's *Ethics* the great book of the BwO?' (153). The crucial problem of Deleuze–Guattari's corporeal politics is distinguishing or selecting between types of BwO, which, as we will see, are not all positive or progressive achievements. The 'plane of consistency' is Deleuze–Guattari's term for an immanent social arrangement of BwOs, but not all BwOs qualify for inclusion; the plane of consistency must be constructed as a selection between types of BwOs; in particular, the fascist BwO must be deselected.

Negatively put then, a BwO is 'the limit of a given process of destratification' (DeLanda 1997, 261), the point at which a particular organisation of organs called an organism no longer holds and matter–energy flows are arranged immanently without reference to a transcendence profiting from the siphoning action of the organism. Positively, a BwO is the matter–energy flow itself subtending a body, and also its 'phase space', its virtual field, the pool of potentials for organization of that body: organismic organisation, and other types of organisations as well (Massumi 1992, 70). The latter sense of the BwO as virtuality is why the BwO is not regressive, but is there besides the organism, waiting to be reached.

Now we must distinguish three types of BwO: full, empty, cancerous. Only the full body is productive. To avoid the others, caution is necessary, for the construction of a BwO is dangerous. The strata must be partially maintained: the body that is not an organism must still be a body, must still have a relative consistency, a difference in intensity of matter–energy flow from the surroundings. Otherwise, we would have pure death, entropy, no energy differences.

The three types of BwOs are as follows:

1 A full BwO is reached by careful experimental destratification, which causes waves of intense matter-energy to flow in immanence. When linked with other selected full BwOs, the plane of consistency is constructed, that is, a collectivity of freely self-organising bodies, continually producing their own connections. This full BwO is the BwO as 'egg' (164) or as field of 'desire' (165). In a full BwO one finds 'a distribution of intensive principles of organs, with their positive indefinite articles, within a collectivity or multiplicity, inside an assemblage, and according to machinic connections operating on a BwO' (165). As we can see from Deleuze–Guattari's insistence on collectivity, multiplicity, and assemblage, the full BwO is never a solitary achievement but always a communal project, a political event. To select only full BwOs for the plane of consistency is 'the test of desire' (165).

2 An empty BwO is reached by too sudden destratification, which empties bodies of its organs. Examples include the hypochondriac body, the paranoid body, the schizo-catatonic body, the drugged body, the masochist body: 'a dreary parade of sucked-dry, catatonized, vitrified, sewn-up bodies.... Emptied bodies instead of full ones' (150). These bodies do not connect with others, for they have no energy flowing; no plane of consistency is possible between these mortified bodies. As points of zero intensity, they are instances of lunar nihilism.

3 The cancerous BwO is the strangest and most dangerous BwO. It is a BwO that belongs to the organism that resides on a stratum, rather than being the limit of a stratum. It is runaway self-duplication of stratification. Such a cancer can occur even in social formations, not just in the strata

named organism, signifiance, subjectification (163). The key to tracking down fascism lies here, in the cancerous BwO, which forms under conditions of runaway stratification, or more precisely, runaway sedimentation, the first 'pincer' of a stratum: 'all a stratum needs is a high sedimentation rate for it to lose its configuration and articulations, and to form its own specific kind of tumor, within itself or in a given formation or apparatus. The strata spawn their own BwOs, totalitarian and fascist BwOs, terrifying caricatures of the plane of consistency' (163). The cancerous BwO breaks down the stratum on which it lodges by endlessly repeating the selection of homogenised individuals in a runaway process of 'conformity'. Social cloning. Assembly-line personalities.

To follow the rhizome here, we need to extract a few simplified concepts from the exceedingly complex 'Geology of Morals' plateau, where Professor Challenger tells us about double articulation: sedimentation/folding or content/expression, each of which has both substance and form. A substance is a 'formed matter', and refers to territorialities or spatial bindings; a form, on the other hand, implies a 'code', or temporal ordering. Content is also 'formed matter', matter selected (territorialised) and formed (coded), while expression is a 'functional structure' that utilises this content to produce a new entity by an 'overcoding', resulting in 'phenomena of centering, unification, totalization, integration, hierarchization, and finalization' (41).

Content/expression or territorialisation/coding/overcoding is the abstract machine of stratification, operant in any register from geological to social as the way to appropriate matter–energy flows from the Earth and build a layer that regulates the flow. The machine has four components in two articulations. The first articulation is sedimentation, which determines: (a) a substance of content, that is, the selection of homogenous materials from a subordinate flow; and (b) a form of content, that is the deposition of these materials into layers. The second articulation is 'folding',[4] in which there is (c) a form of expression, that is, the creation of new linkages; and (d) a substance of expression, the creation of new entities with emergent properties.

The cancerous BwO occurs with too much sedimentation, that is, too much content or coding and territorialising, with insufficient overcoding. The result is a cancer of the stratum, a proliferation of points of capture, a proliferation of micro-black holes. Thousands of individuals, complete unto themselves. Legislators and subjects all in one. Judge, jury, and executioner – and policeman, private eye, home video operator, Neighborhood Watch organiser.... Watching over themselves as much as over others in runaway conscience-formation. Deleuze–Guattari call this situation 'micro-fascism'. To follow this path, move to Plateau 9, 'Micropolitics and Segmentarity', where we will also encounter a phenomenon we neglected in our brief extract from the 'Geology of Morals', namely, the line of flight, or the deterritorialising and decoding of flows.

The fascist line of flight

The danger of fascism is that a line of flight, the source of creativity that moves us away from territory and code (from home and habit), and from resonance and overcoding (from bureaucracy and State), can become a 'passion for abolition', 'suicide... presented not as a punishment but as the crowning glory of the death of others' (231). Deleuze–Guattari explore this danger in Plateau 9, dated 1933: 'Micropolitics and Segmentarity'.

The basic notion beginning Plateau 9 is 'segmentarity', the divisibility and internal borders inherent to all strata. Deleuze–Guattari isolate three types: binary, circular, and linear. Segmentarity tends to be supple – heterogeneous, local, flexible – in 'primitive' societies, and rigid in State societies. Now these types of segmentarity, which are also roughly interchangeable with molecular (supple) and molar (rigid), are, while *de jure* separable, *de facto* interwoven.

The implications of these distinctions are developed later in the plateau. At 217, Deleuze–Guattari use a new term for molecular composition, 'quantum flow', which they distinguish from the molar segmented line. Between two they locate a 'power center', which effects translations between the quantum flow and the segmented line. As always the conceptual distinction finds a real interweaving, as flow and quanta 'can be grasped only by virtue of indexes on segmented line, but conversely, that line and those indexes exist only by virtue of the flow suffusing them' (218). A further twist comes when Deleuze–Guattari discuss flow and line in terms of coding, decoding, overcoding. The mutant flow is the process of escaping a coding process, while quanta are 'signs or degrees of deterritorialization in decoded flow' (219). If we recall the abstract machine of stratification at this point, a mutant flow is a flow that escapes the sorting (territorialising or substance of content) and layering (coding or form of content) processes of the first articulation (sedimentation or the production of a formed matter.) The rigid line corresponds to the other pincer of stratification (expression, the construction of a functional structure); the rigid line is an 'overcoding that substitutes itself for the faltering codes', while its segments 'are like reterritorializations on the overcoding or overcoded line' (219).

This reworking of line and flow in terms of coding, decoding, and overcoding leads to a distinction between connection and conjugation of flows. A 'connection' of flows indicates the self-catalysing of a set of decoded and deterritorialised flows, which 'boost one another, accelerate their shared escape, and augment or stoke their quanta' (220). A connection is a mutiny, a prison break, a bank panic: the more that join the flight, the faster it goes. 'Conjugation', on the other hand, relates to the same mutant flows, but from the point of view of their recapture and overcoding; it 'indicates their relative stoppage, like a point of accumulation that plugs or seals the lines of flight, performs a general reterritorialisation, and brings the flows under the dominance of single flow capable of overcoding them' (220). A conjugation is the rounding up and returning to prison of the escapees, or better, the formation of a new State among them: the King Rat effect. Indeed, it is always, Deleuze–Guattari assert, the most deterritorialised flow that brings about conjunction and reterritorialisation, as was the case, they claim, with the European bourgeoisie during the capitalist takeoff (220–1).

Deleuze–Guattari soon proclaim the possibility of drawing a map of three lines (222). The first line is the supple line of interlaced codes and territories characteristic of primitive segmentarity. This line corresponds to the first articulation of social stratification, which is coupled to the second line, the rigid line of the State apparatus which overcodes and reterritorialises. The third line is the line of flight of decoding and deterritorialisation effectuated by a 'war machine' (222). To insist on the map nature of this discussion ('geography, not history'), Deleuze–Guattari recall that 'primitive' societies are not temporally first. Rather, coding, overcoding and decoding are coexistent functions of any existing society; they insist 'there is a space in which the three kinds of closely intermingled lines coexist: tribes, empires, and war machines' (222). The 'task of the historian' (or schizoanalyst, or rhizomatic analyst, or pragmatics analyst ...) is the consideration of the relative speeds and strengths of these functions; it is to 'designate the "period" of coexistence or simultaneity' of the three functions (221). To drive home the point, Deleuze–Guattari provide a simplified description of a historical example of the coexistence of tribes, empires, war machines in the interchanges between migrants, Rome, Huns. But coexistence is not all: the lines transform themselves, as in the case of the Vandals, the only tribe to cross the Mediterranean, only there to produce 'the most startling reterritorialization: an empire in Africa' (223).

Given such coexistence and transformation of the lines, Deleuze–Guattari finally say that 'it would be better to talk about simultaneous states of the Abstract Machine' (223), which they designate as: (1) abstract machine of overcoding that produces a rigid segmentarity and is effectuated by State apparatus, which is a reterritorialising assemblage; (2) an abstract machine of mutation, which operates by decoding and deterritorialisation, creating lines of flight and erects war machines on its lines (to inhibit State formation); (3) the realm of molecular negotiation between molar lines and lines of flight (223–4).

The fourth element on the map, in addition to the three lines, is the power centre, the analysis of which illustrates the entanglement of lines. A power centre is a point of negotiation between the quantum flow and the rigid segmented line, a place of conversion and translation of flow into segmented line. First, power centres involve rigid segments, whose resonance in the State does not destroy segmentarity; on the contrary, 'centralization is always hierarchical, but hierarchy is always segmentary' (224). This is the power centre's 'zone of power'. Next, power centres are not just molar, but also function in the molecular field, the micrological fabric of society where Foucault's disciplines operate. This field is a 'zone of indiscernability', at once molar and molecular (225). Third, the limit of power centres, their zone of impotence, is their act of conversion itself. Since power centres only translate and do not govern the flow, they are defined by their impotence, by what escapes them. But their relative impotence is also their relative effectiveness: power centers govern the assemblages that effectuates the abstract machine of overcoding, of chasing down the mutant flows.

The example of the flow of money helps concretise the discussion. The zone of power, the setting up of segments, is the concern of the central banks, the conversion of credit flow into payment money by the setting of interest rates, and so on. This is the realm of the State apparatus, the 'abstract machine of molar overcoding' (227). The zone of indiscernability is the micrological texture of money, the series of private relations between banks and borrowers. This is the realm of 'the molecular fabric immersing the State assemblage' (227). The zone of impotence is the 'desiring flow of money, whose quanta are defined by the mass of economic transactions' (226–7). This flow of panic, fad, fashion, is the function of the 'abstract machine of mutation, flows and quanta' (227).

The simultaneity and interweaving of the elements of the map, the states of the abstract machine, lead Deleuze–Guattari to state that 'everything is political, but every politics is simultaneously a *macropolitics and a micropolitics*' (213). As one of their typically loose diagrams illustrates, 'the segmented line (macropolitics) is immersed in and prolonged by quantum flows (micropolitics) that continually reshuffle and stir up its segments' (218). But this *de facto* interweaving means that one cannot simply privilege suppleness or molecularity as ready-made universal principles of the good; everything for Deleuze–Guattari is a matter of practice, of experimentation and *ex post facto* evaluation. The first, 'axiological' error of the 'four errors' to be avoided concerning molecularity and suppleness make this 'pragmatism' of Deleuze–Guattari clear: don't believe that 'a little suppleness is enough to make things "better"' (215). Indeed, concerning the molar line and the molecular flow, we must remember not only their coexistence ('the flow continues beneath the line, forever mutant, while the line totalizes' [221]) and their interdependence ('politics and its judgments are always molar, but it is the molecular and its assessment that makes it or breaks it' [222]), but most importantly, the amorality of the distinction ('there are just as much relations of force, and just as much violence, on one side as the other' [221]).

With these warnings against an *a priori* privilege of the molecular and supple, Deleuze–Guattari come to distinguish molecular fascism from molar totalitarianism. They name points for historical investigation of molecular or microfascism as 'molecular focuses in interaction ... rural fascism and city or neighbourhood fascism, youth fascism and war veteran's fascism, fascism of the Left and of the Right, fascism of the couple, family, school, and office' (214). Such microfascisms spread throughout a social fabric prior to the centralising resonance that create the molar State apparatus. Deleuze–Guattari describe micro-fascism as a proliferation of tiny centres of command; each body is a 'micro-black hole that stands on its own and communicates with the others' (228). Such communication between 'a thousand little monomanias, self-evident truths, and clarities' creates a sort of static, which inhibits State resonance by a kind of 'rumble and buzz, blinding lights giving any and everybody the mission of self-appointed judge, dispenser of justice, policeman, neighborhood SS man' (228). This static of microfascism keeps it below the level of the State: a thousand independent and self-appointed policemen do not make a Gestapo, though they may be a necessary condition for one. Although D/G do not do so, we can call microfascism 'molecular molarity': each unit is self-contained, oriented to unity, an individual (molar), but they interact in solely local manner, independently (molecular).

In a move that might shock those who read Deleuze–Guattari as privileging certain terms, microfascism is defined as the state of a social fabric 'when a *war machine* is installed in each hole, in every niche' (214; *original italics*). A brief trip to Plateau 12, the 'Treatise on Nomadology' is needed here. A particular war machine is a form of social organisation, a concrete social assemblage that preserves immanent self-organising and wards off the transcendent ordering effectuated by the State. Thus 'State' and 'war-machine' are names of functions – overcoding and line of flight respectively – that are aspects of the abstract machine and are instanciated by concrete war machines and States. As aspects of the abstract machine they are co-existent; there have always been packs and States in interaction: the State tries to appropriate the war machine and turn it into an Army, while war machines form in the interstices between States.

Now we must remember that war machines are not unorganised; it is just that they are not organismically organised for the benefit of a despot: their leaders are *ad hoc* and challengeable, rather than reified and deified. War machines occupy and extend 'smooth space', a form of spatial organisation that is locally dense and flexible rather than homogenous and pre-demarcated, as in the gridded or striated space established by States. In smooth space, a law of distance disperses figures across a zone; in striated space, the space is demarcated prior to occupation, and figures are assigned to marked spots.

War machines are thus the key to creation, to mutation in an open future. They constantly throw off lines of flight that move systems off territorial bindings and away from coded behaviour. Now all physical processes are self-organising, but social formations can be transcendent (top-down), and give the illusion that physical production is transcendent too. In the terms of *AO*, this illusory totality arrogating credit for production to itself is the 'socius': the earth, despot, or capital in the primitive, imperial or modern systems. A war-machine is a way of organising social production that prevents the formation of a socius. In concrete terms, this means the war machine wards off capture by State by occupying the smooth space of immanent relations. As we have seen, the war machine is Deleuze–Guattari's term for immanent social relations that instigate mutation and creativity and ward off State resonance. But here, to rejoin Plateau 9, the microfascist spread installs war machines everywhere, in each cell, so that there is only a 'a molecular and supple segmentarity, flows capable of suffusing every cell', a 'molecular or micropolitical power [*puissance*]' (214–15). Microfascism is the social fabric punctuated by thousands of war-machines, each dedicated to its own movement; paradoxically, the movement of the microfascist war-machines is not that of creating connections, but that of sealing off, of molarising self and others. Understanding, recognising, microfascism is of the greatest importance, for 'only microfascism provides an answer to the global question: why does desire desire its own repression?' (215). Desire, the movement of connection and immanence, is repressed by microfascism; in its place arises the strange cancer of a thousand 'cells' or self-contained units. Of course, for Deleuze–Guattari, desire is never a given, a natural resource, a Romantic surge; desire is never an 'undifferentiated instinctual energy', but is engineered from 'complex assemblages'. In this way, desire is a 'supple segmentarity that processes molecular energies and potentially gives desire a fascist determination' (215). Thus we must be on guard against 'the fascist inside you' (215).

The important point of articulation between Plateaus 6 and 9 appears when microfascism is described as a 'cancerous body rather than a totalitarian organism' (215). But to be precise, the cancerous body of proliferating microfascism and the centralised body of the totalitarian organism are not the end of the story. The empty, suicidal BwO also has a fascist correlate, the perverted line of flight, the 'fourth danger'. Deleuze–Guattari lay out the principles of a pragmatics or schizoanalytic analysis of the dangers of each of the four elements of the map: rigid molarity, supple molecularity, the power centre, and the line of flight, at the end of the 1933 Plateau (227–31). The four dangers draw their names, in a typical Deleuze–Guattari monstrous marriage, from 'Nietzsche's Zarathustra and Castenada's Indian Don Juan': Fear, Clarity, Power, Disgust (227).

In fear we cling to molar segmentation, to the rigid outlines of our binary, circular and linear social position. We cling to our binary identities: man/woman, white/black, straight/gay; to our circular locations: to home, neighbourhood, city, region, country; to our linear stations, acting our age. The recording of these molarities is the concern of the power centres, the State apparatuses whose zone of power overlooks those processes that issue us our birth, marriage and death certificates, that collect our taxes and study our demographics in the census. In fear, we cling, rigidly, to our individuality, to our selves.

But being supple rather than rigid is no guarantee of salvation, for the second danger, clarity, comes precisely from supple molecularity, in which we 'invent all kinds of marginal reterritorializations even worse than the others' (228). This is the micrological fabric, the zone of indiscernability in which microfascisms breed. Here we find the static of molecular communication of individual black holes prior to resonance in the State, microfascism as the realm of the cancerous BwO, the breeding of tiny command posts.

The third danger is easily foreseen: Power (*pouvoir*), the stopping of the lines of flight by the totalitarian State. This is the closing off of the society, the search for 'autarky', or national self-sufficiency, the withdrawal from global capitalism to ensure a national destiny; this operation 'is never an ideological operation, but rather an economic and political one' (223). This danger is the danger of the power centres themselves, rather than the segmented lines they produce and to which we cling in fear; power is the danger of macropolitics, of the great resonating black hole of the State which has appropriated a war-machine and tamed it into an Army.

The fourth danger is the greatest, however; it happens when, conversely, a war machine takes over a State and posits war and war alone as its object. This is the 'great Disgust, the longing to kill and die, the Passion for abolition' (227). The fourth and greatest danger is the danger of the lines of flight themselves, which 'emanate a strange despair, like an odour of death and immolation, a state of war from which one returns broken' (229). Here we find the war machine, the concrete machinic assemblage of mutation, social immanence, failing at mutation: 'war is like the fall or failure of mutation' (230). Here we find the analogue of the suicidal, empty BwO in a fascist war machine that has mobilised an incipient microfascist social fabric to take over the State and has thereby found, suicidally, nothing but war as its object. Both suicides – the empty BwO and the fascist State – are nihilistic, both tend to zero, but on different trajectories: one direct and depressive, the other indirectly, after a manic ascension into a war frenzy.

Thus the Deleuze–Guattari map of fascism shows how the fascist leader is faced with a 'paradox' (230). The leader must mobilise the interaction of the micro-black holes, the multiple, self-encased war machines of microfascism, before they resonate in a State, but also before they settle into the 'rumble and buzz' of mere grumbling. These dispersed war machines must be mobilised as a social war machine, but this tends to take off on a suicidal line of flight that captures a State of its own and posits war as its only object. Better still to put it in terms of the strengths and tendencies of concrete assemblages: Hitler had to construct and maintain the momentum of the Nazi war machine (let's say the SS) to overcome the reterritorialisations of hold-over aristocrats (the Wehrmacht officer corps) and the totalitarian resonance chamber of the State (the bureaucratic elements). Or more precisely still, the momentum of the line of flight had to overcome the other elements within the SS war machine itself so that it could overpower the other factors, themselves sites of struggle of the three aspects of the abstract Machine, and create a war machine stronger than the State. Only then, on the suicidal line of flight leading through war to State suicide – the indirect route to an empty BwO – is there a 'realized nihilism' (230). Such fascist sucidal nihilism is qualitatively different from the freezing, reflective, depressive, 'lunar' nihilism diagnosed by Nietzsche, which sinks relentlessly and entropically to zero; rather, fascist nihilism is a frantic, 'solar' nihilism, which burns out to zero on a trajectory through an super-intensity of heat produced by its own manic motion, its fascinated pursuit of war.

A materialist theory of fascist nihilism

The uniqueness and importance of *Capitalism and Schizophrenia* as a whole lies in its materialism. *Anti-Oedipus* opened the field of historical-libidinal materialism, a spectular shattering of the easy Marx–Freud synthesis of the French left by the interjection of Nietzschean energetics, *A Thousand Plateaus* maintained this thrust, but changed much of the terminology of *AO* in the bold attempt to harness the materialist 'new science' of the 1960s and 1970s expressed by thinkers such as Simondon (1964) and Prigogine (1984). In this third section I will show the materialist basis of *ATP*'s two main treatments of fascism: the proliferation of microfascisms as the cancerous BwO, and the suicidal line of flight resulting from a war machine taking over State. Deleuze–Guattari insist that politics, and of course, their 'political science', is 'a problem not of ideology but of pure matter' (165). What is then the materialism behind their accusation that in fascism there lies a 'realized nihilism'?

The materialism invoked here is not the determinist bogey of nineteenth-century thought, but the materialism of 'complexity theory',[5] a materialism that is neither mechanistic nor determinist, but that recognises both the emergent properties (contra the mechanist reduction of a system to its parts – for example, the claim that 'nouns are neurons') and unpredictability of complex systems. According to DeLanda's historical reconstruction (1991, 234, n9), in the late 1960s Deleuze began to formulate some of the philosophical significances of this 'new science', the study of 'open' matter–energy systems which move from simple to complex patterning and from complex to simple patterning. Although post-modern appropriations of science – to say nothing of critiques – have been the focus of much negative attention lately, due to the notorious Sokal hoax, there does seem to be good cause to take seriously the work of Deleuze and Deleuze–Guattari.[6]

To explain the new materialism of complexity theory, some elementary terminology is necessary. First, assume that there are three forms of physical systems: closed (determined), open (random or self-organising). Closed systems have constant matter and energy. They were models for classical modern physics, nature posited as a determinate system, as figured in the story of LaPlace's demon, whereby knowledge of the initial conditions and basic laws of a system would yield knowledge of all possible ('past' or 'future' – but here the terms lose their meaning) states of the system. Open systems, on the other hand, have a flow of matter and energy through them, and are of two types. Open random systems are exemplified by the laminar flow of fluids or diffusion of gases. There are no models for predicting the precise behavior of open random systems, but there are methods for arriving at statistical probabilities of the behavior of the system. In such randomness we find the classic image of 'chaos'. Open self-organising systems, on the other hand, are those in which a matter–energy flow arrives at qualitatively discernable patterns without outside interference. These systems are those studied by 'chaos/complexity theory'. Here we find short-term predictability and long-term unpredictability, the new image of 'chaos'.[7]

A second important term in understanding complexity theory is 'phase space', an idea developed by Henri Poincaré in the late nineteenth century. Improved computer technology, the material support of mathematics, has allowed new uses of this idea. There are five steps in constructing a phase space portrait of a system:

1 Identify important aspects of a system's behaviour, which are called its 'degrees of freedom';
2 Imagine or model a space with as many dimensions as the degrees of freedom of the system to be studied;
3 Each state of the system can then be represented as a single point, with as many values as there are dimensions;
4 The changing states of the system then trace a line, a trajectory, through phase space;
5 We can then try to solve the equations governing the line and pin down the system's behavior as in closed deterministic systems. Sometimes we can't solve the equations, and no patterns emerge, as in open random systems.

Sometimes though, in studying the system we can't solve the equations, but we can identify the evolution of some patterns, as is the case with open self-organising systems. These patterns have various features, some of which are named 'attractor', and 'bifurcator'.

Briefly put, as De Landa explains, the actual/virtual distinction Deleuze appropriates from Bergson (Deleuze 1988) is put to use in *Logic of Sense* and *Difference and Repetition* to distinguish between the (actual) traits of a physical system (its long-term tendencies) and the (virtual) thresholds at which it either adopts or changes those traits. Thus an actual system might, say, oscillate at one frequency within a certain range of parameters, and at another within another range. The actual behavior of the system, its oscillation at frequency #1 or #2, would be a trait, while oscillation frequencies #1 and #2 would be virtual 'attractors', and the transition between #1 and #2 would be a virtual 'bifurcator'. 'Attractors' receive their name by capturing the behaviour of systems within a range of values of parameters – their 'basin of attraction' – while 'bifurcators' are named because they are the events by which a system moves from one attractor to another. DeLanda isolates three types of attractors: point, loop, and chaotic, corresponding to three states: steady state, oscillation, and turbulence.[8]

The virtual/actual distinction enables Deleuze–Guattari to account for unpredictability in physical systems while still maintaining a consistent materialism; the virtual is 'real but abstract'. Attractors are forms of self-organisation of matter; physical systems of matter–energy flow can become organised, even if currently random or laminar.[9] Even turbulent fluids, for instance, which were classic symbols of 'chaotic' matter, are embodiments or actualisations of virtual attractors, albeit 'fractal' or 'strange' ones. There's no real chaos in turbulence; rather, fiendishly complex interactions of matter. However, laminar flows (paradoxically, 'calm' fluids) or gases come close to the original sense of chaos. In the phenomena of self organising systems, we find creativity, novelty, and so on, but this creativity is inherent in matter itself; bifurcators, Events, lines of flight, are changes triggered unpredictably when sensitive systems pick up slight cues that move them onto another basin of attraction, or keep them moving about within a zone of unpredictability.

With this notion of self-organizing matter, Deleuze–Guattari critique 'hylomorphism', the notion that matter needs the imposition of a transcendent form to organise its putative chaos. Hylomorphism lives by the forced choice or exclusive disjunction between chaos or transcendent form. *Après nous, le déluge.* By overthrowing long-term determinism in locating innovation, novelty, creativity in matter (albeit in its virtual thresholds), complexity theory disrupts the materialism = determinism equation and its concomitant forced choice of monistic materialist determinism or spiritualist dualist freedom. Common sense dictates (literally): since monistic materialism is determinism, and since we must preserve the phenomena of freedom, then we must pay the price of a spiritualist dualism. The new materialism of Deleuze–Guattari escapes this forced choice by critique of its hylomorphic presuppositions.

DeLanda's work on complexity theory thus offers us the following way of glossing Deleuze's terminology in *Logic of Sense* (Deleuze 1990). Trait, singularity and Event ('emission of singularities'), line up roughly with that of behaviour pattern, attractor and bifurcator. The terms adopted by Deleuze–Guattari in *ATP* are slightly different, with 'black hole' naming 'attractor' and 'line of flight' naming 'bifurcator'. Further, we can see the BwO as matter–energy flow, and the 'Abstract Machine' as the set of self-organising processes inherent in that flow and effectuated by various concrete social assemblages, as for example the war machine drawing a line of flight by decoding and deterritorialising a flow and occupying a smooth space, that is, warding off transcendent ordering to allow immanent self-organisation. After the scanty nature of this preliminary, the following materialist treatment of fascist nihilism can only be provisional.

Nonetheless, we can say that both the proliferation of micro-black holes and attendant multitude of war-machines (the cancerous BwO of microfascism) and the suicidal line of flight (the war machine that has taken over the State and posited war as its only object) are amenable to materialist explanations.

The cancerous BwO of microfascism occurs with a sedimentation rate that overwhelms the articulatory power of the stratum. In political terms, microfascism occurs when the selecting of homogenised individuals surpasses the overcoding power of the State so that these law-abiding individuals come to enforce their own laws in a proliferation of command centres that inhibits State formation. In complexity theory terms, in microfascism the social system reaches a point whereby a proliferation of attractors fragments the system into mutually communicating but independent sectors. Here there is no resonance in a giant attractor, but only the static of many small attractors. Microfascism is the body politic that moves frenetically without going anywhere.

The suicidal line of flight of fascism occurs when a war machine captures a State apparatus and turns to war. In political terms, this is the end game in which a fascist regime, which has succeeded in mobilising the microfascist proliferation, sacrifices itself even after its defeat in a war is certain. In complexity theory terms, we can say that here the social system has – after escaping the futility of the static zone of too many microattractors (microfascism), and after avoiding the self-conserving basin of attraction of the totalitarian state in which sub-command posts resonate and amplify a central attractor or 'giant black hole' – fallen instead into a zone of complete disorder. In other – mythological – words, the suicidal line of flight has avoided the Scylla of microfascism and the Charybidis of totalitarianism, only to fall into the void of Chaos.

Finally, to complete this section, what is a materialist account of the 'realised nihilism' of fascism? It is relatively easy to see the suicidal line of flight as a realised nihilism: it is the pushing of the social body into nothingness. Instead of a careful destratification to set matter–energy flowing in immanent self-organisation (the full BwO), destratification itself – the decoding and deterritorialising line of flight – becomes the goal; the war machine aims at war, the empty BwO becomes realised through war rather than depression. A solar, flaming, nihilism rather than lunar depressive freezing.

The adjective 'realised' is important in understanding fascist nihilism: as the discussion in *Bergsonism* makes clear, the possible is realised, while the virtual is actualised (Deleuze 1988, 97). Instead of keeping the BwO in reserve ('have a small plot of new land at all times' [Deleuze and Guattari 1987, 161]) as a field of virtual potentials some of which could be actualised on occasion as a cautiously experimental shake up, suicidal fascism realises the pure flow, brings it forth frozen in reality. But this realisation is impossible: as Deleuze–Guattari 'cautiously' note, a system cannot survive without a BwO, but it also cannot live AS a BwO either. There must be some organisation of the body politic, for the BwO is nothing, no-thing. It is prior to all determinate organisation, for it is the matter–energy flow and self-organising capacity of organised bodies. For it to be realised would be to realise nothing. Suicidal, solar, State fascism is a realising of no-thing, a realised nihilism.

Conclusion: fascist nihilism now?

How does this recapitulation of *ATP* (written in the mid to late 1970s) help us understand the contemporary (late 1990s) situation with regard to fascist nihilism? First, two conceptual difficulties need to be cleared up, concerning the type of 'political science' Deleuze–Guattari pursue and the status of history in *ATP*; then we can consider the positive accomplishments of *ATP* in addressing fascist nihilism.

To evaluate *ATP*'s usefulness in understanding contemporary fascist nihilism, we must first be clear what they are doing. *ATP* brings into sharp relief the difference between types of 'political science' (the study of politics, and the politics of science). Deleuze–Guattari name them State or royal science and nomad science. The former is an axiomatic/theorematic approach which isolates constants from variables to develop laws governing phenomena; the latter is a problematics exemplified by metallurgists, who treat variables by putting them into continuous variation (establishing all their ranges without privileging one as the standard or constant) and then 'track' the singularities (virtual thresholds) and traits (actual behaviours) of a material system. Nomad science treats the 'machinic phylum', the convergence of singularities and traits in various 'assemblages' that effectuate sets of operations that actualise the potentials of matter in particular traits.

Now Deleuze–Guattari's treatment of fascism is nomadic: they don't pretend to lay out eternal conditions for fascism, as if it were a platonic idea, a possibility to be realised if only the proper 'laws' of politics are obeyed. Rather, the nomad political science of Deleuze–Guattari consists in tracking the 'machinic phylum' of fascism: the ways in which the potentials inherent in human 'matter' (the potentials of human behaviour tapped into by social training), can be arranged so that a certain human behaviour becomes the content for the expression of a fascist war machine. They ask, in other words, about the construction of a fascist assemblage, the way in which a social machine taps into human potentials by constructing a pedagogy that produces fascist individuals[10] and then mobilises them, rousing them from their microfascist buzz into a war machine capable of appropriating a State.

Second, we must be clear about the historicity of the historical-libidinal materialism of Deleuze–Guattari and how it entails their relatively greater concern with microfascism than with the fascist State. The 'current situation' addressed in *ATP* is of course that of the late 1970s, of Mutual Assured Destruction (MAD), that is, the peace of nuclear terror. Now everything about Deleuze–Guattari's work dissuades us from teleologising that stalemate: they knew as well as anyone that the situation they diagnosed was not the end of history, in large part because for Deleuze–Guattari history is only the transformation of coexistence into succession (430). The important thing is always the map, the balance of forces that effectuates the Abstract Machine of coding, decoding, overcoding in assemblages that are at once tribes, war machines and States. However, in privileging 'geography' (drawing maps) over history, Deleuze–Guattari do not neglect the latter. Recognising the coexistence of aspects of the Abstract Machine eliminates the dangers of evolutionism in ethnographic political science, against which they polemicise relentlessly (359), but this does not entail a neglect of history. To draw a map of the current situation is not just to locate aspects of the Abstract Machine, but to estimate their relative strengths and potentials for actualising a shift in forces. And this can only be done in tracing the development of the current situation – in other words, by doing history.

So, in producing a universal history of forms of the State (459; 466–7), Deleuze–Guattari isolate the fascist moment as something over and done with. Various analyses in Plateau 13: The Apparatus of Capture allow us to see why there is no more room for a fascist war-machine-State. In so far as fascism constructs a totalitarian state, it is motivated by the desire for autarky, for subtraction from global flows (223). It seems now that capital flows are too fast and too big for that project even to be broached, even if a war machine were to be formed from microfascisms. Although they refrain from putting it so, Deleuze–Guattari allow us to posit that capital is itself now a war-machine, occupying the world as smooth space, able to pop up at any place at infinite speed (453–4). Any attempt at a 'closed vessel', at a domestic market of *Ersatz* (463), would be laughable given the ability of capital to disentangle itself from any too-self-assertive reterritorialising attempts of States. It is not that capital has completely surpassed the State, but that States are limited to being the 'models of realisation' of the axiomatic of capitalism (454), that is, that States now are only the places where the abstract moments of capital, the deterritorialised and decoded flows of labour and capital, can meet (455). The historical moment of the fascist State is finished: not forever, perhaps, but for the foreseeable future, given the current situation of capitalism. The real problem is microfascism.

With these two conceptual difficulties clarified, let us consider the accomplishments of *ATP* regarding our understanding of fascist nihilism. First, it forcefully reminds us that nihilism – in materialist terms, an orientation to zero intensity – has two vectors: lunar, 'Christian' nihilism: descending, freezing, depressive, paranoid – the type diagnosed by Nietzsche; and solar, fascist–Nazi nihilism: ascending, burning, manic, 'schizo' – the type diagnosed by Deleuze–Guattari. Hence our initial quandary over the gap between the Nietzschean context and the Deleuze–Guattari context of nihilism as an appropriate label for National Socialism has been resolved.

Secondly, we know that contemporary microfascisms abound. The conceptual apparatus of *ATP* allows us to ask what conditions have kept them from forming a war-machine capable of taking over a State. We might say that microfascisms, as long as they are isolated in the 'rumble and buzz' of molecularity, are relatively 'harmless' in State–political terms, even when they reach the miltia-level as in some parts of the USA. Perhaps it is liberal institutions (in either their disciplinary or 'control' aspects) (Deleuze 1995, 177ff) that keep them from organising themselves into a war-machine with a viable chance at appropriating a State of their own? With no movement organising the microfascisms, there is no *arche* of a fascist war-machine–State, just as smooth capital has prevented its *telos*, the 'closed vessel'.

Third, *ATP* helps us understand 'the former Yugoslavia' as an instance of fascist nihilism. We see here the ethnic purity achieved through violence and apparently the formation of a suicidal State. We also, arguably, see macropolitical intervention by capitalist States to prevent the formation of a 'closed vessel' or autarky in the region (I write this during the NATO bombings of March 1999, and am of course discounting the humanitarian cant of 'saving the ethnic Albanians of Kosovo': such PR staples are simply not a credible explanation of military intervention; if they were, then Rwanda or East Timor or scores of other places would have seen such intervention). Much more work than I am able to provide would have to be done, however, to support Deleuze–Guattari's theses about the relations of micro- and macrofascism in this case. Nonetheless, we do see some of their theses fascist nihilism upheld, especially the turning away from fascism nihilism on the part of capitalist States, who recognise the utility of State reterritorialisation–as opposed to the deterritorialising effects of the suicidal State–in providing a stable international business environment (455).

Fourth, lastly, *ATP* shows how the resistance to fascism must be as much micrological and micropolitical as it is also macrological. As we have seen, for Deleuze–Guattari , 'every politics is simultaneously a macropolitics and a micropolitics' (213). The macropolitical resistance to fascism, the prevention of the formation of a fascist State, can never be said to be over and done with, but for them it does seem to be a matter the capitalist axiomatic has well in hand at the present time. This conclusion, of course, needs constant testing and requires a pragmatic flexibility in revising it when needed. Nonetheless Deleuze–Guattari shift their attention to the micropolitcal. Now, Deleuze–Guattari's call to look to the 'fascist within you' is far from an 'individualist' retreat from politics. Rather, microfascism as 'molecular molarity', as runaway sedimentation, is precisely the creation of individuals. *ATP*, in short, refocuses the struggle from a fascist State at whose pretensions capital would only laugh, to microfascism, the production of individuality. Thus Deleuze–Guattari also shift the struggle onto the left: microfascism prevents a progressive war-machine from forming as well as liberal institutions prevent a fascist war machine from mobilising. The progressive war-machine, a progressive revolutionary movement, is blocked as long as contemporary 'progressives' insist on calling for individual rights and recognition. This is only interest group lobbying for a new axiom, a new dispensation of capital. The struggle must be to prevent the axiomatic struggle (which Deleuze–Guattari validate [470–1]) from becoming either a proto-fascist hierarchy (the party will tell you when you're free) or liberal integration (give us our axioms and we'll behave). Axiomatic struggle must be the struggle to release a force of minoritarianisation that would not just change the grid to include a few more points of identification of individuals with rights, nor would dream the sweet utopian dream of an elimination of grids altogether (or the not-so-sweet dystopic dream of the smooth space of global security forces – 'never believe that a smooth space will suffice to save us' [500]), but would increase the force of smoothing relative to that of gridding. This is no prescription, but only a hint as to how to draw our own maps.

To do justice to Deleuze–Guattari's insistence on positivity, we should say that the best resistance to microfascism is not simply to resist, but also to do otherwise. This does not mean non-resistance as craven acquiescence, but, over and above resistance, the positive production of new networks of immanence, following lines of flight out of the molar categories handed us by macropolitics. Resistance is reactive, Deleuze–Guattari imply in one of their few criticisms of Foucault; lines of flight are among the primary elements of a diagram (530–1, n39). But again, experimentation on lines of flight is not individualistic; the key is forming non-organismic bodies. We in English don't have the immediate sense of *corps* as social body that helps the Francophone reader of Deleuze–Guattari understand the political import of *corps sans organes*. The body without organs, or better, the non-organismic *corps*, is a social body of immanent relations, a place for becomings rather than hierarchies: a date, a conversation, a seminar, a corps of (metallurgical) engineers without officers, a movement, a machine to generate minorities, to generate becomings that cannot be counted with molar categories (how do you count 'someone' who is black AND white, gay AND straight ...?), a nondenumerable mass. Not the proclamation that one 'identifies' with the struggles of minorities, those counted under certain categories, but minoritisation, the production of those who do not even fit the tortured stop-gap categories of 'mixed race' and 'bisexual'. Blowing apart the molar categories of the census-takers. Tiger Woods, the uncountable, the unnameable.

Warren Beatty's great Senator Bulworth: 'we'll just have to fuck each other until we're all beige (blackwhiteyellow)'. Produce a network of Amazon-wimps, of girly-men, of wasp-orchids. The politics of '68 without shame.[11]

Notes

1 The *AO* vs. *ATP* treatment of fascism is discussed in Beasley-Murray 1995.
2 On the caution of *ATP*, see Land 1993.
3 May 1991 claims 'life' as the 'core structure' for Deleuze.
4 De Landa (1997, 290n82) proposes a correction of D/G at this point, differentiating 'folding' from 'cementation', which properly belongs with 'sedimentation'. 'Folding' is then said to accompany 'accumulation' on another physical scale.
5 This term is not in current usage among working scientists – who prefer 'nonlinear dynamics' – but has gained enough currency in 'popular science' treatments to warrant its use here.
6 About DeLanda (1992) no less severe critics than Paul Gross and Norman Levitt say: '[although] there is some muddle...[it is] pretty clear and straightforward...a good and honest job, although one might wish for a more careful delineation of how much of this is really speculative' (Gross and Levitt 1994, 267–8n17). As readers of *Higher Superstition* will attest, this is praise indeed from Gross and Levitt. Since DeLanda explicitly links his account with Deleuze–Guattari, and since Gross and Levitt somewhat approve of DeLanda – although admittedly without mentioning Deleuze–Guattari by name (they do contempuously dismiss Deleuze's treatment of Riemann in his *Cinema* series, although they do not mention the similar treatment in *ATP*) – I assume the connection of Deleuze–Guattari and complexity theory is at least an avenue worth pursuing.
7 We have thus broached the question of a reduction of Newtonian physics from ontology to epistemology. All we ever encounter, all that exist, are open systems, but treating some of them as closed – modelling their behaviour by closed model and linear equations – can be technologically helpful. (I restrict my discussion in this paper to the epistemological vocabulary of 'predictability' rather than the ontological vocabulary of 'indeterminacy', for simplicity's sake, and as 'the better part of valor'.)
8 This is of course a tremendously simplified account of a wide-ranging, complicated and changing scientific field. Current work has moved beyond the attractor–bifurcator model to consider the 'mutual bootstrap' effect between the 'landscape' of a particular phase space and the specific trajectories resident within it. I owe this clarification to Francisco Varela of the CNRS, Paris. See also Kauffman, 1993 and 1995.
9 Here a possible reading of Lucretius: the *clinamen* or 'swerve' is the least deviation from the laminar. Thus ancient Greek atomistic physics was a fluid dynamics, not a solid one. See Serres 1977.
10 On the various pedagogies producing both the micro- and macrofascist body, see Theweleit 1987–89.
11 My thanks go to the volume editors, and to David Lindenfeld, Alistair Welchman, Charles Stivale, and Andrew Cutrofello for their careful comments on earlier drafts.

References

Beasely-Murray, J. (1995) 'Deleuze, Guattari, and the Human Security System'. Paper presented at the annual meeting of the International Association of Philosophy and Literature, Villanova University.

DeLanda, M. (1991) *War in the Age of Intelligent Machines*. New York: Zone Books.

——(1992) 'Non-Organic Life' in *Incorporations*. New York: Zone Books. 128–67.

——(1997) *A Thousand Years of Nonlinear History*. New York: Zone Books.

Deleuze, G. (1983) *Nietzsche and Philosophy*. Trans. H. Tomlinson. New York: Columbia University Press.

——(1988) *Bergsonism*. Trans. H. Tomlinson and B. Habberjam. New York: Zone Books.

——(1990) *The Logic of Sense*. Trans. H. Lester with C. Stivale. Ed. C. Boundas. New York: Columbia University Press.

——1995. *Negotiations*. Trans. M. Joughin. New York: Columbia University Press.

Deleuze, G. and Guattari, F. (1983) *Anti-Oedipus*. Trans. R. Hurley, M. Seem, and H.R. Lane. Minneapolis: University of Minnesota Press.

——(1987) *A Thousand Plateaus*. Trans. B. Massumi. Minneapolis: University of Minnesota Press.

Gross, P. and Levitt, N. (1994) *Higher Superstition: the Academic Left and Its Quarrels with Science*. Baltimore: Johns Hopkins University Press.

Holland, E. (1987) "Introduction to the Non-Fascist Life": Deleuze and Guattari's ' "Revolutionary" Semiotics' in *L'Esprit Créateur*. 27.2.

Kauffman, S. (1993) *The Origins of Order*. New York: Oxford University Press.

——(1995) *At Home in the Universe*. New York: Oxford University Press.

Land, N. (1993) 'Making It with Death: Remarks on Thanatos and Desiring-Production' in *Journal of the British Society for Phenomenology*. 24.1: 66–76.

Massumi, B. (1992) *A User's Guide to Capitalism and Schizophrenia*. Cambridge, MA: MIT Press.

May, T. (1991) 'The Politics of Life in the Thought of Gilles Deleuze' in *SubStance* 66: 24–35.

——(1994) *The Political Philosophy of Poststructuralist Anarchy*. University Park, PA: The Pennsylvania State University Press.

——(1997) *Reconsidering Difference*. University Park, PA: The Pennsylvania State University Press.

Prigogine, I. and Stengers, I. (1984) *Order Out of Chaos*. New York: Bantam.

Serres, M. (1977) *Naissance de la physique dans le texte du Lucrèce*. Paris: Les éditions de Minuit.

Simondon. G. (1964) *L'individu et sa genèse physico-biologique*. Paris. Presses Universitaires de France.

Theweleit, K. (1987–89) *Male Fantasies*. 2 vols. Trans. S. Conway, E. Carter and C. Turner. Minneapolis: University of Minnesota Press.

9

The Survival of Nihilism

Howard Caygill

Nihilist und Christ – das reimt sich, das reimt sich nicht bloss...

(Der Antichrist §58)

In a recent encyclical letter *Fides et Ratio* [Faith and Reason] (October 1998) Pope John Paul II issued a call for philosophy to renounce the nihilism of post-modernity and to resume metaphysical research into the truth. In this extended (165 page) 'untimely meditation' on philosophy, the first on the subject to issue from the Vatican since *L'Aeterni Patris* of Pope Leo XIII in 1879, the Pope proposed to revive the alliance between philosophy and Christianity underdone by a secular modernity whose philosophy terminated in nihilism. The issue of the encyclical letter coincided with the controversial canonisation of Edith Stein, a victim of Auschwitz and, with Heidegger, one of the most gifted and innovative students of Husserlian phenomenology. The conditions for the papal appeal to philosophy had been established in two earlier encyclical letters *Veritatis Splendor* [The Splendour of Truth] 1993 and the extremely provocative and radical *Evangelium vitae* [The Evangel of Life] 1995. All three encyclical letters amount to a defence of the concept of 'life' against what are perceived as nihilistic direats to its sanctity, threats typified by the event of the Holocaust.

The cultural revolution prosecuted in the name of 'life' under the pontificate of John Paul II marks a conscious attempt to retrieve the hegemony on this issue surrendered to secular 'nihilistic' thought. The choice of terrain – 'life' – matches exactly that pursued Nietzsche in his attack upon Christianity in *The Anti-Christ* (1895). Indeed, *Fides et Ratio* reverses Nietzsche's text by using the concept of life to expose the nihilism of secular philosophy in the same way that Nietzsche had used it earlier to expose the nihilism of Christianity. *The Anti-Christ* and *Fides et Ratio* both regard nihilism as a historically specific, transitional phenomena which it is possible to survive in order to arrive at a future affirmation of life. This peculiar rhyming between the critiques of nihilism and Christianity suggests an affinity that is intimated but not fully worked through by Nietzsche: Christ and nihilist rhyme, but the ways in which they not only rhyme remain obscure.

Nietzsche's description of the 'ambiguity of nihilism', is usually framed in terms of the simultaneously active and passive character of the phenomenon. He does not find ambiguity residing in the very project of overcoming nihilism. In a draft for the Preface for an unfinished work *The Will to Power: Attempt at a Revaluation of all Values*, he begins to relate 'the history of the next two centuries' as 'the advent of nihilism', or inevitable catastrophe of European culture. As the 'first perfect nihilist of Europe' he reads prophetically the 'hundred signs' of the continent's nihilistic destiny, having 'lived through the whole of nihilism, to the end, leaving it behind, outside himself' (Nietzsche 1968 Preface). The unwritten book would provoke a counter-movement to nihilism, one 'that in some future will take the place of this perfect nihilism' coming after and out of it. The play of movements and counter-movements, completions and substitutions underestimates the phenomenon of nihilism, most crucially in the hope that nihilism can be survived, superseded or in some way placed 'outside' and behind us.

The ambiguity of nihilism has more insidious roots than the opposition between its passive and active character identified by Nietzsche. The governing ambiguity is most clearly exposed in the double genitive of 'the survival of nihilism' which can mean not only that it is possible for us to survive nihilism but also that nihilism may survive our attempts to survive it. Expressed temporally, the ambiguity consists in the tension between the hope that nihilism is but a transitional condition that can be lived through and gone beyond, and the suspicion that it is an ineluctable modality invulnerable to the passage of time. Nietzsche's analyses of nihilism are precisely strung on the ambiguity of survival, that while nihilism is something we can live through and survive the very desire and the means we use to survive it only confirm and enhance its strength. While nihilism can adopt a number of different figures – religious, scientific, political and aesthetic – these are but vectors of a movement that exceeds any given figure. The ambiguity of nihilism consists in a performative contradiction in which negation may confim nihilism more strongly than its affirmation. It is for this reason that Nietzsche describes nihilism as 'the uncanniest guest', it manifests itself in a process of doubling, as a denial and negation that is most at home when it is denied and negated. Thus Nietzsche affirms nihilism when he negates its Christian variant in the same way as John Paul II affirms it when he negates its secular variant.

Nietzsche's notes on nihilism contemporary with *The Anti-Christ* show him suffering the performative contradiction of nihilism. The tone of the notes contrasts sharply with that of the book, which finds in the concept of life a basis from which to mount the critique of Christian nihilism, only to discover that the affirmation of 'life' in itself nihilistic. This movement is evident in Nietzsche's 1887 definition of 'radical nihilism' which marks the inaugural and terminal moments of the nihilistic condition and is vital for understanding both the history and the ineluctability of nihilism:

'Radical nihilism' is the conviction of an absolute untenability of existence when it comes to the highest values one recognises; plus the realisation that we lack the least right to posit a beyond or an in-itself of things
that might be 'divine' or morality incarnate.   (Nietzsche 1968, §3)

In the inaugual moment of nihilism, identified by Nietzsche with Platonism and later its popular form Christianity, the spatio-temporal world is negated when compared with the 'highest values' or ideas. The transcendent ideas of the good, the true and the beautiful negate and so diminish any good, true or beautiful acts or works that we may accomplish under finite conditions. Nietzsche regards the other-worldly character of Christianity as a prime example of a culture in which the 'highest values' diminish life by establish-ing standards that are defined by the impossibility of their ever being real-ised. Every finite act in the light of these values must be a failure, so reducing to nothing any autonomous significance they may possess and judging them only with regard to those highest values that they can never achieve.

Nietzsche saw the inaugural nihilism of Christianity as having a number of possible futures. The first is to continue to negate the finite world in the name of highest values impossible to realise – an intensification of what Nietzsche described as 'passive nihilism'.The second 'radical nihilism' – has two related variants: the first, described in §3, extends the negation of the finite world to the highest values themselves while the second, described in §2 occurs when '*the highest values devalue themselves*' as in science, when the value of truth is turned against truth itself. Radical nihilism is consistent with the Christian inauguration of nihilism in extending its range to include the ruling ideas or turning its own highest values against themselves. The third future is Nietzsche's own 'revaluation of values' in which the prevailing scenario of values – the opposition between the apparent and the true world – is re-drawn, and the highest values succeeded by a set of affirmative values supposedly immune to nihilistic outcomes. Out of these possible futures Nietzsche elaborates a history of nihilism which moves in three stages from Christian inaugural nihilism to a radical nihilism provoked by the development of science and the consequences of the reformation to the intimations of a revaluation of values in his own work.

Much of Nietzsche's discussion in the notes from the late 1880s concerns the implications of radical nihilism and the possibility of surviving it through a revaluation of values. The chronological equivocations that emerge are consistent with the peculiar trope of radical nihilism that sus-tains the moment of inaugural nihilism at the same as turning it against itself. Nihilism can thus be viewed as both a '*normal* condition' and a 'pathological transitional stage' (§13), as the scientific destruction of faith in the prevailing synthesis of values (§1) and as *'a divine way* of thinking' (§15). Nihilism is thus suspended between past, present and future, and in spite of Nietzsche's attempts to imagine a future without it – after its completion – even these intimations of the survival of nihilism fall to its equivocation.

The attempt to survive the inaugural nihilism of Christianity through the negation of its 'highest values' served only to confirm nihilism, indeed to radicalise it. The enlightenment critique of Christian highest values did not deliver liberation but meaninglessless. In the discussion of the 'decline of cosmological values' the radical consequences of this critique are extended to the basic transcendental values that informed our interpretations of the world: 'the categories "aim", "unity", "being" which we used to project some value into the world – we *pull out* again; so the world looks valueless' (§12). Nihilism is present both in the values themselves – as inaugural nihilism – as well as in their radically nihilistic negation. It will also return in a new guise within the revaluation of values itself.

From the perspective of the ineluctability of nihilism it is possible to regard *The Anti-Christ* and *Fides et Ratio* as two anti-nihilistic tracts which succeed in reconfirming nihilism, albeit in different ways. *The Anti-Christ* is a critique of the inaugural nihilism of Christianity from a standpoint between radical nihilism and the 'revaluation of values' while *Fides et Ratio* is a critique of radical nihilism from the standpoint of inaugural nihilism. The former confirms nihilism in its negation of Christianity, the latter in its negation of radical nihilism; while seeking ways to survive nihilism they both contribute to its survival.

Both *Fides et Ratio* and *The Anti-Christ* engage their critiques of nihilism in terms of the concept of life. The former departs from a diagnosis of a nihilistic culture superficially characterised by personal and social fragmentation, and a philosophy which advocates and celebrates this fragmentation. It then discerns within this appearance of fragmentation the operation of a scientific and technological logic which annihilates 'higher values' in the name of technical and productive efficiency. The nihilistic culture criticised by the Church is the fragmentation that follows from the implementation of a nihilistic scientific and technological order. This train of argument is exemplified in the following passage of the encyclical letter where totalitarian social and political projects 'traumatic for humanity' are aligned with nihilism (in the guise of science and technology):

Certain scientists, deprived of all ethical points of reference, risk no longer having the person at the centre of their interests and the globality of their life. What is more, some of them, aware of the potential of technological progress appear to concede, not only to the logic of the market, but also to the temptation of a demiurgic power over nature and humanity. Nihilism thus emerges as a consequence of the crisis of rationalism. (John Paul II 1998, §46).

The encyclical letter returns to these links between scientific and technological nihilism, and the post-modern celebration of 'living within an horizon without any meaning, under the sign of the provisional and the fleeting' (John Paul II 1998, §91) and totalitarianism. It criticises contemporary philosophy for abdicating from its task of contesting the nihilism of science and technology, and thus for being complicit with the nihilism that found confirmation in 'the terrible experience of evil that has marked our epoch' (John Paul 1998, §91) .

The argument of *Fides et Ratio* had been anticipated in the earlier encyclical letter *Evangelium vitae* on 'the value and inviolability of human life'. This criticised the scientific and philosophical reductions of life to biological functions:

> the *body* comes increasingly to be perceived not as the typical reality of a person, the site of the relation with others, with God and with the world. It is reduced to pure materiality, a mere complex of organs, functions and energies to use according to criteria of mere pleasure and efficiency.
>
> (John Paul 1995, 36)

These criteria not only negate the 'highest values' of Christianity, but more insidiously replace them with new ones (pleasure and efficiency) while pretending to abolish all values. The scientific and technological 'revaluation of all values' depends on the hubris that it is theoretically possible to deliver immortality. Against this both encyclical letters insist on finitude, maintaining that 'the first truth of our existence is beyond the fact that we exist is the inevitability of our death' (John Paul II 1998, §26).

I

However, the re-assertion of ultimate values – the Christian revaluation of scientific and technological values itself invites the return of nihilism. Instead of following the argument of one of the many voices in the encyclical letters which points to a thinking of finitude without either fragmentation or illusory synthesis of ultimate values, the Vatican issues a call for philosophy to regain wisdom by returning to a pre-modern defence of ultimate values:

> The dimension of wisdom is today even more important insofar as the enormous growth of technological power demands a renewed and acute consciousness of ultimate values.... A Philosophy that wishes to negate

the possibility of an ultimate meaning of the world is not only inadequate
but also erroneous.

(John Paul II 1998, 81)

After criticising the radical nihilism of science and technology in the guise of
devaluation of traditional values institutes new, even more terrible systems
of value, the encyclical document simply restates the inaugural nihilism of
Christianity. In place of the new higher values of productivity and efficiency
there is a return to traditional values of truth and the good. Both sets of
value, however, are nihilistic in establishing transcendent ideas which can
never be realised and so condemn humanity to failure and self-negation, so
ensuring the survival of nihilism.

In *The Anti-Christ* Nietzsche predicted that any attempt to reform Christianity from within would be vitiated by the nihilistic 'theological instinct'
wherein 'nihilistic values hold sway under the holiest of names' (Nietzsche
1978, §6). However, his own war upon the 'theological instinct' poised
between radical nihilism and the 'revaluation of values' is not itself immune
to 'theology'. The argument in terms of 'life' frees the concept from its
associations with the 'higher values' of Christianity, but only to convert
them into another higher value. Christianity is condemned for 'negating
life' for 'shifting the centre of gravity out of life' for 'poisoning life' but all in
the name of the new higher value of 'life'. The details of the affirmation of
instinct and the body merely conceal that a new highest value has been
insinuated, one that began in the negation of Christian higher values and
that will end, like all values, in the negation of itself. Life destroying itself for
the sake of itself – a formula revealed by Nietzsche in the word 'health'. The
Christian in negating life inaugurates nihilism, with the cross serving
as the sign of recognition for 'a conspiracy against health, beauty, well-
constitutedness, bravery, intellect, *benevolence of* soul, *against life itself*'
(Nietzsche 1978, §62). Yet the negation of this negation in the name of life
does not achieve the *Aufhebung* of nihilism, but only its confimation and
survival.

The argument against Christian nihilism in the name of life is not the only
exit from Christianity essayed in *The Anti-Christ*. Another is immanent to
Christianity itself, and is found in the figure of Christ and the non-figural
concept of life which he both figures and does not figure. The nihilistic trap
consists in figuring negation, thus giving it a site and the possibility to
negate itself. A way Nietzsche finds to avoid this outcome is to refuse figura-
tion and the formula of the 'cosmological values' – aim, unity and being.
Nietzsche's paradoxical exemplar of such absence of figure is Christ. Christianity for him remains 'the tremendous question mark' because it marks the
'opposite of what was the origin, the meaning, the *right* of the Gospel'
(Nietzsche 1978, §36). The origin is precisely one that is without figure and
thus without 'aim, unity and being': Christ's is a faith 'that lives', it does not
'formulate itself' – his life is that of a 'free spirit' (Nietzsche 1978, §32). His

life has no aim no unity, and no interest in being. Christ does not resist, deny or otherwise negate; his Kingdom:

> The 'kingdom of God' is not something one waits for; it has no yesterday or tomorrow, it does not come in a 'thousand years' – it is an experience within a heart, it is everywhere, it is nowhere.... (Nietzsche 1978, §34)

Nietzsche understands the death of Christ in terms of the implied contrast with the death of Socrates. Christ does not debate the meaning of his death, but practices his freedom from the spirit of revenge. He does not subsume his own death under a system of aims, he does not unify with the rest of his life nor does he propose it as a doctrinal test of his divinity. Instead, for Nietzsche:

> His words to the *thief* on the cross contain the whole Evangel. 'That was verity a *divine* man, a child of God!' – says the thief 'If thou feelest this' – answers the redeemer – *thou art in Paradise*, thou art a child of God.'' *Not* to defend oneself, *not* to grow angry, *not* to make responsible.... But not to resist the evil man – to *love* him.... (Nietzsche 1978, §35)

What was 'exemplary' in this manner of dying was 'the freedom from, the superiority over every feeling of ressentiment' (§40). However, this 'exemplarity' did not consist in figuring a higher value but in showing a practice of life informed by cheerfulness and love, that is, without the spirit of revenge. This 'without revenge' was not in itself a vengeful negation of the prevailing cultural 'spirit of revenge' but the practice of a life that was indifferent to it. The Evangel is in this sense 'the existence, the fulfilment, the *actuality* of this 'kingdom' but an actuality which has no place or time.

Yet paradoxically the anti-figure of Christ became the most prominent and powerful source of a revaluation of values. After the death of Christ Nietzsche imagines the disciples 'being shaken and disappointed to their depths' and then posing the vengeful question 'Who killed him?' (§40). With this question the disciples not only look for the forces that negated Christ's life, but they also imagine that the meaning of his life was itself the very negation of these forces – 'one subsequently understood Jesus as having been *in mutiny against the social order*' (§40). The next step, which Nietzsche saw as codified in the Pauline epistles, was to regard Christ's alleged defeat as a ploy in a larger cosmic battle. The meaning of Christ's death was the resurrection and the establishment of a system of higher values which would justify the last judgement. The exemplar of non-negation is thus transformed for Nietzsche into a mighty figure of negation, the founder of a system of higher values. Yet Nietzsche berates Paul for accomplishing precisely a 'revaluation of all values', for declaring vengeful war on a system of higher values md seeking to negate and replace them with a new set. The vengeful war on Christianity waged in *The Anti-Christ* is analogous to Paul's war on '*ruling* Judaism, its upper class' (Nietzsche 1978, §40); it does not exemplify a practice beyond good and evil but instead figures the negation of old and the institution of new values.

In *The Anti-Christ* Nietzsche plays Paul to Pauline Christianity: like Paul, Nietzsche develops a new systems of values based on a biological definition of 'life', one which is reactive and driven by negation. This ensured the survival of nihilism by creating a new, implacable set of biological values policed by its own medical priesthood.

The futural moment of Nietzsche's work relies on the distinction between 'radical nihilism' and the 'revaluation of values', seeing in the latter the possibility of surviving nihilism. However, this assumes that nihilism is a predicament that can be overcome, an assumption that he nowhere defends satisfactorily. Every revaluation of values demands a devaluation or negation of existing values, and this negation prepares the revaluation to serve as a vector for the propagation and survival of nihilism. The negation of radical nihilism by the Vatican in *Fides et Ratio* in the name of truth and the respect for life repeats the gesture of inaugural nihilism and thus reinstates it while Nietzsche's negation of Christianity repeats the gesture of radical nihilism. And as Nietzsche himself showed, even the exemplary affirmative figure of Christ is not immune to generating nihilistic affects.

If the revaluation of values is unable to escape the radical nihilist predicament the question posed to the future changes from revaluation to that of how to live with nihilism. Nietzsche develops some ideas in this direction in the otherwise puzzling comments on Buddhism in *The Anti-Christ*. Both Christianity and Buddhism are nihilistic religions, but the latter, for Nietzsche, 'stands, in my language, *beyond* good and evil' (Nietzsche 1978, §20). It is a religion in which the 'supreme goal is cheerfulness, stillness, absence or desire, and this goal is achieved' (§21).The direction of this argument is consistent with his comments throughout his writings on Meister Eckhart and negative theology. With this view a new future for nihilism is intimated, one which recognises that it will not be overcome in a 'revaluation of values' and which then seeks a way to survive nihilism without overcoming or living beyond it.

The predicament of cheerfully surviving nihilism is described by Nietzsche at the beginning of the fifth book of *The Gay Science*. In an indirect gloss on the rhyme of Christ and nihilist, Nietzsche reviews the various scenarios of the survival of nihilism following the death of the Christian God. In the interstices of the reactive futures of the advent of a 'logic of terror', a revival of Christian belief or the propagation of the new piety of 'belief in science', Nietzsche finds the cheerfulness of the free spirit. Following the catastrophic death of God, the free spirit does not engage in mourning, nor commence a vengeful search for those guilty of the murder nor seek to lay down new laws. Instead, the free spirit looks for the dawn after the shadows, greeting the news of the death of God with a cheerful 'thoughtfulness, astonishment, longing and expectation'. This is not a negation which would fall into the trap of nihilism, but an indifference to it, a cheerfulness that brings into rhyme the anti-figures of Christ and the perfectly nihilistic free spirit.

References

John Paul II (1995) *Evangelium vitae: II valore e l'inviolabilita delta vita umana*, Milan: Paoline Editoriale Libri.
—— (1998) *Fides et Ratio* 11–30 Vatican.
Nietzsche, F. (1978) *The Anti-Christ*, trans. R.J. Hollingdale, Harmondsworth: Penguin Books.
—— (1968) *The Will to Power*, trans. W. Kaufmmn and R.J. Hollingdale, New York: Vintage Books.

10

Skin-Nihilism Now: Flaying the Face and Refiguring the Skin*

David Boothroyd

> In the course of the ecstatic vision, at the limit of death on the cross and of the blindly lived *lama sabatchtani*, the object is finally unveiled as *catastrophe* in a chaos of light and shadow, neither as God nor as nothingness, but as the object that love, incapable of liberating itself except as outside itself, demands in order to let out the scream of lacerated existence.
>
> [Bataille (1936) 1985, 185]

> To be silent, to die slowly, in the conditions of a complete *déchirure*. From there slipping into the depths of silence and with an infinite perspective, you will know from what infamy the world is made.
>
> [Bataille (1947) cited in Wilson 1995, 186]

A slice of life as death

A profound cutting or wounding of the body disrupts the self-control of the mind in its contemplation of a death always on the brink of finality but never quite arriving at it. Thinking articulates each instant of the postponement of such a torturous death, life is the torment and anguish of its forestalling. If Bataille's obsession with this photo, in its focus on the 'most anguishing of worlds accessible to us *through images* captured on film', can be seen as an identification with the instant of ecstatic pain, Artaud might be said to have spoken directly from within such a moment; the moment of his own 'mental' dismemberment and painful struggle against disintegration, experienced in the form of thinking *through the 'flesh'*:

---

* Dedication: to the gruesomely murdered, and all others NOW being hacked, lacerated, chopped, flayed, raped and dismembered; to all those subjected to annihilations of the skin. (The photographer of the illustration on p. 199 is unknown.)

The death of Fou-Tchou-Li by *Leng-Tch'e* (cutting into pieces), from Dumas' *Traité de psychologie* (1923), reprinted in Bataille's *Tears of Eros*, 1989 (1961)

> This photograph had a decisive role in my life. I have never stopped being obsessed by this image of pain, at once ecstatic and intolerable. (Bataille 1989, 206)

> What is this cry like a dog howling in a dream, which makes your skin crawl, gives you this feeling of grief and unnameable uneasiness making you gag in a mad and drowning frenzy. No, it isn't true. It isn't true.... But the worst of it is, it is true. And at the same time there is this feeling of desperate truth, where it seems you are going to die again, you are going to die a second time... at the end of this visceral distillation don't we picture the panic we have already experienced.   (Artaud 1968, 90)

This thinking-event, or 'picturing', is always already disintegration in act: there is no prior original, stable unity of self and no *a priori* coherent 'normality'; hence no peace of mind for poor Artaud, only Artaud in pieces: in the throes of a desperate, frenzied attempt to think his unity. This condition is a horror multiplied by the sense of *déjà vu* which accompanies it. Artaud experiences the groundlessness of his subjective (dis)unity as a kind of panic 'falling', at once horrible and familiar, which he describes in his correspondence with Jacques Rivière as the 'fear of not dying entirely'. (Artaud 1965, 7)

In both cases this 'thought' is experienced in 'the body' and as the attempt to think the body's relation to death; that is, to re-think the body as 'reversible' flesh; as the medium or site of the ambiguous pain/ecstasy of a laceration and dismemberment (*déchirure*) – something which is neither simply physical nor mental but the *limit* of the self tormented by a generalised violence to which it is exposed as exteriority.[1] Bataille's obsession with this image stems not from any truth it might be supposed to represent, for example the amphibology of the pained/ecstatic expression it makes textually available, but from its *undecidability*. Its 'disturbing effect' is neither simply visceral, nor ethical, nor conceptual and yet it is a function of all of these at once, and is, consequently, unsettling of any attempt to decide its 'meaning'. Obsession is, precisely, the response it provokes. Bataille's direct and indirect reflections on this, in these cited works and elsewhere, express the undecidability of a body which could never be fully represented in themes. In themes, for example, such as those articulating and ordering anthropological, sociological, political, or psychological analyses and explanations, of either images, or (body) events, such as this image, for instance, depicts. As a reader of this image, Bataille no more pities the individual it shows, laments 'man's inhumanity to man', nor seeks to explain (away) the incident, or other such instances, of violence and suffering, than readers of Artaud's 'pain-texts', for example, might purposefully lament his not having received during his life, better 'institutional care' for his 'madness'. There is for them both, in their respective discombobulations, an abyssal morbid de-cision of the difference, of the slash, between dying/ life.

It could be argued, of course, that there are only really matters *of literature* to be addressed here; those of the Text and of inter-textual engagements marking the trajectory of the various textual elements which drift together, at a certain moment in a particular literary culture. The expressions of inner experience they provide are not descriptions of, nor speculations on, particular private experiences or consciousnesses; neither are they, nor could they be, 'private languages'. And, such *writings* are surely symbolic dispersals of several themes; of the ecstasy/pain double, of death, the body, the sovereignty of the subject and the 'impossible', and so on. Bataille's picture is itself, after all and explicitly, a simulacrum of what would normally be referred to as the original 'event', of a torture and a suffering, one which is doubled-up again in its literary repetition in his writing. Its reprographing further here, stands to illustrate the manner in which it may serve to return thought, repeatedly, to a moment of undecidability; a point which may give access to what this essay attempts to discuss below under the rubric of 'ethics of the skin' and to the question of nihilism in terms of the annihilation directed at the skin of *the other*, in his/her *vulnerability*.

However, both Bataille and Artaud, albeit differently, do direct their thinking toward a moment in which 'the body' experiences itself, equivocally, as both witness to *and* victim of violence: as a moment of doubling; as an annihilation – the forestalling of an annihilation 'proper'.[2] For Bataille, for example, in the impossibility of a solipsistic death:

> The privileged manifestation of Negativity is death, but death in fact reveals nothing... for a man ultimately to reveal himself to himself, he would have to die, but he would have to do it while living – by watching himself cease to be. (cited in Boldt-Irons 1995, 96)

Negativity as the nihilistic *will to nothing* is incompletable by any *one*[3]: it is an incompletable 'end' for the solitary subject due to the impossibility of coincidence between the singular personal death and (impersonal) death *itself*. As Blanchot says, every death is, in this technical sense, 'voluntary': 'Thus in voluntary death it is still *extreme passivity* that we perceive – the fact that action here is only the mask of a fascinated dispossession' (Blanchot 1982, 102).

The irreducibility of the difference, or the 'non-difference', between the voluntary and the passive, belongs to a series which gives 'literary' access to death, or, the deconstruction of its 'truth'. The *mise en abyme* is, for the willing which falls into it, redoubled at a level on which, for example, we too, as viewers of this 'picture' (for it is no longer certain what is ultimately 'on view' in all this), are implicated in the paradoxes of this reflexivity. *I am*, at once, disturbed by the instability of my identification with the victim (there but for the grace of God...) and my ambivalence with respect to my witnessing of this scene. I am, of course, outside its spatio-temporal frame, its historical and cultural context: I view the 'scene' as a whole (for example in this text, now). But, in my look, I also border on it – I slip in and out of the crowd which looks on. As Blanchot says: 'Whoever wants to die can only want the borders of death, the utilitarian death which is in the world and which one reaches through the precision of the workman's tools' (Blanchot 1982, 105). I may even find myself identifying with the machete-wielding torturer, and being drawn, vertiginously, into a contemplative teetering on the brink of the 'ethical abyss'.[4] Indeed, this is the point at which the witness/victim doubling makes one's skin crawl. It is as if one were, precisely, imagining doing this to oneself. This schizoid imagination experiences difficulty in its manipulation of the simulacra in play here, as it attempts to maintain the distinction between witness and victim by mapping it onto the I-victim/I-perpetrator distinction (I witness witnessing, etc., as well as *being* the witness.) This phenomenon is, perhaps, not dissimilar to that experienced in ghoulish nightmares, in which the disturbance of my identification therewithin is multiplied by the fact that the horror and perversity I am 'exposed to', is in reality, all *of my own making*: it is a form of auto-affection, or, auto-mutilation.

This essay will attempt to show the manner in which this model, or image, of a mutilation which mutilates the very system of its representation, is ethically instructive: one does not fall *down* the tunnel of reflected reflections into literary play without end, one falls *back* into the world of 'real', violent encounters *between* human beings. Exteriority (as everyday life, reality, etc.) is perhaps inseparable from interiority and the structures of interior experience, but it is in no sense dreamed up. As Artaud says: 'the worst of it is it is true'. The image is of an 'incident'; it really happened, as well as being this (other) thing which it is, over and beyond this or any other particular incident: murderous violent mutilation, is happening *now*.

These cursory references to Bataille and Artaud provide a sense of how the mutilated body is neither simply corporeal nor outside of thought, but *abyssal*. The rest of this essay will discuss nihilism and *an*-nihilism (the interruption or reversal of annihilistic nihilism) in relation to the mutilation of the 'flesh' and the violence directed at it, both with respect to auto- and alter-mutilation. And, by shifting the approach to the 'flesh' – a term which marks Artaud's rejection of the physical/mental dichotomy – moreover, to the surface of contact between *the same* and *the other*, it will be possible to engage in a discussion of the ethical significance of the skin, or of 'being-in-a-skin'. Doing so allows an approach to the ethical in terms of *carnate*, rather than *cognate* life; and in a manner uninflected by explanatory reductionism of the discourses of the human sciences. I shall consider the ethical significance of the species of 'mutilatory' violence directed at the visceral body, the flesh, or, the skin. Emmanuel Lévinas' discussion of the skin will provide the key to reinterpreting what it is that 'obsesses' in the visceral violence of annihilistic nihilism, directing this analysis to the moment in which the ethical resistance of the Other 'reverses' into *my* responsibility.

From sensibility to ethics; on being skinned

The turn to the body in contemporary theory, in particular in connection with discussions of the 'end of metaphysics' and postmodernity is, above all, indebted to Nietzsche's tropical deployment of it in his writing to counter the transcendental tendency of modern rational thought. Rethinking the discursive body (Foucault), the carnal body (Merleau-Ponty), the sexed body (Irigaray), as well as a number of specific interpretations of the ecstatic body (Bataille), or the 'body without organs' (Artaud/Deleuze/Guattari) can all, in their various interests and concerns, be figured in relation to the Nietzschean project of the 'revaluation of all values'. I do not propose to undertake here a detailed discussion of this general theoretical indebtedness of recent European thought to Nietzsche's turn to the body. However, this essay does aim, in part, to understand the significance of the widely-acknowledged, nietzschean-inspired rethinking of the body, as that from within which ethics and the idea of the ethical, emerges.[5] And, it recalls Nietzsche's remark expressing this: 'our most sacred convictions, the unchanging elements in our supreme values, are judgments of our muscles' (Nietzsche 1968, 173). The theme of the ethical incarnate will be addressed here, principally, by way of Lévinas' account of ethical subjectivity in terms of its *being-in-a-skin*. I shall argue that this is an idea which is central to his philosophy of ethical an-nihilism, which thinks the ethical moment as the interruption of annihilistic nihilism. This analysis, then, could be said to aim at an ethico-pathology of violence as violence directed against the flesh, or, rather, at *the skin* (the preferred term here as this emphasises the *liminality* of the flesh), considered as the limit between *the same* and *the other*.

In Lévinas' *Otherwise than Being or Beyond Essence*, the skin figures prominently in an account of *vulnerability* as the 'condition' for the ethical relation to the Other. In the 'itinerary' of that work, Lévinas declares his intention to 'disengage the subjectivity of the subject from reflections on truth, time and being...and to present the subject...as *sensibility from the first* animated by responsibilities' (Lévinas 1978, 19, *my emphasis*). Sensibility is, in fact, a constant theme in Lévinas from his earliest works onwards: whether distinguishing sensibility from intuition in the 1930 book on Husserl; discussing its role in the hypostasis and ipseity of the existent in relation to the 'there is' (*il y a*) in the works of the mid-1940s; employing an analysis of touch in his critique of Heidegger in *Totality and Infinity* as well as playing a key role in his later account of my infinite obligation to the Other, in which the significance of *the skin* is brought to the fore.

Three obvious considerations warrant discussing sensibility in relation to the skin and the skin in relation to ethics: locating the skin, so to speak, *between* sensibility and the ethical. Firstly, there is the fact that the skin is, in every sense, the organ of sensibility: it is not the sense of touch alone that is 'of the skin'. The retina of the eye, the tympan of the ear and the mucous membranes of the nose and mouth are all skin-sites of carnate sensational intensity. Secondly, the skin is 'without metaphor' – a phrase Lévinas is fond of and to which we must return – the boundary between the me and the non-me and gives me the sense of my being an interiority *exposed* to exteriority. Thirdly, as a theme, or a trope at the very least, the skin can be figured in relation to the logic of the border and its *undecidablity*, in the sense given above, and with this comes a whole range issues related to the limits of philosophy and the Nietzschean–Heideggerian theme of 'overcoming nihilism'.

These reflections aim to consider what role the skin plays in 'ethical subjectivity' and to see if it is meaningful to speak of 'overcoming' (annihilistic) nihilism in the form of an ethics of carnality – an ethics which emerges from the skin rather than as the 'idea' of a transcendental subject. They seek also to consider how such an ethics may serve an 'ethico-pathological' understanding of violence, the violence which is the *event* of ethical nihilism, or, murderous violence, and in relation to which the *déchirure* of the skin, as both wound and discursive opening, will allow us to approach. The theme of sacrifice is also central to this analysis as it is a form of sacrificial mutilation which links, as does vulnerability in Lévinas' account, sensibility to the possibility of *giving*. Just to indicate how: for Lévinas, only because I am a being which has tasted bread in my mouth am I able to sacrifice my own sustenance and make of it a gift to the other. This is a recurrent figure in *Otherwise than Being or Beyond Essence*:

> The subject is of flesh and blood, a man that is hungry and eats, (is) entrails in a skin, and thus capable of giving the bread out of the mouth, or *giving his skin*. (Lévinas 1978, 77 *my emphasis*.)

Expressions such as this, which abound in Lévinas' revaluation of sensibility, beg the question of the status of the figural in an account that directs us to the ethical realism of face to face relations. Empiricism and the representation of the empirically real are at issue throughout this revaluation of sensibility: the skin is, after all, the substance of sensation and the organ of the empirical. It can also literally be given. For example, in the case of van Gogh's severing of his ear and making of it a gift (see Bataille 1995, 61–72) or, of performance artist Orlan's giving (and merchandising) of body tissue removed in her work of self-transformation,[6] or, in the somewhat less bizarre form of the organ donation sponsored by medicine, we see an indication of the manner in which even 'giving one's skin' *can be* a non-figural form of approach to another person. This is indeed a strange sort of 'empiricism' (and a number of unusual examples of 'generosity'), particularly given Lévinas' often highly figurative style of expression, but the point of referring to them here is that they each refer the reader directly back to 'real life'; to the 'here and now' of the sensual and to life as 'flesh and blood'. In a certain unapologetically unphilosophical kind of way, this is rather like saying that when Lévinas talks about the skin he is talking about the *actual* skin, the skin which can be wounded, which bleeds and which touches. But this 'actual' does not refer to the empiricist naturalism of the *physical* skin – the skin as conceptualised within anatomo-biology – nor does it refer to any *idea* of the skin in terms of *what it is*. Nonetheless, we read: 'the expression "in one's skin" is not a metaphor' (Lévinas 1978, 109). Lévinas' remarks about the skin aim to give an account of it figuring it otherwise than in ontological language. And although it is, arguably, philosophically impermissible in the final analysis, this is expressed in terms of the skin's (being) *signifyingness*: a signifyingness without a signification; something which is 'wholly sign, signifying itself' (Lévinas 1978, 15) – that is, without its being represented in a theme. The skin is thus also described as 'a modality of the subjective' (Lévinas 1978, 26).

Rethinking the sensibility of the skin is, it is proposed here, a key to a non-essentialist notion of 'ethical subjectivity' of the 'me' (*le moi*). A cursory deconstructive reflection on the metaphysical distinction between aesthesiological sensuality and sentience, will show how this sensuality is relegated to a subservient role in relation to knowledge. Empirically speaking, on the one hand, the skin is considered to be the unthought materiality of carnal sensation. But, on the other, from the perspective of theoretical reflection, the skin constitutes the limit of my subjective being and the boundary of the subject enclosed within it. This is attested to in so far as the skin and its diverse sensory surfaces are made an *object* of reflection in *presentifying logos*; the skin is traditionally thought in the terms of dermato*logy*, of one species or another. Against this dehiscence, however, it can be argued that the skin is, quite literally, *in-between* being the empirical – understood as the very substance of empiricity (which reflection thinks as sensation) – and the transcendental object of dermatological thought, which posits it as such. It is both lived *and* reflected in thought; it is at once the limit of immanent egological life and also the surface on which the exteriority of everything which is not me, impresses itself on me.

In this respect, the skin is an allomorph of what Derrida has termed *undecidability*. And a deconstructive re-writing of the skin in terms of its ethicality, must involve the destabilisation of the decision of its meaning within metaphysics. Rewriting the skin requires a rethinking of the sensual and its relation to meaning, so to speak, *beginning with the skin*. But before we start again, in this sense, let us reflect briefly on philosophy's *decision* of the skin, which Lévinas' discourse is in the process of reversing and transfiguring.

How is the meaning of the sensual, sensation and sensibility, expressed by the whole family of terms expressing the aesthesiological in life, determined within metaphysics? Briefly, it is thus: Reason, speaking of itself in modern philosophy, has generally aimed to transcend the subjective experience of sensuality. The transcendence of sensuality rests on Reason's reflective ability to pull this experience apart, differentiating between sensation and sentience; between sensing and the cognition of sensation which it itself is. In this schema, a secondary role is assigned to the former with respect to the knowledge cognition understands itself to be. Whether in, say, phenomenalism, sensationalism, sense-data theory, positivist naturalism, or even on the model of the synthetic *a priori*, sensuality is taken to be *instrumental* in relation to (the act of) meaning (*Sinngebung*). Consequently, it is either determined as the 'subjectivism' of unreflected 'natural experience' and considered to be epistemologically dubious (according to an argument along Cartesian lines), or it is regarded as a mere apparatus supplying thought (consciousness) with value-free, empirical data upon which it acts. Against this move and the ways of thinking which ensue from it, (ranging from naturalism in science to the metaphysical philosophy of the kind Kant

rejected) the fundamental philosophical gesture of Husserl's phenomenology is to attempt a recuperation and revaluation of sensual life from within
lived-experience. Its appeal to non-thetic experience rests on the identification of a level of conscious life, ontologically prior to theoretical thought
and *not yet* relegated – as it is destined – to the instrumental service of
knowledge. It is in sympathy with the anti-epistemological spirit of phenomenology (rather than the philosophy of consciousness) that Lévinas
argues that *any* epistemology gets underway and asserts its prerogative by
'anaesthetizing' the skin (Lévinas 1978, 64).

Any attempt to rethink skinly sensation in relation to sentience (in terms
of sensible intuition, regarded as a pre-reflective 'act', a non-thetic *Sinngebung*) is at pains not to repeat the empiricist sensualism of ontological
metaphysics, which solves the problem of inference (i.e. of the 'externality'
of reality) by collapsing reflection onto its object in the coincidence of
thought and feeling. In view of this, it is worth recalling at least the spirit
of Lévinas' own appropriation of the great leap forward the Husserlian *epoché*
represents over traditional metaphysics. The *epoché* addresses both the naive
empiricism which supposes sensation to be unmediated closeness to the real,
as well as the reflection which takes itself to be true knowledge distinct from
sensation. It rejects the thought/sense distinction central to the empiricist
notion of experience and the epistemology of subject and object that goes
with it, whilst retaining the project of making philosophy a 'rigorous
science', based on a 'return to things themselves'.

But if the *epoché* avoids the trap of sensualism, it does so by ultimately
retaining and (re)privileging theoretical intentionality (something which
Lévinas so consistently associates with the ontological metaphysics he
opposes). Despite this, Lévinas acknowledges the significance of Husserl's
critique of knowledge *as* knowledge. And, most importantly on Lévinas'
account, the Reduction allows the questioning of the representation of
objects of thought in *themes*. It achieves an 'awakening' of thought to its
own 'effects' upon its supposed objects of intuition; this is an awakening as
startling as that which Kant associated with philosophy's need to awaken
from its 'dogmatic slumber' and forgetfulness of the empirical, by means of
critical philosophy. Despite its advantages, then, Lévinas emphasises that
Husserlian phenomenology is ultimately 'motivated only by the naive considerations emerging in understanding' and the need to expose 'the arbit-
rariness of speculative constructions' (Lévinas 1991, 214). The motivation of
this thinking is otherwise than philosophical on every level, and it seeks to
trigger another alarm. This alarm is, literally one might say, to the empirically alarming, calling of me to my responsibility by the Other, a 'fact'
attested to in the *empirical* event of obligation (see Davies 1995, 103).
Lévinas' continuous reference to, and reemphasis of the 'empirical' should
neither be glossed over, nor uncritically regarded as merely a superficial
aspect of his figurative prose style. It is, in fact, part of a reiterative strategy

recalling how the 'violence of the concept' and the representation of the other in themes, is never merely a philosophical problem but a consequence of the carnate viscerality of the 'me' and of the fact that the ultimate extreme violence, murder, can come, as Lévinas says in *Totality and Infinity*, in the banal susceptibility 'to violence from a blade of steel' (Lévinas 1969, 235). The blade of steel, in each instance, in being aimed at any aspect of a skinly exterior, is, ultimately, also being aimed at a 'face' (Lévinas 1969, 225).

Derrida, in his first major response to Lévinas, *Violence and Metaphysics*, spoke of the 'renewal of empiricism' implicit in the appeal to the 'pure signifyingness', which *Totality and Infinity* associates with the face of the other within the ethical relation, the 'face to face'. He spoke also of how any renewal, any re-writing of empiricism, would be wholly dependent on that which it sought to renounce – the ontology of the Same. In other words, it must be asked how such a notion could be both meaningful and yet escape the conclusion that this appeal is, in the final analysis, one of sentiment, or, conscience. Lévinas must therefore undertake to demonstrate how 'obligation' is effectively non-philosophical, or, pre-originary, unthematised signifyingness (literally non-sense): a signifying which *comes* to me without appearing in a theme.

In *Otherwise than Being*, Lévinas does indeed, albeit obliquely, undertake to rethink the empirical, by continuing with the theme of the relation between sensibility and the ethical, but now the approach is largely from the per-spective of reflection (i.e. philosophy). Whereas *Totality and Infinity* had spoken of the I-Other conjuncture as if this had been articulated from *within* the 'face to face' – as if from beyond being, in *Otherwise than Being* sensibility and the ethical are, from the perspective of reflection, shown to be conterm-inal. The relation to the face being thereby brought down to earth: 'Signify-ingness, the one-for-the-other, is exposedness of self to another. . . . It is the immediacy of a skin and a face, a skin which is always a modification of a face, a face that is weighted down with a skin' (Lévinas 1978, 85). This being 'weighted down' is a reference to the autochthony of a being which has its base in 'carnality', and the interface of the ethical and the carnal is sub-sequently referred to the sensibility borne on the skin.

From the perspective of carnal being, the skin, does not appear *as such* at all; it is, in a manner of speaking, pure sensuality.[7] But let's be clear, to describe the skin in terms of its being the 'condition' for sensory perception, moreover, the 'empirical' condition for this, would be a misnomer perpetrated by thematising thought as it claims the sensible as the object of its intuition. Such a privileging of the exterior perspective, is, precisely, what gives rise to the body represented in natural science. Of this 'seen' body, Merleau-Ponty once said: it is 'only a shadow stuffed with organs' (Merleau-Ponty 1962, 138) – a remark echoed in Lévinas' description of this body as 'entrails in a skin' (Lévinas 1978, 77). The term 'sensibility' in

Lévinas names neither the capacity of a subject nor a concept of reflection; it is *in-between* what empiricist sensualism, on the one hand, considers to be unthought 'pure sensation' and what phenomenology, on the other, regards as the object of consciousness.(see Lévinas 1973, 169) He expresses this in the following passage:

> A thermal, gustative or olfactory sensation is not primarily a cognition of pain, a savor, or an odour. No doubt it can take on this signification of being a discovery (but only) by losing its own sense (*sens propre*), becoming an experience *of...*, a consciousness *of...*, 'placing itself' before *the being exposed in its theme.*   (Lévinas 1978, 65 *my emphasis*)

The expression 'losing its own sense' here plays on the double connotation of *sens* as 'meaning' and 'direction': sensibility loses its own 'meaning' by becoming the noematic correlate of a *noesis*, instead of maintaining its *sense* as a pure *noema*: 'it is a noema without a noesis' (Lévinas 1969, 65). Lévinas here targets the Husserlian dictum that 'all consciousness is consciousness of...something' on the ground that it is founded by attributing to sensibility a *mis*-directed intentionality. The point being that both Husserl's phenomenology (explicitly) and Merleau-Ponty's phenomenology (in a less obvious way) remain committed to the 'parallelism' of 'dualities and theses', or, the obverse–reverse structure of sensibility (the Merleau-Pontean 'sensible-sentient'). Against this, Lévinas declares his renunciation of the intentionality which acts as a 'guiding thread toward the *eidos* of the psyche which would command the *eidos* of sensibility', adding that his analyses '*will follow sensibility in its prenatural signification...*' (Lévinas 1978, 68): that is, the signifying of sensibility *before* it is represented in a theme.

The significance of the reversal of intentionality proposed here is that only on the basis of the *individuation* of the subject *in sensibility* can such a subject enter into a relation to an Other which is neither reducible to, nor accountable for, in relation to the movements of the Same. The model of intentionality rejected, is rejected because it makes of the Other another for-me – and all 'for-me's' are but a function of my project. After all, as already noted, from the perspective of aesthesiological experience, the skin is not experienced as such, no more than the eye observes the retina as it delights in its vista. The skin is that within which my separate existence is maintained: the 'I' is sensibility and 'sensibility is enjoyment (*jouissance*)', without, in this moment of enjoyment, the skin appearing as such.

I cannot explain at length here, the detailed account of the hypostasis of the existent and its inherence within the domain of the 'there is' (*il y a*), which these few remarks must partly serve to recall. I do wish to emphasise, though, how the 'separation' of the existent (Lévinas' alternative notion of 'the subject') from existence in general, is held to be the 'condition of possibility' for an 'I' which can enter into an ethical relation. This idea, extensively articulated in *Totality and Infinity*, reappears in *Otherwise than Being*, expressed in terms of the 'superindividuation of the ego (which) consists in being in itself, *in its skin*' (Lévinas 1978, 118). Such 'separation', or, 'superindividuation' – which in *Totality and Infinity* was described in terms of the sensible existence of the 'I' bathing in the elemental 'there is' – without recourse to an act of negation – is the condition for the reversed intentionality which, throughout *Otherwise than Being*, is held to account for my 'obligation', my 'being-for-the-other'. This obligation, which depends on separation at the level of sensibility; on my sensible uniqueness (*sens unique*), comes to me from beyond myself, unsolicited and not *decided* by me. In the language of *Totality and Infinity*, this is an obligation entered into '*anterior posteriorily*', in an 'instant' of time before time began to pass for the 'me' (*le moi*). My point here is that the model of a *non-negational* relation of the individual existent to existence, precisely, the 'pure' sensibility which remains inaccessible to the Husserlian *epoché*, reveals an event of individuation in which *I am* in my world without, in the same moment and thereby, commanding the world of the other; without violating the place of the other: it is an event which is prior to the appearance on the scene of *the will* of each. The movement of annihilation directed at the skin, or 'skin-nihilism', is thus countered by the articulation of an existence which is being-in-skin: prior to any possible 'willing', I am exposed to the touch of the other.

Refiguring the skin and redirecting ethics

The ethical significance of the skin derives from the fact that it is, from the perspective of sensible existence, the limit-surface upon which the drama of individual existence *as* sensibility is played out – for example, as *jouissance* or 'nourishment' and which, from an exterior perspective, is what constitutes my uniqueness, enclosed within a discernible limit. It is then, doubly, the 'condition' for the approach of the other to me (personally). I am uniquely obliged by the ethical demand of the other: even before I *know* myself; before I 'witness' myself; represent myself to myself in a concept and *think* of myself as *a unity enclosed within a skin*. And, I am, by that very same 'fact', exposed to the possibility of wounding and murder: 'exposedness to wounds and outrage characterises (the skinned subject's) passivity' (Lévinas 1978, 108 *my parenthesis*).

The general ethical structure outlined in *Otherwise than Being* would confine Merleau-Ponty's analyses to the realm of the Same and its relation to its world. In this respect Merleau-Ponty would be right, in Lévinas' view, to question the attempt to locate *the limit between the body and the world*, because, as Merleau-Ponty himself says, 'the world (itself) is flesh' (Merleau-Ponty 1962, 138). The notion of *jouissance* in Lévinas effectively describes a similar dissolution of this limit *as it is represented in ontology*. The existent emerges from the 'there is' but remains in a closed circuit of need and satiation with respect to it. The 'solitary' existent 'I' is lost in its sensuality and has no representation of itself; it has no *idea* that there are, as Merleau-Ponty's says, 'landscapes other than its own'. But from the perspective of thematizing thought, *my skin is not the event of sensible jouissance, it is the limit of my vulnerability.* I am for myself a being which is pure surface, a being which, in being-in-my-skin, am every inch vulnerable. Vulnerability and sensibility are thus inseparable – they are the obverse and reverse of the Same, related to one another as two sides of a Möbius strip. From the perspective of sensible existence this vulnerability amounts to 'uncertainty of the morrow' – for example, encountered in my hunger, thirst, fatigue and pain (see Lévinas 1978a). And, as I represent my skin-boundedness to myself in thought, I perceive my situation to be one of essential vulnerability.[8] What may be described as the pure indulgence of the 'I' in sensual existence, becomes self-concern only *on reflection*. Lévinas reminds us that this moment of reflection is not constitutive of the ethical in life, it remains 'internal' to the Same. An integrated thesis in Lévinas, then, is that *the consciousness which comes to itself in theoretical or calculative reflection is concerned only to save its own skin.*[9]

I shall now return to the prospect of re-figuring the skin, beyond its representation in themes. Earlier I suggested this must 'begin with the skin', which appears to be what Lévinas does when he asks 'what *dissimulation* there may be under the exposedness of a skin laid bare?' (Lévinas 1978, 49). But what can a skin already 'laid bare' dissimulate? Or, putting the same question from the perspective of reflection: what is the meaning of being-in-one's-skin? Prior to my formulation of such a question about my being as such, in so far as this concerns me, according to Lévinas, I am already exposed to the other to whom I must respond not by determining her meaning, but with absolute passivity, *like a skin which flinches when wounded.* The sensibility of the existent characterised as enjoyment (*jouissance*) and being-at-home (*chez-soi*), is always turning back into vulnerability. A turning from being satisfied and at home in my skin, into exposedness to the other. This tremulous sensibility is expressed in the hyperbolic language of passivity:

> a passivity more passive still than any passivity that is antithetical to an act, a nudity more naked than all 'academic' nudity.... It is a passivity that is not reducible to exposure to another's gaze. It is a vulnerability and a paining exhausting themselves like a hemorrhage, denuding even the aspect that its nudity takes on, exposing its very exposedness....
>
> (Lévinas 1978, 72)

Bataille perhaps glimpses such a beguiling passivity in what he finds 'undeniable' and 'most anguishing' in the facial/epidermal expression of the torture victim in his disturbing photograph. Such anguished vulnerability, Lévinas says, 'is not the existential "being-for-death" but the constriction of an "entry inwards".... It is not a flight into the void but a movement into fullness, the anguish of contraction and breakup'. This describes the relation in which 'a subject is immolated without fleeing itself' (Lévinas 1978, 108). Passivity expresses the idea that the 'meaning' or 'sense' of sensibility is *decided* elsewhere as 'taking care of the other's needs' to the point of self-sacrifice; this decision is an 'approach' which inverts my 'being-in-my-skin' into 'being-for-the-other' – something referred to above as the 'reversibility of the flesh'. With respect to the hypostasis of the existent, Lévinas says 'sensibility is enjoyment', but the vulnerability of being 'in one's skin' is also said to (re)turn sensibility into 'exposure to the other' and to wounding. The Möbius strip structure invoked earlier is, so to speak, joined end to end by a flip-switch which repeatedly re-directs sensibility into vulnerability, or in Bataille, ecstasy into pain. This leads Lévinas to claim that:

> I am bound to others before I am bound to my (thematic) body.... *The other calls upon that sensibility with a vocation that wounds*, calls upon an irrevocable responsibility, and thus the very identity of the subject. (Lévinas 1978, 76–7)

Let's at this point recall the remark cited earlier from the itinerary of *Otherwise than Being*: the presentation of the subject 'as a sensibility *from the first* animated by responsibilities' (Lévinas 1978, 19). Sensibility is never purely and simply an indulgence of the existent in sensible being: its 'sojourn' in the sensible is always and 'from the first', interrupted by the obligation which disturbs it. Prior to any being conscious of any *thing*, including my being conscious of my own individual being-in-my-skin, this obligation disturbs me directly and (re-)turns my sensibility into vulnerability by bringing me to the surface of my skin in a (self-)conscious reflection on the nature of this essential vulnerability. The disturbance which turns sensibility into self-concern is, in Lévinas' account, 'older' than my concept of myself as 'being-in-my-skin'. Vulnerability is therefore found to belie an openness, or exposure, to the other's alterity 'before' I experience my skin as mine. This thought makes of the skin the site of *obsession* with the other, and it gives us an insight into the 'ethical' nature of Bataille's obsession with the image.

> It is in the passivity of obsession, or incarnated passivity, that an identity individuates itself as unique, without recourse to any system of references, in the impossibility of evading the assignation of the other without blame.... the self is the very fact of being exposed.
> (Lévinas 1978, 112–18)

This retro-intentionality of passivity seeks to account for the alterity of others as *absolute Others*, for whom my ethical obligation is 'real' in that its manifestation is a part of my everyday experience of a movement directed toward me *from* the outside. It is also, therefore, non-sentimental, in the technical sense of non-ideational (i.e. it is *not my idea*). In some ways, it appears this entire ethical edifice holds itself up on the basis of this supposed 'fact' of obligation; an everyday experience, spoken of as if it were independent of culture and history. But rather than focus this issue here, I wish, finally, to reiterate how the self as a sensible-existent or 'being-in-a-skin', individuated at the level of sensibility, is the condition for ethical openness.

Lévinas elucidates the ethical significance of obsession when he argues that only a being in a skin can be 'open' in this way: 'the self in its skin is both exposed to the exterior (which does not happen to things) *and* obsessed by others in this naked exposure' (Lévinas 1978, 112). This account of carnal sensibility directs us to its hitherside – ethical sensibility: this is an explicit philosophical thesis in Lévinas concerning the relationship between sensibility and the ethical. This analysis has attempted to show how it also constitutes Lévinas' response to the philosophical conundrum of 'the real', which involves thinking it as the *relation* between the here and now and the beyond: we have seen how nihilism 'now', as the annihilation directed against the skin, is reversible into an-nihilation, and that the (ethical) moment is discernible in the interruption of such nihilism. The thesis is, so to speak, inscribed on the skin: the meaning (*sens*) of the skin is a direction (*sens*); it is 'a one-way street' down which the Other *approaches me* and has a unique meaning (*sens unique*) for me. (This figure is borrowed from Bernasconi, 1995.) The expression *sens unique* connotes both uniqueness and direction. This ethical refiguring of the skin does not lead to a notion of *general* responsibility for others, but to an insistence on *my* responsibility for her/him. It attempts to show that the responsibility that can be read-off the skin is not a lottery in which 'it *might be* me', it *is* me. This uniqueness is 'felt' as inescapably as a wound to my skin. Bataille's obsession with the moment of ecstasy/pain reversal perhaps *knows* this, but not what it means *ethically*: intensity has the power to obliterate reflection totally. Lévinas' account of ethical sensibility requires philosophy to recover the ethical: to recover 'the openness of the saying exposed like a bleeding wound' (Lévinas 1978, 151).

Notes

1 For a discussion of the 'reversibility' which is never simply of flesh as distinct from the text or the image, see G. Didi-Huberman (1995).

2 L.A. Boldt-Irons (1995, 96–7) discusses the literary aspects of the paradoxical reflections on the witness/victim relation in Bataille, and the limit of integrity of a unitary consciousness divided by reflection on reflection. This 'abyssal' principle manifests itself in Bataille's writing, in which 'one sign mutilates another'; 'in which we encounter the case of the slipping word, whose capacity for self-destruction or auto-mutilation had been silenced by the straightjacket of discourse'. Mutilation is here made, precisely, a matter of discourse, or, of literature.

3   The incompletability of nihilism understood as the interruption or postponement
    of the moment of 'complete nihilism' is expressed here as ethical 'an-nihilism'.
    It could be argued that this ethical an-nihilism is itself a species of the 'complete
    nihilism' as 'anti-nihilism', of which Nietzsche speaks, for example in the *Genealogy
    of Morals* II, 24, and which remains always 'to come'. On the connection between
    Nietzsche and Lévinas' thinking of the ethical see my 'Lévinas and Nietzsche:
    Beyond Love and Contempt' (Boothroyd 1995, 345–57). For a useful typography
    of the term 'nihilism' in Nietzsche, see A. White (1990, 15–25). My use of the term
    here, in any case, is intended to identify the carnate moment of ethical 'undoing'
    of the 'annihilism' which manifests itself in the murderous violence, central to
    Lévinas' account.
4   This marks the shift from the 'figural' abyssal of the *mise en abyme* to what might be
    described as the 'empirical' abyssal, the event of ethical disturbance (see the
    discussion of 'empiricism' below). If this were to be translated into French, then
    the term *mise en abîme* might be appropriate. Boldt-Irons (1995) refers to the
    specificity of what she calls the *mise en abîme* in Bataille's writing, as that 'techni-
    que' by means of which his reader becomes enmeshed in the processes of the text:
    it 'entails a structural *mise en abyme* of an experienced and perceived *mise en abîme*
    that neither sacrifices consciousness nor preserves its integrity' (1995, 96). The
    'teetering on the ethical abyss' I refer to here involves a comparable movement of
    going from the figural always *back* into the 'ethical incarnate'. However, whereas
    Boldt-Irons interest remains that of the 'mutilation of signs', I am attempting to
    exploit the Lévinasian notion of the skin as the sensible site of the 'abyssal' – at
    once a deconstructive 'repetition' and a 'real' abyss – to bridge the supposed gap
    between the figural and the empirical.
5   I undertake a discussion of this theme in relation to the sexed body in the work of
    Irigaray in my 'Labial Feminism: Body Against Body with Luce Irigaray' (Boothroyd
    1996, 3: 65–80).
6   Orlan's 'Reincarnation of St Orlan' involves her undergoing a series of surgical
    operation's on her face, in the process of which pieces of the surplus skin removed
    and have later been made into supplementary artworks, which have been both sold
    and *given* away.
7   Everything that Lévinas had said about sensibility and the sensible being of the 'I',
    in works prior to *Otherwise than Being*, had been aimed at accounting for its
    substantive singularity, or, its *separateness*, and against what in *Totality and Infinity*
    he once described as its 'dissolution' in modern philosophy, against its reduction to
    a function of discourse, or an integrated function of the world (an aspect of both
    structuralism and Heideggerian phenomenology, albeit differently). Even Merleau-
    Ponty's phenomenology, to whose thinking Lévinas' account of sensibility is sub-
    stantially indebted, is found culpable in this respect. When, in the opening pages
    of *Phenomenology of Perception*, Merleau-Ponty says that 'pure sensation corresponds
    to nothing in experience' (Merleau-Ponty 1962, 3), he is recalling how the Husser-
    lian reduction *does not* claim the *direct* intuition of objects, but rather the non-
    separation of consciousness and its world. The important corollary here is not that
    mental life, or, psychic interiority, has precedence, but on the contrary, that the
    absence of the sensed (object) is conterminal with the fact that we cannot find in
    experience 'a psychic individual' or subject – whose reality, he notes, is distinguish-
    able 'only in degree' from more complex perceptions which are 'bound up with
    the larger whole'. (Merleau-Ponty 1962, 9). For Merleau-Ponty, *I am sensible being*
    no less than I am the consciousness of the sensible reflected in thought. The

'intertwining' of the subject in its world, in terms of which he investigates the relation between the carnality and thought, or vision and the visible, is indicative of how the individuation of the subject is abandoned to an integration with being, to the neglect of its sensible uniqueness. Sensible individuation, is not, according to Lévinas, merely a technical matter of philosophy awaiting theoretical resolution. It is rather, the only possible basis upon which an alterity *which does not originate with me*, which does not appear in a theme of mine as another 'for-me', can be acknowledged.

8   This term is scare-quoted here because, far from any metaphysical sense of the essentiality of this vulnerability being invoked here, Lévinas' teaching is that ethics precedes (the idea of) vulnerability. The vulnerability of the 'I' is discernible in its taking up a 'position' in a skin which is identical with its 'exposedness' to another. Lévinasian ethical an-nihilism begins with the sensibility of the skin, rather than from within the discourse of reflected meanings. Such a 'sensibilism' is the visceral basis for the response-ability of the 'me'.

9   This is something that Derrida in his recent writings on responsibility has described as the 'economy of saving oneself' implicit to the concept of 'salvation'. See his essay, 'Tout Autre est Tout Autre' (Derrida 1995, 87). I am disturbed by the suffering of the other before any *thought* of saving my own skin, or reflection on my own possible fate. As suffering exposes a vulnerability which can be increased to infinity, I become aware of the infinity of my reponsibility. Lévinas calls this unreflected form of the ethical incarnate 'being-in-one's-skin, having-the-other-in-one's-skin' (Lévinas 1978, 115); the other as 'the very respiration of my skin' (Lévinas 1978, 49). I am animated, literally 'inspired' by the Other *before* I come to myself in the concept of being skin-bound. I am cast as host(age) in an ethical plot not of my making, which is 'sensible' to me because it is a matter *of my skin*. The skin is the carnate site of my 'irremissible guilt' which 'with regard to the neighbour is like a Nessus tunic my skin would be' (Lévinas 1978, 109).

References

Artaud, A. (1965) *Artaud Anthology*. New York: City Lights.
—— (1968) *Collected Works Vol. 1*. London: Calder.
Bataille, G. (1985) *Visions of Excess*. Trans. A. Stoekl. Minnesota: University of Minnesota Press.
—— (1989) *Tears of Eros*. New York: City Lights.
Bernasconi, R. (1995) 'One-way Traffic: The Ontology of Decolonization and its Ethics' in G.A. Johnson and M.B. Smith. Eds.
Boldt-Irons, L.A. (1995) 'Sacrifice and Violence in Bataille's Erotic Fiction' in C.B. Gill. Ed.
Boothroyd, D. (1995) 'Lévinas and Nietzsche: In-between Love and Contempt'. *Philosophy Today*. 39/4: 345–57.
—— (1996) 'Labial Feminism: Body Against Body with Luce Irigaray' in *Parallax* 3:65–80.
Davies, P. (1995) 'On Resorting to an Ethical Language' in A. Peperzak. ed. (1995).
Derrida, J. (1978) 'Violence and Metaphysics' in *Writing and Difference*. Trans. A. Bass. London: Routledge
—— (1995) *Gift of Death*. trans. D. Wills. Chicago: University of Chicago Press.
Didi-Huberman, G. (1995) 'Comment déchire-t-on la ressemblance?' in D. Hollier. ed. *George Bataille après tout*. Paris: Belin.

Gill, C.B. ed. (1995) *Bataille: Writing the Sacred* London: Routledge.

Johnson, G.A. and Smith, M.B. eds. (1995), *Ontology and Alterity in Merleau-Ponty*. Evanston: Northwestern University Press.

Lévinas, E. (1973) *The Theory of Intuition in Husserl's Phenomenology*. trans. A Orianne. Evanston: Northwestern University Press.

—— (1969) *Totality and Infinity*. trans. A. Lingis. Pittsburgh: Duquesne.

—— (1978) *Otherwise than Being or Beyond Essence*. trans. Lingis, A. The Hague: Martinus Nijhoff.

—— (1978a) *Existence and Existents*. trans. A.Lingis. The Hague: Martinus Nijhoff.

—— (1991) 'Philosophy as Awakening', in Cadava, Connor, Nancy. eds. *Who Comes After the Subject?*. London: Routledge.

Merleau-Ponty, M. (1962) *Phenomenology of Perception*. trans. C. Smith. London: Routledge.

Nietzsche, F. (1969) *Genealogy of Morals*. trans. W. Kaufmann. New York: Random House.

—— (1968) *Will to Power*. trans. W. Kaufmann and R.J. Hollingdale. New York: Random House.

Peperzak, A. ed. (1995) *Ethics as First Philosophy: The Significance of Emmanuel Lévinas for Philosophy, Literature and Religion*. London: Routledge

White, A. (1990) *Within Nietzsche's Labyrinth*. London: Routledge

Wilson, S. (1995) 'Fêting the Wound' in C.B. Gill. ed.

11
Artaud and the Importance of Being Rude
Catherine Dale

> This anger which consumes me and which I learn every day to put to better use must certainly mean something.
>
> Artaud 1976, 400

I

Refusing the twentieth-century's eviscerating professionalisation of anger is one of Antonin Artaud's imperatives.[1]

> To agree to burn as I have burned all my life and as I burn now is also to acquire the power to burn; and I know that I was predestined to burn, this is why I believe I can say that few angers can reach where my anger will be able to rise. (Artaud 1976, 401)

Artaud's display of anger and rudeness, both in his scandalous theatrical performances and on the page in his rancorous diatribes against the narrow-minded and the banal, is possibly the most famous – in the sense of familiar to his contemporaries and present readers alike – of all his putative idiosyncrasies. Despite this renown, Artaud's most identifiable characteristics are usually reduced to biographical information about drug addiction, schizophrenia, celibacy and religious fanaticism, while little mention is made of his ire, which in its fluidity, appears to transcend systematic classification. Thus paradoxically, Artaud's anger is taken up as both an indeterminate force and a familiar feature. It is a paradox that underscores the process whereby anger is captured and categorised as a particular illness, syndrome or crime, or alternatively, deployed as a creative impulse and romanticised as a force of artistic production.

Artaud's very public hostility enhances both his clinical status as a madman as well as the critical reception of his work. Yet the popularity of Artaud's aggressive and violent writings, drawings and performances is limited. Inevitably, his productions are seen as unpalatable or boring and are then categorised as products (symptoms) of mental disturbance or rejected as part of a tedious and nonsensical routine.[2] Despite the vagaries of the art market, however, Artaud continues to encourage the image of the mentally disturbed writer, performer and artist but for reasons other than popularity. Artaud insists that mental disturbances have something of the utmost importance to say. Hence, he is not against the prodigal claims, whether complementary or critical, built around an ideal nexus of the visionary, the genius and the mad-man.

The lucid powers of the imagination are rarely listened to outside the pathologist's clinic. In this sense, Artaud is an important 'mad-man' because he demands to be taken seriously in both critical as well as clinical terms simultaneously.[3] In an early letter to the publisher Jacques Rivière, Artaud writes, 'I am a man who has greatly suffered in the mind, and as such I have the right to speak' (Artaud 1965, 12). Artaud is less interested in the outcome or reception of his speech than in possessing the right to 'speak' at all. He emphasises not teleology (the finished product) but the infinite process of creating because despite popular, romantic and continuous interest in the analysis of insanity, especially in relation to genius, no such sustained curiosity attends those who enact disagreeable public displays of anger, frustration and rudeness.[4] It is this unpopular and unattractive madness – after all madness is both an ethical and an aesthetic affair – that has been allowed to become boring and is for the most part only caricatured, incarcerated and ignored. Artaud's letters to Rivière exercise the right to speak by attempting to explain over and over, and much to the bewilderment of their addressee, the most unpleasant aspects of the process of writing.

A general ignorance towards madness is one of the central issues of Artaud's 'Van Gogh, the Man Suicided by Society', a work for which Artaud received his only literary award.[5] Van Gogh, writes Artaud, 'did no more than cut off his left ear' (Artaud 1965, 135). Van Gogh is not mad, he is only thought so by 'bourgeois inertia' and its 'organised crime' 'in a world in which every day they eat vagina cooked in green sauce or the genitals of a new born child whipped into a rage plucked as it came out of the maternal sex' (Artaud 1965, 135). Artaud includes himself and Van Gogh in an elite coterie of persecuted sages alongside Gerard de Nerval, Friedrich Nietzsche, Edgar Allen Poe and the Comte Lautréamont. These figures have been suicided by a society which cannot distinguish between the idea of madness as an irrational force able to combat the petty, banal and ultimately destructive elements of reason, and the idea of madness as an irrational and incomprehensible force fit only for incarceration and death.

Artaud's essay on Van Gogh implies the introduction of a distinction between aggressive and insane madness.[6] The etymology of both uses of mad, aggression and insanity, is the Old English word for insanity *gemād*. If we take insanity as the primary or fixed meaning of *gemād*, it becomes possible to view aggression, used here as a symptom of insanity or an insanity in itself, as its mutable element. In this sense the flexibility of aggression enables it to negotiate its roles in both madness and anger and as a result distinguish between an aggressive-madness and an insane-madness. While insane-madness is tolerated to a point, due to the romance of the mad-genius, aggressive-madness which is rude and intimidating, is only tolerated once it has been transformed into insane-madness by a myriad of willing institutions be they familial, religious, legal, pedagogical or self-analytical. Without the excuse of madness, the aggressor is considered a responsible agent. And yet ironically, this same aggressor is regarded as insane because he is the director of aggressive acts. In other words, there is supposedly no such thing as an aggressive act which has been chosen reasonably. Consequently, when Artaud's outspoken derision for the world is poured into the template for insanity, the regard with which it is taken becomes a purely therapeutic exercise. Given the pathological diagnosis of his anger, it is not surprising then, to find that Artaud is rarely taken seriously. Artaud's theories on the weakness and uselessness of man, if they are considered at all – which means without the a therapeutic sentimentalism – are invariably viewed with suspicion and disregarded.

Insofar as the 'agent' of an aggression is treated paradoxically as both responsible and irresponsible for his outbursts, any movement which sets out to try to validate anger's peculiarities also initiates a philosophical debate about the relationship between passion and reason. Of the two, it is the latter of which Artaud is suspicious.

> I destroy because for me everything that proceeds from reason is untrustworthy. I believe only in the evidence of what stirs my marrow, not in the evidence of what addresses itself to my reason.   (Artaud 1976, 108)

At the same time as doubting reason, Artaud also dismisses capricious actions governed by personal passions. In his 'theatre of cruelty', improvisation is forbidden because the actor must be 'a kind of passive and neutral element, since he is rigorously denied all personal initiative' (Artaud 1965, 98). Artaud favours disciplined and incisive thought over spontaneity at the same time as rejecting the rigidity of reason. He turns reason into a purely aesthetic element, one which he uses to articulate his aggression and in so doing reject reason's monopoly on mental acuity. Here, Artaud does not reject the potential lucidity which reason claims but the transcendental form it commonly assumes.

As if to demonstrate that the maneuvering of reason and passion is not new but issues from a virtual or unidentifiable power, Artaud proclaims that 'only the madman is truly calm' (Artaud 1976, 109). The madman's world is ubiquitous and his ideas fly in all directions. 'What I am is without differenciation nor possible opposition, it is the absolute intrusion of my body, everywhere' (Artaud XIV, 76). The calm of the madman arises from the lucidity of the mind which is able to go everywhere. Artaud calls this the 'lucidity of unreason'. It is only the instigation of reason as the correct mode for thinking that carves the world in two. Reason over-codes unreason with a world of madness and secures itself in a sane world. Lucidity lies apart from reason and is available only in moments of madness. At the same time, the mind is able to resist undirected personal passion because the lucidity of unreason or the mind's everywhere is not undirected. The mad mind and its direction are coeval thus the work which Artaud demands of the mind is produced by the unique and unidentifiable ontology of 'an untransplantable ego'.

By paying attention to a hitherto barely discernible distinction between aggression and insanity in relation to passion and reason, Artaud's work raises the status of one of anger's most underrated modes: rudeness. Artaud encourages rudeness to gather its own momentum and thus its own import-ance, hence his notion of the right to speak. In other words, Artaud, who views everything as potentially important – there is no such thing as a minor or inconsequential affective act – increases the strength of his rudeness by injecting it with a gravity that allows it jurisdiction over even the most innocuous of situations.

II

> Do you know another Man whose indignation against everything that now exists is as constant or as violent and who is as constantly and as desperately in a state of perpetual fulmination?   (Artaud 1976, 400)

Although there is no one whose publicised/ published overt anger strikes as constantly as Artaud's, he does have allies. Nietzsche is a collaborator with an enduring and fulminating critique of human weakness, of days when he is 'haunted by a feeling blacker than the blackest melancholy – contempt of man' (Nietzsche 1990, 161). Despite the very different manifestations of their 'civil' objections, Nietzsche's quiet but harsh criticisms and Artaud's loud and frenetic outbursts and snarling terms of abuse, what Artaud and Nietzsche share is a keen awareness of the problem of rudeness and an equally keen desire for its perpetuation. Although Nietzsche claims to be polite in his dealings with others, he does not recommend a complete abandonment of rudeness.[7] In *Ecce Homo*, he claims 'the rudest word, the rudest letter are still more benign, more decent than silence' adding that rudeness is, 'by far the most humane contradiction' (Nietzsche 1989, 229). Rudeness is humane because it is candid; it does not wait smouldering in darkness, clothed in the appearance of extinguished fire. Rudeness is contra-dictorily humane because the socially self-protective and tacit rule of humane politeness tries to veto it. Artaud and Nietzsche show that the problem with rudeness is not with rudeness itself but with the fact that nobody knows how to be rude properly. Through this ineptness, rudeness becomes either cancerous resentment or senseless brutality. The problem is not rudeness but its political, social and cultural value. When Nietzsche calls for 'a revaluation of all values,' he asks:

> under what conditions did man invent the value judgments good and evil? And what value do they have themselves? Have they up to now obstructed or promoted human flourishing? Are they a sign of distress, poverty and the degeneration of life? Or, on the contrary, do they reveal the fullness, vitality and will to life, its courage, its confidence, its future?
> (Nietzsche 1994, 5)

Before humanity can prosper, Nietzsche predicts that the immediate future will be one of 'European nihilism'. According to Nietzsche, nihilism is the unavoidable conclusion to our system of values: 'we must experience nihilism before we can find out what their "value" really had' (Nietzsche 1967, 4). We must experience nihilism before we can even begin to acquire new values. But today, it is hard to say something about nihilism that might aid in its renewed significance. Given its fashionable status as integral to 'youth culture', nihilism itself has largely and ironically, become a futile project. Nihilism has forfeited the strength of its affective value to the writs of historical and democratic mediocrity where it is applied as an epithet to almost everything. As a descriptive term nihilism is regularly ascribed to Western spiritual bankruptcy, disaffected youth, callous politics and spurious democracies, self-proliferating capitalist machine, the ubiquity of addiction, the popularity of mind-numbing television, the glut of information technologies and the demise of the welfare state. It is the stability of this image of nihilism that has helped to extinguish the possibility of its vigorous and efficacious renewal at the close of the millennium.

Unlike the highly concentrated stillness of most twentieth-century images of nihilism, Artaud's nihilistic tendencies are constantly changing course, moving back and forth between pessimistic and lumpen despair and active strikes of denunciation. Nietzsche's scheme of nihilism is consistent with Artaud's mobile nihilism in proposing at least two kinds of nihilism, passive and active. The kind of nihilism one practices is crucial because at any given moment, depending on the quality of the nihilism, one's ability to act is either dormant or active. Nietzsche explains that of the two, passive nihilism is dominant because pessimism, its overriding feature, is the necessary instigator for all nihilism. In a letter to Henri Parisot, Artaud writes:

> this world which cheerfully accepts its own suffocation. People are stupid. Literature, exhausted. There is nothing left, there is no one left, the soul is

insane, there is no love, there isn't even hate, all bodies are sated, everyone's consciousness resigned.   (Artaud 1976, 444)

Passive nihilism regards life as valueless and meaningless. The stupidity that
governs is the stupidity of accepting the expectation of happiness as compensation for mediocrity and specious politeness. Artaud points out that this
pessimism is far from harmless when he complains about groups of French-
men who are casting spells on him in order to silence him as the 'rebel poet'.
These figures are dangerous, not as an organisation such as the National
Front is deemed dangerous but as only the middle-class can be. In another
letter to Parisot, Artaud describes the physical and mental illness which
middle-class France forces upon him. He complains that there is no longer
anything to love, to hate or to worry about. Life is led 'by a bunch of dull
people who have wanted to impose their hatred of poetry on all of us, to
impose their love of middle-class absurdity in a society wholly middle-
classified, with all the verbal dronings about soviets, anarchy, churches,
rites, rationing, quotas, black markets and the resistance movement' (Artaud
1963, 71). Even the violence and the atrocities of World War Two could not
counteract the disease of passive nihilism spread by the middle classes.
   Much of Artaud's anger against the middle-class is aimed vehemently at
the art world of publishing and performing. Abusing those of the literary
scene in 'All Writing is Pig shit', Artaud's taunting runs, 'you beard-asses, you
pertinent pigs, you masters of fake verbiage, confectioners of portraits,
pamphleteers, ground-floor lace-curtain herb collectors, entomologists, pla-
gue of my tongue' (Artaud 1965, 39). In order to wage war on the moral
values of sweetmeats and bonbons that support passive nihilism, and ultimately to overcome the need to wage such a war, Nietzsche proposes active
nihilism as a transitional step. While passive nihilism is aggression that cites
its cause as willed by someone or something else, active nihilism is willful
aggression which does not seek a cause. Active nihilism creates a series of
spontaneous and anarchic actions. The question is, how to get from passive
nihilism to active nihilism? Artaud demonstrates that of all the methods of
anger rudeness is potentially the most flexible. This is partially because it is
one of the less obvious and least expected expressions of an active nihilism;
rudeness is most generally regarded as a form of ineffectual complaint or
bombastic and querulous ranting. But rudeness can be extremely subtle and
effective. Rudeness is not as bloody and reactive as rage, as irascible and
longstanding as irritability, as definitive as hatred, as syphilitic as eternal
resentment, as bitter as malice, as paranoid and self-pitying as vexation, nor
as falsely righteous as indignation.[8]
   If Artaud is able to practice active nihilism, even as he continues to suffer
from ressentiment which is one of its debilitating enemies, it is because his
rudeness is too fast and all encompassing to sustain bitterness. 'Hurried and
rapid images speak to me only in words of anger and blind hate but are over

as fast as a knife stabbing, or lightning in congested sky' (Artaud 1965, 42). The idea that Artaud's resentments are not a serious hindrance to an active nihilism is paralleled by Nietzsche's comments on ressentiment and the nobleman. 'Ressentiment, itself, if it should appear in the nobleman (for it can appear in the noble) consummates and exhausts itself in an immediate reaction, and therefore does not poison' (Nietzsche 1989, 39). Artaud's rude complaints are not psychological or personal but cosmological and metaphysical. He rails less against individuals – when he singles out certain odious characters it is because they are emblematic of something greater – than at modern Western thought in general, especially at its scientific ignorance of emotion and imagination. 'No one in Europe knows how to scream anymore' (Artaud 1958, 141). All anyone can do is talk about their own opinions and morsels of knowledge. Talking is a dinner party activity hijacked by the middle-class and regarded as a skill complimentary to twentieth-century advertising copy, the constant dissemination of information and all scientific discourses specialising in the analysis of the subject. If Artaud screams it is not because he has nothing to say but because, unlike the inhibitions of the dinner party where a scream signifies the end of talk, Artaud's scream arises before its beginning. Artaud's linguistic asperity is distinct from his snarls, shouts, cries and horrendous screams. The latter make the sound of the effort to say something which oftentimes does not need to be said precisely because the point being made is the sound of the effort itself.

III

Artaud traffics in a spirit of rudeness that provides him with the stamina to vociferate in words and screams against even the most inflated and unwieldy of concepts: power, life and ethics, and their complements, violence, war and suffering. Rudeness brings these concepts and elements together through the use of contradiction. Because contradiction is multiple, Artaud is able to ramify general conceptions of 'good' and 'bad', 'life', and 'power', and then reformulate them in relation to his theories of cruelty, excess and suffering. Artaud dispenses with orthodox rules of opposition and allows several impressions to participate in a single consideration. Artaud's use of contradiction confuses 'good' and 'bad', by filing 'life', 'power', and 'ethics', through a kind of conceptual turnstile. Because movement is impossible to observe unless one is standing still, the continuous change that constitutes the movement of the conceptual turnstile is only discernible as contradiction. Insofar as contradiction is a purposefully irresolvable antagonism, it is not surprising then, to find rudeness thriving there. Artaud's rudeness is a declaration of war against the reasoned perpetuation of the status quo. He uses contradiction to counteract stability because its antagonism, which will not create a third element of resolve, prevents the mind from standing still.

It must be noted that rudeness is not always serious, after all it is through contradiction that humour first arises. According to Artaud, the theatre, 'has lost the sense of true humour and of the physical and anarchic, dissociative power of comedy' (Artaud 1976, 235). It is within Artaud's seriocomic structures that contradiction indicates the difference that makes a joke slightly more than a joke.[9] In 'A Letter on Artaud,' Paule Thévenin relays two anecdotes about Artaud's sense of humour. The first concerns a journalist who visited Artaud to ask him for his definition of black humour. Artaud ignored the man, continued talking with Thévenin, wrote in his notebook and then ate his meal. The journalist was still waiting when Artaud:

> took his enormous penknife and, after finding the right place under his hair, he held the point against it (this was his usual custom because he said it relieved him of certain pains). Suddenly, and with a rapid gesture, he stuck the knife straight into the table which was near him. 'You asked me, Sir, for my definition of black humour. Well, here it is, black humour is this!' And the journalist left (Thévenin 1965, 105).

The second story concerns Thévenin's concierge who once chastised Artaud because the evening before:

> he had been reciting the poems of Gérard de Nerval with the window open, and his voice had carried beyond the limits of our apartment. She had hardly opened her mouth when he stopped her: 'Be silent! If you persist in forbidding me to declaim the verses of Gérard de Nerval I shall change you instantly into a flat-headed serpent!' (Thévenin 1965, 104)

Artaud's humour is invariably inseparable from rudeness. Unlike irony and sarcasm which work through hidden or supplementary movements, humour is directly funny. For this reason, humour is intimidating, especially when a joke produce produces more than what is funny or when a joke is not quite formed. The adjunct elements of a joke appear in Artaud's idea for a 'theatre of cruelty' which subjects its audience to the shock of humour. Artaud advocates 'HUMOUR AS DESTRUCTION' through laughter, (Artaud 1958, 91) and calls for 'interjections of a poetry and humor poised to disorganize and pulverize appearances', according to anarchistic principles (Artaud 1958, 125). This is brought out clearly in the first of Thévenin's stories. Artaud's visiting journalist comes to Artaud on the strength of his renown as a theoretician of the theatre, in particular of its black humour but what he receives is not a theory nor a piece of knowledge.

On the stage Artaud is not concerned with adhering to an Aristotelean tradition which raises the violence of tragedy and its calamities above humor. He is interested in the shock, in the unexpected that humour can generate. Artaud admired the Marx Brothers but he felt that if an American audience could only enjoy the joke, it was missing out on the anarchic forces of revolt which accompany it. Artaud's 'hymn to anarchy', appears in Monkey Business whose ending 'puts the braying of a calf on the same intellectual level and gives it the same quality of meaningful suffering as the scream of a frightened woman...' (Artaud 1958, 144). Insofar as a surprise, aside from an initial plan to activate it, forecloses on a planned design, an unexpected joke can be less than funny in its impact even as its effect remains humourous.

In terms of the necessity of creating an impact, Artaud suggests that it is the spontaneity of a surprise that will overcome the inertia of pessimism. To have any effect, the surprise must be absolute which means that it must also shock the one who enacts it.

My scruples in the face of all real action?
    These scruples are absolute and they are of two kinds. Strictly speaking, they are based on a deep-rooted sense of the profound futility of any action whatsoever, whether spontaneous or un-spontaneous.
    This is the point of view of total pessimism. But a certain form of pessimism carries with it its own kind of lucidity. The lucidity of despair, the lucidity of senses are exacerbated and as if on the edge of the abyss. And alongside the horrible relativity of any human action, this unconscious spontaneity which drives one, in spite of everything, to action.   (Artaud 1976, 145)

This is precisely the conceptual turnstile at work. What begins as a passive or pessimistic nihilism is driven by the intensity of despair to become active.[10] What happens to colossal but nevertheless reputedly definitive terms is a process of continual radical conversion. Artaud takes the single term 'life', for example, to mean both something which he extols, and something which he detests or cares nothing about. The meaning of 'life' that he boasts is his own, while the meaning he criticises arises from an all too common opinion. The trick of the turnstile is that in writing about 'life', 'power', 'suffering', and 'joy', Artaud does not always make explicit which conception of each term he are referring to, his or the common one. The indeterminacy of Artaud's conception of life is increased by his claim that 'life' is movement rather than matter and its forms. 'When we speak about 'life', it must be understood that we are not referring to life as we know it from its surface of fact but to that fragile, fluctuating center which forms never reach' (Artaud 1965, 13). The formless flickering of the man burning at the stake is the expression of that which traditional and analytical philosophy, the sciences and psychology, call severally, the impossible, the yet to be calculated and the aporetic symptom.

Against the reductionism of analytical positivism, Artaud insists that life is not relative but absolute. To Artaud, accepting the formlessness of life is the only way of making it bearable. This does not mean, however, that one can simply choose to live, that by following the prayers and slogans that praise life's worth, one is therefore living. In terms of contemporary psychology, Artaud's writings would seem to advocate a 'Yes' that differs violently from the 'Yes' shouted by the liberal ideology of the self-made man and his moral right to earn money. What the conceptual turnstile reveals is a general failure to draw a distinction between the splendour of 'life' as material and therefore accidentally full of suffering (hence a Yes) and 'life' as meaningful or worthwhile only when it can be calibrated against the surety of the promised firmament, (hence the Yes). The Christian humanist finds life on earth tolerable only because better and higher things are at stake. In 'I Hate and Renounce as a Coward', Artaud writes, 'I hate and renounce as a coward every being who is only willing to be for being's sake and does not want to live to work' (Artaud 1965, 222).[11] Those who will themselves to be, are simply awaiting heaven or some rare moment of an earthly fulfillment of ideal forms.

The turnstile reveals that it is not the affections upon it, such as suffering and hatred, that threaten 'life', nor is it the objects with whom Artaud is in hostile opposition. What threatens 'life' is the use of these feelings to found a moral system of thought: a political, legal, pedagogic, familial and theological system of thought, which kills life by dictating the limits at which it can be lived. Although Artaud assaults specific individuals, general character types, the human race – especially the Occidental – and finally, God, the focus of his furious attack is explicitly man's system of prioritisation. 'And finally last night / at the new Athens / the great revelation concerning the whole system of forming / god in the slimey eggwhite of my left ball / after the revelation of the antichrist abyss' (Artaud 1965, 188). Despite Nietzsche's declaration of the death of God, the theological system remains perversely alive in Artaud, hence the specificity and the tawdriness of 'my left ball'.[12] The tenacity of 'God the Absolute' is confirmed by the absurdity of his reflection or blueprint in the monadic singularity of Artaud's left testicle. Artaud positioning of God in his testicle attests to an unappeasable, ontological disagreement with the system that prioritises god as a demonstrable tier of the Platonic system of ideal forms governing the existence of positive experiences of the world.

IV

In contradistinction to the idea of a materiality of the world grounded exclusively in the physical, Artaud's notion of a theatre of cruelty positions the material cruelty of tragedy in the mind and not just in the Blood on the stage. 'There is no cruelty without consciousness and without the application of consciousness' (Artaud 1965, 101). Artaud explains that his notion of cruelty is not created by the use of physical force so much as by a strict and necessary determining of things. This is not to say that cruelty is the logical naming of the world in order to have it make sense. Cruelty is less a controlled enterprise and more an ineluctable becoming of things: 'These monsters are wicked as only blind forces can be, and the theater exists, I think, only on a level that is not yet human' (Artaud 1976, 307). Artaud's idea of theatre is interested in the qualities of power rather than its so-called holders. If these qualities are monstrous, it is because they are disinterested, joyful and rude unlike the pessimism of humanity which is miserably afraid of them. That these monsters are blind is testament to the disingenuous character of the humanist notion of choice and its solipsistic declaration of self-control:

> True culture has never had a native land, it is not human but spiritual... there is no legacy to be defended... true culture would not cease to survive the disappearance of all these forms, all these petrified signs.... True culture has never been bound up with the preservation of individual freedom, and in my opinion it is greatly underestimating culture to believe that it is weakened by the loss of a few men or the destruction of a few writings'. (Artaud 1976, 346)

The implications of Artaud's theory of improving humanity through annihilation are not simply homicidal or flippant or both. Artaud's desire for the annihilation of useless cultural figures and their works is more seriously a proposal for a metaphysical revolution.

Artaud's revolution differs radically from the idea of the communist revolution belonging to his early surrealist colleagues. Artaud's revolution claims that it will revitalise a culture to the point where guns and planes will be useless against it. Artaud's revolution uses the conceptual turnstile which sees that 'life' is existing alongside the mind, while 'the human being is inside the circle this mind turns on, and joined to it by a multitude of fibers' (Artaud 1965, 45). Because Artaud cannot conceive of work as separate from life, he wonders if surrealism did not die 'on the day when Breton and his adepts decided to join the Communist movement and to seek in the realm of facts and of immediate matter the culmination of an action that could normally develop only within the inmost confines of the brain' (Artaud 1976, 139). The mental revolution of the brain is not external to the material revolution of mind: as the mind/brain changes, so the world changes. 'For each man to refuse to consider anything beyond his own deepest sensibility, beyond his inmost self, this for me is the point of view of the complete Revolution' (Artaud 1976, 140). Artaud regards a revolution that tries to improve material states of affairs through a cowardly avoidance of suffering, as old fashioned. All that will ensue from this type of insurgency is a re-enactment of the most reductive aspects of the progressive Enlightenment project, its reformism and its fundamental suspicion of metaphysics.

The 'inmost self' refers to the thinking self of the mind in contradistinction to the being self of an Enlightenment interiority or the being self of a psychoanalytic unconscious. Artaud follows his hatred and renunciation of 'every being who is only willing to be for being's sake' with 'I'd rather work than feel myself alive' (Artaud 1965, 222). The inmost self is where an effort towards a mental intuition takes place. Intuition is that which does not separate an inner self from an outer self nor an inner self from another self which might observe it.[13] Intuition is given importance only rarely because it lies beyond the illusory choices made by the intellect, hence Artaud's emphasis on work, on the mental work needed in order to thinking intuitively.

The illusion of the choice of being and the greatness of the suffering of being are illustrated in Artaud's claim that he chooses his own suffering. Artaud contends, for instance, that it is the dread of the fever that one ought to love.

> I have been sick all my life and I only ask that it continue, / room motto, i.e., / for the states of privation in life have always told me a great deal more about the plethora of my powers than the middle-class drawing – AS LONG AS YOU'VE GOT YOUR HEALTH.   (Artaud 1965, 192)

To accept suffering is not to cease to fight nor to give up on recognising one's enemies. Artaud claims that by accepting suffering, he is simultaneously willing suffering. 'I have chosen the domain of sorrow and shadow as others have chosen that of the glow and the accumulation of things' (Artaud 1965, 47). Given that Artaud pays little heed to the ideology of man's 'freedom of choice', his notion of choosing suffering can only mean, to accept suffering. Acceptance is akin to what Nietzsche refers to as *amor fati*.[14] The emphasis on choice requires that one act as if one has chosen. Acting as if affirms not only what happens but also one's inseparability from it. An acceptance of one's place in the world conforms to an espousal of what Nietzsche also calls 'Russian fatalism'.

Insofar as Artaud is a Russian fatalist he is also a whiner. He rallies viciously against everything that has and has not been done to him, variously and numerously, by initiates of secret sects, by psychiatrists, by administrators of the arts and culture, by God and by his audience. In terms of hatred of the establishment and therefore of the world and everyone in it, the various fields and persons of the establishment all meld into a single authoritarian, progressive and interfering institution. Because he must 'live' in the world, Artaud knows of what he suffers, why he suffers and how he suffers. According to Ronald Hayman, when Artaud begged for money he would accost passers by with, 'Monsieur, the world has done me much harm. You are part of the world, so you have harmed me. Please give me five francs' (Hayman 1977, 1). Artaud is vehemently opposed to both his condition and his situation because he knows these are inseparable from the rest of the world and everyone in it. And yet he also embraces his madness and suffering because he feels has something extraordinary to say.

In one of his last performances in 1947, Artaud intended to describe the barbarity he had suffered since his arrest in 1937 and to accuse those under whom he had suffered during the almost nine subsequent years he spent in asylums. The event The Story Lived by Artaud-Mômo drew over 900 spectators including many of his friends. The performance included poetry, screams, gestures, abuses and invented words. Above all else what this event showed Artaud and his audience is that any apprehension of what he was saying was doomed to failure. Artaud follows up an image of god and his pranks against the poet Artaud and the 'balls in his cunt' with,

> And if you don't get the image,
>
> and that's what I hear you saying
> in a circle,
>
> that you don't get the image
>
> which is at the bottom
>
> of my cunt hole, –
>
> it's because you don't know the bottom,
>
> not of things,
>
> but of my cunt,
>
> mine,
>
> although since the bottom of the ages
>
> you've been lapping there in a circle
>
> as if badmouthing an alienage,
>
> plotting an incarceration to death
> > (1995, 99–101).

The reviews of The Story Lived by Artaud-Mômo were mixed: some said it was literally and figuratively a stunning performance while others saw it as yet another attempt by Artaud to shock his audience with a childish lack of subtlety (Barber 1993, 136–9). Shortly after the performance, Artaud complained in a letter to André Breton about the lack of impact he has made. He wanted to abandon the theatre because, 'the only language which I could have with an audience was to bring bombs out of my pockets and throw them in the audience's face with a blatant gesture of aggression' (Barber 1993, 139). In another letter to Breton he wrote, '[b]esides gathering people together in a room, it remains for me to hurl abuse at this society in the street . . .' (Barber 1993, 138). One such occasion of a violent public spectacle happened in Ireland in 1937 when Artaud was deported back to France and incarcerated in the first of a number of psychiatric institutions for brandishing a sacred sword associated with Saint Patrick, and shouting about it to passers by.[15]

V

According to Paul Arnold, 'our avant-garde has learned from Artaud only his vehemence, his scandalous aspect – flinging bile and excrement at all institutions, beliefs, ideas, feelings, without having any substitute idea or feeling to offer us' (Arnold 19 28). To Arnold, Artaud made a huge 'philosophical error' in trying to turn the abstract, his idea of a magical sphere of affections in expression, into the concrete, an efficacious event in the theatre which would affect both the actors and the audience violently and with a kind of contagious quality of delirium. While Arnold may be right in expressing the frustration of finding that Artaud's ideas have not been successfully rendered by the many who read him, such an 'attitude' delimits any further work. What is in question is not the gulf between what Artaud intends to say and what Arnold thinks he fails to say since there is no place where one can arrest and investigate. What needs to be asked is what happens to what he does say? Jane Goodall points out that:

> Artaud's currency in the major debates of post structuralism has to do with the ways in which he serves as a focus for many of their preoccupations: alterity, the exchange of presence for absence, the demise of constituted subjectivity, the rift between the real and the symbolic, the rediscovery of the body, the potency of a discourse driving into excess and semiotic anarchy.
> (Goodall 1994, 218)

There is a good thirty years between the time of Arnold's essay, written in the early sixties when experimental theatre groups were attempting to enact, unsuccessfully it seems, Artaud's dramatic theories, and the time of Goodall's insightful summary of a post structural adoption of Artaud for any and all of their concerns. Looking across those thirty years from the first wave of excitement towards Artaud since his death and then to the inadequate self-revealing agenda of the post structuralists, one gets the feeling that in effect very little reading of Artaud has been done. The 'conditions of modernity', for want of a better phrase, that shaped Artaud and his ideas about destiny, genius, madness and rudeness, have not left him nor our reading of him. If it is true, as Arnold claims, that Artaud has left us no substitute feeling or idea other than his anger, two vital questions must be addressed. First, why should Artaud offer us a substitute idea when it is us, his readers and his critics, who must be substituted? Second, if Artaud has left us with only the rudeness of his vocalic bile, why does his popularity continue? Perhaps it is because of, rather than in spite of, the convoluted movements Artaud makes through madness and genius towards rudeness? In other words, the problem is not Artaud's rudeness but our reading of it.

Artaud's rudeness towards audiences and the public in general involves a frustrating lack of sympathy or deficit of feeling between the addresser and the addressed. This lack manifests itself as the opacity of Artaud's explanations and theories which are said to make for arduous reading. In her introduction to the *Selected Writings*, Susan Sontag alludes to a fundamental difficulty in reading Artaud who becomes overpowering if read too much which is why she suggests that Artaud is impossible to read beyond a few catchy quotes and ideas (Sontag 1976, lix). According to Eric Sellin, other readers find a 'threshold in the development of Artaud's concepts beyond which the ideas become rarified' (Sellin 1968, 101).[16] While frustrating to positivists, writes Sellin, who dislike the vanishing of Artaud's ideas the closer one gets to them, some find his incandescent concepts opaque enough to become the very ground of a generous inspiration.

The idea that Artaud is engulfed in vague ideas which appear to serve little purpose is the point upon which his readers divide. It is also the point at which Artaud's rudeness becomes less overt and more menacing. Artaud's periodic but recurrent popularity certainly implies an historical curiosity and ensures a fascination with both his insane and his angry madness but it is his rudeness, along with its humour, contradiction and lucidity that disrupts supposedly uncomplicated matters of reading. Why is Artaud hard to read? Sontag suggests that Sade, Wilhelm Reich and Artaud are in some sense 'intrinsically unreadable' because the nature of their work may be boring, morally monstrous or 'terribly painful to read' (Sontag 1976, lix). The problem with reading Artaud needs to be directed away from the difficulty of the work towards the difficult, in other words obtuse and narrow, process of reading itself? If Artaud shows us that no one knows how to be rude properly anymore, more importantly, he demonstrates that no one knows how to read. If we suffer at all from reading Artaud, as Sontag suggests, is it through our inability to read rudeness or because of our socially tacit inability to appreciate the rigours of being rude?

Notes

1 The reformation and relocation of anger is specific to end of the millennium capitalist fervour. Demoted from its eighteenth and nineteenth century position as a reckoning force of political grievances and potential for social revolution, anger is regulated by a global market which can only consider aggression and rudeness by filtering it through scientific understanding. Although it is absurd to try and delineate the twentieth-century demise of anger, there are certain phases wherein the use and status of anger has undergone significant change. In Europe before World War I, during what Roger Shattuck calls 'the banquet years', anger threw itself at the feet of multiple epithets: desirable, monstrous, artistic, fashionable, theatrical, ubiquitous and predictable. In the Dadaist and Surrealist periods between the two World Wars, anger attracted political attention and flaunted itself alongside and as, art. Anger was shocking but also ludicrously funny, unavoidable and necessary. After World War II, the search for stability denounced anger which reminded it of war. Anger retreated into the fifties suburban plot and the female malady of depression whose psychiatric definition of 'anger turned inwards' was treated with one of several members of the tranquilizer family. The sixties was inundated with antiwar protests and conscientious objectors, the outcome of which was the caricatured hippie, still the butt of the economic joke. There, anger entertains the likes of psychotherapy, psychiatry, criminology, feminism, the men's movement and the management of human resources. Antonio Negri's proposal that the twentieth-century can be characterised as a period of transition, between a nineteenth-century romanticism and nostalgia and a futurist aim toward the year two thousand, puts this century's beginnings at the 'Wall Street crash' of 1929 and its culmination with international capitalist reformism (Negri 1985, 64). This epochal reckoning is apposite to the twentieth-century's revaluation and transformation of anger. The morbid events which claimed the historical imaginary of 1929 produced a legacy of economic anxiety, helplessness and despair as demonstrated by capital's utilisation of anger as a tool for its profit based morality. Uncontrolled ('unresolved' or 'excessive') anger is located within the so-called marginal identities of neuroticism, depression and suicide while self-controlled anger has become a lucrative commodity identified with the 'aggressive sell' and the necessity to 'drive a hard bargain'. Locally, the Worker's Union is invited to the employer's negotiation table only to watch their solidarity turn sadly to nostalgia and their unionism become a series of 'individual' and deregulated contracts. Internationally, the President of the United States cheers his way through a world-wide-walkabout armed with a diplomatic immunity that allows him to warn, threaten, praise and console with the kudos of a Hollywood 'peacemaker'. The peace maker', is the name of a recent American movie starring Nicole Kidman and George Clooney. The latter is supposedly 'the peace maker' but by the end of the film it becomes clear that the peacemaker is a much bigger enterprise. 'The Peacemaker' is America itself. Justin Clemens suggested to me that a peacemaker is full of sadness. In relation to psychology and women, sadness is the counter-will of anger. The clinical definition of this kind of sadness is depression or 'anger turned inwards'. If 'The Peacemaker' is not Clooney or Kidman, then it is America herself the feminine overseer of the world depressed and saddened by all that she sees. Both locally and internationally, peace-making tours, conferences and meetings aim to quell and incite anger through economic bribery, blackmail and righteous proselytising. The violence effected by an internationally prominent country such as America is economic.

Artaud claims to have uncovered an American plot to gather up school-boys' sperm in order to create huge populations of soldiers that will be trained to protect the country's capitalism. (See Artaud's 'To have done with the judgement of God' 1976, 555–71.) America sends violence in a packaged message of universal denunciation emptied speciously of all aggressive provocation and loaded instead with moral outrage. The aim of slander (the US counter-accusing Iraq of harbouring aggression) or economic violence (the US placing severe economic sanctions on Cuba) is not the eradication of entire countries but the winning of economic control through deprivation and boycotting of exports and imports. America's instances of power brokering are designed as palimpsests of provocation to ensure that any act(s) of aggression be sighted as those of the responding country and consequently disseminated by the media as instigated by the other country, the country in disgrace. Anger is assigned a place rather than a time hence countries outside direct US jurisdiction are regarded as 'unchristian' (Iraq's reaction to the USA) or poor and ignorant (India's refusal to stop nuclear testing). On a local level, the management of anger is equally spatially coordinated: corporate funded therapy courses are offered to all private employees while government funded anger management 'workshops' are set up in prisons, various other asylums and drug, alcohol and criminal rehabilitation centres. Psychology assures us that anger is not necessarily a harmful emotion: with the correct self-management strategies anger can, and of course should, be expressed and can even be beneficial. Healthy anger is divided into categories of controlled and uncontrolled, acceptable and unacceptable. Anger is presented via a strange and paradoxical syllogism. First, it is proposed that anger is entirely natural and therefore not a problem. Second, anger is a problem because it is naturally unsafe and excessive. Lastly, anger can be controlled which means that it is not a problem. All this is to say that anger is a problem but it is a normal problem because it is good to be angry but only in a certain way. The management of anger is an integral part of any contemporary personal development programme. For the last forty years, middle-men of the psyche have been selling potential 'experiences' back to their clients within the 'safe' environment of therapy. Managing one's angry 'impulses' is the tacit rule of every social programme overseen by the State and its corporate allies. Psychology is the marketing consultant for a commercial technique which folds consumption into structures of therapeutic self-improvement. As a consequence, the idea of individual choice is given meaning and made tangible. Moreover, the individual comes to represent choice, for example, in Gestalt therapy emphasis is placed on the relationship between parts and the whole, 'you are the total sum of your choices'. Similarly, consumerist therapy, disseminates the slogans: 'Just Do It!' 'Say Yes to Life', 'You can be anything you want to be' and 'Where do you want to go today?' Controlling one's anger is the key to productivity but only insofar as it becomes the key to the production of consumption. Say 'Yes' to a new deal and have others say 'Yes' to yours.

2   The things for which Antonin Artaud is famous, his writings on the theatre, his sublime film presence, his delusions, his opiate addiction and his mad rages, were all extraordinary once. But the assimilation of Artaud's madness into the 'madness' of the twentieth century, via the proliferation of quasi-experimental theatre and the codification of addiction as a ubiquitous social illness, mean that Artaud's suffering is now available as 'common experience', experience as prevalent as it is ordinary. A similar outcome plagues the idea of nihilism. In 'La Vie Pue, Messieurs!' Mathew Hyland's looks at the anachronism of rebellion and suggests for example, that Artaud's suffering is now more than ever, less than extraordinary.

Artaud's suffering is divided 'among hapless anonymous millions.... While most of the world's population keep on struggling for bare survival in the accustomed way, Artaud's misfortunes have been democratized to the point that they're no longer experienced as suffering' (Hyland 1997, 2).

3 As part of a larger study on Artaud and philosophy, I argue that one of the profound things about Artaud's work is its insistence on a critical and not just a clinical apprehension of the madness of the mind. In effect, Artaud's work is able to renew the waning interest in all things mad.

4 The epitome of the unattractiveness of madness can be found in Doctor Gaston Ferdière's description of Artaud's arrival at the asylum at Rodez. In 'I looked after Antonin Artaud', Ferdière complains that when he brought Artaud home to lunch with he and his wife, Artaud presented a disgusting spectacle of grunting, shoving food into his mouth, spitting, belching, rubbing food into the tablecloth and ending the meal by kneeling down to sing psalms (Marowitz 1977, 109).

5 Artaud won the Prix Sainte-Beuve for best essay of 1947.

6 A similar point is considered by Anaïs Nin. In her journal Nin wonders whether only Artaud's anger is an insanity or if it is not more correctly all anger which is insane (Nin 1966, 187).

7 In particular, three of Nietzsche's last five books, *Twilight of the Idols*, *The Anti-Christ* and *Ecce Homo*, include instances of, and comments on, rudeness. Nietzsche asks of the Germans, 'do they still think at all?' (Nietzsche 1990, 71), calls the Christian, 'the domestic animal, the herd animal, the sick animal man' (Nietzsche 1990, 128), and the English, those behind the times (rather than ahead of them like his untimely self) who do not even know that there may be a problem with morality (Nietzsche 1990, 81). He also singles out certain hopeful figures, especially English personages such as George Eliot whom he calls a little blue stocking (Nietzsche 1990, 80), and John Stuart Mill whom he refers to as 'the flathead' (Nietzsche 1967, 21).

8 In light of Nietzsche's two nihilisms, one could say that the professionalisation of anger employs a passive nihilism, one intent on deactivating anger. This demonstrates unwittingly, that passive nihilism regards everything, even the fierceness of anger, as pointless unless it commits itself to sending out a 'positive', productive, consumable and profitable message.

9 To offset the image of Artaud as a curmudgeon, Arthur Adamov and Roger Blin, Artaud's associate and friend respectively, comment on Artaud's optimism, wit and predilection for playing tricks on people. For example, one evening some of Artaud's friends thought they had upset him greatly when he left them abruptly after they complained about his ridiculous flights of paranoid fancy but when they saw Artaud a few days later he simply laughed about the event and remarked about funny it had been (Marowitz 1977, 78, 81–2). The more common view of Artaud's 'sensibility' is of an extremely desperate and violent man. This is exemplified in Bernard-Henri Lévi's *Adventures on the Freedom Road*. Lévi uses Artaud to frame the aesthetic violence of the time and the specific madness of World War I. Having placed Artaud at the extreme nadir and apogee of 'the times,' Lévi does not talk about Artaud again, except as a 'name' associated with surrealism (Lévi 1995, 11–12).

10 This touches on an interesting problem between Spinoza, Artaud and Nietzsche. Spinoza emphasises the difference between affects and passions. Passions are divided into joyful passions and sad passions and only joyful passions are affirmative enough to transform themselves into active affects. Given that only joyful

passions can move and change, perhaps the notion of 'joyful suffering' and of an active nihilism found in both Artaud and Nietzsche, will have to be re-thought in Spinozist terms by emphasising not only the power that both suffering and joy can produce but also what kind of power.

11 This essay is called a 'variant text', suggesting that there is no end to a conceivable accumulation of suffixes for, 'I hate and renounce as a coward...'

12 Even during his most devout Christian acts such as the trip to Ireland with the cane of Saint Patrick and his most devout years in the hospital at Rodez, Artaud is always constructing zealous affairs with God, calling some of them hate and some of them love.

13 Artaud's idea of intuition refers to a Bergsonian notion of that which cannot be grasped but can only be felt in its duration. Artaud was greatly influenced by Henri Bergson's theories of intuition and duration. The relationship between Artaud and Bergson is dealt with in a much larger work of mine which is in progress.

14 Consider the final words of 'On Suicide'. 'I can neither live nor die, nor am I capable of not wishing to die or live. And all mankind resembles me' (Artaud 1965, 58).

15 To catch the attention of a passer by surely only one thing necessary, to shout.

16 In addition to Sellin's comments on the frustration of reading Artaud's theories, see Hayman 1977, 61–2.

References

Artaud, A. (1995) *Watchfiends and Rack Screams*. Ed. and Trans. Clayton Eshleman with Bernard Bador. Boston: Exact Change.

Artaud, A. (1978) *Œuvres Complètes* XIV. Paris: Gallimard.

Artaud, A. (1976) *Selected Writings*. Ed. Susan Sontag. Trans. Helen Weaver. USA: California University Press.

Artaud, A. (1965) *Artaud Anthology*. Ed. Jack Hirshman. San Francisco: City Lights.

Artaud, A. (1963) 'To Henri Parisot' (1945) in *Tulane Drama Review*. Trans. Victor Corti. (8: 70–3).

Artaud, A. (1958) *The Theater and its Double* Trans. Mary Caroline Richards. New York: Grove Press.

Barber, S. (1993) *Antonin Artaud: Blows and Bombs*. London: Faber and Faber.

Deleuze, G. (1997) *Essays Critical and Clinical*. Trans. D.W. Smith and M.A. Greco. Minneapolis: University of Minnesota Press.

Hayman, R. (1977) *Artaud and After*. London: Oxford University Press.

Hyland, M. (1997) *La Vie Pue, Messieurs!* Test-strip Monograph Series. New Zealand: Teststrip Gallery.

Marowitz, C. (1977) *Artaud at Rodez*. London: Marion Boyars.

Negri, A. (1989) *The Power of Subversion*. Trans. James Newell. UK: Polity Press.

Nietzsche, F. (1990) *Twilight of the Idols/The Anti-Christ*. Trans. R.J. Hollingdale. London: Penguin.

Nietzsche, F. (1989) *Genealogy of Morals/Ecce Homo*. Trans. Walter Kaufmann and R.J. Hollingdale. Trans. Walter Kaufmann. USA: Vintage.

Nietzsche, F. (1968) *The Will to Power*. Ed. Walter Kaufman. Trans. Walter Kaufmann and R.J. Hollingdale. USA: Vintage.

Nin, A. (1966) *The Journals of Anaïs Nin Volume I*. Ed. Gunther Stuhlmann. England: Peter Owen.

Shattuck, R. (1969) *The Banquet Years*. London: Jonathan Cape.

Thévenin, P. (1965) 'A letter on Artaud' in *Tulane Drama Review*. (9: 99–117).

12

'Epidemics of Enough': Beckettian Sufficiencies

Daniel Katz

'Man has often had enough; there are actual epidemics of having had enough'.

Nietzsche, On the Genealogy of Morals (121)

For a discussion of nihilism, Beckett's work offers no shortage of entry points. In a philosophical key, one can evoke his two favourite tags: Democritus' 'Nothing is more real than nothing', and the Belgian Arnold Geulincx's 'Ubi nihil vales, ibi nihil velis' ('There where you are worth nothing, there you should want nothing') both used in *Murphy* and the trilogy, and recommended by Beckett himself as the best starting places for a critic faced with the task of interpreting his work.[1] Recent biographies only confirm Beckett's deep and ongoing exchanges with the continental philosophical tradition, and his interest in Schopenhauer has long been known.[2] Moreover, Beckett's concern to place his work under a philosophical aegis stressing 'nothing' rhymes with his progressive technical elimination of so many of the traditional props of both prose and theatre, producing texts and dramatic works which if not 'nothing', certainly seem to be striving after *less*, as a title like 'Lessness' makes clear, along with the claim in the very late *Wortstward Ho* to be travelling 'leastward' (Beckett 1983, 33). However, the very care with which Beckett emphasises the remainder, or the 'least', should prevent us from seeing him as seeking some sort of literary presentation of an ideal nothing, of forging in words or on stage the 'reality' of this 'nothing' which Democritus' sentence seems to promise. 'Naught not best worse' (ibid., 32) *Worstward Ho* acknowledges, 'Least best worse. Least never to be naught. Never to naught be brought. Never by naught be nulled. Unnullable least. Say that best worse. With leastening words say least best worse' (ibid., 32). No messianic nihilistic dream of wiping the slate clean is to be found in Beckett; no totality is tolerated even in a negative, or negated mode.

But in sketching a Beckettian nihilism one is certainly not limited by his explicitly philosophical ruminations; one could just as well mention the stark final words of the woman's voice in the play 'Rockaby' – 'fuck life / stop her eyes / rock her off / rock her off' (Beckett 1984b, 282) – in which the question of the value of the world, the value of values, the value of life, pales before an imperious desire: that it end. 'Oh all to end' is how Beckett ended his final prose work, 'Stirrings Still', and Beckett can at times seem like a parody of Nietzsche's nihilist, systematically disparaging all lofty values and goals, merciless to those claiming the right to authority and power, disdainful of all established modes of affirmation. Of course, the irony is that in all this he greatly resembles Nietzsche himself, and this irony is one which should be kept in sight. For, if the problem of nihilism calls Beckett to mind for many reasons and in many registers, it still seems preferable to avoid the temptation of assigning him a secure place within its history. As Simon Critchley has emphasised in his recent discussion of Adorno's writings on Beckett, anything that seems in appearance to be the most severe depreciation of life, transcendent values, existence, and meaning can always be recuperated as precisely the *refusal* of a particular set of conditions and ideology which is intolerable, and therefore the implicit affirmation of the possibility of something other and better than the degraded space of our lives. Thus for Adorno, 'Thought has its honour by defending what is condemned as nihilism' (cited in Critchley 1997, 24) and Beckett becomes, not the nihilist, but the truly political writer. Similarly, as Deleuze makes abundantly clear, for Nietzsche the violent or weary rejection of all transcendent values and ideals is not *simply* nihilism, for the very act of erecting otherworldly values seen as worthy of investment and sacrifice is nihilist in and of itself.[3] Adorno perhaps dialectically echoes Nietzsche by asserting that a certain 'nihilism' is actually a form of affirmation.

Yet Critchley cannot fail to notice the violence of Adorno's recuperation of Beckett, a recuperation which, securely placing Beckett's work within the camp of affirmation, forecloses much of the disturbing violence of Beckett himself, in a manoeuvre which oddly mirrors what Adorno considers to be the true and profound nihilism of the forced intelligibility of socialist realism. Critchley, attempting to preserve Adorno's sense of Beckett's engaged radicality while at the same time protecting Beckett's texts from Adorno's critical precipitation, argues that Beckett is emphatically 'not a nihilist' in that he 'indicates how meaninglessness can be seen as an achievement' (ibid., 27). With this phrase Critchley endeavours to avoid Adorno's near immediate abrogation of the problem of meaninglessness he began by emphasizing, but as elegant as his formulation is, Critchley seems warily conscious all the same of having committed a similar recuperation to that of Adorno, albeit with greater subtlety and a clearer sense of his transgression. The very concept of achievement, if inevitable, also inevitably establishes 'meaninglessness' as a teleological goal in a manner somewhat at odds with both Beckett's work and the claims for the value of 'meaninglessness' itself.

Concerning this debate, two problems must be considered at this point. First, if Beckett's work, especially in the later years, consistently moves in the direction of the reduction of sense, his work nevertheless maintains a clear legibility throughout, and is largely amenable to interpretive projects although, as Critchley and many others have noted, it does present extremely sophisticated and ingenious obstacles to them. It seems that it is precisely the density and surplus of 'meaning' in Beckett's work, along with the intricate philosophical layering to which both Critchley and Adorno are sensitive, which has made it seem such an ideal centerpiece for the 'nihilist' debate. It is quite probably the most conventional quality of Beckett's work – its intense imbrication in canonical literary and philosophical history – which vehiculates Adorno's reading. That this surplus itself makes Beckett's works extraordinarily resistant to theoretical recuperations of all sorts is undeniable, and indeed, to the considerable extent that both Adorno and Critchley engage the strategies of this resistance – what Critchley calls 'redemption from redemption' (27) – I wholly concur with their emphasis, but resistance and 'meaninglessness' are not entirely the same thing. Indeed, what literary 'meaninglessness' might be is not a question I can answer here, but staying on a rather elementary level, much of the work of John Cage or Gertrude Stein, for example, is much more evidently 'nihilist' in a formal or linguistic manner than Beckett's. 'Endgame' is a lot easier to understand than 'Tender Buttons', and Adorno's insistence on 'understanding its unintelligibility, concretely reconstructing the meaning of the fact that it has no meaning' (Adorno 1991, 243) seems at once hyperbolic and misplaced.[4]

More important than a literary-historical parlour game dedicated to sighting the true nihilist, however, is the realisation that the sort of expressive negativity or nihilism which Critchley and Adorno sometimes seem to have in mind is, as such, impossible – that one cannot avoid attributing a sense, role, or function to the meaningless, and thereby negating it, as Derrida has observed in his discussion of Bataille and the 'general economy'. Derrida evokes what Bataille calls the 'minor game': 'The minor play consisting in still attributing a meaning, within discourse, to the absence of meaning' (Derrida 1981, 262)/ *'Le jeu mineur consistant à attribuer encore un sens, dans le discours, à l'absence de sens'* (Derrida 1967, 384) and goes on to point out that for this reason the 'absolute non-discourse' is an impossibility to which any particular discourse can do more than acknowledge its relation, in a fashion which Bataille deems 'sovereign': 'The writing of sovereignty places discourse *in relation* to absolute non-discourse. Like general economy, it is not the loss of meaning, but, as we have just read, the 'relation to the loss of meaning'' (ibid., 270)/ *'L'écriture de souveraineté met le discours en rapport avec le non-discours absolu. Comme l'économie générale, elle n'est pas la perte de sens, mais, nous venons de le lire, "rapport à la perte de sens"'* (ibid., 397). These terms bear a great resemblance to Beckett's 1949 statement on the task of the 'maker': 'The expression that there is nothing to express, nothing with which to express, nothing from which to express, no power to express, no desire to express, together with the obligation to express' (Beckett 1984a, 139). When it is suggested that art could in consequence become 'expressive of the impossibility to express' Beckett rejects such an idea as an 'ingenious method' of fleeing the 'ultimate penury' (ibid., 143) and refuses to reduce the impossibility of expression itself to an expressive 'occasion'. From this contradiction, Beckett is forced to conclude that to be an artist is 'to fail' but he then immediately also refuses to allow a 'fidelity to failure' (ibid., 145) to become the new touchstone of the true artist. The force with which Beckett's work strives to maintain this relationship to a loss which would not be immediately recuperated as a positive value renders Adorno's reading of it facile in comparison. And seen in this light, Adorno and Critchley's question as to whether Beckett is a nihilist is answered in its very asking. Beckett is certainly not a nihilist (whatever that would be) but, as is the case with Bataille, much of his work can be seen as the mourning of the impossibility of the nihilism to which it aspires. Beckett understood the dialectic well in the *Texts for Nothing*, lamenting, '. . . ah if no were content to cut yes's throat and never cut its own' (Beckett 1967, 113–14), and like Bataille's, his work strives to acknowledge its relationship to a negativity, a loss, a 'nothing' which it can never present or embody as such. 'For the only way one can speak of nothing is to speak of it as though it were something' Beckett notes in *Watt* (Beckett 1981, 77), and it is the consciousness of violating a negativity which by definition cannot be inscribed, and not a logocentric suspicion of language's betrayal of the idea and the Ideal, which motivates the many misgivings concerning the integrity of the expressive act found throughout Beckett.

In what follows, then, rather than focus on the various Beckettian 'nothings', I will attempt to work from the obverse, and, not asking why in Beckett there should be nothing rather than something ask instead what in the end is a quite similar question: for Beckett, can there be enough? 'Enough' is the title of a short prose work from the sixties and consists of the bizarre, unworldly reminiscences of an apparently female[5] narrator's common life with an uncommunicative companion, half-husband, half-father, who half abducts, half adopts her ('I cannot have been more than six when he took me by the hand' (Beckett 1974, 54) is the entire description of their meeting) only to have her leave him years later, in an incident which is perhaps only a misunderstanding. As many critics have noticed,[6] the title itself mirrors the many ambivalences of the narrative in being divided between contradictory meanings: 'enough' can express either sufficiency or surfeit, satisfaction or disgust. Throughout the short tale, it is hard to decide if the narrator is implying that her meagre, demeaned life was nevertheless 'enough' for her, or that now she has definitively 'had enough', her final exclamation of the word being another variation on 'Oh all to end'. And given this indeterminacy, equally troubled is the status of the ironic oscillations it permits. Do we read the text as implying that the narrator should have said 'enough!' rather than accept her lot, or that on the other hand she should have realised that this was indeed 'enough' – all anyone can ask? The text presents little occasion for securing a firm purchase on either side, and perhaps what needs to be emphasised is that the tension between the sense of 'enough' as surfeit and that as satisfaction functions here as more than a simple ambiguity, suggesting as it does that not *wanting* anything anymore, to be not wanting, to have enough, is always also not to want *anything* anymore, to have had enough. What Beckett examines here is the uneasy cohabitation of self-sufficiency and mastery with the death drive. The satisfaction of desire is of course its own death and thus ours, that is, *nothing*, while desire itself is inevitably incompletion, division, dependence and lack. The question Beckett asks throughout his work, a question which links him intimately to the problematics and history of nihilism, is: what might it mean not to want anything? Tortured by lack, would an end to desire imply a sort of Nietzschean mastery, or would it on the contrary imply the equally Nietzschean will-lessness and apathy that Nietzsche excoriates under the name 'Buddhism'?[7] To put it another way, is the nihilist position a resentful and dissatisfied 'nothing is enough', depreciating all it encounters, or rather is it the extreme passivity of *nothing* is enough? As Beckett's Irish forebear Oscar Wilde pointed out, 'The only way to get rid of a temptation is to yield to it' (Wilde 1985, 23), and Wilde's scandalous decadence resides precisely in his haste not so much to gratify desire but to thereby annul it. Nihilism, perhaps, is nothing other than the satisfaction of desire, its completion. And 'Enough' is nothing other than an inquiry into the spacings, distances, and delays which make desire possible and which desire seeks to annul.

If 'Enough' is the story of the short-circuiting of desire, it also unfolds as a grueling investigation of the psychic economies of hierarchical relationships, as laconically delivered from the ambivalent and bereft subaltern position. This ambivalence is so masterfully maintained that in a generally brilliant article on Beckett, Alain Badiou can with no discernible irony qualify this story as 'entirely consecrated to love' (Badiou 1992, 361) – a claim passages like the following would seem at least to nuance:

> I did all he desired. I desired it too. For him. Whenever he desired something so did I. He only had to say what thing. When he didn't desire anything neither did I. In this way I didn't live without desires. If he had desired something for me I would have desired it too. Happiness for example or fame. I only had the desires he manifested. But he must have manifested them all. All his desires and needs. When he was silent he must have been like me. When he told me to lick his penis I hastened to do so. I drew satisfaction from it. We must have had the same satisfactions. The same needs and the same satisfactions.   (Beckett 1974, 53)

This very rich passage is, to start with, a reduction: for the narrator, the entire field of desire is reduced to the desire of the nameless old man. Desire is only and exclusively *his* desire, leaving no room for the existence of any desire outside this field: 'When he didn't desire anything neither did I'. But this reduction is then immediately subjected to a re-expansion, with the rather sinister evocation of the breadth and magnitude of the old man's wanting: 'I only had the desires he manifested. But he must have manifested them all'. As the narrator herself says, she does not live *without* desire, but is rather wracked and overwhelmed by desires which nevertheless are not entirely hers. Beckett here gives us an allegory of the sort of narcissistic displacement often sketched by Freud, not only when he laconically suggests that: '... it seems very evident that another person's narcissism has a great attraction for those who have renounced part of their own narcissism and are in search of object-love' (Freud 1984, 82–3) but even more so when he talks about egoic diminution in extreme cases of 'being in love':

> Contemporaneously with this 'devotion' of the ego to the object ... the functions allotted to the ego ideal entirely cease to operate. The criticism exercised by that agency is silent; everything that the object does and asks for is right and blameless. Conscience has no application to anything that is done for the sake of the object; in the blindness of love remorselessness is carried to the pitch of crime. The whole situation can be completely summarised in a formula: *The object has been put in the place of the ego ideal.*
> (Freud 1985, 143–4, *Freud's emphasis*)

Such a schema, in which the love object becomes the source and measure of all desire, value, and even morality, entirely erasing the independence of the ego, seems to correspond neatly to the situation elaborated by Beckett, yet a crucial proviso must be added: according to Freud, this intense and impoverishing idealisation is only possible because it is *precisely one's own narcissism*, the boundlessness of one's own self-love and desire, which is displaced onto the idealised object in the place of the ego–ideal. The narrator's seeming renunciation can thus be read also as an enormous narcissistic annihilation of the beloved object, who exists only as a screen of projection for the narrator's own displaced narcissism. As the paths of will, power, and violence become more complex, we see not only how Beckett re-reads Freud, but also the extent to which Freud's text re-mobilises Nietzsche's, in particular in relation to the whole problematic of *ressentiment*.

However, if the narrator's subjective stance can thus be seen not only as a renunciation of desire but also as a protection of it – a protection whose enormous efficacy is in fact acknowledged ('He must have manifested them all') – we must nevertheless avoid seeing this as a simple dialectical resolution of the question of desire and narcissism, and focus on the remainder and imbalance created by this narcissistic displacement, by this transfer of agency. After all, despite her implication in the couple's dynamics of desire, the narrator ruefully notes that nothing was ever desired *for her*: 'Happiness for example or fame'. The question then is, what is lost in or changed by this detour which chooses to locate desire in the other, and how can its route be measured? What does it mean to be unable to posit oneself as being on the *receiving* end of desire, on the other side of the preposition 'for'? Without using the term 'projection', Nietzsche in fact links nihilism precisely with the habit of sourcing desire in an 'outside':

> The nihilistic question 'for what?' is rooted in the old habit of supposing that the goal must be put up, given, demanded *from outside* – by some *superhuman authority*. Having unlearned faith in that, one still follows the old habit and seeks *another* authority that can *speak unconditionally* and *command* goals and tasks. (Nietzsche 1968, 16)

However, in a move which parallels Freud's tropisms, this new 'outside authority' will be placed precisely on the inside: 'The authority of *conscience* now steps up front (the more emancipated one is from theology, the more imperativistic morality becomes)...' (ibid., 16).[8] In this passage at least, 'conscience' for Nietzsche is nothing but an 'outside' within, an invasive alien parasite, which should presumably be thrown out once and for all. This is the symmetrical obverse of the desiring economy we see in 'Enough', where it appears that an 'inside' has been projected without. And indeed, in the passage quoted above what is most disturbing is the violent, quiet stridency with which the narrative voice insists on preserving its identification with this projection. For what is obscene in the phrase, 'When he told me to lick his penis I hastened to do so' is not the act, nor even the fact that the request is delivered as a command, but rather the *haste* with which it is accomplished, the precipitation in gratifying the desire of the other, made even clearer in Beckett's original French version 'Quand il me disait de lui lécher le pénis je me *jetais* dessus' (emphasis mine; literally, 'I threw myself on it', but the verb 'jeter' preserves connotations of falling and dropping).[9] As we have already seen, when we read 'he' we must also ask to a certain extent 'who?', but still, what needs to be noted here is the location of desire as such: not in the act, not in the other's desire for the act, but rather in the hastening to perform it, in one's recoiling to embrace the otherness of the command. To fully gauge what for Beckett is 'enough' we must measure this moment of haste, this movement which itself both measures and annuls the space between the asking and the act, the *motion* from command to action. Desire here is not simply *haste*, but *hastening*, the advent of haste. Should we linger on this hastening, we may hear it as the affirmation of enough, the enactment of the sufficiency of the demand of the other, of the other demand.

For Nietzsche, in fact, 'enough' can be itself a kind of affirmation. The passage from which I draw my epigraph merits an extended citation:

Man has often had enough; there are actual epidemics of having had
enough (as around 1348, at the time of the dance of death); but even
this nausea, this weariness, this disgust with himself – all this bursts from
him with such violence that it at once becomes a new fetter. The No he
says to life brings to light, as if by magic, an abundance of tender Yeses;
even when he *wounds* himself, this master of destruction, of self-destruction – the very wound itself afterward compels him *to live*.

(Nietzsche 1969, 121)

With regard to such a passage, Beckett's 'if no were content to cut yes's throat
and never cut its own' reverberates suggestively. In the 'Genealogy'
Nietzsche is pointing to the manner in which the sickness, weariness and
wound become themselves a principal of affirmation – the ascetic ideal, by
which the *ressentiment* of the weak is turned back against themselves rather
than towards others, as they are led to identify themselves as the guilty
source of their misfortune and suffering. The meaning bestowed upon
their suffering thus becomes another fetter binding them to life. It is in
this context that the Beckettian 'meaninglessness' which Critchley rightly
champions takes on its full significance, in the sense of a refusal to redeem
suffering through the attribution of a superior meaning or value to it within
a larger structure of sense. Enough is simply enough, a statement which is far
from simple or even entirely ponderable, as its own formulation demonstrates. Just as Nietzsche's 'enough' exists in a perpetual and almost inevitable slide between No and tender Yeses, so Beckett's cannot help but wander
between a courageous recognition of senselessness and the ascetic position
which would recuperate this courage as a positive value. As we shall see
shortly, Beckett's rigour will lead him still further – to the dismantling
even of the consolation of not seeking consolation.

In 'Enough', a recurrent image is that of the flowers which the narrator
describes as a dominant element in her endless wanderings with her
infirm companion. As he can only walk hunched over, his entire 'horizon'
is the ground he treads: 'Tiny moving carpet of turf and trampled flowers'
(Beckett 1974, 55); later, to give a few other examples, we find 'But he
wished everything to be heard including the ejaculations and broken
paternosters that he poured out to the flowers at his feet' (ibid., 55) and
'I see the flowers at my feet and it's the others I see. Those we trod down
with equal step. It is true they are the same' (ibid., 56). Having begun her
tale, 'All that goes before forget' (ibid., 53), referring, apparently, to all that
preceded her meeting with her companion) she ends her tale in a similar
vein:

We lived on flowers. So much for sustenance. He halted and without
having to stoop caught up a handful of petals. Then moved munching
on. They had on the whole a calming action. We were on the whole calm.

More and more. All was. This notion of calm comes from him. Without him I would not have had it. Now I'll wipe out everything but the flowers. No more rain. No more mounds. Nothing but the two of us dragging through the flowers. Enough my old breasts feel his old hand.

(ibid., 60).

The question to be asked here is that of the status of this violent gesture of erasure, and of that which withstands it. Two contradictory interpretations present themselves. First, one might argue that this erasure implies that the narrator has 'had enough' and has chosen to annihilate and nullify. In this case, two further questions become inevitable: first, is this action to be taken as in some way liberating, or rather is it self-destructive, and second, why do the flowers resist this movement? The second interpretation would instead focus on reconciliation, arguing that the narrator has now determined what for her is 'enough'. To simply oppose these two readings is perhaps to miss the point – Beckett's text here asks us to think through the suspension of the distinction between reconciliation and rupture which it enacts. What survives erasure here is the flowers, of course, but flowers which have been literally perverted, or turned away from their habitual function: no longer the nonfunctional aesthetic object *par excellence,* here they have become a source of food, the degree zero of utility and need. What is allowed to survive is 'sustenance' and the text could be read as eliminating all that is non-essential, asserting that the minimum necessary for physical survival is enough, even plenty. On the other hand, eating the flowers could be read as a figure for nourishing oneself precisely on beauty, which would assert the opposite: that the true minimum is 'spiritual' and not physical at all. In any event, what certainly survives this opposition is the mouth. Despite the title 'Enough', the text finishes on an emblem of the lack of self-sufficiency or self-containedness, on the orifice which figures the insatiable and interminable hunger for the other and the outside. Indeed, in *Molloy* Beckett had already stigmatised the mouth for these very qualities, comparing it unfavourably to the anus:

> We underestimate this little hole, it seems to me, we call it the arsehole and affect to despise it. But is it not rather the true portal of our being and the celebrated mouth no more than the kitchen-door [the French *entrée de service* is perhaps stronger]. Nothing goes in, or so little, that is not rejected on the spot, or very nearly. Almost everything revolts it that comes from without and what comes from within does not seem to receive a very warm welcome either. Are not these significant facts.
>
> (Beckett 1965, 80)[10]

Whether penises or flowers, the mouth accepts that there is not yet, that there will not be, enough. Interestingly, what I have been rather loosely calling the 'narrator' begins the story by emphasising the written nature of her text, as a scene of dictation, seems to be staged:

> All that goes before forget. Too much at a time is too much. That gives the pen time to note. I don't see it but I hear it there behind me. Such is the silence. When the pen stops I go on. Sometimes it refuses. When it refuses I go on. Too much silence is too much. Or it's my voice too weak at times. The one that comes out of me. So much for the art and craft. (ibid., 53)

'Enough' is when the mouth has finally closed, accepting no more of the physical world's dubious gifts, and now a sufficient barrier against the voice which exits from me and which I call mine. The narrator's final silent 'enough' is also perhaps an oblique reply to Molly Bloom's celebrated 'Yes' which closes *Ulysses*, as she evokes in memory the first time she made love. 'Enough', both less and more affirmative than 'yes', implies not Molly's 'giving' of herself, but perhaps a certain refusal, a distance now mediated by the intact borders of the two protagonists' bodies, ('My old breasts feel his old hand'), at a moment when the violation of the generational difference evoked earlier on has been erased ('I belonged to an entirely different generation. It didn't last' (ibid., 53)).

'Enough', then, might mean a certain mouthlessness, but also the capacity to forget, abandon, and relinquish – what Nietzsche, very much like Beckett, often refers to in terms of digestion and excretion: 'A strong and well-constituted man digests his experiences (his deeds and misdeeds included) as he digests his meals, even when he has to swallow some tough morsels' (Nietzsche 1969, 129). Similarly, while asserting that there could be 'no happiness, no cheerfulness, no hope, no pride, no *present* without forgetfulness' Nietzsche claims that the man who is without the positive faculty of repression is like a 'dyspeptic – he cannot "have done" with anything' (Nietzsche 1969, 58). If both Nietzsche and Beckett seem to slide toward the 'true portal of our being', however, crucial differences remain in their valorisations of the 'little hole'. For Nietzsche, despite manifold extremely subtle complications, often tends to work within a normative discourse of Health against which Beckett remains steadfastly inoculated.[11] Indeed, the prevalence of illness and infirmity in Beckett is not only indexical of inevitable mortality, or allegorical of subjective lack of self-mastery, but also a constant protest against all the discourses which deem themselves authorised to separate the Normal or Healthy from its other – a tendency at the core of every discourse on decadence. If Beckett's work has so often been the target of violent repudiation and censorship it is because his 'moribunds' are not simply objects of ridicule or subjects of pity but dangerously subversive dismantlings of the systems of values of authoritarian regimes, whether political or philosophical. It is to my mind a dubious Nietzsche who rails against the 'salves and balm' (Nietzsche 1969, 126) of the Priest and the desire for anesthesia, when his very own analysis can easily show that the refusal to allow pain to be deadened is the most powerful religious anesthetic of all. Nietzsche's vision of mastery and health often seems to imply an individual who is supremely self-sufficient yet who has never had enough, at once entire and insatiable. Beckett prefers a 'calming action', such as that attributed precisely to the flowers in the last paragraph of 'Enough'. The flowers here, the last thing allowed to remain, seem in fact assimilated to a sort of a medicine or drug, the effect of which would be similar to the final gift of the old man: 'The notion of calm comes from him'. This is perhaps clearer in the French text, where Beckett writes of the flowers, *'Elles exerçaient dans l'ensemble une action calmante'* (Beckett 1972a, 47) which recalls the title of Beckett's early story, 'Le Calmant', translated by Beckett as 'The Calmative' although a more colloquial translation, at least to American ears, would have been 'The Sedative'.[12] There, the narrator who claims to be speaking from the grave, attempts to dispel his fright through narrative: 'So I'll tell myself a story, I'll try and tell myself another story, to try and calm myself . . . ' (Beckett 1967, 27). Within the story he tells, the vagabond narrator is given a phial, apparently containing the title's sedative, by a stranger who exchanges it in return for a kiss.

> He took off his hat, a bowler, and tapped the middle of his forehead. There, he said, and there only. He had a noble brow, white and high. He leaned forward, closing his eyes. Quick, he said? I pursed up my lips as mother had taught me and brought them down where he had said. Enough, he said. (ibid., 43)

For both Nietzsche and Beckett, the creation of narrative serves to anaesthetise, to calm the pain rather than to heal, and this desire is one for which Beckett has a singular lack of contempt.

Beckett's diminished modulations, his willingness to embrace the symptom and interpret the desire for its eradication as symptomatic itself, tends to separate him from Nietzsche. The 'energy' which Nietzsche seeks constantly to liberate is, in Beckett, most often presented as inevitably tyrannical and oppressive. The application of the mouth to the world permits of no easy solution, and it is this dis-ease which Beckett figures as disease. However, where Beckett and Nietzsche seem joined, along with Freud, as key figures in our contemporaneity is in their interrogation of the relationship of the subject to its desire. All three ask if a phrase such as 'my desires were my desires' is even sayable, and Beckett's work in the trilogy and after quite literally explores what such a syntax would entail on the level of name, pronoun, and complement through its intensive evacuation of the linguistic mechanics of appropriation. It is not only the 'desires' that cannot be appropriated by an 'I' for Beckett, but also the 'I' itself which no enunciation can lock or fix, as Beckett makes clear throughout his long dismantling of subjective self-identity. The mediations, detours, and subterfuges of want which enrage Nietzsche are accepted by Beckett as the fundamental economy of exchange and debt into which any subject is already written. Beckett's obsessional energy is invested in hopes of a return on mildness, and for Beckett enough, if epidemic, is also (that is, never) enough (as for Nietzsche).

If Beckett, then, seems inevitably fit to remain at the centre of contemporary discussions of nihilism, this is perhaps largely due to his lack of fit within them. Not in some way 'meaningless', Beckett's work is rather in profound ways irrecuperable by larger philosophical discourses, and this despite the amazingly energetic and numerous attempts to recuperate it. Rather than being an impossible and ideal meaningless embodiment of negativity, Beckett's work, for now, stands out as a notable if inevitably compromised site of resistance to our critical endeavours – a 'no' which we inevitably betray by tenderly saying 'yes' to it. Let me emphasize – Beckett's work, *now*, resists *now*; the recent rash of work on Beckett is entirely called for. And let us ponder this contingency, for before too long this moment of resistance, like Joyce's, will have seemed brief. The Beckett industry, since Adorno at least and even working against him, is chipping away at it. And to refuse to do so, or to succeed in our task, to postpone it for a 'later' or to insist that 'now' is the moment of moments, all seem equally 'nihilist' acts. Now I'll wipe out everything but the flowers.

Notes

1 See Lawrence Harvey (1970, 267–8) for this anecdote.
2 See James Knowlson's recent biography, or P.J. Murphy's 'Beckett and the Philosophers' in Pilling 1996.
3 Deleuze returns to this point often in *Nietzsche et la philosophie*. For example, see the early sections of Chapter 5, in which Deleuze explains how the 'active nihilism' of religious values is undone by the negative and passive nihilisms which disqualify at once belief in the suprasensible and in the importance of 'life'.
4 Indeed, the statement seems hyperbolic even within the context of Adorno's own discussions of Beckett, which, as Critchley points out, tend more often to focus on the way Beckett's plays *debate* meaning, and the meaning of meaning (see Critchley 1997, 151–2). This they certainly do, but such a description would equally apply to many other canonical modernist works, and thus tells us little about the specificity of Beckett's writing. Moreover, 'debating' meaning hardly seems 'nihilist' in and of itself, though one can see why it is a necessary preliminary to more emphatic negations.
5 Leslie Hill has recently pointed out that the narrator's gender is impossible to determine, as in both the French and English Beckett has systematically eliminated all grammatical markers of it (Hill 1990, 156–8). It is not entirely justifiable to systematically refer to the narrator as female, which I have chosen to do here in the interests of a reading which emphasises the pressure the story applies to traditional hierarchised social relationships, notably older/younger, male/female, parent/child. Other readings which would more forcefully mobilize the gender ambiguity are to be encouraged.

6　For example, Leslie Hill (1990, 158).

7　See, for example, Nietzsche (1968 §I, 1).

8　This is, of course, far from the only parallel between Freud and Nietzsche on the question of subjectivity. For a brilliant look at subjective architectonics in Freud and Nietzsche, see Chapter 3 of Butler 1997.

9　Thomas Hunkeler has recently discussed the importance of the word 'precipitate' in Beckett, implying at once haste but also droppings of all sorts; everything that tends to go down.

10　Beckett's evocation here of an anal hostility to what comes from the outside could be read as a denial of the homosexual potential opened by the indeterminate gender of the narrator of *Enough*. On the contrary, nothing could be further from the truth: 'Nothing goes in, *or so little*, that is not rejected on the spot, or very nearly'. The qualifier here, 'or so little', is of course a denigration of the object which escapes the general rule the sentence establishes, that is, the penis, referred to in similar terms in the early 'What a Misfortune' from *More Pricks than Kicks*: ' "It's a small thing, Hairy", he said . . . "separates lovers" ' (Beckett 1972, 1360).

11　The question of the status of 'health' in Nietzsche is extremely complex, and it is crucial to note how often Nietzsche highlights the importance of decadence and illness in the process of development and advance. A notable example of this would be §224 from *Human, All Too Human*, in which Nietzsche emphasises how the 'weaker' or 'degenerate' further evolution: 'Every progress of the whole has to be preceded by a partial weakening' (Nietzsche 1986, 107). In *Viroid Life*, Keith Ansell Pearson has persuasively shown the importance of this sort of reasoning for Nietzsche's 'evolutionary' schemas, which end not only with an emphasis on the importance of decay and degeneration for all progress (Ansell Peason 1997, 99) but even with the seemingly paradoxical assertion that the 'higher type' actually ' . . . goes against the grain of evolution, which favours the gradual selection of that which endures' (ibid., 101) – a statement which implies that the terms 'higher' and 'lower', 'stronger' and 'weaker', are in some way reversed. Still, these formulations all tend to view the 'degenerate' as an investment in a movement toward a greater advance which in itself is never questioned, just as on the level of the individual, illness – whatever benefits it may provoke – provokes them in the context of an improved and stronger health. In a long discussion of health in Nietzsche, David Farrell Krell also shows well how often Nietzsche relativises the values of health and illness, giving as an example this passage from the notebooks: 'Only when we have an *ideal* in view, an ideal we wish to attain, does it make sense to say "healthy" and "sick" ' (quoted in Krell, 1996, 191). Yet another passage from the drafts for *Ecce Homo* shows Nietzsche again striving to maintain against the recognised necessity of illness and degeneration the possibility of an absolute 'health': 'I took myself in hand, made myself healthy again: the condition for that – as every physiologist will concede – is *that one at bottom be healthy*. A creature that is morbid by type cannot become healthy, still less make itself healthy; as opposed to that, for one who is healthy by type, illness can be an energetic *stimulans* to life, more life (cited in Krell 1996, 209). It is the possibility of the 'healthy type' that Beckett's works call radically into question.

12　'Calmant' in French designates both tranquilisers and pain-killers, the distinction between physical and psychic pain here not being linguistically inscribed (a fact of obvious potential interest to Nietzsche, given his constant focus on somatic groundings and resonances of what is usually called character, history, or mind).

In the context of the story, the sense of *sedation* is clearly privileged, if the others are nevertheless present as well.

References

Adorno, T. (1991) *Notes to Literature, volume 1.* trans. S.W. Nicholsen. New York: Columbia University Press.

Ansell Pearson, K. (1997) *Viroid Life: Perspectives on Nietzsche and the Transhuman Condition* London: Routledge.

Badiou, A. (1992) *Conditions.* Paris: Les Editions du Seuil.

Beckett, S. (1965) *Three Novels by Samuel Beckett: Molloy, Malone Dies, The Unnamable.* New York: Grove Press.

—— (1967) *Stories and Texts for Nothing* New York: Grove Press.

—— (1972a) *Têtes-Mortes* Paris: Les éditions de Minuit.

—— (1972b) *More Pricks than Kicks* New York: Grove Press.

—— (1974) *First Love and Other Shorts* New York: Grove Press.

—— (1981) *Watt* New York: Grove Press.

—— (1983) *Worstward Ho* New York: Grove Press.

—— (1984a) *Disjecta: Miscellaneous Writings and a Dramatic Fragment.* ed. Ruby Cohn. New York: Grove Press.

—— (1984b) *Collected Shorter Plays* New York: Grove Press.

Butler, J. (1997) *The Psychic Life of Power: Theories in Subjection* Stanford: Stanford University Press.

Critchley, S. (1997) *Very Little . . . Almost Nothing: Death, Philosophy, Literature.* London and New York: Routledge.

Deleuze, G. (1961). *Nietzsche et la Philosophie.* Paris: Presses Universitaires de France.

Derrida, J. (1967) *L'Ecriture et la différence.* Paris: Les Editions du Seuil. (1981).

—— *Writing and Difference* trans. A. Bass, London/ NY: Routledge.

Freud, S. (1985) *Civilization, Society and Religion (Pelican Freud Library, vol. 12).* ed. Angela Richards, trans. James Strachey. London: Penguin Books.

Freud, S. (1984) *On Metapsychology: The Theory of Psychoanalysis (Pelican Freud Library, vol. 11).* ed. Angela Richards, trans. James Strachey. London: Penguin Books.

Harvey, Lawrence. (1970) *Samuel Beckett: Poet and Critic* Princeton: Princeton University Press.

Hill, L. (1990) *Beckett's Fiction: In Different Words.* Cambridge: Cambridge University Press.

Hunkeler, T. (1997) *Echos de l'ego dans l'oeuvre de Samuel Beckett.* Paris: Editions L'Harmattan.

Krell, D.F. (1996) *Infectious Nietzsche.* Bloomington: Indiana University Press.

Nietzsche, F. (1986) *Human, All Too Human.* trans. R.J. Hollingdale. Cambridge: Cambridge University Press.

Nietzsche, F. (1969) *On the Genealogy of Morals* and *Ecce Homo.* trans. W. Kaufmann. New York: Vintage.

Nietzsche, F. (1968) *The Will to Power.* ed. W. Kaufmann, trans. W. Kaufmann and R.J. Hollingdale. New York: Vintage.

Knowlson, J. (1996) *Damned to Fame: The Life of Samuel Beckett.* London: Bloomsbury.

Pilling, J., ed. (1996) *The Cambridge Companion to Beckett.* Cambridge: Cambridge University Press.

Wilde, O. (1985) *The Picture of Dorian Gray.* Harmondsworth: Penguin Books.

Index